Table of Contents

What is Lean and Green Diet?

Lean and Green is a weight loss or maintenance plan that prescribes eating a mix of purchased, processed food called "fuelings" and homemade "lean and green" meals. There's no counting carbs or calories. Instead, followers add water to powdered food or unwrap a bar as part of six-or-so mini-meals per day. Lean and Green also offers guidance from coaches to help you learn their trademarked "Habits of Health." The plan additionally recommends doing about 30 minutes of moderate-intensity exercise per day.

"Lean and Green works because it's simple and easy to follow. Five of your daily meals are Lean and Green Fuelings. You'll choose from more than 60 delicious, convenient, nutritionally interchangeable, scientifically-designed Fuelings. Your body will enter a gentle, but efficient fat-burning state, essential for losing weight. Each Fueling contains high-quality protein which helps retain lean muscle mass, and probiotic cultures, which help support digestive health, as part of a balanced diet and healthy lifestyle."

How Does The Lean and Green Diet Work?

The Lean and Green diet subscribes to the idea that eating several small meals or snacks every day leads to manageable and sustained weight loss, and ultimately habit change. The thinking is that instead of eating three huge meals every day, you'll never get that hungry because you're eating six or seven small, filling, and nutritious meals throughout the day. While this may work well for some people, we're all different and there isn't a ton of convincing research to back this method up. The efficacy of eating small meals and found that, ultimately, weight loss is directly related to restricting calories, and the timing and sizing of the meals themselves don't have a meaningful impact on weight loss.

When it comes to successful long-term weight loss, experts seem to agree on one thing: The emotional and behavioral aspects of eating not just the specific meals you're eating are incredibly important. They also stress the importance of looking at whole-body wellness as a path to safe and sustainable weight loss.

What To Eat

- Lean and Green fuelings
- Lean meats
- Greens and other non-starchy vegetables
- Healthy fats
- Low-fat dairy, fresh fruit, and whole grains (on some plans)

What Not To Eat

- Indulgent desserts
- High-calorie additions
- Sugary beverages
- Alcohol

What Kinds Of Foods Can I Eat On The Lean and Green Diet?

- Lean meats, like turkey, lamb, or chicken
- Fish and shellfish, like salmon, crab, shrimp
- Tofu
- Low-carb veggies, including spinach, cauliflower, mushrooms, and cabbage
- Healthy fats, like avocados and pistachios
- Sugar-free beverages and snacks, including coffee and tea
- Vegetable oils
- Eggs

What Foods Should I Avoid On The Lean and Green Diet?

- Fried foods
- Refined grains, like white bread, pasta, and white rice
- Alcohol
- Butter
- Coconut oil
- Milk
- Cheese
- Soda, fruit juice, and other sugar-sweetened beverages

Pros And Cons

Pros

- Packaged products offer convenience
- Achieves rapid weight loss
- Takes guesswork out of what to eat
- Offers social support

Cons

- High monthly cost
- Includes a lot of processed food
- Weight loss may be unsustainable

- Calorie restriction may leave you hungry or fatigued
- Mealtimes can become boring or feel isolating

Health Benefits

Lean and Green's program might be a good fit for you if you want a diet plan that is clear and easy to follow, that will help you lose weight quickly, and offers built-in social support.

- **Packaged Products Offer Convenience**

Lean and Green's shakes, soups, and all other meal replacement products are delivered directly to your door, a level of convenience that many other diets do not offer. Although you will need to shop for your ingredients for "lean and green" meals, the home delivery option for Lean and Green's "fuelings" saves time and energy. Once the products arrive, they're easy to prepare and make excellent grab-and-go meals.

- **Achieves Rapid Weight Loss**

Most healthy people require around 1600 to 3000 calories per day to maintain their weight. Restricting that number to as low as 800 essentially guarantees weight loss for most people. Lean and Green's 5 & 1 plan is designed for quick weight loss, making it a solid option for someone with a medical reason to shed pounds fast.

- **Eliminates Guesswork**

Some people find that the hardest part of dieting is the mental effort required to figure out what to eat each day—or even at each meal. Lean and Green alleviates the stress of meal planning and "decision fatigue" by offering users clear-cut approved foods with "fuelings" and guidelines for "lean and green" meals.

Health Risks

There are also some potential downsides to Lean and Green's plan, especially if you are worried about cost, flexibility, and variety.

- **Includes Processed Food**

Although Lean and Green's "fuelings" are engineered with interchangeable nutrients, they're still undeniably processed foods, which may be a turn off for some users. Nutrition research has shown eating a lot of processed food can have detrimental effects on one's health, so this aspect of the diet plan may pose a disadvantage.

- **Weight Loss May Not Be Sustainable**

One challenge familiar to anyone on a diet is determining how to maintain weight loss once they've completed the program. The same goes for Lean and Green's program. When users go back to eating regular meals instead of the plan's meal replacements, they might find that the weight they lost is quickly regained.

- **Effects Of Calorie Restriction**

Even though Lean and Green's diet plan emphasizes eating frequently throughout the day, each of its "fuelings" only provides 110 calories. "Lean and green" meals are also low in calories. When you're eating fewer calories in general, you may find the plan leaves you hungry and unsatisfied. You may also feel more easily fatigued and even irritable.

- **Boredom And Isolation At Mealtimes**

Lean and Green's reliance on meal replacements can interfere with the social aspects of preparing and eating food. Users might find it awkward or disappointing to have a shake or bar at family mealtime or when dining out with friends.

Lean and Green Fuelings

The majority of the food you'll eat on the Lean and Green Diet will take the form of its pre-packaged "feelings." According to Lean and Green's online guide, you can choose from over 60 soups, bars, shakes, pretzels, and other products (even brownies!) as meal replacements.

The company states that "each item has a nearly identical nutrition profile," which means they can be eaten interchangeably.

Lean and Green

The "lean and green" meals you'll prepare need to include a five-to-seven-ounce portion of cooked lean protein. Lean and Green distinguishes between lean, leaner, and leanest protein sources using the following examples:

- Lean: Salmon, lamb, or pork chops
- Leaner: Swordfish or chicken breast
- Leanest: Cod, shrimp, and egg whites

Lean and Green's 5 & 1 program allows for two non-starchy vegetables alongside the protein in your "lean and green" meal. The veggies are divided into lower, moderate, and higher carbohydrate categories, with the following as examples:

- Lower carb: Salad greens
- Moderate carb: Cauliflower or summer squash
- Higher Carb: Broccoli or peppers

On the Lean and Green 5&1 Plan, the only foods allowed are the Lean and Green Fuelings and one Lean and Green Meal per day.

These meals consist mostly of lean proteins, healthy fats, and low carb vegetables with a recommended two servings of fatty fish per week. Some low carb condiments and beverages are also allowed in small amounts.

Foods allowed in your daily Lean and Green meal include:

- **Meat:** chicken, turkey, lean beef, game meats, lamb, pork chop or tenderloin, ground meat (at least 85% lean)

- **Fish and shellfish:** halibut, trout, salmon, tuna, lobster, crab, shrimp, scallops

- **Eggs:** whole eggs, egg whites, Egg Beaters

- **Soy products:** only tofu

- **Vegetable oils:** canola, flaxseed, walnut, and olive oil

- **Additional healthy fats:** low carb salad dressings, olives, reduced fat margarine, almonds, walnuts, pistachios, avocado

- **Low carb vegetables:** collard greens, spinach, celery, cucumbers, mushrooms, cabbage, cauliflower, eggplant, zucchini, broccoli, peppers, spaghetti squash, jicama

- **Sugar-free snacks:** popsicles, gelatin, gum, mints

- **Sugar-free beverages:** water, unsweetened almond milk, tea, coffee

- **Condiments and seasonings:** dried herbs, spices, salt, lemon juice, lime juice, yellow mustard, soy sauce, salsa, sugar-free syrup, zero-calorie sweeteners, 1/2 teaspoon only of ketchup, cocktail sauce, or barbecue sauce

A Lean & Green meal includes 5 to 7 ounces of cooked lean protein plus three (3) servings of non-starchy vegetables and up to two (2) servings of healthy fats, depending on your lean protein choices. Enjoy your Lean & Green meal any time of day — whatever works best for your schedule.

How to follow the Lean and Green diet

Initial steps

For weight loss, most people start with the Optimal Weight 5&1 Plan, which is an 800–1,000 calorie regimen said to help you drop 12 pounds (5.4 kg) over 12 weeks. On this plan, you eat 5 Lean and Green Fuelings and 1 Lean and Green meal daily. You're meant to eat 1 meal every 2–3 hours and incorporate 30 minutes of moderate exercise most days of the week. In total, the Fuelings and meal provide no more than 100 grams of carbs per day.

Lean and Green meals are designed to be high in protein and low in carbs. One meal offers 5–7 ounces (145–200 grams) of cooked lean protein, 3 servings of non-starchy vegetables, and up to 2 servings of healthy fats. This plan also includes 1 optional snack per day, which must be approved by your coach. Plan-approved snacks include 3 celery sticks, 1/2 cup (60 grams) of sugar-free gelatin, or 1/2 ounce (14 grams) of nuts.

Maintenance phase

Once you reach your desired weight, you enter a 6-week transition phase, which involves slowly increasing calories to no more than 1,550 calories per day and adding in a wider variety of foods, including whole grains, fruits, and low fat dairy. After 6 weeks, you're meant to move onto the Optimal Health 3&3 Plan, which includes 3 Lean and Green meals and 3 Fuelings daily, plus continued Lean and Green coaching.

Those who experience sustained success on the program have the option to become trained as an Lean and Green coach.

1. Lean and Green "Breakfast Recipes"

1. Egg White Muffins | Healthy Breakfast Meal Prep

Prep Time: 15 mins

Cook Time: 25 mins

Total Time: 40 mins

Servings: 12 muffins

Calories: 34kcal

Ingredients

- 1 cup baby spinach, chopped
- 1/2 cup diced bell peppers
- 1/2 cup baby tomatoes, diced
- 2 cups egg whites
- 1/2 cup cottage cheese
- 1/2 teaspoon kosher salt
- 1/2 teaspoon black pepper
- 1/2 teaspoon garlic powder

Instructions

- Pre-heat oven to 300ºF.
- Coat a 12-cup muffin tray with cooking spray.
- Combine all prepared veggies in a medium mixing bowl and then evenly divide the veggie mixture amongst the 12 muffin cups.
- Combine egg whites, cottage cheese, salt, pepper, and garlic powder in a blender and blend until light and frothy.
- Pour the egg mixture over the veggies, again, doing your best to divide the eggs as evenly as possible amongst all 12 muffin cups.
- Place tray in the oven and bake for 25 minutes or until the eggs have fluffed up and are cooked through.
- Cool before removing from the pan. They should pop out easily if you greased your pan well.
- Serve immediately or pop into the fridge or freezer. To reheat, microwave the muffins for 45-60 seconds or until thawed. Enjoy!

Nutrition

Serving: 1muffin | Calories: 34kcal | Carbohydrates: 1g | Protein: 6g | Fat: 1g | Saturated Fat: 1g | Cholesterol: 1mg | Sodium: 199mg | Potassium: 117mg | Fiber: 1g | Sugar: 1g | Vitamin A: 493IU | Vitamin C: 9mg | Calcium: 13mg | Iron: 1mg

2. Classic Bacon And Eggs

Cooking Time: 10 minutes

Servings: 4

Ingredients

- 8 eggs
- 9 oz. bacon, in slices
- cherry tomatoes (optional)
- fresh thyme (optional)

Instructions

- Fry the bacon in a pan on medium-high heat until crispy. Put aside on a plate. Leave the rendered fat in the pan.
- Use the same pan to fry the eggs. Place it over medium heat and crack your eggs into the bacon grease. You can also crack them into a measuring cup and carefully pour them into the pan to avoid splattering of hot grease.
- Cook the eggs any way you like them. For the sunny side up leave the eggs to fry on one side and cover the pan with a lid to make sure they get cooked on top. For eggs cooked over easy flip the eggs over after a few minutes and cook for another minute. Cut the cherry tomatoes in half and fry them at the same time.
- Salt and pepper to taste.

Nutrition

- Net carbs: 1 % (1 g)
- Fiber: 0 g
- Fat: 78 % (32 g)
- Protein: 21 % (20 g)
- kcal: 377

3. Chicken Fajita Lettuce Wraps

Prep Time: 15 Mins

Cook Time: 30 Mins

Total Time: 45 Mins

Servings: 2 People

Calories: 180.0 Kcal

Ingredients

- lb chicken breast (thinly sliced into strips)

- bell peppers (thinly sliced into strips)
- tsp olive oil
- 2.0 tsp fajita seasoning
- tbsp fresh lime juice
- 6.0 leaves romaine heart
- 1/4 cup non-fat Greek yogurt (optional)

Instructions

- Preheat. Preheat oven to 400°F
- Combine. Combine all ingredients (except romaine) into a large plastic bag and seal. Mix well to evenly coat.
- Prep. Empty the bag content onto a foil-lined baking sheet and bake 25-30 minutes until chicken is thoroughly cooked.
- Serve. Serve on romaine leaves topped with Greek yogurt (if desired).

Nutrition

- Calories: 180.0 kcal
- Carbohydrates: 2.0 g
- Cholesterol: 80.0 mg
- Fat: 5.0 g
- Fiber: 2.0 g
- Protein: 40.0 g
- Serving Amount: 1
- Serving Unit: serving
- Sodium: 300.0 mg
- Sugar: 5.0 g

4. Lean Green Lettuce Tacos

Prep: 15 mins

Cook: 11 mins

Total: 26 mins

Yield: Makes 8 appetizer servings

Ingredient

- 1 small zucchini, diced
- 1 small yellow squash, diced
- ½ pound extra-lean ground beef
- 1 tablespoon olive oil
- 1 (1.25-oz.) taco fresco seasoning
- 1 (8-oz.) can no-salt-added tomato sauce
- 2 tablespoons chopped fresh cilantro
- 1 tablespoon lime juice
- 8 romaine lettuce leaves

- **Toppings:** diced tomato, chopped fresh cilantro, chopped red onion, crumbled queso fresco

Instructions

- Sauté first 3 ingredients in hot oil in a large nonstick skillet over medium-high heat 5 to 6 minutes or until meat crumbles and is no longer pink. Stir in seasoning until blended; cook 1 minute.
- Reduce heat to low; stir in tomato sauce, and cook, stirring often, 3 to 4 minutes or until thoroughly heated. Remove from heat, and stir in cilantro and lime juice.
- Serve meat mixture in romaine lettuce leaves with desired toppings.
- 2% reduced-fat shredded Cheddar or Monterey Jack cheese may be substituted.
- Note: For testing purposes only, we used Nueva Cocina Taco Fresco Ground Beef Seasoning.

Nutrition

Per Serving: Calories: 93; Calories From Fat 0%; Fat 4.5g; Saturated Fat 1.3g; Mono Fat 2.4g; Poly Fat 0.4g; Protein 6.7g; Carbohydrates 6.2g; Fiber 1g; Cholesterol 10mg; Iron 1mg; Sodium 227mg; Calcium 14mg.

5. Crustless Spinach Quiche

Active Time: 20 Mins

Total Time: 30 Mins

Ingredients

- 1 tablespoon olive oil
- 4-8 ounces white mushrooms, sliced
- 1 clove garlic, minced
- 10 oz box frozen spinach, thawed and squeezed dry
- 6 eggs
- 3/4 cup milk, I used 2%
- 3/4 cup heavy cream
- 1/3 cup sharp cheddar, diced
- 3/4 cup shredded Gouda cheese
- Salt and pepper to taste, I used 3/4 teaspoon kosher salt and a generous 1/4 teaspoon freshly ground black pepper

Instructions

- Preheat the oven to 350ºF. Grease a 9-inch pie plate and set it aside.
- Add olive oil to a non-stick skillet and saute the mushrooms, garlic, and a pinch of salt until mushrooms are lightly browned and have given off all their liquid. Add the spinach and mix and heat for a minute to remove any excess moisture.
- Place the spinach mixture in the bottom of the pie dish, followed by the cheddar chunks.
- In a medium bowl, whisk together the eggs, milk, cream, salt, and pepper.
- Pour the egg mixture into the pie plate. Top with the shredded Gouda cheese.
- Bake for 45-55 minutes, or until the top is golden brown (ovens may vary). Slice and serve.

Nutrition

Yield: 6 ,Serving Size: 1 Large Slice ,Calories: 367 ,Total Fat: 27g, Saturated Fat: 14g , Trans Fat: 1g ,Unsaturated Fat: 11g ,Cholesterol: 250mg ,Sodium: 1794mg ,Carbohydrates: 14g , Fiber: 5g ,Sugar: 5g ,Protein: 20g

6. Spaghetti Squash Carbonara

Prep Time: 10 Mins

Cook Time: 20 Mins

Total Time: 30 Mins

Serves: 4 Servings

Ingredients

- 1 large spaghetti squash (about 2 lbs.)
- 6 slices bacon (or ⅓ cup cooked pancetta)
- 2 large eggs
- ¾ cup grated Parmesan cheese
- 4 cloves garlic, minced (optional)
- salt and pepper to taste
- 2 tsp chopped fresh parsley
- extra Parmesan cheese for garnish if desired

Instructions

- Slice spaghetti squash in half, lengthwise, from stem to tail. Remove seeds and stringy flesh. Place squash flesh side down in a microwave-safe glass baking pan. Cook 10-12 min. until flesh is soft. Let squash cool to touch, turn over and "rake" a fork through the flesh to create the "noodles".

- While the squash is cooking, use kitchen shears to cut bacon into small pieces. Cook bacon in a large skillet. Place on a paper towel-lined plate when cooked. Reserve a small amount of bacon drippings in a frying pan.
- Combine eggs, cheese, salt, and pepper in a small bowl.set aside.
- Just before serving, add garlic to the frying pan and cook until fragrant (about 1 min.) Add the spaghetti squash and bacon and heat thoroughly. Turn off heat, and add egg/cheese mixture. Toss to combine. (The egg will cook when combined with the hot squash).
- Garnish with parsley and additional Parmesan cheese.

Nutrition

Serving size: ¼ of recipe (approx. 1¼ cup spaghetti squash per serving) Calories: 244.3 Fat: 13.9 Saturated fat: 6.4 g Carbohydrates: 15.9 g Sugar: 6.0 g Sodium: 559 mg Fiber: 3.3 g Protein: 16.2 g Cholesterol: 119.1 mg

7. Spinach and Turkey Bacon Omelette

Prep Time: 10 minutes

Cook Time: 10 minutes

Total Time: 20 minutes

Servings: 1

Calories: 237kcal

Ingredients

- 3 extra-large egg whites
- 2 slices pre-cooked turkey bacon
- 5-6 spinach leaves
- 1/4 cup reduced-fat mexican cheese
- 1 t pico de gallo
- 1 t skim milk
- Salt to taste
- Pepper to taste
- Pam cooking spray

Instructions

- Start by placing the turkey bacon on a paper plate lined with a paper towel, with an additional paper towel on top, place in the microwave, and cook for 2 minutes.

- Next in a small bowl, crack and separate the egg whites and add 1 T. pico de gallo, salt, and pepper to taste and milk. Whisk for approximately 1 minute, or until the mixture appears slightly frothy.
- Spray a small skillet with cooking spray and turn on medium heat and add egg mixture to heated skillet.
- Chop up the cooked turkey bacon and spinach leaves.
- After the eggs in the skillet are turning white and not so opaque, gently flip the eggs over to the other side. Try to not break up the formed omelet. (I know, this can be tricky. You can do it!)
- After several minutes when the eggs appear cooked on both sides, sprinkle 3/4 of the measured cheese on top of the omelet and add the chopped spinach and turkey bacon to only one side of the omelet. Fold the other side over and sprinkle the remaining cheese on top of the omelet.
- Cook for an additional minute or two, and transfer omelet to plate and enjoy!

Nutrition

Per Serving: Calories: 93; Calories From Fat 0%; Fat 4.5g; Saturated Fat 1.3g; Mono Fat 2.4g; Poly Fat 0.4g; Protein 6.7g; Carbohydrates 6.2g; Fiber 1g; Cholesterol 10mg; Iron 1mg; Sodium 227mg; Calcium 14mg.

8. The Best Cloud Bread Recipe

Prep Time: 10 Minutes

Cook Time: 15 Minutes

Total Time: 25 Minutes

Servings: 10 Pieces

Ingredients

- 4 large eggs, separated
- 1/2 teaspoon cream of tartar
- 2 ounces low-fat cream cheese
- 1 teaspoon Italian herb seasoning
- 1/2 teaspoon sea salt
- 1/4 - 1/2 teaspoon garlic powder

Instructions

- Preheat the oven to 300 degrees F. If you have a convection oven, set it on convect. Line two large baking sheets with parchment paper.
- Separate the egg whites and egg yolks. Place the whites in a stand mixer with a whip attachment. Add the cream of tartar and beat on high until the froth turns into firm meringue peaks. Move to a separate bowl.
- Place the cream cheese in the empty stand mixing bowl. Beat on high to soften. Then add the egg yolks one at a time to incorporate. Scrape the bowl and beat until the mixture is completely smooth. Then beat in the Italian seasoning, salt, and garlic powder.
- Gently fold the firm meringue into the yolk mixture. Try to deflate the meringue as little as possible, so the mixture is still firm and foamy. Spoon 1/4 cup portions of the foam onto the baking sheets and spread into even 4-inch circles, 3/4 inch high. Make sure to leave space around each circle.
- Bake on convect for 15-18 minutes, or in a conventional oven for up to 30 minutes. The bread should be golden on the outside and firm. The center should not jiggle when shaken. Cool for several minutes on the baking sheets, then move and serve!

Nutrition

Calories: 36kcal, Carbohydrates: 0g, Protein: 2g, Fat: 2g, Saturated Fat: 1g, Cholesterol: 68mg, Sodium: 167mg, Potassium: 63mg, Sugar: 0g, Vitamin A: 125iu, Calcium: 18mg, Iron: 0.3mg

9. Skinny Chicken Salad

Active Time: 30 Mins

Ingredients

- 4 ounces shredded or diced (cooked) boneless, skinless, chicken breast (abt 1 cup)
- 1/4 cup diced celery
- 2 tablespoons sliced green onion
- 1/4 cup diced sweet, crisp apple
- 1 tablespoon light mayo
- 1 tablespoon light sour cream or greek yogurt
- Optional: 1/2-1 tablespoon chopped fresh parsley or cilantro
- 1/8 teaspoon curry powder
- 1/4 teaspoon red wine vinegar

- 1 tablespoon toasted sliced almonds
- Salt and pepper to taste

Instructions

- Combine all ingredients except almonds and stir to combine. If possible, chill for an hour or so before eating.
- Before serving, mix in almonds.
- Eat-in a lettuce wrap, on whole-grain bread, in a wrap, or a pita.

Nutrition (Salad Alone)

Cal: 267g, Protein: 28g, Fat: 12g, Carbs: 8g, Fiber:2g, Sugar: 6g, Serving Size: 1

10. Low Carb Cloud Bread With Greek Yogurt

Prep Time: 10 Mins

Cook Time: 25 Mins

Total Time: 35 Mins

Ingredients

- 3 eggs separated (room temperature)
- 3 tablespoons Greek Yogurt plain
- ¼ teaspoons baking powder

Instructions

- Before you begin, preheat your oven to 300 degrees. I use a Silpat baking mat on top of my cookie sheet, but parchment paper works too.
- Mix egg yolks (yolks only) and Greek yogurt until blended smooth. I'd almost say over blend these, try to get rid of as many lumps as you can.
- Beat egg whites and ¼ teaspoon baking powder (some have used cream of tartar instead) until fluffy. Again, I'd over blend these and make sure to get the same consistency from top to bottom of your bowl.
- Fold the egg white mixture into the yolk and Greek yogurt mixture carefully. Be careful not to overmix, but know that these need to be fully mixed for your cloud bread to come out fluffy and beautiful. I recommend using a large whisk of some kind to do this.
- Using a cookie scooper, take a scoopful of batter out of the bowl and tap it a few times lightly on the counter to let the big air bubbles out before baking. Drop the batter on your Silpat baking mat, leaving a little room in between.

- Bake for 25 minutes at 300 degrees, or until golden brown. Sprinkle sea salt on the cloud bread as soon as they come out of the oven, then move to a cooling rack.

Nutrition

Calories: 224kcal | Carbohydrates: 3g | Protein: 21g | Fat: 13g | Saturated Fat: 5g | Cholesterol: 494mg | Sodium: 207mg | Potassium: 283mg | Sugar: 2g | Vitamin A: 713IU | Calcium: 170mg | Iron: 2mg

11. Easy Whole30 Breakfast Bake (Paleo Keto)

Servings: 8 Servings

Prep Time: 10 Minutes

Cook Time: 35 Minutes

Total Time: 45 Minutes

Ingredients

- 1 lb homemade turkey sausage (or compliant sausage), see recipe below
- 1 1/2 cups shredded russet potatoes, about 2 medium potatoes (omit for keto)
- 1 cup diced bell peppers
- 1/2 cup diced onions
- 12 eggs, beaten
- 1/4 cup nutritional yeast (optional)

Homemade Turkey Sausage

- 1 lb ground turkey
- 1 teaspoon Italian seasoning
- 1 teaspoon ground sage
- 1/2 teaspoon all-purpose salt-free seasoning, see recipe below
- 1/2 teaspoon sea salt
- 1 tablespoon avocado oil

Instructions

- Preheat the oven to 350 degrees. Prepare a 9x13 baking dish with cooking spray.
- To cook the sausage, heat oil in a large skillet over medium-high heat.
- Crumble in the ground turkey, add seasonings, and cook until browned. Remove sausage from pan. In the same skillet, add the onions and peppers. Cook 3-5 minutes until beginning to soften.

- Add sausage, peppers and onions, and remaining ingredients to a large mixing bowl. Combine well.
- Pour mixture into the prepared baking dish and bake for 30-35 minutes, until a knife inserted in the center comes out clean.

Nutrition

Calories: 219kcal, Carbohydrates: 10g, Protein: 23g, Fat: 9g, Saturated Fat: 2g, Cholesterol: 276mg, Sodium: 277mg, Potassium: 445mg, Fiber: 1g, Sugar: 1g, Vitamin C: 19mg, Calcium: 51mg, Iron: 2.2mg

13. Cauliflower Rice-Stuffed Peppers

Active: 40 Mins

Total: 1 hr

Servings: 4

Ingredients

- 4 large bell peppers (about 2 pounds)
- 2 cups small cauliflower florets
- 2 tablespoons extra-virgin olive oil, divided
- Pinch of salt plus 1/2 teaspoon, divided
- Pinch of ground pepper plus 1/4 teaspoon, divided
- ½ cup chopped onion
- 1 pound lean ground beef
- 2 cloves garlic, minced
- ½ teaspoon dried oregano
- 1 (8 ounces) can no-salt-added tomato sauce
- ½ cup shredded part-skim mozzarella

Instructions

- Preheat oven to 350 degrees F.
- Slice off stem ends of bell peppers. Cut the flesh from the stem and chop. You should have about 1 cup. Scoop out seeds from the pepper cavities. Bring about an inch of water to a boil in a large pot fitted with a steamer basket. Steam the peppers until starting to soften, about 3 minutes. Remove the peppers from the pot and set them aside.
- Pulse cauliflower in a food processor until broken down into rice-size pieces. Heat 1 tablespoon oil in a large skillet over medium heat. Add the cauliflower rice and a pinch each of salt and pepper. Cook, stirring until softened

and starting to brown, about 3 minutes. Transfer to a small bowl.
- Wipe out the pan. Add the remaining 1 tablespoon oil, the chopped bell pepper, and onion. Cook, stirring, until starting to soften, about 3 minutes. Add beef, garlic, oregano, and the remaining 1/2 teaspoon salt and 1/4 teaspoon pepper. Cook, stirring and breaking up the beef with a wooden spoon just until no longer pink, about 5 minutes. Add tomato sauce and the cauliflower rice; stir to coat.
- Place the peppers upright in an 8-inch square baking dish. Fill each pepper with a generous 1 cup of the cauliflower rice mixture. Top each pepper with 2 tablespoons of cheese.
- Bake until the filling is heated through and the cheese is melted, 20 to 25 minutes.

Nutrition

Serving Size: 1 Stuffed Pepper, Per Serving: 374 calories; protein 29.3g; carbohydrates 16.5g; dietary fiber 3.5g; sugars 7.2g; fat 21.7g; saturated fat 7.2g; cholesterol 82.8mg; vitamin a iu 621.3IU; vitamin c 250.1mg; folate 81.3mcg; calcium 155.2mg; iron 4mg; magnesium 60.3mg; potassium 1010.5mg; sodium 521.7mg; thiamin 0.1mg.

14. Cauliflower Tortillas

Prep Time: 30 mins

Cook Time: 20 mins

Total Time: 50 mins

Servings: 6 tortillas

Calories: 37kcal

Ingredients

- 3/4 large head cauliflower (or two cups riced)
- 2 large eggs (Vegans, sub flax eggs)
- 1/4 cup chopped fresh cilantro
- 1/2 medium lime, juiced, and zested
- salt & pepper, to taste

Instructions

- Preheat the oven to 375 degrees F., and line a baking sheet with parchment paper.
- Trim the cauliflower, cut it into small, uniform pieces, and pulse in a food processor in batches

until you get a couscous-like consistency. The finely riced cauliflower should make about 2 cups packed.

- Place the cauliflower in a microwave-safe bowl and microwave for 2 minutes, then stir and microwave again for another 2 minutes. If you don't use a microwave, a steamer works just as well. Place the cauliflower in a fine cheesecloth or thin dishtowel and squeeze out as much liquid as possible, being careful not to burn yourself. Dishwashing gloves are suggested as it is very hot.
- In a medium bowl, whisk the eggs. Add in cauliflower, cilantro, lime, salt, and pepper. Mix until well combined. Use your hands to shape 6 small "tortillas" on the parchment paper.
- Bake for 10 minutes, carefully flip each tortilla and return to the oven for an additional 5 to 7 minutes, or until completely set. Place tortillas on a wire rack to cool slightly.
- Heat a medium-sized skillet on medium. Place a baked tortilla in the pan, pressing down slightly, and brown for 1 to 2 minutes on each side. Repeat with remaining tortillas.

Nutrition

Serving: 1tortilla, Calories: 37kcal, Carbohydrates: 2g, Protein: 3g, Fat: 1g, Saturated Fat: 0g, Cholesterol: 62mg, Sodium: 39mg, Potassium: 182mg, Fiber: 1g, Sugar: 1g, Vitamin A: 135IU, Vitamin C: 25.9mg, Calcium: 21mg, Iron: 0.5mg,

---

15. Zucchini Shrimp Scampi

Yield: 4 Servings

Prep Time: 15 Minutes

Cook Time: 10 Minutes

Total Time: 25 Minutes

Ingredients

- 2 tablespoons unsalted butter
- 1 pound medium shrimp, peeled and deveined
- 3 cloves garlic, minced
- 1/2 teaspoon red pepper flakes, or more, to taste
- 1/4 cup chicken stock
- Juice of 1 lemon

- Kosher salt and freshly ground black pepper, to taste
- 1 1/2 pounds (4 medium-sized) zucchini, spiralized
- 2 tablespoons freshly grated Parmesan
- 2 tablespoons chopped fresh parsley leaves

Directions

- Melt butter in a large skillet over medium-high heat. Add shrimp, garlic, and red pepper flakes. Cook, stirring occasionally, until pink, about 2-3 minutes.
- Stir in chicken stock and lemon juice; season with salt and pepper, to taste. Bring to a simmer; stir in zucchini noodles until well combined, about 1-2 minutes.
- Serve immediately, garnished with Parmesan and parsley, if desired.

Nutrition

- Calories 214.3
- Calories from Fat 77.4
- Total Fat 8.6g
- Saturated Fat 4.7g
- Trans Fat 0.3g
- Cholesterol 232.7mg
- Sodium 338.1mg
- Total Carbohydrate 7.8g
- Dietary Fiber 1.9g
- Sugars 4.8g
- Protein 27.0g

---

16. Mexican Cauliflower Rice

Prep Time: 10 mins

Cook Time: 15 mins

Total Time: 25 mins

Servings: 4

Calories: 105

Ingredients

- 1 head cauliflower, riced
- 1 tbsp olive oil
- 1 medium white onion, finely diced
- 2 cloves garlic, minced
- 1 jalapeno, seeded and minced
- 3 tbsp tomato paste
- 1 tsp sea salt

- 1 tsp cumin
- 1/2 tsp paprika
- 3 tbsp fresh chopped cilantro
- 1 tbsp lime juice

Instructions

- Rice the cauliflower. Slice the florets from the head of the cauliflower. Fit a food processor with the s-blade. Place half the florets into the bowl of the food processor and pulse until riced, scraping down the sides once halfway through to catch any larger pieces. Scrape out the riced cauliflower and repeat with the remaining florets.
- Heat a skillet over medium-high heat. Add the oil and heat until it shimmers. Add the onion and saute until soft and translucent, stirring occasionally, 5-6 minutes.
- Add the garlic and jalapeno and saute until fragrant, 1-2 minutes.
- Add the tomato paste, salt, cumin, and paprika and stir into the vegetables.
- Add the cauliflower rice and stir continuously until all ingredients are incorporated. Continue sautéing, stirring occasionally, until the cauliflower releases its liquid and is dry and fluffy.
- Remove the Mexican cauliflower rice from heat. Stir in the cilantro and lime juice. Serve immediately.

To Use Frozen Cauliflower Rice:

- Defrost in the fridge overnight or in a fine-mesh sieve under cool running water.
- Shake the rice to remove as much moisture as possible.
- Transfer the cauliflower rice to a cotton kitchen towel and wring out excess moisture.
- Frozen cauliflower rice will cook more quickly.
- To use store-bought cauliflower rice:
- Look for bright white cauliflower rice, without a hint of a green tint
- Store packaging may cause the rice to sweat and release moisture, so be sure to wring it out before using it.

Storage Instructions

- Store in a tightly sealed container in the fridge for up to 3 days.

- Reheat in the microwave in 30-second intervals or a skillet over a medium-high flame for 2-3 minutes.
- If making for meal prep, reserve fresh cilantro and add it just after reheating.

Nutrition

Calories: 105kcal, Carbohydrates: 15g , Protein: 4g , Fat: 4g, Saturated Fat: 1g , Polyunsaturated Fat: 0g, Monounsaturated Fat: 3g, Trans Fat: 0g, Cholesterol: 0mg, Sodium: 500mg , Potassium: 713mg , Fiber: 5g , Sugar: 6g , Vitamin A: 950g, Vitamin C: 113g, Calcium: 90g , Iron: 1.8mg

---

17. Bacon & Cheddar Waffle Biscuits

Prep Time: 5 minutes

Cook Time: 5 minutes

Total Time: 10 minutes

Servings: 16

Calories: 171

Ingredients

- 2 cups of flour
- 1 tablespoon baking powder
- 1/2 cup butter
- 1/2 teaspoon salt
- 1 cup cheese
- 2/3 cup milk
- 5 slices bacon cooked and sliced

Instructions

- Preheat your waffle iron.
- Combine all the dry ingredients well; take a whisk to them or sift. Then cut in the butter until the mixture is coarse crumbs.
- Once the butter is cut in, pour the milk in, add the cheese and combine.
- You have a few options now when it comes to shaping. You can roll out the dough until it's about 1/4 of an inch thick then cut out circles that fit in your waffle iron or squares if wanted.
- Place the dough shape in the waffle iron and close. If you have a setting for the color or crispness of the waffle, choose the middle setting.

- Cook in the waffle iron until nicely browned on the outside. The biscuits will puff up slightly and cook. Enjoy!

Nutrition Facts

Serving: 16g, Calories: 171kcal, Carbohydrates: 12g, Protein: 4g, Fat: 11g, Saturated Fat: 6g, Cholesterol: 28mg, Sodium: 218mg, Potassium: 126mg, Vitamin A: 265IU, Calcium: 99mg, Iron: 0.9mg

18. Skinny Shrimp Scampi With Zucchini Noodles

Prep Time: 20 Minutes

Cook Time: 10 Minutes

Yield: 4 Servings

Ingredients

- 2 Tablespoons olive oil
- 1 pound jumbo shrimp, shelled and deveined
- 1 Tablespoon minced garlic
- 1/4 teaspoon crushed red pepper flakes (optional)
- 1/4 cup white wine
- 2 Tablespoons freshly squeezed lemon juice
- 2 medium zucchini, cut into noodles (See Kelly's Notes)
- Chopped parsley, for garnish

Instructions

- Place a large sauté pan over medium-low heat. Add the olive oil and heat it for 1 minute. Add the garlic and crushed red pepper flakes and cook them for 1 minute, stirring constantly.
- Add the shrimp to the pan and cook them, stirring as needed, until they are cooked throughout and pink on all sides, about 3 minutes. Season the shrimp with salt and pepper and then using a slotted spoon, transfer them to a bowl, leaving any liquid in the pan.
- Increase the heat to medium. Add the white wine and lemon juice to the pan. Using a wooden spoon, scrape any brown bits from the bottom of the pan, cooking the wine and lemon juice for 2 minutes. Add the zucchini noodles and cook, stirring occasionally, for 2 minutes.

Return the shrimp to the pan and toss to combine. Season with salt and pepper, garnish with parsley, and serve immediately.

Nutrition

- Calories: 170
- Total Fat: 8g
- Saturated Fat: 1.5g
- Trans Fat: 0g
- Total Carbohydrate: 6g
- Dietary Fiber: 1g
- Total Sugars: 3g
- Protein: 17g

19. Egg Roll In A Bowl

Yield: 4 Servings

Prep Time: 5 Minutes

Cook Time: 10 Minutes

Total Time: 15 Minutes

Ingredients

- 1 lb (16 ounces) ground pork or beef
- 1 teaspoon minced garlic
- 14 ounces shredded cabbage or coleslaw mix
- 1/4 cup low-sodium soy sauce
- 1 teaspoon ground ginger
- 2 teaspoons sriracha
- 1 whole egg
- 1 tablespoon sesame oil
- 2 tablespoons sliced green onions

Instructions

- In a large skillet, brown the pork or beef until no longer pink. Drain the meat if it's wet. Add the garlic and saute for 30 seconds. Add the cabbage/coleslaw, soy sauce, ginger, and saute until desired tenderness. You can add a little water if you need more liquid to sautee the coleslaw down.
- Make a well in the center of the skillet and add the egg. Scramble until done over low heat.
- Stir in sriracha. Drizzle with sesame oil and sprinkle with green onions. Add additional soy sauce and sriracha if desired.

Nutrition

- Yield: 4
- Calories: 331

- Total Fat: 23.4g
- Carbohydrates: 4.9g
- Fiber: 1.9g
- Protein: 24.3g

20. Baked Blueberry Donuts

Prep Time: 5 Mins

Cook Time: 10 Mins

Total Time: 15 Mins

Ingredients

- 1 1/4 cups whole wheat pastry flour, spoon in, and level off the top (all-purpose, spelled or whole wheat flour will also work, as well as Kodiak Cake pancake mix)
- 1 teaspoon baking powder
- 1/2 teaspoon salt
- 1/4 cup sugar
- 1 egg
- 1/2 cup milk (I like almond milk or cashew milk)
- 1 teaspoon vanilla extract
- 2 tablespoons coconut oil, melted (any oil or even melted butter will work)
- 1/2-1 cup fresh blueberries
- Powdered sugar, optional topping

Instructions

- Pre-heat oven to 350° F.
- In a large bowl, combine flour, baking powder, salt, and sugar. Stir in egg, milk, vanilla extract, and coconut oil. I add the coconut oil last and stir swiftly, as to avoid it hardening up. Gradually, stir in blueberries.
- Spoon batter into a liberally greased donut pan (nonstick spray works fine). You can also use a piping bag or a freezer bag with the tip snipped off to pipe the donut batter into the pan. Divide equally to create 10 donuts. The batter should fill donut molds to the center (but not cover it).
- Bake for 9-10 minutes. Let donuts cool for about 5 minutes before removing them from the donut pan. You may need to use a knife to remove each donut from the pan.
- To make the donut glaze, mix all glaze ingredients in a medium bowl. You may need to add a bit more water 1-2 teaspoons at a time for the right consistency.
- Dip warm donuts into the glaze, making sure to coat both sides, if desired. Place onto wire cooling rack to allow excess glaze to drip down. The glaze will eventually set + harden on the donuts after about 20 minutes.
- Donuts are best enjoyed the same day, though they keep at room temperature for a couple of extra days in an airtight container.

Nutrition

- Calories; 117
- Calories from fat: 35
- Fat: 3.9g
- Saturated Fats; 2.8g
- Cholesterol: 19.8mg
- Sodium:165.6mg
- Carbohydrates: 19g
- Fiber: 2.3g
- Sugar: 7.3g
- Protein: 2.6g

21. Low Carb Hatch Chile Rellenos Casserole

Prep Time: 30 Mins

Cook Time: 45 Mins

Total Time: 1 Hr 15 Mins

Servings: 8

Calories: 303 Kcal

Ingredients

- 1 1/2 pounds chiles, Hatch, poblanos, pasilla, or Anaheim chiles, charred, skins and seeds removed.
- 6 ounces queso fresco or cotija cheese, you can also substitute ricotta cheese for a similar texture and flavor.
- 12 ounces sharp cheddar cheese, grated
- 4 large eggs, beaten
- 1 teaspoon kosher salt
- 1/2 teaspoon black pepper
- 2 Tablespoons olive oil

Instructions

- Roast chiles under the broiler or on a charcoal grill, turning often until the skin is blackened. Place them in a paper bag and close tightly. When chiles are cool enough to handle, pull away and discard the seed and inside veins.

- Roasted, skinned, and seeded chiles.
- Preheat oven to 425 degrees F.
- Brush olive oil on the bottom of a 10.5" x 7.5" baking dish. Line with chiles.
- Hatch chiles in a casserole
- Cover chiles with about 2 ounces of crumbled cotija and 4 ounces of shredded cheddar. Repeat once, ending with cheeses on top.
- Hatch Chile casserole
- In a bowl, beat 4 eggs, salt, and pepper. Pour mixture over chiles and cheese. Cover with foil. Bake at 425 degrees F. For 40 minutes, or until cheese is hot and bubbly. Remove from oven and let rest 5-10 minutes to set.
- Low carb chile cheese casserole
- The casserole can be frozen. Cut into squares and wrap well.

Nutrition

- Serving: 1g
- Calories: 303kcal
- Carbohydrates: 7g
- Protein: 16g
- Fat: 23g
- Saturated Fat: 12g
- Cholesterol: 160mg
- Sodium: 896mg
- Potassium: 103mg
- Fiber: 2g
- Sugar: 3g
- Vitamin A: 675IU
- Vitamin C: 10.2mg
- Calcium: 366mg
- Iron: 0.9mg

22. Spinach Artichoke Dip

- Prep Time: 5 minutes
- Cook Time: 25 minutes
- Total Time: 30 minutes
- Servings: 12
- Calories: 65kcal

Ingredients

- 8 ounces reduced-fat cream cheese room temperature
- ½ cup plain non-fat Greek yogurt
- ½ cup sour cream full-fat or reduced-fat
- 10 ounces frozen spinach defrosted and drained
- ½ cup jarred artichokes drained and chopped
- ¼ cup freshly grated Parmesan cheese
- ⅓ cup shredded Mozzarella Cheese
- ⅓ cup Feta cheese crumbled
- 2 teaspoons minced garlic
- ¼ teaspoon crushed red pepper flakes optional
- 1 teaspoon fresh lemon juice
- ½ teaspoon kosher salt

Instructions

- Preheat oven to 350 degrees and grease a 1-quart baking dish.
- Defrost frozen spinach in the microwave or overnight in the refrigerator. Place defrosted spinach in cheesecloth or clean kitchen towel and squeeze out excess moisture over the sink.
- Drain a 10-ounce jar of artichoke hearts and chop well, measure out ½ cup of artichokes to use for the dip.
- In a large mixing bowl cream the cream cheese, sour cream, and yogurt together until creamy and smooth.
- Add the spinach, artichokes, cheese, salt, lemon juice, garlic cloves, and red pepper flakes to the cream cheese mixture and mix until all the ingredients are well incorporated.
- Transfer the mixture to the greased baking dish.
- Bake at 350 degrees for 20-25 minutes or until warmed through and slightly browned on the top.
- Serve with veggies, tortilla chips, or pita chips.

Nutrition

Calories: 65kcal | Carbohydrates: 3g | Protein: 6g | Fat: 3g | Saturated Fat: 1g | Cholesterol: 11mg | Sodium: 250mg | Potassium: 152mg | Sugar: 1g | Vitamin A: 2855IU | Vitamin C: 1.7mg | Calcium: 127mg | Iron: 0.5mg

23. Healthy Bruschetta Chicken

Prep Time: 10 Mins

Cook Time: 20 Mins

Total Time: 30 Mins

Servings: 4

Ingredients: Chicken

- 2 tbsp olive oil, extra virgin

- 4 chicken breasts
- salt & pepper to taste
- 1 tbsp dried basil
- 1 tbsp minced garlic

Bruschetta

- 3 ripe Roma tomatoes, diced
- 7 basil leaves, chopped
- 1 sprig oregano, chopped
- 2 tsp minced garlic
- 1 tbsp olive oil, extra virgin
- 1 tsp balsamic vinegar
- 1/4 tsp salt
- 1/4 tsp pepper

Balsamic Glaze

- 1 cup balsamic vinegar

Instructions: Chicken

- Add olive oil to saute pan or cast-iron skillet. Heat pan to medium-high heat.
- Add chicken to the hot pan. Sprinkle salt, pepper, and dried basil on top of each cutlet. Cook until browned, about 5 minutes. Flip chicken. Add garlic to the pan. Cook until the remaining side of the chicken is browned, about 5 minutes.

Bruschetta

- Add all ingredients to a bowl and stir together until combined.
- Pour over your cooked chicken breasts.

Balsamic Glaze

- Add 1 cup balsamic vinegar to a small saucepan. Bring to a boil over medium-high heat. Reduce heat to medium. You should see bubbling along the outside of your pan. Let simmer for 10 minutes. Stir occasionally as vinegar begins to thicken and coat the spoon. Remove from heat and set aside to cool for a few minutes. It will thicken a bit more as it sits and you'll end up with around 1/4 cup of balsamic glaze.
- Drizzle over bruschetta topped chicken.

Nutrition

Serving: 1chicken Breast + 1/4 Bruschetta Topping And Glaze, Calories: 283kcal,

Carbohydrates: 11g, Protein: 25g, Fat: 13g, Saturated Fat: 2g, Cholesterol: 72mg, Sodium: 291mg, Potassium: 595mg, Sugar: 8g, Vitamin A: 460iu, Vitamin C: 8.8mg, Calcium: 49mg, Iron: 1.5mg

24. Spaghetti Squash Lasagna

Prep Time: 10 mins

Cook Time: 1 hr

Total: 1 hr 10 mins

Serving: 4 –6 servings

Ingredients

- 2 medium spaghetti squash
- 1 tablespoon plus 2 teaspoons olive oil divided
- 2 teaspoons kosher salt divided
- ¾ teaspoon black pepper divided
- 1 pound ground turkey
- 2 teaspoons Italian seasoning
- ¼ teaspoon red pepper flakes
- 2 cloves garlic minced
- 1 (24-ounce) jar good-quality tomato pasta sauce I like roasted garlic
- 1 tablespoon red wine vinegar
- 1 (10-ounce) pack frozen spinach drained and pressed as dry as possible
- 1 cup part-skim ricotta cheese or low-fat 1% or 2% cottage cheese
- 1 cup shredded fontina, mild provolone, mozzarella, or similar melty cheese divided
- ¼ cup grated Parmesan cheese
- Chopped fresh parsley

Instructions

- Place a rack in the center of your oven and preheat the oven to 400 degrees F. Roast the spaghetti squash according to this recipe for Roasted Spaghetti Squash.
- While the squash is baking, heat the remaining tablespoon of oil in a large skillet over medium-high. Add the turkey, 1 teaspoon salt, remaining ½ teaspoon pepper, Italian seasoning, and red pepper flakes. Stir and cook, breaking apart the meat into small pieces, until it is fully cooked through and browned on all sides, about 4 minutes. Stir in the garlic and cook until fragrant, about 1 minute more. Reduce the heat to low.

Stir in the pasta sauce and red wine vinegar. Let simmer for 1 minute. Taste and adjust the seasoning as desired.

- Place the spinach in a large mixing bowl. Use a fork to separate any large clumps. Add the ricotta, ½ cup fontina, and remaining ½ teaspoon salt. Stir with the fork to combine. When the squash is cool enough to handle, use a fork to fluff the insides into strands and add the strands to the bowl. With the same fork, stir to combine, evenly distributing the ingredients as best you can. Return the squash halves to the baking sheet, cut sides up.
- Fill the squash: Pile the ricotta/squash filling evenly into each of the four halves. Top with tomato sauce, remaining shredded cheese, and Parmesan. Return to the oven and bake until the filling is fully heated through and the cheese is melty about 10 to 15 minutes.
- Brown the top (optional): Turn the oven to broil. Broil the squash until the cheese is extra bubbly and lightly browned, about 2 minutes. Watch it carefully, and do not walk away so that it doesn't burn. Sprinkle with parsley and enjoy!

Nutrition

- Calories: 555KCAL
- Carbohydrates: 39G
- Protein: 48G
- Fat: 25G
- Saturated Fat: 12g
- Cholesterol: 125mg
- Potassium: 967mg
- Fiber: 8g
- Sugar: 14g
- Vitamin A: 1283iu
- Vitamin C: 11mg
- Calcium: 551mg
- Iron: 3mg

25. Healthy Chicken Breakfast Sausage

Total Time: 15 min

Prep Time: 5 min

Cook Time: 10 min

Servings: 4 (2 patties each)

Ingredients

- 1 pound lean ground chicken
- 1 teaspoon dried sage
- 1 1/4 teaspoons garlic powder
- 1 teaspoon freshly cracked black pepper
- 1/2 teaspoon crushed red pepper flakes
- 2 teaspoons pure maple syrup
- 2 teaspoons olive oil

Preparation

- In a large bowl, stir together all ingredients except for oil. Form into eight round patties.
- Heat a nonstick skillet over medium heat. Add one teaspoon of oil. Working four patties at a time, cook sausage until browned on one side, about 3-5 minutes, then flip and brown on the other side. Continue the process until cooked through, about 5 minutes. Remove from skillet and repeat with remaining oil and patties.
- Serve hot or store extra sausage in the refrigerator in an airtight container.

Nutrition

- Servings: 4 (2 patties each)
- Calories: 179
- Total Fat: 11g
- Saturated Fat: 3g
- Cholesterol: 84mg
- Sodium: 60mg
- Total Carbohydrate: 3g
- Dietary Fiber: 0g
- Total Sugars: 2g
- Protein: 18g
- Calcium: 13mg
- Iron: 1mg
- Potassium: 554mg

26. Spaghetti Squash Casserole

Prep Time: 5 Minutes

Cook Time: 35 Minutes

Total Time: 40 Minutes

Servings: 6 Servings

Ingredients

- 1 spaghetti squash cooked
- 1 pound lean ground beef
- 1 onion diced
- 2 cloves garlic minced

- 15 ounces diced tomatoes canned
- 1 tablespoon tomato paste
- 1 cup marinara sauce or pasta sauce
- 1 teaspoon Italian seasoning
- 1 ½ cups mozzarella cheese shredded

Instructions

- Preheat oven to 375F.
- Cook squash until tender. Cut in half. Using a fork, remove spaghetti squash strands from the squash and set them aside.
- In a medium saucepan, cook ground beef, onion, and garlic until no pink remains. Drain any fat.
- Add diced tomatoes, tomato paste, pasta sauce, and seasoning. Simmer 5 minutes.
- Stir in squash. Place in a casserole dish (or back into the squash halves) and top with cheese. Bake for 20 minutes or until golden and bubbly.

Nutrition

Calories: 286, Carbohydrates: 19g, Protein: 25g, Fat: 12g, Saturated Fat: 4g, Cholesterol: 56mg, Sodium: 530mg, Potassium: 748mg, Fiber: 4g, Sugar: 9g, Vitamin A: 630IU, Vitamin C: 15.1mg, Calcium: 358mg, Iron: 3.5mg

27. Crustless Broccoli Quiche with Cheddar And Onions

Prep Time: 10 Mins

Cook Time: 30 Mins

Rest time: 15 Mins

Total Time: 55 Mins

Ingredients

- 1 tablespoon butter for pan
- 1 (16 oz) package frozen chopped broccoli
- 8 large eggs
- ½ cup sour cream (or full-fat Greek yogurt)
- 1 teaspoon Diamond Crystal kosher salt (or ½ teaspoon fine salt)
- ¼ teaspoon black pepper
- 1 teaspoon garlic powder
- ¼ cup chopped scallions white and green parts
- 1 cup shredded sharp cheddar cheese (4 oz)

Instructions

- Preheat oven to 400 degrees F. Generously butters a 9-inch pie dish.
- Place the broccoli in a large microwave-safe bowl. Add ¼ cup water. Cover and microwave on high for 6 minutes, stirring after the first 3 minutes. Drain well.
- In a large bowl, whisk together the eggs, sour cream, Kosher salt, black pepper, and garlic powder. Stir in the broccoli, the scallions, and the cheese.
- Transfer the mixture to the prepared pie dish. Bake until golden brown and a knife inserted in center comes out clean, about 30 minutes.
- Allow the quiche to cool and set in pan on a wire rack, about 15 minutes, before slicing into 8 triangles and serving.

Nutrition

- Calories: 196
- Fat: 14g
- Saturated Fat: 8g
- Sodium: 317mg
- Carbohydrates: 5g
- Fiber: 2g
- Sugar: 2g
- Protein: 12g

28. Keto Meatloaf

Servings: 8 Slices

Prep Time: 10 Mins

Cook Time: 1 Hr 5 Mins

Total Time: 1 Hr 15 Mins

Ingredients

- 2 pounds 80/20 Ground beef
- 1 medium Onion, diced
- 2 cups Crushed Pork rinds
- 1 large Egg
- 2 tablespoons Worcestershire sauce
- ½ teaspoon Garlic powder
- 1 teaspoon salt
- ⅓ cup Reduced sugar ketchup

Instructions

- Preheat oven to 350 degrees F.
- In a large bowl combine all ingredients except ketchup. Mix ingredients until fully combined.

- Press ingredients into a parchment paper-lined loaf pan.
- Bake for 30 minutes. After 30 minutes add ketchup on top and bake for 25-35 minutes more.
- Remove from oven and let rest for 15 minutes.
- Enjoy!

Nutrition

- Serving: 1slice, Calories: 351kcal, Carbohydrates: 3g, Protein: 25g, Fat: 25g, Saturated Fat: 10g, Cholesterol: 110mg, Sodium: 672mg, Potassium: 369mg, Fiber: 1g, Sugar: 2g, Vitamin A: 34iu, Vitamin C: 2mg, Calcium: 34mg, Iron: 3mg.

29. Zucchini Lasagna Recipe

Prep Time: 35 Min

Cook Time: 22 Min

Servings: 9

Calories: 212kcal

Ingredients

- 2 medium zucchini
- 1 pound beef, ground, 95% lean
- 1/2 medium onion
- 1/2 medium bell pepper, red
- 2 medium carrot
- 3 clove garlic
- 15-ounce tomato sauce
- 1 tablespoon Worcestershire sauce
- 1 teaspoon oregano, dried
- 1 teaspoon basil, dried
- 1/8 teaspoon salt
- 1/8 teaspoon black pepper, ground
- 2 cup cottage cheese
- 1 large egg
- 1/4 cup Parmesan cheese, grated
- 2 cup mozzarella cheese, shredded

Instructions

- Wash and cut zucchini into very thin strips. Line a colander with paper towels and place it in the sink. Place zucchini into the colander and salt generously. Allow zucchini strips to sweat for 30 minutes.
- Dice onion and red bell pepper (enough for 1/2 cup), grated carrots (enough for 1/2 cup), and mince garlic.
- Pre-heat oven to 350* F and grease a 9×13 inch pan.
- In a large skillet over medium-high heat, brown ground beef until cooked completely, making sure to chop into small pieces as you go. Remove beef onto a paper towel-lined plate and set aside.
- Remove most of the remaining fat from the skillet, place it back on the stove, and saute the onion, pepper, carrot, and garlic until the onion is translucent.
- Add tomato sauce, Worcestershire sauce, spices, and the cooked ground beef back into the skillet. Bring to a simmer, and allow to simmer for 10 minutes.
- Meanwhile, mix cottage cheese, egg, and parmesan in a small bowl.
- Once the zucchini have sweat for 30 minutes, wipe clean and dry with a clean cloth. Place one layer of zucchini strips on the bottom of the greased pan.
- On top of the zucchini, spread half of the tomato-beef sauce. Then spread a layer of half of the cottage cheese mixture. Then sprinkle half of the mozzarella cheese. Repeat layers once more: zucchini, sauce, cottage cheese, mozzarella.
- Place in the oven for 20 minutes at 350* F, then turn the oven to broil and crack the oven door. Allow the top of the lasagna to bubble and brown, watching carefully. Should take 2 minutes or less.
- Remove from the oven and allow to sit for 20-30 minutes before serving.

Nutrition

Calories: 212kcal | Carbohydrates: 11g | Protein: 24g | Fat: 8g | Saturated Fat: 4g | Cholesterol: 72mg | Sodium: 663mg | Fiber: 2g | Sugar: 7g

30. Mashed Potato Flatbread

Prep Time: 15 Mins

Cook Time: 20 Mins

Total Time: 35 Mins

Servings: 8 Flatbreads

Ingredients

- 1 cup Mashed Potatoes (about 8.5 ounces/240 grams fresh potatoes)
- 1 cup All-Purpose Flour (Plain Flour + extra for dusting (about ½ cup))

Instructions

- Place the flour and potato mash onto your work surface. Using your hand(s) start bringing the ingredients together until you form a sticky dough.
- Roll this into a sausage and cut it into 8 pieces. Form each piece into a round shape.
- Make sure the worktop and dough are dusted with flour before you start rolling it out. Roll it out thin.
- Cook on medium to high heat on a dry frying pan for about 2 minutes (1 minute per side) or until done.
- Best served right away while still warm.

Nutrition

- Calories: 83
- Sodium 8mg
- Potassium 99mg
- Carbohydrates 18g
- Protein 2g
- Vitamin C 6.1mg
- Calcium 4mg
- Iron 0.8mg

31. Fried Cabbage With Sausage

Prep Time: 10 minutes

Cook Time: 20 minutes

Total Time: 30 minutes

Ingredients

- 12 ounces smoked sausage
- 2 tablespoons olive oil divided
- 1/2 yellow onion
- 2 cloves garlic
- 1 medium head cabbage
- 1 teaspoon salt
- 1 teaspoon ground pepper

Instructions

- Slice the smoked sausage into thin rounds.
- Heat 1 tablespoon olive oil in a dutch oven or large, deep skillet over medium heat. Add the sausage to the skillet and cook, stirring often, until sausage is browned on both sides, about 4 minutes.
- Add the onion and garlic to the skillet and cook for 3 more minutes to soften onions.
- Add the remaining tablespoon of oil to the skillet along with the cabbage and sprinkle with salt and pepper.
- Cook the cabbage, stirring constantly, until it becomes tender, about 10 minutes.
- Serve immediately.

Nutritional Value

- Calories: 304
- Fat: 24g
- Protein:
- Carbs: 13g
- Fiber: 5g
- Net carbs: 8

32. Salmon Florentine

Prep: 12 Min

Inactive: 10 Min

Cook: 20 Min

Yield: 4 Servings (1 Serving = 1 Piece Salmon)

Ingredients

- Deselect All
- 2 (10 ounce) packages frozen spinach, thawed
- 1 tablespoon olive oil
- 1/4 cup minced shallots
- 2 teaspoons minced garlic
- 5 sun-dried tomatoes, chopped
- 1/4 teaspoon red pepper flakes
- 1/2 teaspoon salt
- 1/4 teaspoon black pepper
- 1/2 cup part-skim ricotta cheese
- 4 (6-ounce) salmon fillets, rinsed and patted dry

Directions

- Preheat oven to 350 degrees F. Using your hands, squeeze spinach of all excess liquid.
- Heat olive oil in a large skillet over medium heat. Add shallots and garlic and cook for 3 minutes

until they begin to soften. Add garlic and cook for 1 minute more. Add spinach, sun-dried tomatoes, red pepper flakes, 1/2 teaspoon salt, and 1/4 teaspoon pepper, and cook an additional 2 minutes. Remove from heat and let cool for approximately 10 minutes. Add ricotta and stir to combine. Season with additional salt and pepper, to taste.

- Using your hands, pack approximately 1/2 cup spinach mixture on top of each salmon fillet, forming mixture to the shape of the fillet. Place fillets on a rimmed baking sheet or glass baking dish and bake for 15 minutes, until salmon is cooked through.

33. Slow Cooker Everything Chicken

Prep Time: 5 Minutes

Cook Time: 4 Hours

Total Time: 4 Hours 5 Minutes

Yield: 9 People

Serving Size: 0.75 Cup

Ingredients

- 3 pounds boneless and skinless chicken breasts
- 1/4 cup extra-virgin olive oil
- 1-2 tablespoons garlic chopped
- 1 1/2 teaspoons kosher or sea salt
- 1 teaspoon pepper
- 1/2 cup vegetable broth or chicken broth, low-sodium
- Instructions
- Place chicken in the slow cooker. Drizzle with olive oil being sure to coat all sides. Add garlic, sea salt, and pepper. Pour broth around the outside of the chicken. Cover and cook on low for 6-8 hours, or on high for 3-4 hours, or until chicken reaches an internal temperature of 170 degrees.
- When the chicken is tender and cooked through, remove it from the slow cooker and slice or shred it with a fork.
- Serve in tacos, soup, or chili, with your favorite gravy & mashed potatoes, cook it into a chicken casserole, or top it with teriyaki sauce and serve it over brown rice for an Asian twist. Enjoy!

Nutrition

Serving: 0.75cup | Calories: 228kcal | Carbohydrates: 1g | Protein: 32g | Fat: 10g | Saturated Fat: 2g | Cholesterol: 97mg | Sodium: 616mg | Potassium: 559mg | Fiber: 1g | Sugar: 1g | Vitamin A: 73IU | Vitamin C: 2mg | Calcium: 9mg | Iron: 1mg

34. Quick Chicken Marsala

Active Time: 20 Mins

Total Time: 20 Mins

Yield: Serves 4 (serving size: 1 cutlet and about 1/4 cup sauce)

Ingredients

- 2 tablespoons olive oil, divided 4 (4-oz.) skinless, boneless chicken breast cutlets 3/4 teaspoon black pepper, divided 1/2 teaspoon kosher salt, divided 1 (8-oz.) pkg. presliced button mushrooms 4 thyme sprigs 1 tablespoon all-purpose flour 2/3 cup unsalted chicken stock 2/3 cup Marsala wine 2 1/2 tablespoons unsalted butter 1 tablespoon chopped fresh thyme (optional)
- How To Make It
- Heat 1 tablespoon oil in a large nonstick skillet over medium-high. Sprinkle chicken with 1/2 teaspoon pepper and 1/4 teaspoon salt. Add chicken to pan; cook until done, about 4 minutes per side. Remove chicken from pan (do not wipe out pan).
- Add the remaining 1 tablespoon oil to the pan. Add mushrooms and thyme sprigs; cook, stirring occasionally until mushrooms are browned, about 6 minutes. Sprinkle flour over mixture; cook, stirring constantly, 1 minute.
- Add stock and wine to pan; bring to a boil. Cook until slightly thickened, 2 to 3 minutes. Remove pan from heat. Stir in butter, remaining 1/4 teaspoon pepper, and remaining 1/4 teaspoon salt. Add chicken to pan, turning to coat. Discard thyme sprigs before serving. Sprinkle with chopped thyme, if desired.

Nutrition

- Calories: 344
- Fat:17g
- Satfat: 6g

- Unsat: 9g
- Protein: 28g
- Carbohydrates: 9g
- Fiber: 1g
- Sugars: 7g
- Added sugars: 0g
- Sodium: 567mg
- Calcium: 19g
- Potassium: 16mg

35. Zucchini Chips

Prep Time: 5 minutes

Cook Time: 50 minutes

Total Time: 55 minutes

Servings: 2 servings

Ingredients

- 1 medium zucchini washed and dried
- 1 tbsp. olive oil
- Scant ½ tsp. kosher salt
- ½ tsp. black pepper
- ¼ tsp. onion powder
- ½ tsp. paprika

Instructions

- Preheat the oven to 450 degrees. Line two baking sheets with parchment paper.
- Thinly slice the zucchini with a knife or mandolin.
- In a large bowl, combine the oil, salt, pepper, onion powder, and paprika. Stir to combine.
- Add the zucchini slices to the bowl and toss well so that each slice is coated with the seasoned oil.
- Place the zucchini slices on the prepared baking sheets.
- Bake for 8-15 minutes watching very closely. When the zucchini starts to show some brown spots remove from the oven and set aside.
- Reduce the oven temperature to 180-200 degrees. Return the zucchini to the oven and cook for an additional 20-40 minutes or until the slices are crispy.
- Remove from the oven and cool.

Nutrition

Serving: 1g | Calories: 80kcal | Carbohydrates: 4g | Protein: 1g | Fat: 7g | Saturated Fat: 1g | Polyunsaturated Fat: 6g | Sodium: 586mg | Fiber: 2g | Sugar: 2g

36. Heavenly Halibut

Prep Time: 15 Mins

Cook Time: 10 Mins

Total Time: 25 Mins

Servings: 8

Ingredients

- ½ cup grated Parmesan cheese
- ¼ cup butter softened
- 3 tablespoons mayonnaise
- 2 tablespoons lemon juice
- 3 tablespoons chopped green onions
- ¼ teaspoon salt
- 1 dash hot pepper sauce
- 2 pounds skinless halibut fillets

Instructions

- Preheat the oven broiler. Grease a baking dish.
- In a bowl, mix the Parmesan cheese, butter, mayonnaise, lemon juice, green onions, salt, and hot pepper sauce.
- Arrange the halibut fillets in the prepared baking dish.
- Broil halibut fillets 8 minutes in the prepared oven, or until easily flaked with a fork. Spread with the Parmesan cheese mixture, and continue broiling 2 minutes, or until topping is bubbly and lightly browned.

Nutrition

- Servings Per Recipe: 8
- Calories: 235.3
- Protein: 25.7g
- Carbohydrates: 0.9g
- Dietary Fiber: 0.1g
- Sugars: 0.2g
- Fat: 13.9g
- Saturated Fat: 5.5g
- Cholesterol: 58mg
- Vitamin A Iu: 397.7IU
- Niacin Equivalents: 11.2mg
- Vitamin B6: 0.4mg

- Vitamin C: 2.2mg
- Folate: 15.3mcg
- Calcium: 112.6mg
- Iron: 1mg
- Magnesium: 97.6mg
- Potassium: 530.1mg
- Sodium: 281.7mg
- Thiamin: 0.1mg

37. Baked Zucchini Fries

Prep Time: 15 Mins

Cook Time: 30 Mins

Total Time: 45 Mins

Servings: 4 Servings

Ingredients

- Zucchini Fries
- 2 Medium Zucchini
- 1 Egg
- 1 Cup Grated Parmesan Cheese
- 1 Tsp Garlic Powder
- 1 Tsp Italian Spice
- Lemon Parsley Aioli
- 1/2 Cup Mayonnaise
- 1 Lemon, Juiced
- 1 Garlic Clove, Minced
- 1 Tbsp, Finely Chopped Parsley
- Salt And Pepper

Instructions

- Preheat the oven to 425 degrees Fahrenheit and line two baking trays with parchment paper.
- Slice the zucchini in half, then half again, then into quarters. You should have 16 slices per zucchini.
- Crack the egg in a small bowl or container and lightly beat it.
- Add the parmesan and spices to a separate bowl or container and stir to combine.
- Dip a slice of zucchini in the egg wash and transfer to the parmesan. Use your other hand to coat the zucchini in the cheese and transfer to the baking tray. Repeat this process until all zucchini is coated.
- Bake for 25-30 minutes, flipping halfway through on the cut side. Serve immediately.

- To make the optional lemon parsley aioli, add all ingredients to a small bowl and stir together.

Nutrition

Calories: 156.8KCAL, Carbohydrates: 6.2g, Protein: 12.5g, Fat: 9.8g, Saturated Fat: 6.5g, Cholesterol: 66.6mg, Sodium: 258.4mg, Fiber: 1.6g, Sugar: 4.2g

38. Roasted Delicata Squash

Yields: 4 servings (as a side dish)

Prep Time: 10 mins

Cook Time: 30 mins

Total Time: 40 mins

Ingredients

For The Roasted Squash:

- 2 Delicata squash 1 pound each, rinsed, seeds removed, and cut into ½-inch slices
- 3 tablespoons extra virgin olive oil
- 2 tablespoons of honey
- ¾ teaspoon kosher salt
- ¼ teaspoon black pepper
- For the sweet & sour (agrodolce) drizzle sauce: (optional)
- 1 small ½ teaspoon red habanero (or any other hot) chili, minced
- ⅓ cup white wine vinegar
- Zest of a lime
- Juice of a lime 2-3 tablespoons, freshly squeezed
- Pinch of salt
- 2 tablespoons pepitas aka pumpkin seeds

Instructions

- Preheat the oven to 375 degrees. Line a baking sheet with parchment paper.
- Place the squash onto the baking sheet. Drizzle it with olive oil and honey. Sprinkle it with salt and pepper. Toss to coat evenly. Make sure that all the delicata squash slices are evenly distributed throughout the sheet pan.
- Bake for 12-15 minutes on each side (25-30 min. in total), flipping the squash halfway through the baking process.
- If preferred, while the squash is baking make the sweet and sour drizzle sauce. Place the chili, vinegar, zest, and juice of a lime, and salt in a

small saucepan and heat in medium heat. Let it come to a boil, turn down the heat to medium-low and simmer until the mixture is syrupy, 10-12 minutes.

- When ready to serve, arrange the slices of roasted delicata squash on a large plate, drizzle it with the sweet and sour sauce, and sprinkle it with pepitas.
- Serve immediately.

Nutrition

Calories: 235kcal | Carbohydrates: 29g | Protein: 4g | Fat: 13g | Saturated Fat: 2g | Sodium: 448mg | Potassium: 833mg | Fiber: 4g | Sugar: 14g | Vitamin A: 3120IU | Vitamin C: 31mg | Calcium: 63mg | Iron: 2mg

---

39. 10 Minute Garlic Bok Choy Recipe

Prep Time: 2 Mins

Cook Time: 8 Mins

Total Time: 10 Mins

Servings: 6 As A Side

Ingredients

- 1 tbsp vegetable oil
- 5 cloves garlic (minced)
- 2 large shallots (minced)
- 2 pounds baby bok choy (halved or quartered)
- 2 tbsp soy sauce
- 1 tsp sesame oil
- 1 tsp crushed red pepper (optional)

Instructions

- Add the oil to a large wok or skillet over medium-high heat. Swirl to coat the entire surface of the pan. Add the garlic and shallots, stirring continuously for 1-2 minutes, or until fragrant.
- Add the bok choy, soy sauce, and sesame oil. Toss to coat and cover. Cook for 1-2 minutes, uncover and toss, and then cover and continue to cook until bok choy is cooked to desired doneness (approximately 3-5 minutes more).
- Sprinkle with crushed red pepper and serve immediately. Enjoy!

Nutrition

Calories: 54kcal | Carbohydrates: 4g | Protein: 2g | Fat: 3g | Saturated Fat: 1g | Cholesterol: 0mg | Sodium: 439mg | Potassium: 29mg | Fiber: 1g | Sugar: 1g | Vitamin A: 6825IU | Vitamin C: 68.8mg | Calcium: 171mg | Iron: 1.3mg

---

40. Keto Reuben In A Bowl

Prep Time: 5 Minutes

Cook Time: 10 Minutes

Total Time: 15 Minutes

Ingredients

- 1 lb Finely Sliced Corned Beef
- 1 Tablespoon Olive Oil
- 1 bag 16 Oz Coleslaw Mix
- 2 Tablespoons Butter, salted
- 2 cups Swiss Cheese, grated
- ½ Cup Green Onion, chopped

Russian Dressing

- 1 cup Mayonnaise
- ¼ Cup Sugar-Free Ketchup
- 4 Teaspoons Horseradish
- 2 Tablespoons Diced Dill Pickle
- 1 Teaspoon Worcestershire Sauce
- Salt, to taste

Instructions

- In a large skillet over medium-high heat, pour olive oil into a skillet and add corned beef. Cover and saute for 5 minutes. Remove skillet from heat and drain the corned beef.
- Return skillet to medium-high heat and add butter. Stir.
- Once butter is melted, add coleslaw to the corned beef and cook for 5 minutes stirring frequently.
- Adjust heat to low and add Swiss cheese. Cover the skillet and allow the cheese to melt until it's bubbly. Optionally, move the skillet to the oven and set the oven to BROIL. Heat until the cheese is melted and bubbly.
- Combine all the Russian Dressing Ingredients then drizzle the skillet ingredients with Russian Dressing and top with Green Onions.

Nutrition

- Yield: 8 Serving Size
- Calories: 514
- Total Fat: 46g
- Carbohydrates: 6g
- Fiber: 1g
- Protein: 18g

41. Healthy Homemade Spaghetti Sauce

Prep Time: 15 minutes

Cook Time: 50 minutes

Total Time: 1 hour 5 minutes

Servings: 20 servings

Ingredients

- 1 1/2 pounds ground beef
- 3 teaspoons minced garlic
- 2 cans tomato puree 29 ounces each
- 2 cans diced tomatoes, with juice 14.5 ounces each
- 2 teaspoons salt
- 2 teaspoons lemon juice
- 2 tablespoons olive oil
- 2 teaspoons oregano
- 2 teaspoons basil
- 1 teaspoon thyme
- 1 teaspoon crushed red pepper

Instructions

- In a large saucepan, brown the ground beef along with the garlic. Drain.
- Add in the rest of the ingredients and bring to a low boil, stirring often.
- Once the sauce is heated through and at a low boil, reduce the burner temperature to low and simmer uncovered for 45 minutes.
- Serve immediately or allow the sauce to cool, then package it in freezer-safe containers for easy storage.

Nutrition

Calories: 112kcal | Carbohydrates: 9g | Protein: 9g | Fat: 5g | Saturated Fat: 2g | Cholesterol: 22mg | Sodium: 284mg | Potassium: 554mg |

Fiber: 2g | Sugar: 5g | Vitamin A: 505IU | Vitamin C: 13mg | Calcium: 36mg | Iron: 3mg

42. Olive Oil Scrambled Eggs With Feta And Tomatoes

Prep Time: 5 mins

Cook Time: 5 mins

Total Time: 10 mins

Ingredients

- 1 Tablespoon Extra-Virgin Olive Oil
- 2 Tablespoons Diced Onion
- 1/2 Cup Cherry Tomatoes Halved
- 2 Eggs Beaten
- Kosher Salt To Taste
- Black Pepper To Taste
- 2 Oz. Feta Cheese Crumbled (About 1/4 Cup)
- 1 Tablespoon Chopped Fresh Parsley Or Dill, Basil, Or Chives
- More Extra Olive Oil, Feta, And Parsley, For Serving Optional

Instructions

- Season the two beaten eggs with a little bit of salt and pepper. Set aside.
- Sauté diced onion in a nonstick skillet in the 2 tablespoons olive oil over medium heat until softened (try not to brown them), about 1 minute.
- Add the halved cherry tomatoes (1/2 cup) to the skillet and continue sautéing until softened about 2 minutes.
- Add the beaten eggs to the skillet. Use a wooden spoon or spatula to push the eggs into the center of the skillet from the outside, working your way around as they cook.
- When the eggs are almost cooked (after about 1 minute), add the feta cheese (2 oz.) and chopped fresh parsley or other herbs (1 tablespoon). Stir and finish cooking until the eggs are only just underdone, about 30 seconds more (they will finish cooking completely on the plate from the residual heat).
- Transfer eggs to a plate and sprinkle with extra feta cheese and parsley, drizzle with olive oil, and season with more salt and pepper, if desired. Eat immediately.

Nutrition Facts

Calories:421kcal|Carbohydrates:8.6g|Protein:20.3g|Fat:35.1g|Saturated Fat: 13.2g |Cholesterol: 378mg |Sodium: 763mg |Fiber: 1.6g| Sugar: 6.3g

43. Low Carb Zuppa Toscana Soup

Prep Time: 10 Mins

Cook Time: 20 Mins

Total Time: 30 Mins

Ingredients

- 1 Lb. Ground Italian Sausage
- 4 Slices Thick-Cut Bacon, Diced
- 1 Small Onion, Diced
- 5 Cups Chicken Broth
- 2 Cups Water
- 5 Cups Cauliflower Florets, Medium-Sized Head Of Cauliflower
- 1 1/2 Cups Chopped Kale
- 1 Cup Heavy Cream
- Salt And Pepper To Taste
- Pinch Of Red Pepper Flakes
- Parmesan Cheese For Serving

Instructions

- In a large dutch oven or stock, pot brown the sausage until crumbled and cooked through. Use a slotted spoon to remove the sausage to a paper towel-lined plate and set it aside.
- Turn the pot to medium-high heat and add the bacon, cooking until fat is rendered and bacon begins to crisp. Add the onion and cook an additional 2 to 3 minutes.
- Return the sausage to the pot and pour in the chicken broth, water, and cauliflower florets. Bring mixture to a boil, then reduce heat to simmer, cover, and cook for 10 minutes, until the cauliflower is fork-tender.
- Stir in the kale and let cook an additional 2 minutes until softened slightly. Finally stir in the heavy cream, salt, and pepper to taste and the red pepper flakes. Simmer for 2 more minutes until heated through. Enjoy with fresh parmesan on top.

Nutrition

Calories: 327kcal | Carbohydrates: 6g | Protein: 11g | Fat: 29g | Saturated Fat: 13g | Cholesterol:

77mg | Sodium: 888mg | Potassium: 470mg | Fiber: 1g | Sugar: 1g | Vitamin A: 1359IU | Vitamin C: 46mg | Calcium: 61mg | Iron: 1mg

44. Chicken And Ginger Congee (Gf)

Serves: 6

Prep Time: 5 mins

Cook Time: 1 hr

Total Time: 1 hr 5 mins

Ingredients

- 1 Cup Long-Grain Rice (White Or Brown)
- 8 Cups Water
- 6 Chicken Thighs (Bone-In)
- 1 Piece Of Ginger About 1 Inch By 1 Inch (2.5 Cm By 2.5 Cm) - Peeled And Sliced Into Large Pieces
- Salt - To Taste
- Scallions - For Garnish

Instructions

- Rinse and drain the rice. Pour the rice into a heavy stockpot (a cast iron pot works great).
- Add in the water, ginger, and chicken thighs.
- Bring the pot to a boil then immediately turn down the heat. Allow the pot to simmer, covered, for 1-1 1/2 hours, or until the rice has absorbed most of the liquid and has started breaking apart. It will take white rice for about 1 hour, and brown rice for about 1 1/2 hours.
- Remove the chicken thighs into a bowl and allow to cool. When the chicken thighs are cool enough for you to handle, shred the meat and remove the bones.
- Add the shredded chicken back into the congee and mix well.
- Add salt, if desired.
- Serve the congee into individual bowls and garnish with green onions, if desired.

45. Homemade Cheddar Biscuits

Prep Time: 20 minutes

Cook Time: 15 minutes

Total Time: 35 minutes

Yield: 8-10 biscuits

Ingredients

- 2 and 1/2 cups (312g) all-purpose flour, plus extra for hands and work surface
- 2 Tablespoons aluminum-free baking powder (yes, Tablespoons)
- 1 teaspoon garlic powder
- 1 teaspoon salt
- 1/2 cup (1 stick; 115g) unsalted butter, cubed and very cold (see note)
- 1 cup + 2 Tablespoons (270ml) cold buttermilk, divided
- 2 teaspoons honey
- 1 cup (125g) shredded cheddar cheese

Topping

- 1/4 cup (4 Tablespoons; 60g) unsalted butter, melted
- 1 garlic clove, minced
- 1 teaspoon dried parsley

Instructions

- Preheat oven to 425°F (218°C).
- Make the biscuits: Place the flour, baking powder, garlic powder, and salt together in a large bowl or a large food processor. Whisk or pulse until combined. Add the cubed butter and cut into the dry ingredients with a pastry cutter or by pulsing several times in the processor. Cut/pulse until coarse crumbs form. If you used a food processor, pour the mixture into a large bowl.
- Fold in the shredded cheese. Make a well in the center of the mixture. Pour 1 cup (240ml) buttermilk and drizzle honey on top. Fold everything together with a large spoon or rubber spatula until it begins to come together. Do not overwork the dough. The dough will be shaggy and crumbly with some wet spots. See the photo above for a visual.
- Pour the dough and any dough crumbles onto a floured work surface and gently bring together with generously floured hands. The dough will become sticky as you bring it together. Have extra flour nearby and use it often to flour your hands and work surface in this step. Using floured hands or a floured rolling pin, flatten into a 3/4 inch thick rectangle as best you can. Fold one side into the center, then the other side. Turn the dough horizontally. Gently flatten into a 3/4 inch thick rectangle again. Repeat the

folding. Turn the dough horizontally one more time. Gently flatten into a 3/4 inch thick rectangle. Repeat the folding one last time. Flatten into the final 3/4 inch thick rectangle.
- Cut into 2.75 or 3-inch circles with a biscuit cutter. (Tip: Do not twist the biscuit cutter when pressing down into the dough– this seals off the edges of the biscuit which prevents them from fully rising.) Re-roll scraps until all the dough is used. You should have about 8-10 biscuits. Arrange in a 10-inch cast-iron skillet (see note) or close together on a parchment paper-lined baking sheet. Make sure the biscuits are touching.
- Brush the tops with remaining buttermilk. Bake for 15-20 minutes or until the tops are golden brown.
- Make the topping: Mix the topping ingredients. Generously brush on the warm biscuits.
- Cover leftovers tightly and store at room temperature or in the refrigerator for up to 5 days.

2. Lean and Green Recipes Main & Lunch Recipes

46. Grilled Chicken Cauliflower Alfredo With Zucchini Noodles

Prep Time: 10 Minutes

Cook Time: 15 Minutes

Total Time: 25 Minutes

Servings: 4

Ingredients: Chicken

- 1 lb boneless (skinless chicken breast, sliced thin and then cut into slices)
- 1/2 tsp sea salt
- 1/4 tsp garlic powder
- 1/4 tsp paprika
- 1/8 tsp black pepper

Garnishment

- ❖ Shaved parmesan cheese
- ❖ Chopped parsley
- ❖ Serve with your favorite dipping bread

Instructions

- Rinse chicken in water and pat dry. Slice chicken to desired strip thickness. Or wait to cut until after cooking.
- Using a brush, coat the chicken with approximately 1/2 tablespoon of olive oil and season with salt, garlic powder, paprika, and pepper.
- Place a grill pan (or regular pan) over medium heat. Add olive oil and allow it to heat.
- Once heated, add the chicken to the pan allowing to cook 8-10 minutes, or until done.
- Place a separate large pan over medium-low heat with olive oil. Once heated, add the roasted red peppers and zucchini noodles - stirring to cook them through.
- If desired, season noodles with additional garlic powder and a dash of sea salt.
- When the noodles have cooked (yet still have some firmness), add the chicken and cauliflower alfredo sauce. Stir to combine.

Nutrition

- Calories: 270
- Calories From Fat: 103
- Fat: 11.4g
- Saturated Fat: 2.6g
- Polyunsaturated Fat: 6.5g
- Cholesterol: 60mg
- Sodium: 1001.2mg
- Carbohydrates: 15.3g
- Fiber: 3.7g
- Sugar: 8.7g
- Protein: 28g

47. Low Carb Italian Wedding Soup

Prep Time: 10 Minutes

Cook Time: 30 Minutes

Total Time: 40 Minutes

Servings: 10 Servings

Ingredients

- Meatballs
- 1 lb. ground turkey or beef
- 1 large egg
- 1 tsp. onion powder
- 1 tsp. garlic powder
- 1/2 tsp. dried basil

Italian Wedding Soup Base

- 8 cups chicken broth
- 1/4 cup sliced baby carrots
- 1 cup sliced celery
- 6 oz. Bag fresh baby spinach
- 2 tsp. Garlic powder
- 2 tsp. Onion powder
- Salt & pepper to taste after cooking

Instructions

- Bring the broth to boil in a large soup pot.
- While that warms up, mix your meatballs in a medium mixing bowl.
- When the broth is boiling, gently drop the meatballs into the broth.
- Add the chopped vegetables (not the spinach) and spices. Simmer until everything is cooked through (about 20-30 minutes. The meatballs should be at least 165 F. and the carrots should be soft.)
- When everything is done cooking, quickly stir in the spinach and allow the soup to boil for approximately 1-2 more minutes to cook the spinach down.
- Remove from heat and allow to cool.
- Serve with salt and pepper as needed.

Nutrition

- Calories: 85
- Calories From Fat: 18
- Fat: 2g
- Saturated Fat: 1g
- Cholesterol: 46mg
- Sodium: 745mg
- Potassium: 459mg
- Carbohydrates: 4g
- Fiber: 1g
- Sugar: 1g
- Protein: 13g

48. Mexican Zucchini And Beef

Prep Time: 5 mins

Cook Time: 25 mins

Total Time: 30 mins

Servings: 6 servings

Ingredients

- 2 medium zucchini sliced and quartered
- 1 ½ pounds ground beef
- 2 cloves garlic minced
- 10 ounces mexican style diced tomatoes with green chilis (salsa or diced tomatoes could be used), canned
- 1 tablespoon chili powder
- 1 teaspoon ground cumin
- 1 teaspoon salt
- ½ teaspoon black pepper
- ½ teaspoon onion powder
- ¼ teaspoon crushed red pepper flakes

Instructions

- Brown ground beef with minced garlic, salt, and pepper. Cook over medium heat until meat is browned.
- Add tomatoes and remaining spices. Cover and simmer on low heat for another 10 minutes.
- Add the zucchini. Cover and cook for about 10 more minutes until zucchini is cooked, but still firm.

Nutrition

Serving: 1cup (approx) | Calories: 315 | Carbohydrates: 5g | Protein: 21g | Fat: 23g | Saturated Fat: 9g | Cholesterol: 81mg | Sodium: 498mg | Potassium: 597mg | Fiber: 2g | Sugar: 3g | Vitamin A: 606IU | Vitamin C: 16mg | Calcium: 55mg | Iron: 3mg

49. Low Carb Pho – Vietnamese Beef Noodle Soup

Prep Time: 15 minutes

Cook Time: 3 hours

Total Time: 3 hours 15 minutes

Servings: 5 servings

Ingredients

- The Broth (4-5 servings)
- 5-6 beef soup bones browned and roasted - the more connective tissue, the better!
- 1/2 Onion charred
- 1 tablespoon Fresh Ginger sliced
- 1 tbsp Salt
- 3 tbsp Fish Sauce
- 2 pods Star Anise
- 1 gallon Water

Instructions

- Preheat oven to 425 degrees F.
- Cover beef bones in water and boil for 15 minutes in a large stockpot on the stovetop while the oven preheats. Discard water.
- Place parboiled beef bones and onion on a baking sheet or casserole dish and roast for 45 - 60 minutes, until bones are browned and onion is blackened.
- Toss bones, onion, fresh ginger, salt, fish sauce, star anise, and freshwater into the pressure cooker.
- Set pressure cooker to high pressure for 2 hours. If you are using a stovetop, you will simmer for 6-8 hours instead.
- Strain broth with a fine colander.
- Place shirataki noodles and meat of choice in a bowl, pour broth over the top into the bowl while it is still very hot.
- Stir and let sit until raw meat is no longer pink and noodles are cooked 1 to 2 minutes.
- Serve with condiments and veggies of choice on the side.

Nutrition

Calories: 172kcal | Carbohydrates: 3g | Protein: 25g | Fat: 5g | Saturated Fat: 2g | Cholesterol: 67mg | Sodium: 2342mg | Potassium: 461mg | Sugar: 1g | Vitamin A: 135IU | Vitamin C: 5.8mg | Calcium: 62mg | Iron: 2.2mg

50. Olive Oil Seared Scallops

Total Time: 9 min

Prep Time: 5 min

Cook Time: 4 min

Servings: 2 (1/2 pound each)

Ingredients

- 1 pound sea scallops
- 1/4 teaspoon kosher salt (or to taste)
- 1/4 teaspoon ground black pepper
- 2 tablespoons olive oil (or enough to coat the bottom of the pan)

Preparation

- If not done in advance, remove the small side muscle from each scallop. Rinse scallops under cold water and pat dry with paper towels.
- Season with salt and pepper.
- Add olive oil to a large saute pan and heat on medium-high heat until the oil starts to shimmer but before it smokes. (The pan must be hot enough, otherwise, the scallops will not brown.) Carefully add scallops to the pan, making sure there is space between each scallop.
- Cook the scallops for about 2 minutes, flip carefully to the other side and cook for another 2 minutes. They should have a nice golden crust and still be slightly translucent on the inside. Serve immediately.

Nutrition

- Servings: 2 (1/2 pound each)
- Calories: 185
- Total Fat: 8g
- Saturated Fat: 1g
- Cholesterol: 46mg
- Sodium: 1047mg
- Total Carbohydrate: 6g
- Total Sugars: 0g
- Protein: 23g
- Calcium: 12mg
- Iron: 1mg
- Potassium 356mg

51. One Pot Taco Zucchini Noodles

- Prep Time: 10 Minutes
- Cook Time: 15 Minutes
- Total Time: 25 Minutes

Ingredients

- 1 tbsp olive oil
- 2 large zucchinis spiralized
- 1 lb lean ground turkey
- 1 clove garlic minced
- 1/2 small brown onion peeled and finely chopped
- 3 tbsp of homemade taco seasoning or one packet of your favorite taco seasoning
- 1/4 cup water
- 14 oz can diced tomatoes
- 1/2 cup shredded cheddar cheese
- Fresh cilantro leaves

- One lime sliced into wedges

Instructions

- In a large pan or skillet, add olive oil and bring to medium-high heat. Add zucchini noodles and cook until zucchini releases water and is just cooked. Drain water and remove noodles from the pan, setting them aside for later.
- Add garlic, onions, and ground turkey to your skillet. Cook until ground turkey has browned, crumbling the ground turkey as you cook it. Drain out excess fat.
- Sprinkle taco seasoning across turkey. Add entire contents of the diced tomatoes (including the liquid), 1/4 cup water, and stir into the turkey mixture. Stir and cook on medium heat until everything is evenly mixed, turkey is cooked through, and the sauce has thickened.
- Turn heat down to low and add in zucchini noodles. Gently toss zucchini into the sauce, but be careful not to cook the zucchini further, or else the noodles will release more water and make the sauce watery. Sprinkle cheese over the pasta. Turn off heat and cover with a lid until cheese is melted.
- Garnish with cilantro and squeeze lime juice if desired before serving.

Nutrition

- Serving: 0.25of Recipe, Calories: 318kcal, Carbohydrates: 13.2g, Protein: 29g, Fat: 18.2g, Saturated Fat: 5.7g, Polyunsaturated Fat: 3.5g, Monounsaturated Fat: 7g, Trans Fat: 0.2g, Cholesterol: 92.2mg, Sodium: 927mg, Fiber: 4.9g, Sugar: 7.4g, Vitamin A: 500iu, Vitamin C: 62.7mg, Calcium: 210mg, Iron: 3.6mg, Net Carbs: 8g

52. Best-Ever Cauliflower Stuffing

Yields: 6 Servings

Prep Time: 15 Mins

Total Time: 40 Mins

Ingredients

- 4 tbsp. butter
- 1 onion, chopped
- 2 large carrots, peeled and chopped
- 2 celery stalks, chopped or thinly sliced

- 1 small head cauliflower, chopped
- 1 c. (8-oz.) package baby Bella mushrooms, chopped
- Kosher salt
- Freshly ground black pepper
- 1/4 c. freshly chopped parsley
- 2 tbsp. freshly chopped rosemary
- 1 tbsp. freshly chopped sage (or 1 tsp. ground sage)
- 1/2 c. low-sodium vegetable or chicken broth

Directions

In a large skillet over medium heat, melt butter. Add onion, carrot, and celery and sauté until soft, 7 to 8 minutes.

Add cauliflower and mushrooms and season with salt and pepper. Cook until tender, 8 to 10 minutes more.

Add parsley, rosemary, and sage and stir until combined. Pour over broth and cook until totally tender and liquid is absorbed 10 minutes.

Nutrition (Per Serving)

- Calories: 90
- Protein: 6g
- Carbohydrates:3g
- Fiber: 1g
- Sugar:2g
- Fat:6g
- Saturated fat:2g
- Sodium: 230mg

53. Low Carb Chicken Pot Pies

Prep Time: 15 Minutes

Cook Time: 25 Minutes

Total Time: 40 Minutes

Ingredients: For The Cauliflower Base

- 1 Medium Head Cauliflower (4-5 Cups Cauliflower Rice)
- ¼ Cup Shredded Parmesan Cheese
- 1 Egg
- Pinch Of Salt And Pepper

For The Pot Pie Filling:

- ½ onion, diced
- 1 ½ cups chicken broth
- ¼ cup almond milk, unsweetened
- 1 cup frozen mixed vegetables
- 8oz cooked chicken, diced
- 1 tbs onion powder
- ½ tsp salt
- ½ tsp black pepper
- 2 tbs cornstarch + ¼ cup water

Instructions

- Preheat oven to 400 degrees F. Add the cauliflower to the bowl of a food processor and pulse until you achieve a rice-like consistency. Transfer cauliflower "rice" to a bowl and microwave for 5 minutes. Set aside and allow cauliflower to cool for approx 10 minutes.
- Add the cauliflower rice to a cheesecloth and squeeze out as much of the juice from the cauliflower as possible. If you don't, the bases may end up soggy. (The key here is to get as much of that juice out as you can. Once you have done around with the cheesecloth. Repeat with another dry cheesecloth to ensure you have removed a majority of the liquid. I managed to get 1 ½ cups of cauliflower juice).
- Add the dried cauliflower rice to a bowl with the egg, parmesan cheese, salt, and pepper. Using your hands, combine all of the ingredients thoroughly. Spray a large muffin pan or 4 ramekins and gently press the cauliflower mixture to the sides, creating a cauliflower bowl. Bake for 20-25 minutes or until the centers are dry and the edges are golden brown.
- While the cauliflower bases are in the oven, spray a medium saucepan with cooking spray and saute the diced onion on high heat until slightly tender. Reduce heat to medium and add the chicken broth, almond milk, mixed vegetables, onion powder, salt, and black pepper. Stir and cover for approx 5-8 minutes or until frozen vegetables are soft.
- Mix the cornstarch with the water to make a slurry and add to the sauce with the cooked chicken. Stir in the cornstarch mixture and increase heat to high and cook until sauce begins to boil. Remove from heat.
- Fill each cauliflower base with the pot pie filling and serve!

Nutrition

- Yield: 4 Pot Pies
- Serving Size: 1 Pot Pie
- Calories: 205
- Total Fat: 6g
- Saturated Fat: 2g
- Cholesterol: 73mg
- Sodium: 491mg
- Carbohydrates: 17g
- Net Carbohydrates: 13g
- Fiber: 4g
- Sugar: 5g
- Protein: 20g

54. Roasted Vegetable Medley

Prep Time: 10 minutes

Cook Time: 35 minutes

Total: 45 minutes

Serves: 8

Ingredients

- 3 zucchini squash cut lengthwise into fourths, and then slice into bite-size pieces
- 3 yellow squash sliced same as zucchini
- 1 red pepper cut into 1" pieces
- 1 red onion cut into wedges
- 8 ounces whole mushrooms
- 1 garlic clove minced
- 1 tablespoon balsamic vinegar (more to taste)
- 1 tablespoon olive oil
- 1 tablespoon rosemary leaves
- 1 teaspoon kosher salt

Instructions

- Preheat oven to 450 degrees.
- Spray a large baking sheet with cooking spray (or you can foil line the baking sheet and spray the foil).
- Mix all of the cut-up vegetables and garlic in a large bowl.
- Add olive oil and balsamic vinegar. Toss until all the vegetables are covered.
- Add rosemary leaves and salt, and toss again.
- Roast the vegetables for about 30-40 minutes, stirring once. You will know the vegetables are done when they are brown on the outside edges and tender on the inside.

Nutrition

Calories: 59kcal | Carbohydrates: 8g | Protein: 3g | Fat: 2g | Saturated Fat: 1g | Sodium: 301mg | Potassium: 526mg | Fiber: 2g | Sugar: 6g | Vitamin A: 768IU | Vitamin C: 47mg | Calcium: 29mg | Iron: 1mg

55. Roasted Carrots And Parsnips

Prep Time: 15 minutes

Cook Time: 20 minutes

Total: 35 minutes

Serves: 8

Ingredients

- 4 large parsnips
- 4 large carrots
- 2 tablespoons oil olive, sunflower, canola, grapeseed
- 3 teaspoons rosemary
- 2 teaspoons kosher salt
- 1 teaspoon thyme

Instructions

- Preheat oven to 425 degrees.
- Peel the parsnips and carrots. Quarter the thick end of the carrots, and half them on the thinner end. Quarter the parsnips. Cut out the thick, fibrous center, then cut them the same as the carrots.
- Combine parsnips and carrots in a large bowl and toss with oil, rosemary, salt, and thyme.
- Spread onto a baking sheet.
- Roast for approximately 20-30 minutes, turning the vegetables after the first 10-15 minutes. The vegetables will be tender and slightly browned.

Nutrition

Calories: 96kcal | Carbohydrates: 17g | Protein: 1g | Fat: 3g | Saturated Fat: 1g | Sodium: 643mg | Potassium: 388mg | Fiber: 5g | Sugar: 5g | Vitamin A: 5232IU | Vitamin C: 15mg | Calcium: 38mg | Iron: 1mg

56. Parmesan Baked Potato Halves

Prep Time: 10 minutes

Cook Time: 45 minutes

Total: 55 minutes

Serves: 6

Ingredients

- 6 small potatoes scrubbed and cut in half
- 1/4 cup butter
- Grated parmesan cheese
- Garlic powder
- Other seasonings to personal preference
- Instructions
- Preheat oven to 400 degrees.
- Melt butter and pour into a 9x13 inch pan and spread evenly across the bottom.
- Generously sprinkle parmesan cheese and lightly sprinkle other seasonings all over the butter.
- Place potato halves face down on the butter and seasonings.
- Place in preheated oven and bake for 40 to 45 minutes.
- Cool for at least a full 5 minutes before removing from the pan, otherwise, the parmesan crust won't stick to the potato.
- Serve on a plate with a side of sour cream or ranch dressing for dipping.

Nutrition

Calories: 204kcal | Carbohydrates: 22g | Protein: 8g | Fat: 10g | Saturated Fat: 6g | Cholesterol: 28mg | Sodium: 212mg | Potassium: 719mg | Fiber: 4g | Sugar: 1g | Vitamin A: 310IU | Vitamin C: 19.4mg | Calcium: 146mg | Iron: 5.6mg

57. Roasted Potatoes With Brussels Sprouts And Bacon

Prep Time: 10 minutes

Cook Time: 35 minutes

Total: 45 minutes

Serves: 6 servings

- Ingredients
- 2 pounds red potatoes Yukon Gold or Russets work well too
- 1 pound Brussels sprouts
- 1/4 cup olive oil
- 3 cloves garlic minced
- 1 teaspoon rosemary optional
- 1 teaspoon kosher salt
- 1/2 teaspoon ground black pepper
- 1/2 pound bacon lightly cooked and cut into pieces

Instructions

- Preheat oven to 400 degrees.
- Scrub and rinse the potatoes. Pat dry and dice into one-inch pieces.
- Wash Brussels sprouts and trim off the ends, slice in half length-wise.
- Whisk olive oil, garlic, rosemary (optional), salt, and pepper in a large bowl until well combined.
- Add potatoes and Brussels sprouts and stir until potatoes and Brussels are coated in the oil mixture.
- Place potatoes and Brussels sprouts on a baking sheet and sprinkle bacon pieces over the top.
- Roast for 35-40 minutes. Potatoes should be golden and soft and Brussels should be well roasted and lightly charred-- bacon should be nice and crispy.

Nutrition

Calories: 378kcal | Carbohydrates: 32g | Protein: 10g | Fat: 24g | Saturated Fat: 6g | Cholesterol: 25mg | Sodium: 684mg | Potassium: 1063mg | Fiber: 5g | Sugar: 4g | Vitamin A: 595IU | Vitamin C: 78mg | Calcium: 51mg | Iron: 2mg

58. One Pan Balsamic Chicken And Veggies

Servings: 4 Servings

Prep Time: 10 minutes

Cook Time: 13 minutes

Ready in: 23 minutes

Ingredients

- 1/4 cup + 2 Tbsp Italian salad dressing (I recommend using Kraft light Italian it's the perfect consistency for this and it's what I used)
- 3 Tbsp balsamic vinegar

- 1 1/2 Tbsp honey
- 1/8 tsp crushed red pepper flakes (more or less to taste)
- 1 1/4 lbs chicken breast tenderloins
- 2 Tbsp olive oil
- Salt and freshly ground black pepper
- 1 lb fresh asparagus, trimmed of tough ends, chopped into 2-inch pieces (look for thinner stalks. Green beans are another good option)
- 1 1/2 cups matchstick carrots
- 1 cup grape tomatoes, halved

Instructions

- In a mixing bowl whisk together salad dressing, balsamic vinegar, honey, and red pepper flakes, set aside.
- Heat olive oil in a 12-inch skillet over medium-high heat. Season chicken with salt and pepper to taste, then place chicken evenly in skillet.
- Cook about 6 - 7 minutes, rotating once halfway through cooking, until chicken has cooked through (meanwhile, chop asparagus and tomatoes). Add half the dressing mixture to skillet and rotate chicken to evenly coat.
- Transfer chicken to a large plate or a serving platter while leaving sauce in skillet. Add asparagus and carrots to skillet, season with salt and pepper to taste, and cook, stirring frequently, until crisp-tender, about 4 minutes. Transfer veggies to plate or platter with chicken.
- Add remaining dressing mixture to skillet and cook, stirring
- constantly, until thickened, about 1 minute. Add tomatoes to chicken and veggies and drizzle dressing mixture in pan over top (or return chicken and veggies to the pan and toss to coat).

Nutrition

- Calories: 342
- Calories from Fat: 126
- Fat: 14g
- Saturated Fat: :2g
- Cholesterol: 90mg
- Sodium: 351mg
- Potassium: 1021mg
- Carbohydrates: 20g

- Fiber: 4g
- Sugar: 15g
- Protein: 33g
- Vitamin C: 16mg
- Calcium: 57mg
- Iron 3.3mg

---

59. Vegetarian Chili

Prep Time: 20 Minutes

Cook Time: 30 Minutes

Total Time: 50 Minutes

Servings: 6 -8 servings

Ingredients

- 2 tablespoons olive oil
- 1 small yellow onion, diced (1 cup)
- 1 tablespoon minced garlic (reduce depending on garlic sensitivity)
- 1 red bell pepper, diced (heaping cup)
- 2 tablespoons ground chili powder
- 1/2 tablespoon dried (NOT ground) oregano
- 1 teaspoon ground cumin
- 1/2 teaspoon EACH: dried basil, seasoned salt, cayenne pepper, paprika
- 1/4 teaspoon cracked pepper
- 1/2 tablespoon white sugar
- 2 cans (14.5 ounces EACH) fire-roasted diced tomatoes
- 2 cans (14.5 ounces EACH) black beans, drained and rinsed
- 1 can (14.5 ounces) pinto beans, drained and rinsed
- 1 can (4 ounces) fire-roasted diced green chiles, optional
- 1 cup frozen corn
- 1 cup vegetable stock (vegetable broth will work)
- 1 bay leaf
- 2 tablespoons fresh lime juice
- Toppings: cheddar cheese, fat-free sour cream, avocado, cilantro, chives, tortilla strips, etc.

Instructions

- Place a large heavy-bottomed pot (or dutch oven) over medium heat. Pour in the olive oil and wait until shimmering, about 20 seconds. Add in the diced onion and stir for 3-4 minutes.

Add in the diced pepper and cook these veggies, stirring occasionally, until they are all very tender, about 6-9 minutes.

- While the veggies are getting soft, mince the garlic and measure out all your spices, combining them into a small bowl: the chili powder, oregano, cumin, dried basil, salt, cayenne pepper, paprika, pepper, and sugar. Stir together and set aside until onion/pepper are tender.
- Add in the garlic and all the seasonings you've already measured and set aside. Cook, stirring constantly, until the seasonings and garlic are fragrant, about 45 seconds - 1 minute. Be careful to not burn.
- Carefully add in the UNDRAINED diced tomatoes (they might sizzle splatter up a bit) and stir. Add in the drained and rinsed black beans, drained and rinsed pinto beans, chiles (if desired), frozen corn, and vegetable stock. Add in the bay leaf.
- Stir to combine everything. Reduce the heat as needed to maintain a gentle simmer, and stir occasionally, for 25-30 minutes.
- Remove 1 and 1/2 cups of the chili and transfer to a blender. To avoid a mess, remove your blender lid's center insert and hold a kitchen towel firmly over the top. Ensure the lid is securely fashioned and blend while holding the towel. Once smooth, pour this mixture back into your chili. Stir to combine.
- Add fresh lime and fresh cilantro as desired. Season to taste (I always add in a little bit more salt & pepper). Garnish individual bowls with everyone's favorite toppings. For us, sour cream and cheddar cheese are a must-have!
- Nutrition
- Calories: 264 kcal
- Total Fat: 7.4g
- Cholesterol: 0mg
- Sodium: 717.9mg
- Total carbohydrates: 39.3g
- Dietary Fiber: 15g
- Sugar: 3.8g
- Protein: 12. 1g

60. Instant Pot Low Carb Corned Beef And Cabbage

Prep Time: 15 minutes

Cook Time: 1 hour 35 minutes

Total Time: 1 hour 50 minutes

Servings: 8 servings

Ingredients

- 4 pounds corned beef brisket
- 6 cups water
- 2 tsp black peppercorns
- 4 cloves garlic
- 2 tsp dried mustard
- 1 cabbage cut into wedges or 8 cups
- 1 cup onions sliced
- 1 cup carrots sliced into thirds
- 1 cup celery stalks chopped

Instructions

- Place the beef brisket into the pot. Discard the spice packet that comes with the meat.
- Cover the beef with water, add more to cover if needed.
- Add the spices into the pot.
- Cover and set on "Meat/Stew" for 60 minutes on high.
- Hit Cancel then use the Natural Release method, about 20 minutes.
- Remove cover carefully, watch for steam, remove the brisket and keep warm.
- Add the vegetables to the pot and press the "Soup" setting for 15 minutes.
- Use the "Quick" Release method.
- Uncover and add the beef back to the pot to warm through.
- Enjoy immediately!

Nutrition

- Calories: 499
- Calories from Fat: 306
- Fat: 34g
- Saturated Fat: 10g
- Cholesterol: 122mg
- Sodium: 2812mg
- Potassium: 1000mg
- Carbohydrates: 11g
- Fiber: 4g
- Sugar: 5g
- Protein: 35g
- Vitamin A: 2840IU
- Vitamin C: 106.1mg
- Calcium: 89mg

- Iron: 4.6mg

61. Jicama Tortilla Chicken Tacos

Prep Time: 10 Mins

Total Time: 10 Mins

Ingredients

- 8 jicama tortillas
- 1 cup Crock Pot Salsa Chicken
- 0 Point toppings (salsa, pico de gallo, cilantro, red onions, diced peppers, black beans, jalapenos, etc)

Instructions

- Stack two of the jicama tortilla on top of each other.
- Top with a ¼ cup crock pot salsa chicken, and add on any additional toppings you'd like.

- Nutrition

- Servings: 4 Servings
- Calories: 87 kcal
- Carbohydrates: 5.5 g
- Protein: 12.4 g
- Fat: 1.4 g
- Saturated Fat: g
- Trans Fat: g
- Cholesterol: 36.5 mg
- Sodium: 177 mg
- Potassium: 65 mg
- Fiber: 2.4 g
- Sugar: 1 g
- Calcium: 10 mg
- Iron: 1.1 mg

62. Best Oven-Roasted Broccoli With Nutritional Yeast

Prep Time: 5 minutes

Cook Time: 20 minutes

Total Time: 25 minutes

Ingredients

- 1 large head of broccoli; approx 4 heaping cups of broccoli florets
- 1 TBSP olive oil
- 3 TBSP nutritional yeast
- 1/2 tsp garlic salt, give or take

Instructions

- Pre-heat oven to 425° F.
- Cut broccoli down into bite-sized florets. In a colander, rinse them off and give them a good shake to dry them off; transfer them to a large bowl.
- Drizzle the florets with the olive oil and sprinkle the florets with 2 TBSP of nutritional yeast, followed by the garlic salt. With a large spoon, give the broccoli a good toss to evenly coat the florets. You could also cover the bowl and shake the contents until evenly coated. When done, spread the florets out onto a baking sheet. Sprinkle the rest of the nutritional yeast over the broccoli florets.
- Bake in the oven for 15-20 minutes, tossing the broccoli halfway through.
- Season with a bit of extra garlic salt if needed, and cracked black pepper if desired.

63. Spinach Artichoke Dip

Prep Time: 5 minutes

Cook Time: 25 minutes

Total Time: 30 minutes

Servings: 12

Ingredients

- 8 ounces reduced-fat cream cheese room temperature
- ½ cup plain non-fat Greek yogurt
- ½ cup sour cream full-fat or reduced-fat
- 10 ounces frozen spinach defrosted and drained
- ½ cup jarred artichokes drained and chopped
- ¼ cup freshly grated Parmesan cheese
- ⅓ cup shredded Mozzarella Cheese
- ⅓ cup Feta cheese crumbled
- 2 teaspoons minced garlic
- ¼ teaspoon crushed red pepper flakes optional
- 1 teaspoon fresh lemon juice
- ½ teaspoon kosher salt

Instructions

- Preheat oven to 350 degrees and grease a 1-quart baking dish.
- Defrost frozen spinach in the microwave or overnight in the refrigerator. Place defrosted spinach in cheesecloth or clean kitchen towel and squeeze out excess moisture over the sink.

- Drain a 10-ounce jar of artichoke hearts and chop well, measure out ½ cup of artichokes to use for the dip.
- In a large mixing bowl cream the cream cheese, sour cream, and yogurt together until creamy and smooth.
- Add the spinach, artichokes, cheese, salt, lemon juice, garlic cloves, and red pepper flakes to the cream cheese mixture and mix until all the ingredients are well incorporated.
- Transfer the mixture to the greased baking dish.
- Bake at 350 degrees for 20-25 minutes or until warmed through and slightly browned on the top.
- Serve with veggies, tortilla chips, or pita chips.

Nutrition

Calories: 65kcal | Carbohydrates: 3g | Protein: 6g | Fat: 3g | Saturated Fat: 1g | Cholesterol: 11mg | Sodium: 250mg | Potassium: 152mg | Sugar: 1g | Vitamin A: 2855IU | Vitamin C: 1.7mg | Calcium: 127mg | Iron: 0.5mg

64. Zucchini Pasta With Creamy Avocado Pesto

Prep: 10 Minutes

Cook: 5 Minutes

Total: 15 Minutes

Servings: 2

Ingredients

- 1 avocado ripe
- 1 clove garlic
- ½ cup fresh basil leaves
- 1 Tbsp lemon juice 15 mL
- 2 Tbsp extra virgin olive oil 30 mL
- Water as needed
- Salt and pepper to taste
- 2-3 zucchinis spiralized or cut into ¼ inch wide strips

Instructions

- Sauce: In a food processor, blend avocado, garlic, basil leaves, and lemon juice until smooth, then mix in extra virgin olive oil. Add water, 1 Tbsp at a time, until sauce reaches a fluid yet thick consistency. Season with salt and pepper, to taste.

- Zucchini Noodles: Saute zoodles with a splash of olive oil over medium/high heat until slightly soft and bright green, 3 to 5 minutes. Drain excess water.
- Serve: Toss zoodles with sauce and top with parmesan cheese (you may not need all of the sauce).

Nutrition Value

Serving: 1serving (half recipe) Calories: 362kcal, Carbohydrates: 16g, Protein: 4.6g, Fat: 34.1g, Saturated Fat: 6.3g, Cholesterol: 0mg Sodium: 28mg, Potassium: 1043mg, Fiber: 9.1g, Sugar: 4.1g, Calcium: 40mg, Iron: 1.4mg.

65. Air Fryer Garlic Zucchini

Prep Time: 5 mins

Cook Time: 15 mins

Total Time: 20 mins

Servings: 2 servings

Ingredients

- 2 zucchini 455g
- Olive oil or cooking spray
- 1/2 teaspoon garlic powder
- Salt, to taste
- Black pepper, to taste

Instructions

- Trim the ends of the zucchini, if desired. Cut the zucchini into 1/2" thick slices (either into lengthwise slices or into coins). If cutting into lengthwise slices, cut to length to fit the width of your air fryer basket if needed.
- Lightly oil or spray the zucchini slices on both sides and then season with garlic powder, salt, and pepper.
- Air Fry at 400°F for 8-14 minutes or until browned and cooked through.

Nutrition

Calories: 36kcal | Carbohydrates: 7g | Protein: 2g | Fat: 1g | Saturated Fat: 1g | Sodium: 16mg | Potassium: 512mg | Fiber: 2g | Sugar: 5g | Vitamin A: 390IU | Vitamin C: 35.1mg | Calcium: 31mg | Iron: 0.7mg

66. Healthy Sloppy Joes (Homemade in 30 minutes)

Prep Time: 5 minutes

Cook Time: 25 minutes

Total Time: 30 minutes

Servings: 8 Servings

Ingredients

- 1 ½ pounds lean ground beef
- 1 small green pepper finely diced
- 3/4 cup ketchup
- 1 tbs worcestershire sauce
- 1 tbs brown sugar
- 1/2 teaspoon garlic powder
- ½ tsp onion powder
- ½ tsp garlic salt
- 1 tsp dijon mustard
- ¼ tsp ground black pepper
- 8 buns

Instructions

- In a small bowl mix together ketchup, Worcestershire sauce, brown sugar, garlic powder, onion powder garlic salt, mustard, and black pepper. Set aside.
- Add ground beef to a medium skillet and cook over medium-high heat until it begins to brown.
- Add green pepper and cook until soft.
- Drain liquids and stir in the mixture made in step 1. Mix until combined.
- Reduce heat, and simmer covered for 20 minutes.
- Remove the lid and simmer for about 5 minutes more or until the mixture thickens (if you like thicker sloppy joes)!
- Serve with your favorite garnishes on your favorite rolls!

Nutrition

Calories: 176.3kcal | Carbohydrates: 10.7g | Protein: 18.2g | Fat: 5.3g | Saturated Fat: 2.3g | Cholesterol: 48.8mg | Sodium: 442.2mg | Potassium: 35.3mg | Fiber: 0.2g | Sugar: 7.9g | Vitamin A: 50IU | Vitamin C: 17.5mg | Calcium: 3mg | Iron: 1.5mg

67. Sheet Pan Baked Tilapia And Roasted Veggies

Prep Time: 10 mins

Cook Time: 15 mins

Total Time: 25 mins

Ingredients

- 4 6 ounce tilapia fillets
- 3 cups broccoli florets, cut into 1-inch pieces
- 1 yellow squash, sliced
- 1 1/2 cups carrots, thinly sliced
- 4 Tablespoons olive oil, (divided)
- 2 Tablespoons lemon juice
- 1 Tablespoon garlic, minced
- 1 Tablespoon fresh parsley, (1 1/2 teaspoons dried)
- 1/4 teaspoon dried red pepper flakes
- 1/4 teaspoon onion powder
- Salt & pepper

Instructions

- Preheat oven to 400 degrees F.
- Place veggies on a baking sheet and drizzle with 2 tablespoons olive oil. Sprinkle with salt and pepper, mix, and then push to the sides of the pan.
- In a small bowl, mix the remaining 2 tablespoons of olive oil, lemon juice, garlic, parsley, red pepper flakes, and onion powder. Place tilapia on the pan between the veggies and rub the marinade on all sides of the fillets. Sprinkle tilapia with salt and pepper.
- Bake for 12-15 minutes or until fish reaches 145 degrees F and flakes easily. Serve immediately.

Nutrition

- Calories: 343
- Calories from Fat: 153
- Fat: 17g
- Saturated Fat: 3g
- Cholesterol: 85mg
- Sodium: 148mg
- Potassium: 1011mg
- Carbohydrates: 12g
- Fiber: 3g
- Sugar: 4g
- Protein 37g
- Vitamin A: 8600IU
- Vitamin C: 75.9mg
- Calcium: 76mg
- Iron: 1.8mg

68. Kicked-Up Tuna Melts

Prep Time: 5 minutes

Cook Time: 5 minutes

Total Time: 10 minutes

Servings: 4 people

Ingredients

- 12 ounces canned albacore white tuna, packed in water, drained
- 1/4 cup mayonnaise, more to taste (or substitute half mayo, half plain greek yogurt)
- 1/4 cup red onion, finely chopped (or yellow onion)
- 2 teaspoons fresh lemon juice
- Pinch dried oregano leaves
- Salt and pepper, to taste
- 4 slices crusty bread
- 4 slices cheese, cheddar, or provolone
- Avocado, optional, for topping
- Tomato, optional, for topping

Instructions

- Turn oven to Broil on High.
- In a medium bowl, combine tuna, mayonnaise, onion, lemon juice, salt, pepper, and oregano and stir until thoroughly combined.
- Arrange bread on a baking sheet and smooth a big spoonful of tuna mixture onto each slice.
- Top with thin slices of tomato or avocado, if desired, and then a slice of cheese.
- Broil until cheese is melted and bubbly.

Nutrition

Calories: 325kcal | Carbohydrates: 15g | Protein: 29g | Fat: 15g | Saturated Fat: 7g | Cholesterol: 67mg | Sodium: 721mg | Potassium: 272mg | Sugar: 2g | Vitamin A: 300IU | Vitamin C: 1.7mg | Calcium: 279mg | Iron: 1.9mg

69. Easy Healthy Taco Salad Recipe With Ground Beef

Prep Time 10 minutes

Cook Time 10 minutes

Total Time 20 minutes

Servings: 6 servings

Ingredients

- 1 lb ground beef
- 1 tsp avocado oil (or any oil of choice)
- 2 tbsp taco seasoning (store-bought or home-made)
- 8 oz Romaine lettuce (chopped)
- 1 1/3 cup Grape tomatoes (halved)
- 3/4 cup Cheddar cheese (shredded)
- 1 medium Avocado (cubed)
- 1/2 cup Green onions (chopped)
- 1/3 cup salsa
- 1/3 cup Sour cream

Instructions

- Heat oil in a skillet over high heat. Add ground beef. Stir fry, breaking up the pieces with a spatula, for about 7-10 minutes, until the beef is browned and moisture has evaporated.
- Stir taco seasoning into the ground beef until well combined.
- Meanwhile, combine all remaining ingredients in a large bowl. Add the ground beef. Toss everything together.

Nutrition

- Calories: 332
- Fat: 25g
- Protein: 20g
- Total Carbs: 9g
- Net Carbs: 5g
- Fiber: 4g
- Sugar: 2g

70. Fried Cabbage With Sausage

Prep Time 10 minutes

Cook Time 20 minutes

Total Time 30 minutes

Servings 5

Ingredients

- 12 ounces smoked sausage
- 2 tablespoons olive oil divided
- 1/2 yellow onion
- 2 cloves garlic
- 1 medium head cabbage
- 1 teaspoon salt
- 1 teaspoon ground pepper

Instructions

- Slice the smoked sausage into thin rounds.
- Heat 1 tablespoon olive oil in a dutch oven or large, deep skillet over medium heat. Add the sausage to the skillet and cook, stirring often, until sausage is browned on both sides, about 4 minutes.
- Add the onion and garlic to the skillet and cook for 3 more minutes to soften onions.
- Add the remaining tablespoon of oil to the skillet along with the cabbage and sprinkle with salt and pepper.
- Cook the cabbage, stirring constantly, until it becomes tender, about 10 minutes.
- Serve immediately.

Nutrition

- Calories: 304
- Fat: 24g
- Protein: 12g
- Carbs: 13g
- Fiber: 5g= 8 net carb

---

71. Korean Ground Beef Recipe

Prep Time: 10 mins

Cook Time: 10 mins

Total Time: 20 mins

Ingredients

Sauce:

- ¼ cup reduced-sodium soy sauce (or use a gluten-free alternative and add salt as needed)
- 1 tablespoon honey or a liquid sugar-free alternative
- 1 teaspoon cornstarch
- ½ teaspoon crushed red pepper flakes

Stir-Fry:

- 2 tablespoons avocado oil
- 1 lb. lean ground beef (85/15)
- 1 tablespoon minced fresh garlic
- 1 tablespoon minced fresh ginger root

To Finish The Dish:

- 1 tablespoon sesame oil
- ¼ cup thinly sliced green onions, green parts only

Instructions

- In a small bowl, prepare the sauce by whisking together the soy sauce, honey, cornstarch, and red pepper flakes. Set aside. In a large skillet, heat the oil over medium-high heat.
- Add the beef and cook, stirring, until no longer pink, breaking it up into crumbles as you cook, about 5 minutes.
- Drain the beef. Return to the skillet. Add the garlic and the ginger to the skillet and cook, stirring, for 1 minute.
- Stir the sauce into the beef. Cook 2 more minutes, until heated through and the sauce thickens.
- Off heat, drizzle the dish with sesame oil, sprinkle it with green onions, and serve.

Nutrition

- Calories: 370
- Fat: 27g
- Saturated Fat: 8g
- Sodium: 651mg
- Carbohydrates: 7g
- Fiber: 0.3g
- Sugar: 4g
- Protein: 22g

---

72. Mexican Green Beans

Prep Time: 15 minutes

Cook Time: 10 minutes

Total Time: 25 minutes

Servings: 6

Ingredients

- 1 pound green beans, trimmed and cut
- 1/2 cup roma tomato, seeded and diced (4 oz)
- 1/4 cup chopped onion (1 oz)
- 1 clove garlic, minced
- 2 tbsp avocado oil or good olive oil
- 1 tbsp butter, ghee, or another tbsp of oil
- 2 tbsp water
- 1 whole bay leaf, crumbled
- 1 tsp chicken base
- 1 tsp fresh oregano, minced (or 1/4 tsp. Dry but fresh tastes different)
- 1/4 tsp ground cumin
- Salt and pepper to taste

Instructions

Preparation:

- Wash, trim and cut beans. Cut the tomato in half and squeeze gently over the trash can to remove seeds, then dice. Chop onion and minced garlic and fresh oregano (if using).

Method:

- Heat 1 tbsp of oil in a large frying pan over medium heat. When hot, add the onion, garlic, tomato, and bay leaf until the onion begins to soften. Add the chicken base, water, another tablespoon of oil, oregano, cumin, and green beans. Stir to coat the beans and loosely cover with a piece of foil or a lid. Cook for 4 minutes or until the beans are cooked to your preference.
- Add butter adjust seasoning by adding salt, pepper, or more oregano and cumin. Serve.

Nutrition

Calories 84, Calories from Fat 63, Fat 7g, Carbohydrates 6g, Fiber 3g, Protein 1g

73. One Pot Unstuffed Cabbage Roll

Prep Time: 5 Mins

Cook Time: 30 Mins

Total Time: 35 Mins

Yield: 3-4 Servings

Ingredients

- 1 lb ground beef
- 1 medium onion, diced
- 2 cloves garlic, minced
- 1 cup cauliflower, riced (using a food processor, or pre-riced)
- 1 large green cabbage, cored and chopped
- 1/2 cup beef broth
- 2 cups tomato sauce (sub tomato sauce for AIP)
- 1 tsp sea salt
- 2 tsp parsley

Instructions

- Using a large dutch oven, brown the ground beef on medium heat. Remove the beef and set aside, reserving the fat in the pan.

- Next, saute the onion and garlic for 5 minutes or until translucent
- Add the riced cauliflower and saute for 5-8 minutes or until softened
- Add back in the ground beef as well as the broth, tomato sauce, cabbage slices, parsley, and sea salt. Stir well to combine
- Place the lid over the dutch oven and simmer for 15 minutes to allow cabbage to soften and flavors to incorporate.
- Remove the dish from the heat and serve warm.

Nutrition

Calories: 271, Fat: 5.5g, Carbohydrates: 18.8g Fiber: 4.6g Protein: 37.1g

74. Cabbage Roll Soup

Prep Time: 10

Cook Time: 40

Total Time: 50 Minutes

Yield: 4 Servings

Ingredients

- 1 lb ground beef
- 1 tsp sea salt
- 1/4 tsp black pepper (omit for AIP)
- 1 onion, diced
- 3–4 cloves garlic, minced
- 1 cup carrots, roughly chopped
- 1 cup cauliflower, riced
- 1 medium green cabbage, chopped (about 4 cups)
- 5 cups beef broth
- 1 1/2 cup tomato sauce (sub tomato sauce for AIP)
- Juice of half a lemon
- 2 tsp oregano
- 2 tbsp parsley, chopped

Instructions

- Using a large, heavy cast iron pan or stockpot, brown the ground beef over medium heat. Lightly season and use a wooden spoon to crumble. Once browned, set aside and leave about 2 tbsp of fat in the pan (or add avocado if needed).

- Add the onion to the same pot and cook for 3-4 minutes or until lightly translucent. Add in the garlic, carrots, and cauliflower rice and cook for another 3-4 minutes to lightly soften. Stir in the cabbage and allow to wilt for 2 minutes
- Add the beef back to the pot and stir in the broth, tomato sauce, lemon juice, and oregano. Stir well and bring to a low simmer.
- Allow simmering for 30-35 minutes. The vegetables should be softened and the soup should lightly reduce.
- Season the soup to taste and top with fresh parsley to serve.

Nutrition

Calories: 269, Fat: 4.3g, Carbohydrates: 27.2g, Fiber: 9.3, Protein: 33.3g

75. Healthy Chicken Piccata

Prep Time: 30 Minutes

Cook Time: 25 Minutes

Total Time: 30 Minutes

Yield: 4 Servings

Ingredients

- 1 lemon
- 1 pound boneless skinless chicken breasts
- ¼ cup all-purpose flour
- ½ teaspoon salt
- ½ teaspoon ground pepper
- 1 tablespoon plus 4 teaspoons extra-virgin olive oil, divided
- 1 large sweet onion, sliced
- 1 clove garlic, minced
- 1 cup reduced-sodium chicken broth
- ¼ cup dry white wine
- 4 teaspoons drained capers
- ¼ cup chopped parsley

Instructions

- Prepare Lemon And Chicken: Cut lemon in half. Juice half of it, and cut the remaining half into thin slices. Cut chicken breasts into 8 thin cutlets.
- Dredge Chicken: Whisk flour, salt, and pepper in a shallow dish or pie plate. Dredge chicken in the flour mixture, turning to coat. Discard 2 teaspoons dredging flour and reserve the rest to thicken the sauce in step 5.
- Brown Chicken: Heat 2 teaspoons oil in a large non-stick skillet over medium-high heat. Add half the chicken and cook until the bottom is browned, 2 to 4 minutes. Turn over and continue cooking until browned on the bottom, 2 to 3 minutes. Set aside on a plate. Repeat with 2 teaspoons oil and the remaining 4 pieces of dredged chicken, adjusting the heat to medium-low to prevent the chicken from burning. Transfer the second batch of chicken to the plate.
- Cook Onions And Garlic: Wipe out the skillet with a clean paper towel. Add the remaining 1 tablespoon oil and place the skillet over medium-high heat. Add onion, and cook, stirring often until soft and browned 5 to 7 minutes. Add garlic, and cook, stirring constantly until the garlic is fragrant and just starting to brown, 30 to 90 seconds.
- Make Sauce: Sprinkle the remaining dredging flour over the onion mixture and stir to coat. Stir in broth, white wine, capers, lemon slices, and lemon juice, increase heat to high and bring to a simmer, stirring constantly.
- Finish Dish: Add the chicken and any accumulated juices from the plate to the skillet and turn to coat in the sauce. Bring to a simmer while turning the chicken in the sauce until the sauce is thickened, and the chicken is completely cooked through and hot, 3 to 4 minutes. Stir in parsley, remove from the heat and serve.

Nutrition

Calories: 264 Sugar: 2g, Sodium: 550 Mg, Fat: 9 G, Saturated Fat: 1 G, Carbohydrates: 14 G, Fiber: 1 G, Protein: 28 G

76. Seared Scallops Recipe

Prep Time: 5 mins

Cook Time: 10 mins

Total Time: 15 mins

Servings: 4

Ingredients

- 1 pound large sea scallops

- 1 tablespoon salted butter
- 1 tablespoon olive oil
- For the pan sauce: (optional)
- 1/4 cup chicken stock or broth
- 2 tablespoons salted butter
- 1 clove garlic minced
- 1 medium shallot finely diced
- ❖ Salt and pepper to taste

Instructions

- Rinse scallops to remove any potential grit and drain well. Pat both sides of scallops dry with paper towels.
- Heat 12-inch skillet over medium heat. Add butter and olive oil into a heated skillet and allow butter to melt.
- Add scallops to the skillet in a single layer, taking care to leave plenty of room between each scallop. Cook for about 3 to 5 minutes and then gently turn scallop with tongs or a small spatula to sear the second side for an additional 3 to 5 minutes or until the scallop is firm to the touch and well-browned.
- Remove the scallops from the skillet to a serving platter and keep warm.

Nutrition

Calories: 190kcal | Carbohydrates: 4g | Protein: 14g | Fat: 12g | Saturated Fat: 6g | Cholesterol: 50mg | Sodium: 541mg | Potassium: 248mg | Vitamin A: 260IU | Vitamin C: 0.2mg | Calcium: 7mg | Iron: 0.4mg

77. Scalloped Potatoes Recipe

Prep Time: 15 mins

Cook Time: 1 hr 30 mins

Cooking Time: 15 mins

Total Time: 2 hrs

Servings: 10

Ingredients

- 4 large Russet or Yukon Gold potatoes sliced thinly to 1/8-inch thick
- 1/4 cup butter
- 1/4 cup all-purpose flour

- 2 cups whole milk or heavy cream
- 1/2 teaspoon Kosher salt
- 1/2 teaspoon ground black or white pepper
- 1/8 teaspoon cayenne pepper

Instructions

- Preheat oven to 350º F. Spray 9×13 casserole dish with nonstick cooking spray and set aside.
- Place potato slices in a bowl of cold water to keep from turning brown while making the cream sauce.
- Make Cream Sauce
- Melt butter in a medium saucepan set over medium heat. Whisk in flour until well-combined, then whisk in milk, salt, pepper, cayenne pepper. Reduce heat to simmer and continue to whisk until sauce bubbles slightly around the edges of the saucepan and has thickened slightly.
- If you are adding cheese (making Potatoes Au Gratin), stir them in at this point.

Make Casserole: Drain cold water from the potato slices and arrange the slices in the 9×13 casserole dish. Pour cream sauce over potato slices and cover the casserole dish with foil.

Cook

- Bake covered for 45 minutes. Remove the foil and bake until the top is golden brown and the potatoes are fork-tender. If additional browning is desired, you may broil the casserole for 3 to 5 minutes.
- Remove from the oven and allow to cool for 15 minutes to allow the sauce to thicken for easier serving. Serve warm.

Nutrition

Calories: 199kcal | Carbohydrates: 31g | Protein: 5g | Fat: 6g | Saturated Fat: 4g | Cholesterol: 17mg | Sodium: 185mg | Potassium: 680mg | Fiber: 2g | Sugar: 3g | Vitamin A: 231IU | Vitamin C: 8mg | Calcium: 76mg | Iron: 1mg

78. Pot Roast Recipe

Prep Time: 15 mins

Cook Time: 3 hrs

Total Time: 3 hrs 15 mins

Servings: 6

Ingredients

- Olive oil
- 1 (3-5) pound boneless roast beef (chuck or round roast) brisket, chuck, or round
- 3 cups beef stock or broth divided
- 3 tablespoons worcestershire sauce or coconut aminos
- 2 teaspoons stone house seasoning
- 1 pound red potatoes cut into bite-sized pieces
- 2 medium onions cut into wedges
- 1 pound carrots cut into 1 1/2 inch slices
- 4 stalks celery cut into 1 1/2 inch slices
- 3 sprigs fresh thyme or 1/2 teaspoon dried thyme
- 1 sprig of fresh rosemary

Instructions

- Preheat oven to 350º F. Sear roast.
- Drizzle olive oil into the bottom of a heavy Dutch oven over medium heat.
- Add roast and sear on all sides, about 3 minutes per side.
- Carefully remove the pot roast from the Dutch oven using tongs and place it onto a large platter or a rimmed baking sheet. Deglaze the pan by pouring 1 cup of beef broth or red wine into the Dutch oven.
- Using a wooden spoon, scrape up all of the cooked bits on the bottom of the pan.
- Add the beef, and any juices, back into the Dutch oven.
- Add the remainder of the beef broth and/ or red wine to the pot.
- Add in the Worcestershire sauce, Stone House Seasoning, vegetables, and herbs.
- Cover and place in the oven for 3 hours, until the roast is fork-tender and reaches 202º F when checked with an internal thermometer.

Slow-Cooker Classic Pot Roast

- If the slow cooker doesn't have an in-pot browning method (see your slow cooker's instructions), follow the instructions above for searing the roast.
- Then, transfer the seared pot roast to the insert of a slow cooker.

- Deglaze the pan as instructed above and pour into the slow cooker along with the remaining beef broth and/ or red wine, Worcestershire sauce, Stone
- House Seasoning, the vegetables, and the herbs. Cook on the low setting for 6-8 hours, depending on your slow cooker.

Instant Pot Classic Pot Roast

- Set your Instant Pot to the Saute function. Drizzle olive oil into the Instant Pot insert pot.
- Add your roast and sear on all sides until browned, about 3 minutes per side.
- Carefully remove the roast from the Instant Pot using tongs and place onto a large platter or a rimmed baking sheet.
- Deglaze the pot by pouring 1 cup of beef broth or red wine into the pot.
- Using a wooden spoon, scrape up all of the cooked bits on the bottom of the pan. Add the beef, and any juices, back into the pot.
- Add the remainder of the beef broth and/ or red wine to the pot.
- Add in the Worcestershire sauce, Stone House Seasoning, vegetables, and herbs.
- Seal the Instant Pot and cook on High pressure for 60 minutes.
- Then, allow the pressure to release naturally for 20 minutes.
- Carefully release any additional pressure using the quick-release method. Remove the lid and serve.

Nutrition

- Serving: 2g | Calories: 425kcal | Carbohydrates: 19g | Protein: 27g | Fat: 19g

79. Best French Toast Recipe

Prep Time: 5 mins

Cook Time: 5 mins

Total Time: 10 mins

Servings: 4

Ingredients

- 2 large eggs
- 1 cup milk, half and half, coconut milk, or almond milk
- Pinch salt

- 1 tablespoon granulated sugar, honey, or maple syrup
- 1 teaspoon vanilla extract
- 1 teaspoon ground cinnamon
- 8 slices sandwich bread
- Butter
- Instructions
- Whisk together eggs, milk, salt, sugar, vanilla, and cinnamon in a flat-bottomed pie plate or baking dish. Place bread slices, one or two at a time, into the egg mixture and flip to make sure both sides of bread are well-coated.
- Melt butter in a large skillet or on a griddle. Place bread slices in skillet or on the griddle and cook on medium heat until golden brown on each side, about 2-3 minutes.
- Serve immediately or keep warm in the oven until ready to serve, but no longer than about 30 minutes.

Nutrition

Calories: 225kcal | Carbohydrates: 32g | Protein: 9g | Fat: 5g | Saturated Fat: 2g | Cholesterol: 99mg | Sodium: 307mg | Potassium: 172mg | Fiber: 1g | Sugar: 10g | Vitamin A: 235IU | Calcium: 218mg | Iron: 2.2mg

80. The Best Instant Pot Chili Recipe

Prep Time: 5 mins

Cook Time: 25 mins

Total Time: 30 mins

Servings: 8 people

Ingredients

- 2 pounds ground beef
- 1/2 medium sweet onion diced
- 2 tablespoons tomato paste
- 3 tablespoons chili powder
- 2 teaspoons Stone House Seasoning
- 2 teaspoons ground cumin
- 2 teaspoons cocoa powder
- 2 cups beef stock or broth
- 2 (28-ounce) can crushed tomatoes
- 1 (15-ounce) can red kidney beans drained and rinsed
- 1 (15-ounce) cans black beans drained and rinsed

Instructions

- Set the Instant Pot to the Sauté setting. Add the ground beef and onion and cook until the beef has browned and the onion is translucent about 3-5 minutes. Drain away excess drippings from the ground beef.
- Stir in the tomato paste, chili powder, Stone House Seasoning, cumin, and cocoa powder. Next, stir in the beef stock, crushed tomatoes, kidney beans, and black beans.
- Set the Instant Pot to 18 minutes at High Pressure. When the chili has finished cooking, use an oven mitt and carefully use the quick-release method to release the pressure according to the manufacturer's directions.
- Serve the Instant Pot Chili with toppings as desired.

Nutrition

Serving: 1cup | Calories: 310kcal | Carbohydrates: 3g | Protein: 21g | Fat: 23g | Saturated Fat: 8g | Cholesterol: 80mg | Sodium: 858mg | Potassium: 525mg | Fiber: 1g | Sugar: 1g | Vitamin A: 955IU | Vitamin C: 0.9mg | Calcium: 41mg | Iron: 3.4mg

81. Beef Tenderloin

Prep Time: 15 mins

Cook Time: 45 mins

Total Time: 1 hr

Ingredients

- 1 beef tenderloin Plan two 2" filets per person
- 1 tablespoon Stone House Seasoning Recipe

Instructions

- Place beef tenderloin on a rimmed baking sheet, pat dry with paper towels, and season both sides of the meat with Stone House Seasoning. Cover tightly with plastic wrap and refrigerate for one hour or up to 4 days before you plan on cooking and serving.
- Remove from the refrigerator, unwrap and allow to stand for about an hour to come to room temperature.

- Meanwhile, preheat grill or oven to approximately 400º F.
- Place tenderloin onto the grill or in the oven. Allow the beef tenderloin to cook until it reaches 145º F when checked with an internal meat thermometer in the thinner areas and 140º F in the thicker area, about 45 minutes.
- Remove from grill and cover loosely with aluminum foil and allow to rest on the carving board for about 15 minutes before carving and serving.

Nutrition

Calories: 238kcal | Protein: 35g | Fat: 10g | Saturated Fat: 1g | Cholesterol: 105mg | Sodium: 64mg

---

82. Simple Beef Stroganoff

Prep Time: 5 mins

Cook Time: 25 mins

Total Time: 30 mins

Servings: 6

Ingredients

- 1 tablespoon olive oil
- 2 pounds beef (roast, sirloin, or beef tenderloin) sliced into 1/4-inch slices
- 1 teaspoon Stone House Seasoning
- 1 cup sour cream
- 1 package egg noodles cooked according to package directions

Instructions

- Add olive oil to a medium skillet (or Dutch oven) set over medium heat. Add beef slices and sprinkle with Stone House Seasoning. Cook the beef until browned and cooked for about 8 minutes.
- Stir in the sour cream until smooth to make the sauce.
- Serve over egg noodles or mashed potatoes. You can also add the egg noodles to the skillet or Dutch oven and mix them into the sauce if you prefer. Top with fresh parsley, if using.

Nutrition

Calories: 584kcal | Carbohydrates: 41g | Protein: 38g | Fat: 30g | Saturated Fat: 13g |

Cholesterol: 172mg | Sodium: 553mg | Potassium: 694mg | Fiber: 2g | Sugar: 2g | Vitamin A: 294IU | Vitamin C: 1mg | Calcium: 88mg | Iron: 4mg

---

83. Chicken Pot Pie With Puff Pastry Recipe

Prep Time: 10 mins

Cook Time: 45 mins

Total Time: 55 mins

Servings: 6

Ingredients

- 2 tablespoons olive oil divided
- 3 skinless, boneless chicken breasts cut into 1-inch pieces
- 1/2 medium onion diced
- 1 large baking potato peeled and cut into chunks
- 3 large carrots cut into chunks
- 3 tablespoons butter
- 1/4 cup all-purpose flour
- 1 teaspoon salt
- 1/2 teaspoon black pepper
- 3 cups chicken stock or broth
- Puff pastry thawed

Instructions

- Preheat oven to 425º F.
- Drizzle the olive oil into a heavy Dutch oven or pot set over medium heat. Add the chicken and cook until browned. Using a slotted spoon, remove from the Dutch oven to a plate.
- Add the onions, potatoes, and carrots and cook until the onions are translucent and the potatoes and carrots are slightly tender about 8 minutes. Add the butter and allow to melt. Then, stir in the flour, salt, and pepper and cook until thickened, about 2 more minutes. Pour in the chicken stock and bring to a boil. Add back in the chicken and their juices.
- Ladle the chicken pot pie filling into a 3-quart casserole dish or individual dishes set on a parchment or foil-lined baking sheet. Top with puff pastry. Trim the edges of the puff pastry to about 1/2-inch overhang of the rim of the baking dish. Using a sharp knife, cut a slit in the puff pastry as a vent to allow steam to escape during

baking. Bake until golden brown and the pot pie is bubbling, about 30 minutes.

Nutrition

Calories: 276kcal | Carbohydrates: 23g | Protein: 18g | Fat: 11g | Saturated Fat: 4g | Cholesterol: 85mg | Sodium: 715mg | Potassium: 731mg | Fiber: 2g | Sugar: 4g | Vitamin A: 6250IU | Vitamin C: 7.3mg | Calcium: 35mg | Iron: 1.5mg

84. Easy Skillet Lasagna Recipe

Prep Time: 5 mins

Cook Time: 25 mins

Total Time: 30 mins

Servings: 8

Ingredients

- 1 tablespoon olive oil
- 1/2 medium onion chopped
- 1 1/2 pounds ground beef
- 1 teaspoon stone house seasoning
- 1 1/2 teaspoons chopped fresh oregano (divided) or 1/2 teaspoon dried oregano
- Pinch red pepper flakes optional
- 4 cups tomato sauce
- 8 lasagna noodles broken into 2-inch pieces
- 3/4 cup grated parmesan cheese
- 1/2 cup ricotta cheese divided

Instructions

- Drizzle olive oil into a medium skillet set over medium heat. Add chopped onion and cook until translucent, about 3 minutes. Add the ground beef and cook until browned throughout, about 5 more minutes. Discard any excess drippings.
- Stir in the Stone House Seasoning, 1 teaspoon of the fresh oregano, red pepper flakes (if using), tomato sauce, and the broken noodle pieces. Bring to a boil and then reduce the heat to medium-low. Simmer, cover, and cook until the noodles are tender about 20 minutes.
- Remove from the heat and top with Parmesan cheese, ricotta, and remaining fresh oregano

Nutrition

Calories: 434kcal | Carbohydrates: 28g | Protein: 25g | Fat: 24g | Saturated Fat: 9g | Cholesterol: 76mg | Sodium: 1147mg | Potassium: 735mg | Fiber: 2g | Sugar: 6g | Vitamin A: 680IU | Vitamin C: 9.1mg | Calcium: 174mg | Iron: 3.4mg

85. Roasted Turkey Recipe

Prep Time: 15 mins

Cook Time: 2 hrs 30 mins

Resting Time: 30 mins

Servings: 8

Ingredients

- 1 (12-pound) turkey
- 8 tablespoons butter softened
- 1 1/2 teaspoons kosher salt
- 1 teaspoon freshly ground black pepper

Instructions

- Preheat oven to 325º F. Mix softened butter, salt, and pepper together until well combined. Set aside.
- Prepare the turkey for roasting
- Remove neck and any other items from the inside cavity of the fully thawed turkey. Pat the turkey dry with paper towels and arrange the turkey on a rack in roasting pan, breast side up. Carefully separate the skin at the breast of the turkey away from the meat, taking care not to tear the skin.
- Spoon one tablespoon of the butter mixture under the skin at each breast. Carefully massage the butter to completely cover the breast of the turkey and make sure that the skin covers the breast completely. Spread the remaining butter mixture onto the outside of the turkey.
- Tie the legs of the turkey to help the turkey roast more evenly.
- Roast Turkey
- Bake the turkey until juices run clear when pricked between the leg and breast of the turkey and the internal temperature reaches 165º F when checked at the thickest part of the breast, about 2 1/2 to 3 hours.
- Remove from the oven. Cover turkey with foil and allow to rest for 20 – 30 minutes.

- Slice and serve.

Nutrition

Calories: 782kcal | Carbohydrates: 1g | Protein: 105g | Fat: 39g | Saturated Fat: 14g | Cholesterol: 378mg | Sodium: 1513mg | Potassium: 1082mg | Sugar: 1g | Vitamin A: 620IU | Calcium: 56mg | Iron: 4mg

86. Mississippi Roast Recipe (Pepperoncini Roast)

Prep Time: 5 mins

Cook Time: 8 hrs

Total Time: 8 hrs 5 mins

Ingredients

- 1 (3 pounds) chuck roast
- 1 tablespoon Stone House Seasoning
- 1 (25.5-ounce) jar Pepperoncinis peppers including juices
- Optional Ingredients
- 1 1/2 teaspoons ranch seasoning mix
- 1 tablespoon cornstarch

Instructions

- Add chuck roast to the slow cooker. Add Stone House Seasoning and optional Ranch Seasoning to the roast and pour in peppers and their juices.
- Set a timer and cook on a low setting for 8 hours.
- To serve, shred the beef using two forks and serve with peppers.

Nutrition

Calories: 268kcal | Protein: 28g | Fat: 17g | Cholesterol: 94mg | Sodium: 668mg | Potassium: 349mg

87. Perfect Prime Rib Recipe

Prep Time: 1 hr

Cook Time: 2 hrs

Resting Time: 20 mins

Total Time: 3 hrs

Ingredients

- 1 (3 – 4 bone) bone-in prime rib, about (10 – 10.5 pounds)
- 1 tablespoon kosher salt
- 2 teaspoons freshly ground black pepper

Instructions

- Salt prime rib from one hour to up to five days before cooking and serving your prime rib. Once salted, wrap tightly in plastic wrap and refrigerate until an hour before cooking.
- An hour before cooking, remove the prime rib from the refrigerator, unwrap and place, bone side down, on a roasting pan and allow to reach room temperature. If cooking a boneless roast, place onto a roasting rack inside the roasting pan. At this point add pepper or other seasonings, if using.
- Preheat oven to 475º F. Then, roast your prime rib for 15 minutes and reduce to 325º F until your prime rib reaches the desired internal temperature, usually 11 – 12 minutes per pound, about 1 hour and 50 minutes. Using an internal meat thermometer, remove your prime rib from the oven about 2 – 4 degrees less than the desired serving final temperature you desire. The temperature of the prime rib will continue to rise due to carryover cooking. Tent prime rib with foil and allow to rest for 20 minutes.
- Place on a carving board for slicing and serve.

Nutrition

Serving: 3ounces | Calories: 340kcal | Protein: 19g | Fat: 29g | Saturated Fat: 12g | Polyunsaturated Fat: 1g | Monounsaturated Fat: 12g | Cholesterol: 72mg | Sodium: 55mg | Potassium: 258mg

88. Cola Glazed Ham Recipe

Prep Time: 5 mins

Cook Time: 1 hr

Total Time: 1 hr 5 mins

Servings: 16

Ingredients

- 1 (8-pound) fully cooked, spiral-sliced ham
- 1 (12-ounce) can Coca-Cola
- 1 cup brown sugar firmly packed

Instructions

- Preheat oven to 325º F. Place ham in a roasting pan. Combine Coca-Cola and brown sugar and pour over ham. Cover tightly with aluminum foil. Every 30 minutes, uncover the ham and baste well with the pan juices and then recover the ham. Bake 20 minutes per pound, until the thickest part of the ham registers 140º F on a meat thermometer, about 2 hours. Remove the foil for the last 10 minutes of cooking time so that after the final glaze, the glaze can caramelize on the ham
- Remove roasting pan from the oven and baste again. Let the ham stand for about 15 minutes, remove the ham from the roasting pan and onto a platter for serving.

Nutrition

Calories: 52kcal | Carbohydrates: 13g | Sodium: 4mg | Potassium: 18mg | Sugar: 13g | Calcium: 11mg | Iron: 0.1mg

89. White Chicken Chili Recipe

Prep Time: 5 mins

Cook Time: 25 mins

Total Time: 30 mins

Servings: 8

Ingredients

- 4 medium skinless, boneless chicken breasts
- 4 cups chicken stock or broth
- 1 clove garlic minced
- 1 medium onion diced
- 1 (15-ounce) can white beans, drained
- 1 (4-ounce) can dice green chilis, with liquids from chilis
- 1 teaspoon dried oregano
- 1 teaspoon ground cumin
- 1/2 teaspoon chili powder
- 1 teaspoon salt
- 1 teaspoon ground black pepper
- 1 teaspoon chopped fresh oregano

Instructions

Stovetop White Chicken Chili Recipe

- Add chicken to a 4-quart, heavy-bottomed Dutch oven or stockpot over medium heat. Add chicken stock and cook until tender, about 15 minutes. Shred chicken with two forks and then add back to the liquid.
- Add garlic and onion to the stockpot, white beans, green chilis, dried oregano, cumin, chili powder, salt, pepper, and chopped fresh oregano. Stir until well-combined. Taste for flavor and adjust to your preference.
- Simmer over low heat for about 5 minutes. Remove from heat and serve.

Slow Cooker White Chicken Chili Recipe

- Add chicken, chicken stock, garlic, onion, chilis, oregano, cumin, chili powder, salt, and pepper to a 6-quart slow cooker. Cook for 8 hours on low. Shred chicken with two forks and stir in white beans and fresh oregano and cook for another 10 minutes. Serve.

Instant Pot White Chicken Chili Recipe

- Add the chicken, chicken stock, garlic, onions, beans, chilis, oregano, cumin, chili powder, salt, and pepper to your Instant Pot and secure the lid with the vent closed.
- Set your Instant Pot to High pressure for 20 minutes. Allow the pressure to release naturally for 10 minutes and then, using a potholder, carefully use the quick release. Remove the lid from the Instant Pot and shred the chicken using two forks. Stir to combine all of the ingredients and serve.

Nutrition

Calories: 152kcal | Carbohydrates: 6g | Protein: 3g | Fat: 1g | Cholesterol: 3mg | Sodium: 466mg | Potassium: 150mg | Sugar: 2g | Vitamin A: 35IU | Vitamin C: 1.4mg | Calcium: 13mg | Iron: 0.6mg

90. Chili Rubbed Chicken Skewers Recipe

Prep Time: 10 mins

Cook Time: 10 mins

Total Time: 20 mins

Servings: 4 servings

Ingredients

- 2 chicken breasts boneless, skinless, and cut into 1-inch pieces
- 1 teaspoon Stone House Seasoning

- 1 teaspoon chili powder
- 1/2 teaspoon paprika
- 1/2 teaspoon cumin
- pinch cayenne pepper
- 2 medium red peppers cut into 1-inch pieces
- 1 small red onion cut into 1-inch pieces
- 4 medium zucchini cut into 1-inch pieces

Instructions

- Place the chicken pieces into a large zip-top bag. Add Stone House Seasoning, chili powder, paprika, cumin, and cayenne pepper to the chicken. Remove as much air as possible as you are sealing the bag. Massage the seasoning onto the chicken, making sure that each piece is coated. Place into the refrigerator until ready to build your skewers.
- Build your skewers by alternating vegetable pieces with the chili-rubbed chicken. (Zucchini, chicken, pepper, chicken, onion, chicken, and zucchini works well as the zucchini holds the skewer ingredients in place.)
- Preheat the grill, grill pan, or skillet to medium heat. Spray or brush with olive oil spray.
- Cook the chili-rubbed chicken skewers on the grill, grill pan, or skillet for five minutes. Flip and cook an additional five minutes or until the chicken has cooked through.

Nutrition

Calories: 183kcal | Carbohydrates: 10g | Protein: 27g | Fat: 3g | Cholesterol: 72mg | Sodium: 157mg | Potassium: 1064mg | Fiber: 3g | Sugar: 7g | Vitamin A: 2560IU | Vitamin C: 112.4mg | Calcium: 41mg | Iron: 1.7mg

91. Slow Cooker Beef Bourguignon Recipe

Prep Time: 10 mins

Cook Time: 6 hrs

Total Time: 6 hrs 10 mins

Servings: 6

Ingredients

- 3 slices bacon diced
- 1 3-4 pound chuck roast, cut into 2-inch cubes
- 1 1/2 tablespoons all-purpose flour
- 1 1/2 teaspoons stone house seasoning plus more to taste

- 2 cups sliced mushrooms
- 2 cups about 3 medium sliced carrots
- 2 cups about 3 medium diced red potatoes
- 1 medium onion peeled and cut into 2-inch chunks
- 2 tablespoons tomato paste
- 4 stalks fresh thyme
- 2 bay leaves
- 1 cup red wine
- 4 cups beef stock or broth
- Fresh parsley optional garnish

Instructions

- Cook bacon until crispy in stove top-compatible slow cooker insert or a skillet set over medium heat. Using a slotted spoon, remove the bacon from the slow cooker insert (or skillet) and set it aside. Add the beef to the bacon drippings, along with the flour and Stone House Seasoning. Stir to coat the beef and then cook the beef until it is well-browned about 6 minutes.
- Transfer the slow cooker insert over to the slow cooker and add bacon to your bacon. If you do not have a stove top-compatible insert, you'll transfer the crispy bacon and cooked beef from your skillet into the slow cooker.
- Add in the mushrooms, carrots, onions, red potatoes, and onion. Then, add the tomato paste, fresh thyme, bay leaves, burgundy (or your favorite hearty red wine), and beef broth. Set timer for 6 to 8 hours on the low setting.

Nutrition

Serving: 2cups | Calories: 506kcal | Carbohydrates: 13.9g | Protein: 63.2g | Fat: 17.6g | Saturated Fat: 5.4g | Fiber: 2g | Sugar: 3.6g

92. Hamburger Sliders With A Spicy Cilantro Lime Spread

Prep Time: 10 mins

Cook Time: 15 mins

Total Time: 25 mins

Ingredients

- 1 pound ground beef
- 1 clove garlic minced
- 1 tablespoon worcestershire sauce

- 1/2 cup mayonnaise
- 1/4 cup cilantro
- 2 tablespoons lime juice
- 4 dashes of tabasco sauce
- Salt and pepper
- Slider buns or rolls
- Lettuce
- Cheese
- Tomato

Instructions

- Mix ground beef, garlic, and Worcestershire sauce until well-combined.
- Form into 8 small patties. Refrigerate until ready to cook.
- Blend mayonnaise, cilantro, lime juice, Tabasco sauce, salt, and pepper until creamy. Adjust to your taste preference.
- Cook hamburger patties. Open slider buns or rolls and spread spicy cilantro-lime spread on top and bottom of the bun.
- Add hamburger patty and lettuce, cheese, and tomato.
- Serve warm.

Nutrition

Calories: 484kcal | Carbohydrates: 1g | Protein: 19g | Fat: 43g | Saturated Fat: 11g | Cholesterol: 92mg | Sodium: 296mg | Potassium: 340mg | Sugar: 1g | Vitamin A: 85IU | Vitamin C: 3.3mg | Calcium: 25mg | Iron: 2.5mg

93. Skillet Pork Chop Recipe

Prep Time: 5 mins

Cook Time: 25 mins

Total Time: 30 mins

Ingredients

- 6-8 Pork Chops Bone-In, Thick Sliced
- 2-3 Tablespoons Olive Oil
- Salt
- Pepper

Instructions

- preheat oven to 350 degrees.
- Pour olive oil into a skillet over medium heat.
- Add pork chops and season with salt and pepper.

- Cook about 3-5 minutes on each side, until each side has browned well.
- Place skillet in the oven for about 15 minutes.
- Serve immediately.

Nutrition

Calories: 249kcal | Protein: 29g | Fat: 14g | Saturated Fat: 4g | Cholesterol: 90mg | Sodium: 64mg | Potassium: 500mg | Calcium: 9mg | Iron: 1mg

94. One Pot Penne Pasta Recipe

Prep Time: 5 mins

Cook Time: 10 mins

Total Time: 15 mins

Ingredients

- 1 pound smoked sausage cut into bite-sized slices
- 1/2 medium onion diced
- 2 cloves garlic minced
- 1 cup sliced mushrooms
- 3 cups penne pasta uncooked
- 2 cups chicken stock or broth
- 1 (10-ounce) jar roasted red peppers undrained
- 2 cups Monterey Jack cheese
- 1/2 cup Parmesan cheese
- 2 cups fresh spinach

Instructions

- Add sausage, onions, garlic, and mushrooms to a medium pot over medium heat. Cook until onions are slightly tender, stirring often. Add in penne pasta, chicken stock, roasted red peppers, along with the liquid from the jar. Stir to combine and cover for about 5-8 minutes. Remove lid, stir and continue to cook until penne pasta is al dente or at the amount of tenderness you prefer.
- Stir in the cheeses and fresh spinach until well combined and the spinach is tender. Serve.

Nutrition

Calories: 482kcal | Carbohydrates: 36g | Protein: 23g | Fat: 26g | Saturated Fat: 11g | Cholesterol: 71mg | Sodium: 822mg | Potassium: 302mg | Fiber: 1g | Sugar: 2g |

Vitamin A: 265IU | Vitamin C: 0.8mg | Calcium: 302mg | Iron: 1.5mg

| Sugar: 3g | Vitamin A: 275IU | Vitamin C: 2.4mg | Calcium: 47mg | Iron: 1.7mg

95. Buffalo Chicken Enchiladas Recipe

Prep Time10 mins

Cook Time20 mins

Ingredients

- 2 chicken breasts cooked and shredded
- 1 teaspoon Stone House Seasoning
- 1 cup enchilada sauce divided
- 1 cup buffalo sauce divided
- 1 (10-ounce) can diced tomatoes with green chilis drained
- 10-12 corn or flour tortillas
- 1 1/2 cups Monterrey Jack Cheese or Colby Jack Cheese shredded
- 4 green onions sliced (optional)
- Blue cheese (Optional)

Instructions

- Preheat the oven to 350º F. Spray a 9x13 baking dish with nonstick cooking spray and pour 1/4 cup of enchilada sauce into the bottom of the baking dish and set aside.
- Add the chicken, Stone House Seasoning, 1/2 cup of enchilada sauce, 1/2 cup of buffalo sauce, and diced tomatoes with green chilis to a medium bowl. Stir until well combined.
- Spoon about 2 tablespoons to 1/4 cup chicken mixture into the center of each flour tortilla. Top with about 2 tablespoons of grated cheese and fold two ends of tortilla over the filled center. Place the tortilla seam side down into the baking dish. Repeat until all tortillas have been filled.
- Pour remaining enchilada sauce and buffalo sauce over the assembled tortillas. Top with grated cheese. Place in oven and bake for about 20 minutes, until cheese has melted thoroughly and has become bubbly.
- Garnish with sliced green onions and crumbled blue cheese, if desired.

Nutrition

Calories: 191kcal | Carbohydrates: 22g | Protein: 15g | Fat: 3g | Cholesterol: 36mg | Sodium: 1794mg | Potassium: 282mg | Fiber: 1g

96. Skillet Mediterranean Chicken Recipe

Prep Time: 5 mins

Cook Time: 25 mins

Total Time: 30 mins

Ingredients

- 4 boneless, skinless chicken breasts
- 1 tablespoon Italian Seasoning Mix
- 4 tablespoons olive oil
- 2 garlic cloves minced
- ½ onion diced
- 2 cups tomato sauce
- 1 cup pitted green olives

Instructions

- Sprinkle both sides of the chicken generously with Italian Seasoning Mix.
- Heat 2 tablespoons of the olive oil in a large heavy skillet over medium heat. Add the chicken, and cook for several minutes on each side until browned on both sides. Remove the chicken from the skillet onto a plate and set aside.
- Add the remaining olive oil, garlic, and onion and cook until the onion is just tender about 2 minutes. Stir in the tomato sauce and olives and return the chicken to the skillet. Cover and cook until the chicken has cooked throughout, about 15 more minutes.

Nutrition

Calories: 448kcal | Carbohydrates: 9g | Protein: 55g | Fat: 20g | Saturated Fat: 3g | Cholesterol: 146mg | Sodium: 770mg | Potassium: 881mg | Fiber: 2g | Sugar: 5g | Vitamin A: 590IU | Vitamin C: 10.1mg | Calcium: 68mg | Iron: 3.6mg

97. Sheet Pan Teriyaki Salmon Green Beans Recipe

Prep Time: 5 mins

Cook Time: 15 mins

Total Time: 20 mins

Servings: 4

Ingredients

- 3 - 4 (6-ounce) salmon fillets
- 1 pound green beans ends trimmed
- 1 tablespoon olive oil
- 1/2 teaspoon kosher salt
- 1/2 teaspoon freshly ground black pepper
- 6 - 8 tablespoons teriyaki sauce + more if desired

Instructions

- preheat oven to 425ºF. Line a rimmed baking sheet with parchment paper.
- Arrange salmon fillets on the lined sheet pan and arrange green beans around the salmon. Drizzle the olive oil over the green beans and sprinkle the green beans and salmon with salt and pepper.
- Spread the teriyaki sauce, about 2 tablespoons per fillet, over the salmon.
- Bake the salmon and green beans until the salmon easily flakes with a fork, about 15 minutes. Remove from the oven and drizzle with additional teriyaki sauce, if desired.

Nutrition

Calories: 244kcal | Carbohydrates: 10g | Protein: 19g | Fat: 14g | Sodium: 396mg | Potassium: 319mg | Fiber: 4g | Sugar: 4g | Vitamin A: 1045IU | Vitamin C: 18.5mg | Calcium: 56mg | Iron: 1.6mg

98. Balsamic Roast Beef Recipe

Prep Time: 5 mins

Cook Time: 4 hrs

Total Time: 4 hrs 5 mins

Ingredients

- 1 (3-4 pound) boneless roast beef (chuck or round roast)
- 1 cup beef stock or broth
- 1/2 cup balsamic vinegar
- 1 tablespoon Worcestershire sauce
- 1 tablespoon soy sauce
- 1 tablespoon honey
- 1/2 teaspoon red pepper flakes
- 4 cloves garlic chopped

Instructions

- Place roast beef into the insert of your slow cooker. In a 2-cup measuring cup, mix all remaining ingredients. Pour over roast beef and set the timer for your slow cooker. (4 hours on High or 6-8 hours on Low)
- Once roast beef has cooked, remove it from the slow cooker with tongs into a serving dish. Break apart lightly with two forks and then ladle about 1/4 - 1/2 cup of gravy over roast beef.
- Store remaining gravy in an airtight container in the refrigerator for another use.

Nutrition

Calories: 432kcal | Carbohydrates: 6g | Protein: 43g | Fat: 35g | Saturated Fat: 1g | Cholesterol: 1mg | Sodium: 181mg | Potassium: 57mg | Fiber: 1g | Sugar: 5g | Vitamin A: 37IU | Vitamin C: 1mg | Calcium: 11mg | Iron: 1mg

99. Chili Stuffed Baked Potatoes Recipe

Prep Time: 10 mins

Cook Time: 1 hr

Total Time: 1 hr 10 mins

Ingredients

- 6 russet potatoes
- Olive oil or butter
- Sea salt
- Black bean chili
- 1/2 cup sour cream
- 1 cup shredded cheddar cheese
- Fresh parsley or cilantro for garnish optional

Instructions

- preheat oven to 375º F. Adjust oven rack to the center of the oven. Place the second oven rack underneath with a baking sheet lined with aluminum foil to catch any drippings.
- Scrub potatoes with a medium bristled brush. Rub with olive oil or butter and sprinkle with sea salt. Pierce the potato with a sharp knife or fork about 3-5 times around the potato to allow steam to escape as cooking. Place directly onto the oven rack placed in the center of the oven.
- As potatoes are cooking, prepare black bean chili according to recipe instructions.
- Test potatoes for doneness by squeezing the center of the potato while using a potholder to

- determine if they tender or checking the internal temperature of the potato with an instant-read thermometer. The potato should register 210º F.
- Remove potatoes from the oven and place them on the sheet pan used on the rack underneath or another platter for serving.
- To serve, split open potatoes with a knife and gently squeeze the potato from both ends to open the contents. Using a large spoon, ladle black bean chili into the center of the potato. Top with sour cream, cheese, and optional garnish.

Nutrition

Calories: 281kcal | Carbohydrates: 39g | Protein: 10g | Fat: 10g | Saturated Fat: 6g | Cholesterol: 30mg | Sodium: 143mg | Potassium: 934mg | Fiber: 3g | Sugar: 2g | Vitamin A: 308IU | Vitamin C: 12mg | Calcium: 185mg | Iron: 2m

100. Thanksgiving Recipes

Prep Time: 1 hr

Cook Time: 50 mins

Total Time: 1 hr 50 mins

Ingredients

- Cranberry Sauce
- 2 cups fresh or frozen cranberries
- 1 cup water
- 1 cup Sugar
- 1 tbsp fresh lemon juice
- 1 tsp orange zest

Cole Slaw

- 1 head of cabbage – cored and sliced very thinly
- ½ small carrot grated
- ½ cups mayonnaise
- 2 tablespoons apple cider vinegar
- ¼ cup sugar
- 1 teaspoon sea salt or to taste
- ½ teaspoon black pepper or to taste
- Roasted Sweet Potatoes and Apples
- 4 large sweet potatoes – peeled and sliced

- 3 large apples – peeled and sliced
- 1 small onion – large chop
- Sea Salt to taste
- Black Pepper to taste
- 1 tbsp brown sugar
- 1 tsp cinnamon
- olive oil

Mashed Sweet Potatoes

- 6 large sweet potatoes
- 1/2 cup apple butter
- 4 tbsp butter
- sea salt to taste
- 1/2 tsp cinnamon optional

Cole Slaw

- Mix mayonnaise, sugar, vinegar, sea salt, and black pepper in a small bowl, blend the ingredients completely. Allow to sit for about 5 minutes so sugar fully dissolves, then remix the ingredients
- Mix cabbage and grated carrot, then add in coleslaw dressing and mix well to make sure the mixture is thoroughly coated.
- Refrigerate until ready to use.
- Coleslaw needs to sit at least 4 hours before eating, and it's best to make it the day before.

Roasted Sweet Potatoes

- Peel and cut sweet potatoes into medium-sized chunks, coat with olive oil, and season with salt and pepper add onion chunks, and place on a cookie sheet in a 350-degree oven for 15 minutes before adding apples.
- Peel and cut apples into medium-sized chunks, coat with brown sugar and cinnamon, and place on a cookie sheet with sweet potatoes after they have cooked 15 minutes and cook for an additional 15 minutes.
- Remove from oven and mix both, place on a serving platter, and sprinkle with chopped parsley.
- Mashed Sweet Potatoes with Apple Butter
- Peel and cut sweet potatoes into medium-sized chunks.
- Place sweet potatoes in boiling salted water and cook for 15-20 minutes or until tender

- Drain potatoes well and in a mixing bowl add the potatoes and butter and whip until butter is melted.
- Add in apple butter, salt, and cinnamon and whip until fully incorporated
- Place in a serving bowl and serve immediately or keep warm in a 200-degree oven until ready to serve

Nutrition

Calories: 280kcal | Carbohydrates: 55g | Protein: 3g | Fat: 6g | Saturated Fat: 3g | Cholesterol: 13mg | Sodium: 262mg | Potassium: 638mg | Fiber: 7g | Sugar: 34g | Vitamin A: 11810IU | Vitamin C: 31.6mg | Calcium: 76mg | Iron: 1.4mg

3. Lean and Green Recipes Side Dishes & Dinner Recipes"

101. Medifast Lean And Green Recipe: Broccoli Taco Bowl

Prep Time: 2 minutes

Cook Time: 10 minutes

Total Time: 12 minutes

Servings: 1

Ingredients

- 4- oz lean ground hamburger
- oz shredded cheddar cheese
- 1 1/4 cup broccoli cut into bite-sized pieces
- 1/4 cup Rotel tomatoes
- 1/4 teaspoon garlic powder
- 1/4 teaspoon onion powder
- 1/4 teaspoon salt divided
- Pinch of red pepper flakes
- 2 tablespoons low sodium chicken stock

Instructions

- Put your broccoli in a bowl with your chicken stock and cover with plastic wrap. Put in the microwave for 4 minutes, or until tender and cooked.
- In a large skillet brown your hamburger and drain the grease if needed when it's done.
- Add your Rotel tomatoes, garlic powder, onion powder, salt, and red pepper flakes and stir well.

- When your broccoli is finished cooking then add it to your skillet and toss with the hamburger mixture.
- Add everything to a bowl and top with your shredded cheddar cheese.

Nutrition

Serving: 0g | Calories: 336kcal | Carbohydrates: 13g | Protein: 36g | Fat: 15g | Saturated Fat: 8g | Cholesterol: 100mg | Sodium: 959mg | Potassium: 929mg | Fiber: 4g | Sugar: 4g | Vitamin A: 1125IU | Vitamin C: 107mg | Calcium: 289mg | Iron: 4.5mg

102. Oven Roasted Cauliflower

Yield: 6 Servings

Prep Time: 10 Minutes

Cook Time: 35 Minutes

Total Time: 45 Minutes

Ingredients

- 1 large head of cauliflower, cut into bite-sized florets (6-8 cups)
- 3 Tablespoons olive oil
- 1/4 teaspoon salt
- 1/4 teaspoon pepper
- 1 teaspoon oregano
- 1/4 teaspoon onion salt
- 1/4 teaspoon garlic powder
- 1/4 teaspoon dried basil

Instructions

- Preheat the oven to 425 degrees. Line a sheet pan with foil.
- Pour the oil over the cauliflower florets in a large bowl. Toss or stir to coat all the pieces.
- Mix all the seasonings. Sprinkle half the mixture on top of the cauliflower. Toss and stir to coat. Sprinkle the remaining seasonings on top and stir again.
- Place the cauliflower on the prepared sheet pan. Make sure the flat sides of the cauliflower are face down on the pan and that the cauliflower is now crowded.
- Bake for 15 minutes. Remove the pan from the oven and use a spatula to flip the pieces of cauliflower over. Return the pan to the oven and

bake for an additional 20 minutes. Serve immediately.

Nutrition

- Calories: 93
- Total fat: 7g
- Saturated fat: 1g
- Trans fat: 0g u
- Unsaturated fat: 6g
- Cholesterol: 0mg
- Sodium: 184mg
- Carbohydrates: 6g
- Fiber: 3g
- Sugar: 3g
- Protein: 3g

103. This Sautéed Spinach

Prep Time:1 Minute

Cook Time:5 Minutes

Total Time:6 Minutes

Serves:4 Servings

Ingredients

- 1 tbsp olive oil
- 10 oz fresh spinach washed
- 2 cloves fresh garlic pressed
- salt and pepper to taste

Instructions

- Heat a large skillet with olive oil over medium-high heat on the stove.
- Add the garlic in and cook stirring for about 30 seconds. Add spinach covering the garlic, piling it all in the pan. Let cook 2-3 minutes, then continue to cook an additional 2-3 minutes, stirring frequently until all spinach leaves have wilted.
- Remove from heat and season to taste with salt and pepper. Serve hot. Enjoy!

Nutrition

Calories: 34kcal, Carbohydrates:1g Protein: 0g, fat: 3g, Saturated Fat: 0g Polyunsaturated Fat: 2g, Monounsaturated Fat: 0g Trans Fat: 0g Cholesterol: 0mg Sodium: 80mg

104. Mexican Green Beans

Prep Time: 15 minutes

Cook Time: 10 minutes

Total Time: 25 minutes

Servings: 6

Ingredients

- 1 pound green beans, trimmed and cut
- 1/2 cup roma tomato, seeded and diced (4 oz)
- 1/4 cup chopped onion (1 oz)
- 1 clove garlic, minced
- 2 tbsp avocado oil or good olive oil
- 1 tbsp butter, ghee, or another tbsp of oil
- 2 tbsp water
- 1 whole bay leaf, crumbled
- 1 tsp chicken base
- 1 tsp fresh oregano, minced (or 1/4 tsp. Dry but fresh tastes different)
- 1/4 tsp ground cumin
- Salt and pepper to taste

Instructions

Preparation:

- Wash, trim and cut beans. Cut the tomato in half and squeeze gently over the trash can to remove seeds, then dice. Chop onion and minced garlic and fresh oregano (if using).

Method:

- Heat 1 tbsp of oil in a large frying pan over medium heat. When hot, add the onion, garlic, tomato, and bay leaf until the onion begins to soften. Add the chicken base, water, another tablespoon of oil, oregano, cumin, and green beans. Stir to coat the beans and loosely cover with a piece of foil or a lid. Cook for 4 minutes or until the beans are cooked to your preference.
- Add butter adjust seasoning by adding salt, pepper, or more oregano and cumin. Serve.

Nutrition

- Calories: 84kcal | Carbohydrates: 6g | Protein: 1g | Fat: 7g | Fiber: 3g

105. Roasted Fennel With Garlic & Herbs

Prep Time: 8 Mins

Cook Time: 30 Mins

Total Time: 38 Mins

Ingredients

- 2 large bulbs of fennel
- 3 tbsp olive oil
- 2 cloves garlic minced
- 3/4 tsp salt
- 1 tsp black pepper
- 1 tsp thyme
- 1/4 cup parmesan

Instructions

- Preheat the oven to 400 degrees Fahrenheit (205 degrees Celsius)
- Remove any of the stalks from the fennel bulbs and then cut them in half lengthwise. Cut each halved fennel bulb into 1 inch thick slices and arrange the slices on a parchment paper-lined baking sheet ensuring that they are all laid out evenly and do not overlap.
- In a bowl combines the olive oil and minced garlic and brush it over the sliced fennel and then sprinkle the thyme, salt, and pepper over top to ensure they are all well seasoned.
- Bake the fennel in the oven for 20 minutes. After 20 minutes if using parmesan, sprinkle it over the fennel and then return the tray to the oven to bake for another 10 minutes.
- After 30 minutes of baking the fennel should be tender and caramelized on the edges. Serve warm.

Nutrition

Calories:121kcal, Carbohydrates:1g, Protein: 2g, Fat: 12g, Saturated Fat: 2g, Cholesterol: 4mg, Sodium: 537mg, Potassium: 24mg, Fiber: 1g, Sugar: 1g

106. Avocado Cauliflower Rice

Prep Time: 5 minutes

Cook Time:15 minutes

Total Time: 20 minutes

Servings: 6 cups

Ingredients

- 6 cups cauliflower rice
- 1 tablespoon cooking fat (avocado oil, coconut oil, ghee...)
- 1 cup diced yellow onion (120 grams)
- 3 cloves garlic, minced
- 2 large avocados, diced (300 grams)
- 1 jalapeño, diced
- 2 1/2 tablespoons lime juice
- 1/2 cup packed cilantro, roughly chopped
- Salt and pepper, to taste

Instructions

- Heat a large sauté pan over medium heat. Add oil and let it get hot. Once hot, add diced onions and sauté for 5 minutes until translucent, stirring occasionally. Add garlic and cook for another minute. Add the cauliflower rice and let cook for 6-7 minutes, stirring occasionally, until softened.
- While the rice cooks, make the avocado mash. Add avocados, diced jalapeno, lime juice, and salt and pepper to a large bowl and mash with a fork until combined, but a little texture remains.
- Once cauliflower rice is cooked to your preference, remove from heat. Add avocado mixture to cauliflower rice and mix well to combine. Stir in cilantro. Top more cilantro and jalapeño if desired. Enjoy!

Nutrition

- Fat: 10g
- Saturated Fat: 2.6g
- Polyunsaturated Fat: 0.1g
- Monounsaturated Fat: 5g
- Potassium: 715.9mg
- Carbohydrates: 14g
- Fiber: 7.4g
- Sugar: 5.4g
- Protein: 4g
- Vitamin A: 230IU
- Vitamin C: 100.6mg
- Calcium: 49mg
- Iron: 1mg

107. Mexican Cauliflower Rice

Prep Time: 10 mins

Cook Time: 15 mins

Total Time: 25 mins

Servings: 4

Ingredients

- 1 head cauliflower, riced
- 1 tbsp olive oil
- 1 medium white onion, finely diced
- 2 cloves garlic, minced
- 1 jalapeno, seeded and minced
- 3 tbsp tomato paste
- 1 tsp sea salt
- 1 tsp cumin
- 1/2 tsp paprika
- 3 tbsp fresh chopped cilantro
- 1 tbsp lime juice

Instructions

- Rice the cauliflower. Slice the florets from the head of the cauliflower. Fit a food processor with the s-blade. Place half the florets into the bowl of the food processor and pulse until riced, scraping down the sides once halfway through to catch any larger pieces. Scrape out the riced cauliflower and repeat with the remaining florets.
- Heat a skillet over medium-high heat. Add the oil and heat until it shimmers. Add the onion and saute until soft and translucent, stirring occasionally, 5-6 minutes.
- Add the garlic and jalapeno and saute until fragrant, 1-2 minutes.
- Add the tomato paste, salt, cumin, and paprika and stir into the vegetables.
- Add the cauliflower rice and stir continuously until all ingredients are incorporated. Continue sautéing, stirring occasionally, until the cauliflower releases its liquid and is dry and fluffy.
- Remove the Mexican cauliflower rice from heat. Stir in the cilantro and lime juice. Serve immediately.

Nutrition

Calories: 105kcal, Carbohydrates: 15g, Protein: 4g, Fat: 4g, Saturated Fat: 1g, Polyunsaturated Fat: 0g, Monounsaturated Fat: 3g, TransFat: 0g, Cholesterol: 0mg, Sodium: 500mg, Potassium: 713mg , Fiber: 5g, Sugar: 6g, Vitamin A: 950%, Vitamin C: 113%, Calcium: 90mg, Iron: 1.8%

108. Garlic Mashed Cauliflower

Prep Time: 20 minutes

Cook Time: 2 minutes

Total Time: 22 minutes

Ingredients

- 1 large cauliflower chopped into small florets
- 3 ounces low fat cream cheese
- 2 tablespoons salted butter
- 1 1/2 teaspoon minced garlic sauteed if you aren't buying it already prepared
- 1 tablespoon fresh rosemary chopped into small pieces, optional

Instructions

- Bring a medium pot of water to boil. Once boiling, cook the cauliflower for 8-10 minutes or until fork-tender. Remove and drain cauliflower.
- Place cauliflower along with all other ingredients into a blender or food processor and pulse until smooth and creamy.

Nutrition

Calories: 101kcal, Carbohydrates: 3g, Protein: 2g, Fat: 9g, saturated fat: 5g, Cholesterol: 26mg, Sodium: 109mg, Potassium: 132mg, Sugar: 1g, Vitamin A: 305IU, Vitamin C: 13.3mg, Calcium: 37mg, Iron: 0.1mg.

109. Low Carb Baked Cauliflower Au Gratin

Prep Time:15 Minutes

Cook Time:30 Minutes

Total Time:45 Minutes

Serve: 4

Ingredients

- 1 Lb Cauliflower, cut into florets (about 4 1/2 cups)
- 2 Tbsp Butter
- 1 Tbsp + 1 tsp Almond flour
- 1 Tbsp + 1 tsp Coconut flour
- 1 1/2 Cups 2% Milk (or Almond)
- 3/4 tsp Salt
- 1/4 tsp Onion powder
- 1/4 tsp Garlic powder

- 1/8 tsp Pepper
- 1 Cup Packed Cheddar cheese, grated and divided (4 oz) (or dairy-free)

Instructions

- Turn your oven to 375 degrees and bring a large pot of salted water to a boil.
- Add the cauliflower (once boiling) and cook until it just begins to become tender, about 5-7 minutes. Drain well and then spread out onto some paper towel. Use another layer of paper towel to gently press as much moisture out of the cauliflower as you possibly can.
- While the cauliflower cooks, melt the butter in a medium pan over medium/high heat. Once melted, add in the almond flour and coconut flour and whisk, stirring constantly, until it just begins to brown, about 1 minute.
- Whisk in the milk, salt, garlic, and onion powder, and pepper until smooth and bring to a boil. Once boiling reduces the heat to medium, stirring occasionally, until VERY thick, about 7-8 minutes.
- Remove the milk mixture from the heat and whisk in 1/2 cup of the cheese until smooth.
- Spread 1/3 of the sauce on the bottom of an 8×8 inch pan. Pack the cauliflower into the pan on top and then spoon the rest of the sauce over top. Sprinkle with the remaining cheese.
- Bake until golden brown and bubbly, about 25-30 minutes.
- Let stand for 5 minutes and DEVOUR!

Nutrition

Calories: 174kcal, Carbohydrates: 8.6g, Protein: 9.1g, Fat: 12.2g, Saturated Fat: 7.2g Polyunsaturated Fat: 0.4g Monounsaturated Fat: 3g Cholesterol: 35mg, Sodium: 467mg, Potassium: 357mg, Fiber: 2.5g, Sugar: 4.6g, Vitamin C: 47mg , Calcium: 220mg, Iron: 0.5mg.

110. Roasted Garlic Mashed Cauliflower

Prep Time: 20 minutes

Total Time: 20 minutes

Servings: 6 servings

Ingredients

- 1 head cauliflower cut into florets
- ¼ cup milk almond or cashew milk
- 3 Tbsp. olive oil
- 1 ½ tsp. rosemary fresh
- 1 ½ tsp. thyme fresh
- 3-4 cloves roasted garlic
- ¾-1 tsp. salt to taste
- 1 pinch black pepper

Instructions

- Roast a head of garlic in the oven. You can do this up to 3 days in advance and store it in the refrigerator until ready to use.
- Bring a large pot of water to a boil. Boil cauliflower for 10-12 minutes.
- Drain water and place cauliflower on a towel and dry cauliflower completely before proceeding.
- In the bowl of a food processor combine cauliflower, milk, olive oil, rosemary, thyme, roasted garlic cloves, salt, to taste, and a pinch of black pepper.
- Puree for 1-2 minutes or until mashed cauliflower is completely smooth. Be sure to scrape down the sides of the bowl every 20-30 seconds to ensure even pureeing.
- If mashed cauliflower has cooled too much, return it to the pot and heat it to your desired temperature.
- Serve mashed cauliflower with a drizzle of olive oil and a few sprigs of rosemary or thyme and enjoy!

Nutrition

Fat: 9g, Saturated Fat: 1g, Sodium: 333mg, Potassium: 59mg, Carbohydrates: 5g, Fiber: 2g, Sugar: 1g, Protein: 1g, Vitamin C: 65.6mg, Calcium: 37mg, Iron 0.5mg

111. Stuffed Zucchini Boats

Prep Time: 10 mins

Cook Time: 30 mins

Total Time: 40 mins

Serves: 3

Ingredients

- 3 zucchinis
- Cooking spray
- 3/4 lb. chicken breast cut into cubes

- 1 Tbsp olive oil
- 1/4 tsp Italian seasoning
- 1/4 tsp garlic powder
- 1/4 tsp salt
- 1/4 tsp ground black pepper
- 3/4 cup pasta sauce
- 1/4 cup grated parmesan cheese
- 1/4 cup shredded mozzarella cheese

Instructions

- preheat oven to 400°F.
- To prepare the zucchini, cut the zucchini in half lengthwise, then use a spoon or melon baller to scoop the center flesh and seeds from the zucchini. Repeat for the remaining zucchini.
- Place the zucchini in a baking dish or cookie sheet cut-side up and lightly coat with cooking spray. Place in the preheated oven for 15 minutes until the zucchini cooks slightly and becomes tender.
- Meanwhile, to prepare the chicken, heat the olive oil in a large non-stick skillet over medium-high heat. Add the chicken along with the seasoning, salt, and pepper.
- Cook for 8-10 minutes until the chicken is cooked through. Add the pasta sauce and cook for an additional 2 minutes, stirring occasionally.
- Scoop the chicken mixture into the zucchini boats. Top the chicken with parmesan cheese and mozzarella cheese. Return the zucchini boats to the oven for 5 more minutes, or until the cheese is melted.
- Sprinkle with fresh basil and parmesan cheese, if desired, and serve.

Nutrition

Serving: 2boats | Calories: 284kcal | Carbohydrates: 10g | Protein: 32g | Fat: 12g | SaturatedFat: 4g | Cholesterol: 87mg | Sodium: 848mg | Potassium: 1133mg | Fiber: 2g | Sugar: 7g | Vitamin A: 825IU | Vitamin C: 40.8mg | Calcium: 185mg | Iron: 1.8mg

112. Sheet Pan Salmon & Green Vegetables

Prep Time:15 mins

Cook Time:15 mins

Total Time:30 mins

Yield: 3-4

Ingredients

For The Sauce

- 2 medium cloves of garlic, grated
- 3 tablespoons of finely chopped parsley (coriander or basil will also work)
- Zest of 1/2 lemon
- Juice of 1/2 lemon
- 3 tablespoons olive oil
- 1/2 teaspoon sea salt
- For the rest
- 1 tablespoon coconut oil or olive oil to grease the pan
- 4 salmon fillets (whatever size suits your pan and appetite)
- 12–14 Brussels sprouts, halved
- 12–14 asparagus spears, hard ends cut off and rinsed
- 1 bunch of broccolini florets (or broccoli rabe or 1/2 head of regular broccoli in florets)
- Extra olive oil, sea salt, pepper, and lemon

Instructions

- Preheat the oven to 200 C / 400 F.
- Mix the sauce in a small bowl and set aside.
- Grease a large sheet pan or flat-ish baking tray with about a tablespoon of olive oil and place the salmon fillets in the middle, leaving about an inch of space in between. Spread even amounts of the sauce over the top of each salmon fillet.
- Scatter the green vegetables around and in between the fillets, overlapping each other is fine. Drizzle the vegetables lightly with olive oil (about 2 tablespoons) and the juice of half of the remaining lemon. Sprinkle with a few pinches of sea salt and pepper.
- Place the tray in the oven for 15 minutes, rotating halfway if your oven is slightly uneven in temperature (like mine).
- Serve while hot with any additional vegetables, salads, or starchy carbs, if you needed.

113. Easy Low Carb Keto Creamed Spinach Recipe

Prep Time: 5minutes

Cook Time: 10minutes

Total Time: 15minutes

Ingredients

- 4 cloves Garlic (minced)
- 10 oz Baby spinach (chopped; about 16 cups)
- 1/2 cup Heavy cream
- 3 oz Cream cheese (cut into small pieces)
- 1 tsp Italian seasoning
- 1/4 tsp sea salt
- 1/4 tsp black pepper
- Parmesan cheese (optional, for topping)

Instructions

- Heat butter in a large saute pan or wok over medium heat. Add minced garlic and saute until fragrant.
- Add spinach. Saute for 2 to 4 minutes, until wilted. If the pan is too full to stir at first, cover it for a minute or two, which will let the spinach at the bottom wilt. Then you can start to stir in a folding motion.
- Add heavy cream, cream cheese, sea salt, black pepper, and Italian seasoning. Stir constantly until the cream cheese melts, then cook a few minutes until thickened.
- If desired, sprinkle with Parmesan cheese for serving.

Nutrition

Calories: 274 | Fat: 27g | Protein: 4g | Total Carbs: 5g | Net Carbs: 4g | Fiber: 1g Sugar: 1g

---

114. Cauliflower Spanish Rice

Prep Time: 10 Minutes

Cook Time: 10 Minutes

Total Time: 20 Minutes

Servings: 3 Cups Rice

Ingredients

- 1 large head of cauliflower*
- 1 tbsp olive oil or avocado oil
- 1/2 cup diced onion
- 3 cloves garlic minced
- 1 tsp cumin
- 1/2 tsp salt + more to taste
- 2 tbsp tomato paste
- 1/4 - 1/2 cup chicken or vegetable broth
- Fresh cilantro for garnish optional

- 1 lime, juiced optional

Instructions

- Cut your cauliflower in half and half again. Remove stem and discard. Chop the head of the cauliflower into chunks (1-2 inch pieces). Place inside a food processor and pulse. You probably need to do this in 2-3 batches. Between each batch, remove and set aside.
- Heat a large skillet to medium heat. Add onion and saute for 3 minutes, then add garlic and saute another 1-2 minutes.
- Add in the riced cauliflower and saute for another 4-5 minutes. salt, and cumin. Stir around the veggie mixture to coat.
- Now add in cumin, salt, tomato paste, then 1/4 cup broth (you might not need broth with frozen rice as it produces enough moisture). Bump up the heat to medium-high. Continue to stir around until the tomato paste dissolves in the mixture. If the mixture is too dry, add in more broth by the tablespoon. If the mixture is slightly wet, continue to cook until the liquid dissolves.
- Serve hot with garnished cilantro, lime juice, and added salt to taste.

Nutrition

Calories:76kcal | Fat:5g | Sodium:872mg | Potassium:277mg | Carbohydrates:7g | Fiber:1g | Sugar:3g | Protein:1g | VitaminA:165% | VitaminC:22.4% | Calcium 29mg | Iron 0.9mg

---

115. Sauteed Green Beans With Mushrooms

Prep Time: 10 minutes

Cook Time: 10 minutes

Total Time: 20 minutes

Servings: 6

Ingredients

- 1 pound fresh green beans, trimmed
- 1 Tablespoon olive oil
- 2 cloves garlic, minced
- 8 ounces mushrooms, white button or cremini, sliced
- Salt and pepper, to taste

Instructions

- Steam or blanch the green beans in boiling water for about 2 minutes, until they are bright green. Immediately transfer the beans to a bowl of ice water, then drain when cool.
- Pat the green beans dry with a kitchen towel. Slice the green beans into bite-size pieces.
- Heat the oil in a skillet over medium heat. Add the garlic and stir until fragrant, about 30 seconds.
- Next, add the mushrooms to the pan and saute until soft.
- Add the sliced green beans to the pan and toss to heat through.
- Season to taste with salt and pepper, then serve.

Nutrition

Calories: 53kcal | Carbohydrates: 6g | Protein: 2g | Fat: 2g | Sodium: 6mg | Potassium: 279mg | Fiber: 2g | Sugar: 3g | Vitamin A: 520IU | Vitamin C: 10.3mg | Calcium: 30mg | Iron: 1mg

116. Best Oven-Roasted Broccoli With Nutritional Yeast

Prep Time: 5 minutes

Cook Time: 20 minutes

Total Time: 25 minutes

Ingredients

- 1 large head of broccoli; approx 4 heaping cups of broccoli florets
- 1 TBSP olive oil
- 3 TBSP nutritional yeast
- 1/2 tsp garlic salt, give or take
- Cracked black pepper (optional)

Instructions

- Pre-heat oven to 425° F.
- Cut broccoli down into bite-sized florets. In a colander, rinse them off and give them a good shake to dry them off; transfer them to a large bowl.
- Drizzle the florets with the olive oil and sprinkle the florets with 2 TBSP of nutritional yeast, followed by the garlic salt. With a large spoon, give the broccoli a good toss to evenly coat the florets. You could also cover the bowl and shake the contents until evenly coated. When done, spread the florets out onto a baking sheet.

Sprinkle the rest of the nutritional yeast over the broccoli florets.
- Bake in the oven for 15-20 minutes, tossing the broccoli halfway through.
- Season with a bit of extra garlic salt if needed, and cracked black pepper if desired.

117. Baby Spinach Caprese Salad

Prep time: 20 min

Total time: 20 min

Serves: 4

Ingredients

- Tomatoes, cherry - 1/2 pint, halved
- Cucumbers - 1/2, chopped
- Mozzarella, fresh - 4 oz, cubed
- Basil - 2 to 3 sprigs, sliced
- Spinach, baby - 5 oz
- Balsamic vinegar - 2 Tbsp
- Honey - 1 1/4 tsp
- Dijon mustard - 1 1/4 tsp
- Cooking oil - 2 Tbsp + 2 tsp

Instructions

Prep

- Tomatoes / Cucumbers / Mozzarella / Basil – Prep as directed.

Make

- Make vinaigrette – Whisk together balsamic vinegar, honey, Dijon mustard, and cooking oil. Season to taste with salt and pepper. (Can be done up to 5 days ahead)
- Toss tomatoes, cucumbers, mozzarella, basil, and spinach with the rest of the vinaigrette. Season to taste with salt and pepper.
- Enjoy your favorite summer meal!
-

Nutrition

- Fat: 10g
- Carbohydrates: 14g
- Fiber: 7.4g
- Sugar: 1g
- Protein: 4g
- Calcium: 49mg
- Iron: 1mg

118. Lemon Basil Chicken

Prep Time: 15 mins

Cook Time: 15 mins

Total Time:30 mins

Servings: 4 servings (about 4 cups total)

Ingredients

- 1 tablespoon extra-virgin olive oil
- 1/2 large yellow onion finely chopped, about 1 cup
- 4 cloves garlic minced
- 1 1/2 pounds boneless skinless chicken breasts, cut into 3/4-inch pieces
- 2 tablespoons low-sodium soy sauce
- 1/4 teaspoon ground black pepper
- 5 cups loosely packed baby spinach about 5 ounces
- 1 tablespoon lemon zest
- 2 tablespoons freshly squeezed lemon juice
- 2 cups fresh basil leaves
- Kosher salt and pepper to taste
- Prepared brown rice for serving

Instructions

- In a large skillet, heat the olive oil over medium. Once hot, add the onion and cook, stirring often until softened, about 4 minutes. Add the garlic and cook until fragrant, about 30 additional seconds.
- Add the chicken, increase the heat to medium-high, and let cook for 3 minutes, browning all sides. Stir in the soy sauce and black pepper. Let cook until the chicken is completely cooked through, about 3 minutes longer.
- Stir in the spinach a few handfuls at a time, letting the heat of the pan wilt it as you go. Stir in the lemon zest, lemon juice, and basil. Cook and stir just until the basil is wilted about 1 additional minute. Taste and season with additional salt or pepper as desired. Serve warm with rice as desired.

Nutrition

Calories: 349kcal|
Carbohydrates:29g|Protein:40g|Fat:8g|Saturat

ed fat: 1g|Cholesterol: 98mg|Sodium: 534mg|Fiber: 4g|Sugar: 3g

119. Garlic Roasted Pork Chops

Prep Time: 10 mins

Cook Time: 15 mins

Total Time: 25 mins

Ingredients

- 1 tbsp olive oil
- 1 tsp sea salt
- 1/2 tsp ground black pepper
- 4 boneless center-cut pork chops
- 6-8 cloves garlic, peeled and whole

Instructions

- Heat the oven to 400 degrees.
- In an oven-safe skillet, heat the olive oil over high heat.
- Season the pork chops with salt and pepper.
- Once the oil is hot, add the pork chops to the skillet and sear for 2-3 minutes, until golden brown.
- Flip the chops over, toss in the garlic cloves, and place the pan in the hot oven.
- Roast the chops for 2 minutes.
- Then, carefully flip the chops and the garlic over and roast for another 2 minutes, or until they are cooked through.
- Carefully remove from the oven. Allow the chops to rest, out of the hot pan, for about 5 minutes, and then serve. Serve the roasted garlic alongside.

Nutrition

Fat:4.5g|SaturatedFat:1g|Cholesterol:5.1mg|Sodium:693.6mg|Carbohydrates 31.9g|Fiber 0.2g|Sugar 0.1g|Protein 39g

120. Cauliflower "Fried Rice"

Prep Time: 20 Mins

Cook Time: 10 Mins

Total Time: 30 Mins

Yield: 4 Servings

Ingredients

- 1 medium head, about 24 oz cauliflower, rinsed

- 1 tbsp sesame oil
- 2 egg whites
- 1 large egg
- pinch of salt
- cooking spray
- 1/2 small onion, diced fine
- 1/2 cup frozen peas and carrots
- 2 garlic cloves, minced
- 5 scallions, diced, whites and greens separated
- 3 tbsp soy sauce, or more to taste Tamari for Gluten Free, Coconut

Instructions

- Remove the core and let the cauliflower dry completely.
- Coarsely chop into florets, then place half of the cauliflower in a food processor and pulse until the cauliflower is small and has the texture of rice or couscous – don't over process or it will get mushy. Set aside and repeat with the remaining cauliflower.
- Combine egg and egg whites in a small bowl and beat with a fork. Season with salt.
- Heat a large saute pan or wok over medium heat and spray with oil.
- Add the eggs and cook, turning a few times until set; set aside.
- Add the sesame oil and saute onions, scallion whites, peas and carrots, and garlic for about 3 to 4 minutes, or until soft. Raise the heat to medium-high.
- Add the cauliflower "rice" to the saute pan along with soy sauce. Mix, cover, and cook for approximately 5 to 6 minutes, stirring frequently, until the cauliflower is slightly crispy on the outside but tender on the inside.
- Add the egg then remove from heat and mix in scallion greens.

Nutrition

Serving: 11/3cup, Calories: 108kcal, Carbohydrates: 14g, Protein: 9g, Fat: 3g, Cholesterol: 47mg, Sodium: 868mg, Fiber: 6g, Sugar: 1g

121. Baked Cod Sheet Pan Dinner

Prep Time:10 Minutes

Cook Time:15 Minutes

Total Time: 25 Minutes

Servings: 4

Ingredients

- 1 pound thin asparagus, ends trimmed
- 1-pint cherry tomatoes halved
- 1 tablespoon extra-virgin olive oil
- 4 4 ounce cod fillets, rinsed and patted dry
- 2 tablespoons lemon juice
- 1 teaspoon lemon zest
- 1/4 cup grated Parmesan cheese
- Salt and pepper

Instructions

- preheat oven to 375 degrees F. Lightly coat a 15x10-inch baking sheet with nonstick spray.
- Toss the asparagus and cherry tomatoes with the olive oil; spread on the baking sheet. Place cod fillets on top.
- Brush the fish with lemon juice; sprinkle with the lemon zest. Sprinkle everything with Parmesan and a little salt and pepper.
- Place in the oven and cook until fish flakes easily with a fork, about 12-15 minutes.

Nutrition

Serving: 4servings | Calories: 141kcal | Carbohydrates: 9g | Protein: 6g | Fat: 5g | Saturated Fat: 1g | Cholesterol: 5mg | Sodium: 111mg | Potassium: 486mg | Fiber: 3g | Sugar: 5g | Vitamin A: 1490IU | Vitamin C: 36.9mg | Calcium: 110mg | Iron: 3.3mg

122. Easy Sauteed Mushrooms

Prep Time: 5 Mins

Cook Time: 15 Mins

Total Time: 20 Mins

Servings: 4 servings

Ingredients

- 1 teaspoon unsalted butter, split into 2 ½ pieces
- 1 teaspoon olive oil
- 2 cloves garlic, minced
- 1 small shallot, peeled and minced
- 1 pound button mushrooms, cleaned and sliced thin can use crimini or baby Bella
- ⅓ cup white wine

- 2 splashes Worcestershire Sauce
- Salt and pepper, to taste
- 1 Tablespoon fresh parsley, chopped can use 1 teaspoon dried parsley

Instructions

- In a medium saute pan, over medium heat add ½ teaspoon unsalted butter and olive oil to melt and hot enough that the butter is beginning to bubble. Add to the pan the garlic and shallot. Saute and stir for about 1 minute.
- Add the other ½ teaspoon unsalted butter to the saute pan. Add the sliced mushrooms and season with salt and pepper. Saute for about 1 minute. Add the white wine and Worcestershire Sauce, increase heat to medium-high. Cover the saute pan and let the flavors blend and the wine reduces about 5 minutes.
- Remove from the heat and add the fresh parsley. Check to the season, re-season if necessary. Add the chopped parsley and serve as a side dish.

Nutrition

Serving: 1serving | Calories: 61kcal | Carbohydrates: 4g | Protein: 3g | Fat: 2g | Saturated Fat: 0g | Cholesterol: 2mg | Sodium: 7mg | Potassium: 374mg | Fiber: 1g | Sugar: 2g | Vitamin A: 115IU | Vitamin C: 4.2mg | Calcium: 6mg | Iron: 0.7mg

123. Healthy Sweet Potato Casserole

Prep Time: 20 mins

Cook Time: 30 mins

Total Time: 50 mins

Servings: 12 servings

Ingredients

Bottom Layer:

- 3 cups sweet potatoes boiled, peeled, and mashed
- ½ cup coconut sugar
- ½ cup butter melted
- 1 tsp vanilla
- ½ cup coconut milk or almond milk
- 2 eggs

Instructions

- Mix the sweet potato, coconut sugar, butter, vanilla, milk, and eggs by hand or with an electric mixer, and place it into a greased pan.
- Melt butter, add coconut sugar and stir until dissolved. Stir in almond flour and pecans. Combine until well mixed and crumbly and sprinkle topping.
- Bake at 350 for 30 minutes in a small casserole dish.

Nutrition

Calories: 251kcal | Carbohydrates: 17g | Protein: 3g | Fat: 20g | Saturated Fat: 10g | Cholesterol: 58mg | Sodium: 151mg | Potassium: 162mg | Fiber: 2g | Sugar: 8g | Vitamin A: 5111IU | Vitamin C: 1mg | Calcium: 32mg | Iron: 1mg

124. One Pan Cabbage Casserole (Low Carb)

Cook time: 20 MINUTES

Total time: 20 MINUTES

Yield: 6

Ingredients

- 1 pound ground beef or turkey, browned and drained
- 1 small onion, diced
- 1/2 head of cabbage chopped into medium chunks (roughly 3 cups)
- 1 can tomatoes with green chilies (undrained)
- 1 8 ounces can of tomato sauce
- 1 teaspoon chili powder
- 1 teaspoon garlic powder
- Salt and pepper to taste
- 1 cup shredded cheese (cheddar or Colby jack is our favorite)

Instructions

- In a medium-size skillet brown your beef or turkey over medium heat, drain off any grease.
- Add the diced onion and sauté for 3-5 minutes.
- Add the cabbage, tomatoes with green chilies, tomato sauce, spices and stir well.
- Cover and reduce heat to medium cooking for 15-18 minutes stirring occasionally.
- Top with cheese!

Nutrition

Fat: 5.3g|Carbohydrates: 9g|Fiber: 1.6g

125. Cucumber Tomato Salad

Prep Time: 10 Minutes

Cook Time: 15 Minutes

Total Time: 25 Minutes

Yield: 10

Serving Size: 1

Ingredients
Salad:

- 6 cucumbers, quartered
- 2 pints grape tomatoes, halved
- 1 purple (red) onion, chopped
- 1 tablespoon dill weed
- 1/2 cup crumbled feta cheese, plus more for topping

Dressing:

- 1 cup apple cider vinegar
- ½ cup balsamic vinegar
- ½ cup olive oil
- 2 cups water
- 2 teaspoons black pepper
- 1 teaspoon granulated sugar

Instructions

- Whisk together the vinegar, olive oil, water, pepper, and sugar; set aside.
- Add the cucumbers, tomatoes, onion, dill weed, and cheese to a large bowl. Pour the dressing over the top and toss until combined.
- Top with feta cheese, dill weed, and salt/pepper to taste. Refrigerate for 15 minutes before serving. Enjoy!

Nutrition Facts:

Total fat: 13g|Saturated fat: 3g|Trans fat: 0g|Fat: 10g|Cholesterol: 7mg

Sodium: 81mgl|Carbohydrates: 11g|Fiber: 2g|Sugar: 7g|Protein: 3g

126. Cauliflower Parmesan Crisps

Prep Time: 30 minutes

Cook Time: 17 minutes

Total Time: 47 minutes

Servings: 4 (Makes 12-13 pieces)

Ingredients

- 3 lb head of cauliflower 1 average head of cauliflower
- 3/4 cup fresh grated Parmesan cheese
- 1 tsp garlic powder
- 1 tbsp dry parsley
- Salt optional

Instructions

- Cut cauliflower florets off the stem.
- Steam cauliflower florets until tender. (10-15 minutes)
- Place steamed cauliflower florets in a food processor and pulse a few times until it looks like fine crumbs. (Make sure there are no chunks left.)
- Transfer cauliflower crumbs in a doubled cheesecloth and squeeze out all the liquid. (You may have to let it cool a bit or it will be too hot for you to squeeze.)
- Place cauliflower in a mixing bowl and add Parmesan cheese, dry parsley, and garlic powder. Mix well, until all evenly incorporated. (Taste to see if you want to add salt. Parmesan cheese is quite salty and you may feel like it's enough salt.)
- Preheat the oven to 425 and line a large baking sheet with parchment paper.
- Use a cookie scoop to scoop out cauliflower "dough." Press it into a ball with your hands and place it on the baking sheet. (I used #40 scoop.)
- Press down to flatten the "dough" into a thin disk, fixing the broken edges. The goal is for the disks to be only about 3 millimeters thin.
- Repeat with all the "dough." You will get about 12 pieces.
- Bake for 15-17 minutes, until deep golden brown.
- Let the cauliflower crisps cool before taking them off the baking sheet. Use a spatula to gently scoop them up.

Nutrition

Calories: 162kcal | Carbohydrates: 18g | Protein: 13g | Fat: 5g | Saturated Fat: 3g | Cholesterol: 12mg | Sodium: 404mg |

Potassium: 1054mg | Fiber: 6g | Sugar: 6g | Vitamin A: 145IU | Vitamin C: 164.5mg | Calcium: 301mg | Iron: 1.7mg

127. Mexican Cauliflower Rice Skillet Dinner

Prep Time: 5 mins

Cook Time: 20 mins

Total Time: 25 mins

Serves:4

Ingredients

- 1 lb ground beef
- 1/4 medium onion diced
- 1/2 red pepper diced
- 3 tbsp taco seasoning
- 1 cup diced tomatoes
- 12 ounces cauliflower rice fresh or frozen
- 1/2 cup chicken broth
- 1 1/2 cups shredded Cheddar cheese or Mexican Blend

Instructions

- In a large skillet over medium heat, brown the ground beef until almost cooked through (just a little pink). Add the onion and pepper and continue to cook until no longer pink. Stir in the taco seasoning.
- Add the tomatoes and cauliflower rice and stir to combine. Stir in the broth and bring to a simmer. Reduce the heat to medium-low and cook until the cauliflower rice begins to soften (8 to 10 minutes for frozen).
- Sprinkle the skillet with the cheese and cover. Let cook until the cheese is melted, 3 or 4 minutes. Remove from heat and top with your favorite toppings like sour cream, avocado, and chopped cilantro.

Nutrition

Food   Energy:352kcal|Total fat:21.71g|Cholesterol: 96mg|Carbohydrate: 7.04g|Total dietary fiber: 2.00g|Protein: 29.09g

128. Low-Carb Twice Baked Cauliflower

Prep Time 20 Minutes

Cook Time 35 Minutes

Total Time 55 Minutes

Yield: 8 Servings

Ingredients

- 1 large head cauliflower
- 4 oz. cream cheese, cut into cubes
- 1/2 cup sour cream
- 1/4 cup green onions, minced
- 1/4 cup freshly grated Parmesan cheese (or more)
- 6 slices bacon, cooked until very crisp, fat blotted with a paper towel and then crumbled
- 1 cup grated sharp cheddar cheese

Instructions

- preheat oven to 350F/180C.
- Spray a glass casserole dish with olive oil or non-stick spray.
- Cut out stem and core from cauliflower, and cut into small pieces.
- Cook in a large pot of boiling salted water until cauliflower is tender, but not overly soft.
- Drain well and mash with a potato masher (affiliate link), leaving some chunks.
- While cauliflower is cooking, cook the bacon and crumble, slice green onions, cube the cream cheese, measure sour cream, and measure Parmesan.
- Mix cream cheese, sour cream, green onion, Parmesan, and 3/4 of the crumbled bacon into the drained cauliflower.
- Spread evenly in a 1.5 Quart Glass Casserole Dish (affiliate link).
- Sprinkle with cheddar cheese and reserved bacon.
- Bake 20-25 minutes covered, or until hot and bubbly.
- ❖ Remove the lid and bake about 10 minutes more, or until the cheese is slightly browned. Serve hot.

Nutrition Information:

Calories: 292|Total Fat: 23g|Saturated Fat: 12g|Unsaturated   Fat: 8g

Cholesterol:62mg|Sodium: 468mg|Carbohydrates: 6.4g|Fiber: 3g|Sugar: 3g|Protein: 14g

129. Sautéed Mushrooms

Prep Time:10 mins

Cook Time:15 mins

Total Time: 25 mins

Ingredients

- 1 lb fresh, firm mushrooms (I like to use cremini mushrooms)
- ¼ cup unsalted butter (or extra virgin olive oil)
- 1 tablespoon minced fresh garlic
- ½ teaspoon Diamond Crystal kosher salt
- ¼ teaspoon freshly ground black pepper
- ½ teaspoon dried thyme
- 2 tablespoons chopped parsley for garnish

Instructions

- Wipe the mushrooms clean with damp paper towels, then slice them into ¼-inch-thick slices.
- In a large skillet, heat the butter over medium heat. When foaming subsides, add the sliced mushrooms, minced garlic, kosher salt, black pepper, and dried thyme.
- Cook, stirring often, over medium heat, until the mushrooms are tender and the liquids they have released have evaporated about 7 minutes.
- Garnish the mushrooms with chopped parsley. Serve immediately.

Nutrition

Calories:261|Fat:24g|SaturatedFat: 14g|Sodium: 295mg|Carbohydrates: 9g|Fiber: 3g|Sugar: 4g| Protein: 7g

130. Loaded Cauliflower Casserole

Yield: 8 Servings

Prep Time: 30 Minutes

Cook Time: 30 Minutes

Total Time: 1 Hour

Ingredients

- 8 slices of bacon, fried crispy
- 1 large head cauliflower, cut into florets
- 1/2 cup sour cream
- 1/2 cup mayonnaise
- 1 tablespoon ranch seasoning
- ¼ teaspoon black pepper
- 1 cup shredded Colby & Monterey jack cheese
- 1 cup sharp cheddar cheese
- 6 tablespoons chopped fresh chives, divided

Instructions

- preheat oven to 370 degrees. Spray an 11×7 (you can also use 13×9) baking dish with non-stick cooking spray.
- Fry bacon in a large skillet until crispy and crumble. Set aside.
- Steam cauliflower until tender, about 15 to 20 minutes.
- Combine your sour cream, mayonnaise, ranch seasoning, black pepper in a large bowl. Add the steamed cauliflower florets, 1/2 of the bacon, 1 cup sharp cheddar cheese, and 3 tablespoons chives; mix well. Transfer mixture to the prepared baking dish and top with your Colby & Monterey jack cheese and the other half of the bacon.
- ❖ Cover the dish with foil and bake for 20 minutes. Remove foil and bake another 5-10 minutes or just until cheese is bubbly and beginning to brown. Garnish casserole with remaining chives.

Nutrition

Calories:297|TotalFat:26.6g|SaturatedFat:9.8g |TransFat:0.4g|UnsaturatedFat:14.8g|Cholesterol:53.6mg|Sodium:798mg|Carbohydrates:3g| Fiber: 0.5g|Sugar: 1.2g|Protein: 11.4g

131. Baked Roasted Radishes Recipe

Prep Time: 5 minutes

Cook Time: 30 minutes

Total Time: 35 minutes

Ingredients

- 2 lb Radishes (trimmed and halved)

- 3 tablespoons Olive oil
- 1 teaspoon Sea salt (plus more to taste when done)
- 1/4 teaspoon Black pepper
- 1/2 teaspoon Smoked paprika
- 1/4 teaspoon Onion powder
- 1/4 teaspoon Garlic powder

Instructions

- preheat oven to 400 degrees F (204 degrees C).
- Toss radishes with olive oil and spices. Arrange in a single layer on a baking sheet, making sure each radish touches the pan.
- Roast for about 30 to 35 minutes, until golden and crispy.
- Season with extra salt and pepper to taste.

Nutrition

Calories: 87|Fat: 7g|Protein:1g|Total Carbs: 5g|Net Carbs: 3g|Fiber:2g

Sugar2g

131. Healthy Chicken Stir-Fry

Total Time:60 minutes

Yield: 4 serving(s)

Ingredients

- 4 chicken breasts, cut into bite-sized pieces
- 2 tablespoons extra virgin olive oil
- 1 cup brown rice
- 1 medium-size bunch of bok choy, washed and diced
- 3 medium-sized carrots, washed and sliced
- 1 medium yellow or white onion, chopped
- 1 yellow or red pepper, washed and cubed
- 1/2 a head of broccoli, washed and the heads cut off into bite-sized pieces
- 1 container or 2 cups snow peas, washed and cleaned
- Stir Fry Sauce
- 1/2 cup reduced-sodium soy sauce
- 1 tablespoon sesame oil
- 1 teaspoon sesame seeds
- 1 tablespoon garlic
- 2.5 tablespoons ginger paste or 1.5 tablespoons fresh ground ginger
- 1 teaspoon red chili pepper flakes

- 1 teaspoon honey

Directions

- Follow package instructions for 1 cup dry brown rice. It will yield 2 cups once cooked. The rice simmers for 40-50 minutes
- Mix the stir-fry sauce ingredients into a measuring cup or bowl and set aside
- Prep the vegetables and the chicken as indicated above then set aside
- Heat a large frying pan add in the 2 tbsp EVOO add chicken breast and brown until fully cooked
- Wait until all the rice is cooked, and cooling. Next, add all the veggies to the cooked chicken and cover your stir-fry with the prepared sauce
- The entire stir-fry will cook 3-5 minutes together until veggies are bright in color but still crisp
- ❖ Plate 1/2 cup rice to each plate and distribute the stir-fry among the 4 plates. This recipe makes 4 healthy-sized servings of stir fry

Nutrition

Calories: 465|Protein: 35g|Fat: 7g|Carbohydrates: 42g

132. How to Cook Bok Choy

Prep Time: 10 mins

Cook Time: 7 mins

Total Time: 17 mins

Servings: 4

Ingredients

- 1 pound baby bok choy
- 2 tablespoon soy sauce
- 2 tablespoons vegetable broth
- 1 tablespoon rice vinegar
- 1 tablespoon sesame oil, divided
- 1 teaspoon honey
- ⅛ teaspoon red chili flakes
- 2 tablespoons vegetable oil, divided
- 1 tablespoon minced garlic
- 2 teaspoons minced ginger
- ¼ cup thinly sliced green onions, white and green parts
- ¼ teaspoon sesame seeds

Instructions

- Rinse the bok choy with water. Shaking off any excess water and then dry using a kitchen towel or paper towels.
- Cut each bok choy, halved lengthwise.
- In a small bowl combine soy sauce, broth, vinegar, 2 teaspoons of sesame oil, honey, and red chili flakes.
- In a wok or 12-inch nonstick skillet add 1 tablespoon vegetable oil and 1 teaspoon of sesame oil over high heat until just smoking.
- Use tongs to carefully place the bok choy cut side down in a single layer in the wok, lightly press down to make contact with the surface.
- Cook until lightly browned without moving, about 1 to 2 minutes.
- Flip the bok choy over and cook the other side until lightly browned for 1 to 2 minutes. Transfer to a plate.
- Add 1 tablespoon vegetable oil to the wok. Add garlic, ginger, and green onions, stir fry until fragrant, about 30 seconds.
- Add the soy sauce mixture to the wok, simmer until thickened, about 30 seconds.
- Add bok choy back to the wok, stir-fry, and cook until the sauce glazes the greens, about 1 to 2 minutes.
- Transfer to a platter and garnish with sesame seeds.

Nutrition

- Fat: 11g
- Saturated Fat: 6g
- Sodium: 608mg
- Potassium: 19mg
- Carbohydrates: 5g
- Fiber: 1g
- Sugar: 3g
- Protein: 2g
- Vitamin A: 5081IU
- Vitamin C: 52mg
- Calcium: 128mg
- Iron: 1mg

133. The Best Creamed Spinach Recipe

Prep Time: 5 minutes

Cook Time: 10 minutes

Total: 15 minutes

Serves: 8 servings

Ingredients

- 20-24 ounces fresh spinach (about 1 1/2 pounds)
- 5 tablespoons butter
- 1 onion finely chopped
- 4 cloves garlic crushed
- 1/4 cup flour
- 2 cups half and half (or whole milk)
- Kosher salt to taste
- Ground black pepper to taste
- 1/2 cup Parmesan cheese (fresh, shredded-- not the powdered kind)
- 1/2 cup Mozzarella cheese
- 5 wedges Creamy Swiss (Laughing Cow)

Instructions

- Bring a large stockpot of water to a boil. Add spinach and cook down for about 2-3 minutes or until spinach is wilted but not soggy.
- Drain spinach well and then wring out using cheesecloth (preferred) or a kitchen towel. You can also press spinach in a fine-mesh strainer to try and remove excess water. Note: the spinach may be VERY hot, handle with care and allow to cool if needed.
- Note: you may be surprised to find that you only have 1-2 cups of spinach. This is normal. Set spinach aside.
- In a large skillet over medium heat, melt butter. Add onions and garlic and cook until onions become soft and transparent.
- Sprinkle flour over the onions and stir until flour is cooked (about 3 minutes).
- Pour in half and half a little at a time, whisking constantly making a bechamel sauce. You want it to be the consistency of a thin gravy. Add more half and a half or milk if needed.
- Add salt and pepper to taste.
- Add spinach and stir until spinach is well mixed in.
- Add Parmesan cheese, Mozzarella cheese, and creamy Swiss cheese (or cream cheese). Stir until all cheeses are melted and completely mixed in.
- Serve immediately.

Nutrition

Calories: 228kcal | Carbohydrates: 10g | Protein: 9g | Fat: 18g | Saturated Fat: 11g | Cholesterol: 52mg | Sodium: 289mg | Potassium: 511mg | Fiber: 2g | Sugar: 1g | Vitamin A: 7175IU | Vitamin C: 21.9mg | Calcium: 256mg | Iron: 2.3mg

134. Sweet Potato Casserole With Coconut Pecan

Prep Time: 10 minutes

Cook Time: 35 minutes

Total: 45 minutes

Serves: 9 servings

Ingredients

- 1 (29-ounce) can sweet potatoes drained (or 3 1/2 cups cooked and mashed sweet potatoes)
- 1/4 cup milk
- 1/4 cup brown sugar
- 3 tablespoons butter melted
- 1 egg
- 1 teaspoon vanilla
- 1/2 teaspoon salt

Topping

- 1/2 cup brown sugar
- 1/2 cup pecans chopped
- 1/2 cup shredded coconut
- 3 tablespoons flour
- 3 tablespoons butter melted

Instructions

- preheat oven to 350 degrees. In a large bowl or mixer, combine sweet potatoes, milk, brown sugar, melted butter, egg, vanilla, and salt. Beat ingredients with a hand mixer (or in a mixer) until the sweet potatoes are light and fluffy.
- Transfer sweet potato mixture into a greased 9x9 inch baking pan.
- Stir all of the topping ingredients together in a small bowl.
- Sprinkle the topping evenly over the sweet potatoes.
- Bake uncovered for 35 minutes.

Nutrition

Calories: 300kcal | Carbohydrates: 42g | Protein: 3g | Fat: 14g | Saturated Fat: 7g | Cholesterol: 39mg | Sodium: 274mg |

Potassium: 387mg | Fiber: 4g | Sugar: 24g | Vitamin A: 13230IU | Vitamin C: 2.2mg | Calcium: 59mg | Iron: 1.1mg

135. Slow Cooker Creamed Corn

Prep Time: 5 minutes

Cook Time: 3 hours

Total: 3 hours 5 minutes

Serves: 10

Ingredients

- 1 lb. corn (about 4-5 cups) fresh or frozen is fine
- 3 Tbsp. butter
- 1/4 c. milk
- 6 oz. cream cheese
- 2 tsp. sugar
- Salt and pepper to taste

Instructions

- Combine all ingredients in a slow cooker.
- Cook on low for 3 to 4 hours, stirring occasionally.
- Serve hot.
- If you need to whip it up faster (without a slow cooker), combine all ingredients in a medium-sized pot and cook over medium heat, stirring often, until heated through and thickened.

Nutrition

Calories: 141kcal | Carbohydrates: 11g | Protein: 3g | Fat: 10g | Saturated Fat: 6g | Cholesterol: 29mg | Sodium: 89mg | Potassium: 130mg | Fiber: 1g | Sugar: 4g | Vitamin A: 470IU | Vitamin C: 2.5mg | Calcium: 26mg | Iron: 0.3mg

136. Cranberry Sausage Stuffing

Prep Time: 15 minutes

Cook Time: 55 minutes

Total: 1 hour 10 minutes

Serves: 16

Ingredients

- 3 cups whole wheat bread cubed
- 8 cups white bread cubed

- 2 pounds sage sausage Bob Evans brand works great
- 2 cups chopped onion
- 2 cups chopped celery
- 1 1/2 tablespoon dried sage
- 1 tablespoon dried rosemary
- 1 teaspoon dried thyme
- 1 golden delicious apple cored and chopped
- 1 1/2 cups dried cranberries (Craisins work great!)
- 1/2 cup chopped fresh parsley
- 1 2/3 cups turkey stock (chicken stock works great too!)
- 1/2 cup butter melted
- 1 cup slivered almonds or walnuts or any kind of nuts, chopped (optional)

Instructions

- Spread bread cubes in a single layer on a baking sheet. Bake 5-7 minutes at 350-degrees or until evenly toasted. Transfer toasted breadcrumbs to a large bowl.
- In a large skillet, cook the sausage and onion over medium heat, stirring until evenly browned. Add the celery, sage, rosemary, and thyme. Cook, stirring for 2-3 minutes.
- Pour sausage mixture over bread in a bowl. Mix in apples, cranberries, parsley, and almonds (optional). Drizzle with turkey stock and melted butter and toss until evenly coated.
- Spoon into two 9x13 baking dishes and cook, covered for 40 minutes, then uncover and bake for another 15 minutes.

Nutrition

Calories: 397kcal | Carbohydrates: 29g | Protein: 14g | Fat: 26g | Saturated Fat: 9g | Cholesterol: 57mg | Sodium: 591mg | Potassium: 341mg | Fiber: 3g | Sugar: 12g | Vitamin A: 455IU | Vitamin C: 5mg | Calcium: 109mg | Iron: 2mg

---

137. Corn Casserole

Prep Time: 10 minutes

Cook Time: 1 hour 30 minutes

Total: 1 hour 40 minutes

Serves: 8

Ingredients

- 2 15 ounce cans creamed corn
- 1 15 ounces can whole corn drained
- 1 cup soda (or saltine) crackers crushed
- 1/2 cup milk
- 1/2 cup sugar
- 3 eggs
- 3 tablespoons flour
- 3 tablespoons butter melted (or bacon grease, see notes above)

Instructions

- preheat oven to 350-degrees.
- Combine all ingredients in a large bowl, mix well.
- Pour mixture into a greased 9x13 glass baking dish.
- Bake for 1 - 1 1/2 hours or until cooked through and golden brown on top.
- ❖ Tip: If you like it more ready, bake longer. It will become more like cornbread. If you like it more like a corn pudding, bake for less time.

Nutrition

Calories: 171kcal | Carbohydrates: 22g | Protein: 4g | Fat: 8g | Saturated Fat: 4g | Cholesterol: 83mg | Sodium: 158mg | Potassium: 58mg | Fiber: 1g | Sugar: 14g | Vitamin A: 253IU | Calcium: 30mg | Iron: 1mg

---

138. Loaded Mashed Potatoes

Prep Time: 10 minutes

Cook Time: 25 minutes

Total: 35 minutes

Serves: 6

Ingredients

- 6 cups prepared mashed potatoes I prepare with butter and milk
- 1 cup sour cream
- 1 envelope ranch salad dressing mix unprepared (I use Hidden Valley brand)
- 2 cups shredded cheddar cheese divided
- 6 slices cooked bacon chopped
- 6 green onions thinly sliced (optional)

Instructions

- preheat oven to 350 degrees.

- In a large bowl, combine mashed potatoes, sour cream, ranch dressing mix, 1 cup cheese, bacon, and onions.
- Spread into a large casserole dish. Bake for 25 minutes or until heated. Remove from oven and sprinkle top with remaining 1 cup cheese.
- Return to oven and bake for an additional 5 minutes, or until cheese on top is melted.
- Garnish if desired with extra bacon and green onions.
- Serves 6-8

Nutrition

Calories: 390kcal | Carbohydrates: 29g | Protein: 19g | Fat: 23g | Saturated Fat: 13g | Cholesterol: 67mg | Sodium: 437mg | Potassium: 1032mg | Fiber: 6g | Sugar: 2g | Vitamin A: 735IU | Vitamin C: 26.6mg | Calcium: 385mg | Iron: 7.4mg

139. Oven Roasted Green Beans

Prep Time: 10 minutes

Cook Time: 20 minutes

Total: 30 minutes

Serves: 6 servings

Ingredients

- 2 Pounds Fresh Green Beans (If Using Frozen, See Notes Above)
- 3 Tablespoons Olive Oil
- 4 Cloves Garlic Finely Minced
- Kosher Salt To Taste
- Black Pepper To Taste

Instructions

- preheat oven to 425-degrees.
- Trim green beans if necessary. Pat green beans completely dry with paper towels.
- Place green beans in a large bowl and toss with olive oil and garlic until evenly coated.
- Place green beans on a baking sheet and spread them out so the green beans aren't touching each other if possible. You can divide them between two baking sheets if needed.
- Sprinkle beans with salt and pepper and place in the oven.
- Roast for 15-20 minutes or until beans start to look toasted and brown spots start to form.

Nutrition

Calories: 112kcal | Carbohydrates: 11g | Protein: 3g | Fat: 7g | Saturated Fat: 1g | Sodium: 10mg | Potassium: 327mg | Fiber: 4g | Sugar: 5g | Vitamin A: 1045IU | Vitamin C: 19.1mg | Calcium: 60mg | Iron: 1.6mg

140. Thanksgiving Stuffing With Bacon

Prep Time: 15 minutes

Cook Time: 1 hour 30 minutes

Total: 1 hour 45 minutes

Serves: 12

Ingredients

- 1 loaf french bread
- 1 lb bacon
- 2 cups chopped celery
- 1 onion chopped
- 1 tsp sage
- Salt and pepper to taste
- 2 cups chicken broth

Instructions

- Preheat the oven to 350.
- Cut the french bread into 1-inch cubes and put it in a large bowl.
- Cut the bacon into small pieces and cook in a skillet.
- Drain the bacon, but DO NOT throw away the grease. Add the bacon to the bread pieces.
- Saute the celery and onions in the leftover bacon grease. Drain excess grease. Mix into the bacon and bread.
- In the large bowl, add sage, salt, and pepper.
- Add 1-2 cups of chicken broth, depending on how moist you like the stuffing.
- Stir until well combined.
- Pour into a greased 9x13 dish and bake covered for 30 minutes. Uncover and bake for another 20 minutes.

Nutrition

Calories: 262.52kcal | Carbohydrates: 20.85g | Protein: 9.08g | Fat: 15.74g | Saturated Fat: 5.22g | Cholesterol: 24.95mg | Sodium: 578.42mg | Potassium: 205.99mg | Fiber: 1.22g

| Sugar: 1.55g | Vitamin A: 89.57IU | Vitamin C: 3.94mg | Calcium: 28.84mg | Iron: 1.51mg

141. Roasted Vegetable Medley

Prep Time: 10 minutes

Cook Time: 35 minutes

Total: 45 minutes

Serves: 8

Ingredients

- 3 zucchini squash cut lengthwise into fourths, and then slice into bite-size pieces
- 3 yellow squash sliced same as zucchini
- 1 red pepper cut into 1" pieces
- 1 red onion cut into wedges
- 8 ounces whole mushrooms
- 1 garlic clove minced
- 1 tablespoon balsamic vinegar (more to taste)
- 1 tablespoon olive oil
- 1 tablespoon rosemary leaves
- 1 teaspoon kosher salt

Instructions

- preheat oven to 450 degrees.
- Spray a large baking sheet with cooking spray (or you can foil line the baking sheet and spray the foil).
- Mix all of the cut-up vegetables and garlic in a large bowl.
- Add olive oil and balsamic vinegar. Toss until all the vegetables are covered.
- Add rosemary leaves and salt, and toss again.
- Roast the vegetables for about 30-40 minutes, stirring once. You will know the vegetables are done when they are brown on the outside edges and tender on the inside.

Nutrition

Calories: 59kcal | Carbohydrates: 8g | Protein: 3g | Fat: 2g | Saturated Fat: 1g | Sodium: 301mg | Potassium: 526mg | Fiber: 2g | Sugar: 6g | Vitamin A: 768IU | Vitamin C: 47mg | Calcium: 29mg | Iron: 1mg

142. Cauliflower Mashed Potatoes

Prep Time: 10 minutes

Cook Time: 20 minutes

Total: 30 minutes

Serves: 8 servings

Ingredients

- 2 cups cauliflower florets
- 2 cups Yukon potatoes medium diced
- ¼ cup Greek yogurt
- 1 tablespoon butter
- Salt and Pepper to taste

Instructions

- Steam or boil potatoes and cauliflower until soft. Strain water if necessary.
- Add all ingredients to a mixer and mix until you have a smooth potato consistency.
- Season with salt and pepper.

Nutrition

Calories: 47kcal | Carbohydrates: 6g | Protein: 2g | Fat: 1g | Cholesterol: 4mg | Sodium: 26mg | Potassium: 259mg | Fiber: 1g | Vitamin A: 45IU | Vitamin C: 16.9mg | Calcium: 25mg | Iron: 1.5mg

143. Gluten-Free Stuffing

Prep Time: 10 minutes

Cook Time: 30 minutes

Total: 40 minutes

Serves: 4

Ingredients

- ¼ cup yellow onion diced
- ¼ cup celery diced
- ¼ cup carrots diced
- ¼ cup mushrooms chopped
- 2 cups gluten-free bread diced
- 3 oz chicken broth low sodium, organic
- 1 T herb mixture see below
- Salt and Pepper to taste

Herb Mixture:

- 1 T thyme chopped
- 1 T rosemary chopped
- 1 T sage chopped
- 1 tsp garlic chopped
- 1 tsp lemon zest

- 1 tsp orange zest
- 1 T grapeseed oil

Instructions

- preheat oven to 350 degrees. In a sauté pan spray a nonstick spray and add the first 4 ingredients.
- Cook until soft, then move to a mixing bowl.
- Add the remaining ingredients to the cooked vegetables in a mixing bowl and mix thoroughly.
- Transfer the mixture to a casserole dish- Cover with foil and bake for about 30 minutes. Herb mixture
- Chop all the herbs. Using a mixing bowl add the herb mixture. Then stir.

Nutrition

Calories: 97kcal | Carbohydrates: 11g | Protein: 2g | Fat: 5g | Saturated Fat: 1g | Cholesterol: 3mg | Sodium: 148mg | Potassium: 103mg | Fiber: 2g | Sugar: 2g | Vitamin A: 1545IU | Vitamin C: 7.6mg | Calcium: 52mg | Iron: 0.8mg

144. Low-Sugar Cranberry Sauce

Prep Time: 5 minutes

Cook Time: 15 minutes

Total: 20 minutes

Serves: 20

Ingredients

- 1 ½ c. cranberries frozen
- 2 c. apples small diced
- ½ c. oranges cut and segmented
- 2 c. raspberries
- ¼ c. maple syrup
- ¼ c. Truvia
- 2 Tbsp. lemon juice
- 1 Tbsp. butter

Instructions

- Add everything but the butter to a sauté pan and cook until most of the liquid has reduced.
- Take off the heat and stir in the butter. Serve hot.

Nutrition

Calories: 49kcal | Carbohydrates: 11g | Protein: 1g | Fat: 1g | Saturated Fat: 1g | Cholesterol: 2mg | Sodium: 6mg | Potassium: 93mg | Fiber: 3g | Sugar: 7g | Vitamin A: 65IU | Vitamin C: 13.4mg | Calcium: 14mg | Iron: 0.2mg

145. The Best Oven Roasted Asparagus

Prep Time: 3 minutes

Cook Time: 10 minutes

Total: 13 minutes

Serves: 4 servings

Ingredients

- 1 bunch asparagus (trimmed)
- 2 tablespoons olive oil (extra virgin)
- 3 cloves garlic (minced)
- 3 tablespoons Parmesan cheese (grated)
- 1/2 teaspoon Kosher salt
- Pepper to taste

Instructions

- preheat oven to 425-degrees. Rinse and trim asparagus. Dry well and set aside.
- In a mixing bowl or shallow dish, combine olive oil, garlic, Parmesan cheese, salt, and pepper. Toss well with asparagus until asparagus is lightly coated with the mixture.
- Place asparagus in a single layer on a lined baking sheet and bake for 8-10 minutes.
- Remove from oven and serve immediately.

Nutrition

Calories: 102kcal | Carbohydrates: 5g | Protein: 4g | Fat: 8g | Saturated Fat: 2g | Cholesterol: 3mg | Sodium: 354mg | Potassium: 236mg | Fiber: 2g | Sugar: 2g | Vitamin A: 880IU | Vitamin C: 7mg | Calcium: 75mg | Iron: 2.4mg

146. One Pot Creamy Garlic Noodles

Prep Time: 10 minutes

Cook Time: 20 minutes

Total: 30 minutes

Serves: 6

Ingredients

- 4 Tbsp. butter divided
- 4-5 cloves garlic minced
- 28 oz chicken broth (3 3/4 cups)
- 2 1/2 c. milk add more if needed
- 1 lb. linguini
- kosher salt and black pepper to taste
- 1 tsp. basil
- 2/3 c. Parmesan cheese
- 4 c. broccoli optional
- 2 chicken breasts grilled and cut into strips

Instructions

- In a large, 5-6 quart skillet, heat 2 Tbsp. butter over medium heat. If you don't have a large skillet, a stock-pot works well, too. Add garlic and cook for about a minute.
- Add chicken broth, milk, remaining 2 Tbsp. butter, pasta noodles, salt and pepper, and basil. Bring to a boil, stirring occasionally.
- Once boiling, reduce heat to a simmer stirring occasionally for 16-20 minutes or until noodles have cooked through. If you are wanting to add broccoli, add it after about 10 minutes into the simmering process.
- Stir in Parmesan when noodles are finished cooking and add a little milk if necessary to reach your desired consistency.

Nutrition

Calories: 664kcal | Carbohydrates: 74g | Protein: 44g | Fat: 22g | Saturated Fat: 12g | Cholesterol: 97mg | Sodium: 1162mg | Potassium: 1214mg | Fiber: 7g | Sugar: 10g | Vitamin A: 1660IU | Vitamin C: 151.6mg | Calcium: 530mg | Iron: 2.9mg

147. Watermelon Feta Salad

Prep Time: 15 minutes

Total: 15 minutes

Serves: 8

Ingredients

- 3 pounds watermelon cut into cubes
- 24 ounces blueberries
- 2 cucumbers sliced and quartered
- 8 ounces feta cheese cut into cubes
- 10 mint leaves sliced
- 5 basil leaves sliced

- 2 limes
- Salt to taste

Instructions

- In a large bowl, combine watermelon, blueberries, cucumbers, and feta cheese.
- Add mint, basil, and the juice from both limes. (Optional: add the zest from the limes as well.) Sprinkle with salt if desired.
- Stir until all ingredients are coated in lime juice. Chill until ready to serve.

Nutrition

Serving: 1g | Calories: 189kcal | Carbohydrates: 30g | Protein: 6g | Fat: 7g | Saturated Fat: 4g | Cholesterol: 25mg | Sodium: 321mg | Potassium: 400mg | Fiber: 4g | Sugar: 21g | Vitamin A: 1262IU | Vitamin C: 30mg | Calcium: 176mg | Iron: 1mg

148. Easy Vinegar Marinated Cucumbers (Cucumber Salad)

Prep Time: 10 minutes

Cook Time: 0 minutes

Total: 10 minutes

Serves: 10 people

Ingredients

- 5 cucumbers
- 1 red onion
- 1 cup apple cider vinegar (or white vinegar, red wine vinegar, rice vinegar)
- 1/2 cup sugar (or more to taste)
- 1/2 cup water
- 1 teaspoon salt

Instructions

- Peel and slice cucumbers into thin slices.
- Cut the onion in half and cut into very thin slices.
- Combine onions and cucumbers in a large bowl.
- In a separate, medium-sized bowl, combine the remaining ingredients.
- Stir until sugar dissolves.
- Pour vinegar mixture over cucumbers and onions.*
- Stir until the cucumbers are evenly coated in the dressing.
- Refrigerate for at least 20 minutes.

- Before serving, drain liquid and place it in a serving bowl to serve.

Nutrition

Calories: 66kcal | Carbohydrates: 14g | Protein: 1g | Fat: 1g | Saturated Fat: 1g | Sodium: 237mg | Potassium: 220mg | Fiber: 1g | Sugar: 13g | Vitamin A: 108IU | Vitamin C: 6mg | Calcium: 25mg | Iron: 1mg

149. Lemon Spaghetti

Prep Time: 5 minutes

Cook Time: 10 minutes

Total: 15 minutes

Serves: 8

Ingredients

- 16 ounces spaghetti
- 2 lemons
- 1/2 cup olive oil
- 1/2 cup grated Parmesan cheese
- 3/4 teaspoon salt more to taste if needed
- Ground black pepper to taste
- 1/4 cup chopped fresh basil

Instructions

- Cook spaghetti according to package directions. Reserve 1 cup of the pasta water and drain the rest from the spaghetti.
- While pasta is cooking, zest, and juice the lemons. You should get about 1/2 cup of lemon juice. If not, fill up the rest of the 1/2 cup with bottled lemon juice.
- In a small bowl, add lemon juice, olive oil, parmesan, salt, and pepper. Whisk until combined.
- Toss spaghetti with the lemon sauce until it is evenly coated. Add lemon zest and basil.
- Add the reserved pasta water a little at a time until the sauce clings to the pasta and thickens a little.
- Top with more fresh basil, lemon zest, parmesan, salt, and pepper. Serve hot.

Nutrition

Serving: 1g | Calories: 365kcal | Carbohydrates: 45g | Protein: 10g | Fat: 16g | Saturated Fat: 3g | Cholesterol: 6mg | Sodium: 318mg |

Potassium: 172mg | Fiber: 3g | Sugar: 2g | Vitamin A: 94IU | Vitamin C: 14mg | Calcium: 90mg | Iron: 1mg

150. Curried Chickpeas

Prep Time: 10 minutes

Cook Time: 8 hours

Soaking: 12 hours

Total: 20 hours 10 minutes

Serves: 4

Ingredients

- 1 cup dry chickpeas (see recipe notes for using canned chickpeas)
- 1/2 cube butter
- 2 teaspoons cumin seeds
- 1/2 onion diced
- 8 cloves garlic finely chopped
- 1/4 jalapeño finely chopped
- 3 tomatoes (medium to large size)
- 1 teaspoon salt or to taste
- 1 teaspoon garam masala or to taste

Instructions

- Soak the chickpeas overnight, then drain excess water.
- Melt butter in a skillet over medium-high heat.
- Sauté the cumin seeds, onion, garlic, and jalapeño in the butter. Cook until onions are caramelized.
- Blend the 3 tomatoes in a blender. Add tomato purée to the onions and garlic sauté.
- Add chickpeas with 2 cups of water, salt, garam masala, and the tomato garlic sauce in a crockpot.
- Cook on low for about 8 hours. If the beans have not popped open and the sauce is not coming together you can move them to the stovetop and cook them at a soft bubbly boil until the sauce comes together. If lacking in flavor, add more salt and Indian spice.
- Serve chickpeas over rice and/or with Naan bread.

Nutrition

Calories: 220kcal | Carbohydrates: 38g | Protein: 11g | Fat: 4g | Saturated Fat: 1g |

Cholesterol: 1mg | Sodium: 602mg | Potassium: 718mg | Fiber: 11g | Sugar: 8g | Vitamin A: 815IU | Vitamin C: 19mg | Calcium: 85mg | Iron: 4mg

4. Lean and Green Recipes "Lean & Green Recipes"

151. Mediterranean Pork Loin With Sun-Dried Tomatoes And Olives

Prep Time: 5 Minutes

Cook Time: 240 Minutes

Total Time: 245 Minutes

Servings: 4-6 Serving

Ingredients

- 1 1/2-2 lbs pork tenderloin (NOT marinated)
- 1 C Broth of your choice (chicken, vegetable, etc.)
- 2 teaspoons Garlic, chives, lemon, salt, pepper, onion, and garlic powder)
- 1/2 teaspoon s Mediterranean Seasoning
- 10 green olives, sliced
- 1 T sun-dried tomatoes (not in oil) sliced thin

Instructions

- Place pork loin in the bottom of the Crock-Pot (slow cooker.)
- Pour the broth over the meat.
- Sprinkle with the seasonings, then scatter the olives and sun-dried tomatoes around the meat.
- Place the lid on and cook on high for 4 hours, or low for 6 hours. Meat may need longer if frozen. It will be done when the internal temperature reaches 155 degrees F.
- Slice the meat thin, drizzle with some of the broth, and garnish with a few olive and sun-dried tomato pieces.
- Serve hot.

Nutrition

- Calories: 210
- Total Fat: 5.6g
- Sat Fat: 1.8g
- Cholesterol: 103mg
- Sodium: 155mg

- Carbohydrates: 0.7g
- Fiber: 0.2g
- Sugar: 0g
- Protein: 37.2g
- Calcium: 18mg
- Iron:2mg
- Potassium: 600mg

152. Creamy Spinach and Garlic Stuffed Chicken

Prep Time: 15 Minutes

Cook Time: 40 Minutes

Total Time: 55 Minutes

Servings: 4 Serving

Ingredients

- 1 1/2 lbs boneless, skinless chicken breast
- 8 I (1/2 of an 8 oz block) light cream cheese
- 1 Tablespoon Garlic, chives, lemon, salt, pepper, onion, and garlic powder)
- 8 ounces raw baby spinach (1 bag)
- 1 pinch of Desperation Seasoning

Instructions

- preheat oven to 375 degrees.
- Place chicken breast on a cutting board and using a sharp knife, cut a pocket into the chicken breast. Repeat on all pieces of chicken.
- Place the cream cheese into a large microwave-safe bowl and heat on high for 10 seconds until soft and spreadable. Repeat in 5-second intervals if necessary. Sprinkle the garlic seasoning over the cream cheese. Stir to combine & smooth out all the lumps.
- Pour the spinach into the bowl. Using a pair of kitchen shears, chop up the spinach into smaller pieces.
- Using a rubber spatula, combine the spinach and the cream cheese into a consistent mixture. Do this gently as to not crush and bruise the spinach.
- Divide the mixture into as many equal portions as you have pieces of chicken. Stuff mixture into the pocket of the chicken breast. Repeat on all pieces of chicken.
- Place chicken in an oven-safe dish side by side. Use a dish that is large enough to leave space

around each piece so they are not touching. (This allows for faster, more even cooking.)

- Using a rubber spatula, get the remaining cream cheese out of the bowl and place a little smear on top of each of the chicken rolls to protect them while baking. Sprinkle each with a pinch of Dash of Desperation seasoning. You can also spray with a little nonstick cooking spray if there doesn't seem to be "enough" cream cheese left.
- Cover the dish with aluminum foil and place it in the center of your preheated oven.
- Bake for 35 minutes, remove the foil and bake for an additional 10 minutes or until chicken has reached an internal temperature of 165 degrees as verified with a meat thermometer.
- Let chicken rest for 5 minutes and then slice and serve.

Nutrition

- Calories: 267
- Total Fat: 11.3g
- Sat Fat: 4.4g
- Cholesterol: 131mg
- Sodium: 15mg
- Carbohydrates: 1.1g
- Fiber: 0.3g
- Sugar: 0.1g
- Protein: 38g
- Calcium: 39mg
- Iron: 1mg
- Potassium: 737mg

153. Cheesy Chicken & Cauliflower Bake

Prep Time: 55 Minutes

Cook Time: 35 Minutes

Total Time: 50 Minutes

Servings: 4 Serving

Ingredients

- 1 1/2 pounds boneless, skinless chicken breasts cut into 3/4" chunks
- 2 teaspoons Garlic and oil of your choice)
- Pinch Garlic, onion, salt, pepper, parsley)
- 6 T Half and Half [/ingrd]

- 1 T Garlic, chives, natural sea salt, onion, and garlic powder)
- 6 cups grated cauliflower (fresh works best, but you can also use frozen)
- 1 C light OR 1/2 C regular shredded cheddar cheese

Instructions

- Preheat oven to 325 degrees.
- In a large skillet, heat roasted garlic oil over medium-high heat.
- Add the chicken to the skillet, season with a pinch of dash of desperation and saute until slightly golden brown and tender (about 10-12 minutes.)
- While chicken is cooking, cut the cauliflower into smaller pieces and grate into "rice" using a box grater into a large bowl. You may also do this by pulsing a few pieces at a time in the food processor
- Spray a 9x11 baking dish with nonstick cooking spray and add the cauliflower into a single layer at the bottom of the dish.
- Sprinkle the chicken in the skillet with garlic and spring onion seasoning. Pour the half and a half into the skillet and stir, scraping up all the browned bits off the bottom.
- Pour the chicken and cream mixture over the cauliflower and sprinkle with the cheese.
- Cover tightly with aluminum foil and bake for 15-20 minutes until hot and melty.
- Serve hot and enjoy
- Nutrition
- Calories: 350
- Total Fat: 14.8g
- Sat Fat: 5.4g
- Cholesterol: 135mg
- Sodium: 232mg
- Carbohydrates: 9.9g
- Fiber: 3.8g
- Sugar: 3.7g
- Protein: 43.5g
- Calcium: 177mg
- Iron: 1mg
- Potassium: 1142mg

154. Finger Licking Slow-Cooked BBQ Chicken

Prep Time: 5 Minutes

Cook Time: 360 Minutes

Total Time: 365 Minutes

Servings: 4 Servings

Ingredients

- 2 pounds boneless, skinless chicken thighs
- 1 T Stacey Hawkins Honey BBQ Seasoning (or a dry, sugar-free substitute)
- 1 Tablespoon of cumin, cayenne, chili powder, salt, pepper, garlic, and onion
- Pinch Alderwood Smoked Sea Salt

Instructions

- Place chicken thighs in a single layer at the bottom of your slow cooker. (You could use an Insta Pot as well, 10 minutes cooking time)
- Sprinkle seasonings over the thighs. Place the cover on the slow cooker.
- Cook on low for 6 hours.
- Remove the lid and using two forks, shred the meat.
- Serve hot with your favorite side dishes, or chilled over a salad.

Nutrition

- Calories: 208
- Total Fat: 7.9g
- Sat Fat: 0g
- Cholesterol: 0mg
- Sodium: 210mg
- Carbohydrates: 2g
- Fiber: 0g
- Sugar: 0.5g
- Protein: 29.9g

155. Skewered Shrimp With Leeks And Yellow Squash

Prep Time: 15 Minutes

Cook Time: 15-20 Minutes

Total Time: 25-30 Minutes

Servings: 4 Servings

Ingredients

- 2 pounds wild-caught shrimp, raw, peeled & deveined
- 2 large leeks, washed, trimmed, and cut into 1/2" chunks
- 2 small, thinner yellow squash, washed, trimmed, and cut into 1/2" chunks
- 1 Tablespoon of tarragon, chives, garlic, lemon, salt, pepper, garlic, and onion)
- 2 1/2 Tablespoons Stacey Hawkins Luscious Lemon or Roasted Garlic Oil
- 8 T fresh grated Parmesan cheese for garnish
- Natural Sea salt & freshly cracked peppercorns (or a pinch of Dash of Desperation) to taste

Instructions

- Preheat outdoor grill or oven to 375 degrees.
- Add the shrimp and veggies to a large bowl. Drizzle with oil and seasonings. Toss to coat. Let sit for 10 minutes, up to all day (refrigerated) to let the flavors develop.
- Skewer shrimp and veggies individually, or pour into a grill basket
- Cook for 20-25 minutes, using a spatula to turn the pieces at least once during cooking. Cook until shrimp is opaque and fully cooked and vegetables are crisp-tender.
- Serve hot, sprinkled with fresh grated Parmesan cheese for a garnish,

Nutrition

- Calories: 352
- Total Fat: 13.3g
- Sat Fat: 3g
- Cholesterol: 455mg
- Sodium: 784mg
- Carbohydrates: 12.3g
- Fiber: 2.4g
- Sugar: 4.4g
- Protein: 47.9g
- Calcium: 53mg
- Iron: 2mg
- Potassium: 449mg

156. Mojo Marinated Flank Steak

Prep Time: 5 Minutes

Cook Time: 10 + marinade time Minutes

Total Time: 20 Minutes

Servings: 4 Serving

Ingredients

- 2 pounds flank steak or skirt steak, trimmed of all excess fat
- 2 T fresh lime juice plus 1 extra lime for garnish
- 1 T fresh garlic, onion, chives, parsley, salt, pepper)
- 1 tsp ground cumin (optional, but will give more flavor)
- 1/3 C low sodium beef broth
- 1 pinch of Desperation Seasoning

Instructions

- Add all ingredients (except beef & Dash) to a large zipper style bag. Zip closed & using your hands, smoosh all the ingredients together to make a uniform marinade.
- Add the beef. Seal again and place on a plate, in the refrigerator for 1 hour up to overnight.
- When ready to cook, preheat outdoor grill (or indoor cast iron pan or grill pan) to medium-high heat. Oil the grates or the pan lightly using nonstick cooking spray before heating.
- Remove the steak from the bag and discard the marinade. Season with the Dash of Desperation. Cook the steak for 2 minutes on each side and check the temperature. Keep cooking/flipping until the internal temperature of the steak is 115-120 degrees for Medium Rare, 125-130 for Medium.
- When finished cooking, remove from the pan and set on a plate. Tent the beef with foil and let it rest for 10 minutes. Finish your other sides during this time.
- Slice the steak on a diagonal, garnish with lime wedges and serve hot with your favorite Green sides.
- Enjoy!

Nutrition

- Calories: 276
- Total Fat: 11.8g
- Sat Fat: 4.9g
- Cholesterol: 78mg
- Sodium: 80mg
- Carbohydrates: 0.4g
- Sugar: 0.1g
- Protein: 39.5g
- Calcium: 22mg
- Iron: 3mg

- Potassium: 484mg

157. Instant Pot Chicken Curry (Green!)

Prep Time: 20 Minutes

Cook Time: 8 Minutes

Total Time: 28 Minutes

Servings: 6 Servings

Ingredients

- 1 ½ pounds boneless chicken thighs
- 1 small onion
- 1 red bell pepper
- 1 green bell pepper
- 2 small zucchini
- 3-4 cloves garlic minced
- 8-10 kaffir lime leaves
- 1 teaspoon coconut oil or vegetable oil
- 4 ounce green curry paste
- 2 tablespoon fish sauce
- 2 tablespoons palm sugar or 1 ½ tb brown sugar
- 14 ounces can coconut milk
- 1 cup canned bamboo shoots drained
- ½ cup Thai basil leaves or sweet basil
- 1 tablespoon cornstarch optional
- 1 tablespoon lime juice optional

Instructions

- Prep work: Cut the chicken into 1-inch chunks. Peel the onion and remove the bell pepper seeds. Chop the onion, bell peppers, and zucchini into roughly 1-inch chunks. Keep them separate to add at different times. Mince the garlic. Crush the kaffir lime leaves in your hand to release the oils. Drain the bamboo shoots.
- Set a large 6+ quart Instant Pot to Sauté. Add the coconut oil, chopped onions, minced garlic, and kaffir lime leaves. Sauté for 2 minutes to soften. Deglaze the bottom of the pot with ¼ cup water.
- Add in the curry paste, fish sauce, palm sugar, and coconut milk. Stir well. Then mix in the chopped chicken.
- Lock the lid into place. Set the Instant Pot on Pressure Cook High for 4 minutes. Once the timer goes off, perform a quick release. When the steam button drops it is safe to open the IP.
- Set the IP back on Sauté. Stir in the bell peppers and bamboo shoots. Simmer for 2 minutes.

- If the sauce seems thin, you can toss the zucchini chunks in 1 tablespoon of cornstarch to thicken the sauce. (This is often dependent on the thickness of the coconut milk and the moisture in the veggies.) Stir in the zucchini chunks. Simmer another 1-2 minutes. Then stir in the Thai basil.
- Taste. Add fresh lime juice if desired. Serve with a side of white rice, cauliflower rice, or broccoli rice.

Nutrition

Calories: 488kcal, Carbohydrates: 18g, Protein: 23g, Fat: 37g, Saturatedfat: 20g, Cholesterol: 111mg, Sodium: 587mg, Potassium: 737mg, Fiber: 4g, Sugar: 11g, Vitamin A: 4543iu, Vitamin C: 69mg, Calcium: 72mg, Iron: 3mg

158. Perfect Baked Chicken Thighs

Prep Time: 5 Minutes

Cook Time: 25 Minutes

Total Time: 30 Minutes

Servings: 6

Ingredients

- 2 tablespoons olive oil
- 6 large, bone-in chicken thighs, or 8-10 small
- 3-5 sprigs of fresh thyme
- 3-5 sprigs of fresh rosemary
- 1 lemon, sliced into rounds
- 1/2 teaspoon garlic powder
- Salt and pepper

Instructions

- Preheat the oven to 450 degrees F. Set a 12- to 14-inch cast-iron skillet on the stovetop over medium-high heat. Add the olive oil.
- Pat the skin on the chicken thighs dry with paper towels. Sprinkle the thighs with garlic powder. Then sprinkle generously with salt and ground black pepper.
- Once the oil is smoking hot, place the thighs in the skillet, skin side down. Sear for 5-7 minutes until the skin is golden-brown.
- Flip the chicken thighs over and add the fresh herb sprigs and the lemon slices.
- Place the entire skillet in the oven and roast for 15-18 minutes. Serve warm.

Nutrition

Calories: 290kcal, carbohydrates: 0g, protein: 18g, fat: 23g, saturatedfat: 5g, cholesterol: 110mg, sodium: 87mg, potassium: 231mg, fiber: 0g, sugar: 0g, vitamin a: 110iu, vitamin c: 2.1mg, calcium: 11mg, iron: 0.8mg

159. Holy Guacamole Recipe

Prep Time: 10 Minutes

Cook Time: 0 Minutes

Total Time: 10 Minutes

Servings: 8

Ingredients

- 3 large ripe Haas avocados
- 1 lime, juiced
- 2-3 cloves garlic, minced
- 1 jalapeno, minced
- 1/4 cup green onions, chopped
- 1/4 cup cilantro, chopped
- 1 plum tomatoes, diced
- Salt and pepper, to taste

Instructions

- Cut the avocados in half, remove the pit, and scoop the flesh out with a spoon. Place the avocado flesh in a medium bowl and pour the lime juice over the top. Use a spoon and fork to mash the avocado until mostly smooth.
- Smell your jalapeño to test the heat... You can usually tell if you got a spicy one. Stir in the garlic, jalapeño (half or all), green onions, and cilantro. Salt and pepper to taste. Stir in the diced tomato at the very end.
- Serve immediately, or press plastic wrap down over the surface of the guacamole, removing all air bubbles, and refrigerate until ready to serve.

Nutrition

Calories: 127kcal, Carbohydrates: 8g, Protein: 1g, Fat: 11g, Saturated Fat: 1g, Cholesterol: 0mg, Sodium: 6mg, Potassium: 401mg, Fiber: 5g, Sugar: 0g, Vitamin A: 260iu, Vitamin C: 14.1mg, Calcium: 15mg, Iron: 0.5mg

160. Thai Chicken Satay With Peanut Sauce

Prep Time: 40 Minutes

Cook Time: 6 Minutes

Total Time: 46 Minutes

Servings: 4

Ingredients

For The Chicken Satay:

- 1/2 pounds chicken tenders
- 1 cup unsweetened coconut milk
- tablespoons brown sugar
- tablespoons fish sauce
- 1 tablespoon ground coriander
- 1 teaspoon cumin
- 1/2 teaspoon turmeric
- 1 teaspoon salt
- Wooden Skewers, soaked
- For the Peanut Dipping Sauce:
- 1/2 cup peanut butter
- 1 tablespoon fresh minced ginger
- 1/3 cup chicken broth
- 1 tablespoon honey
- 1/4 cup low-sodium soy sauce
- tablespoons rice vinegar
- 3 tablespoons sesame oil
- 2 cloves garlic
- 1 tablespoon chile-garlic sauce, optional

Instructions

- Combine the coconut milk, brown sugar, fish sauce, and spices in a large zip lock bag. Shake and add the chicken tenders. Marinate for at least 30 minutes.
- Soak the skewers in water for at least 30 minutes.
- Preheat the grill to direct medium heat. Weave each tender onto a skewer and lay it on a foil-covered cookie sheet.
- Grill the Thai chicken satay for 3 minutes per side.
- Meanwhile, puree all the ingredients for the peanut sauce in the blender and set aside.
- Serve the chicken satay skewers over jasmine rice with spicy peanut sauce for dipping.

Nutrition

Calories: 690kcal, Carbohydrates: 25g, Protein: 47g, Fat: 46g, Saturatedfat: 18g, Cholesterol: 108mg, Sodium: 2458mg, Potassium: 1122mg, Fiber: 5g, Sugar: 16g, Vitamin A: 50iu, Vitamin C: 6.4mg, Calcium: 77mg, Iron: 3.7mg

161. Primavera Mixed Grill

Prep Time: 15 Minutes

Cook Time: 30 Minutes

Total Time: 45 Minutes

Servings: 4 Serving

Ingredients

- 1 3/4 lb boneless skinless chicken breast
- 7 C fresh vegetables, chopped into similar size pieces
- 4 tsp Roasted Garlic Oil (or oil of your choice)
- 1 Tablespoon of seasoning of your choice

Instructions

- Preheat the outdoor grill (or indoor oven) to 400 degrees.
- Peel, seed, and chop the vegetables into 1" chunks. Add to a large bowl.
- Cut the chicken into 1" chunks. Add to the bowl.
- Pour oil and seasonings over the chicken & veg and toss to coat.
- Place the mixture into a grill basket and place it on the grill. (Or baking dish and into the oven)
- Close the lid and cook for 30 minutes, tossing the mixture 1/2 way through cooking for even browning. The meal will be ready when the chicken reaches 165 degrees (verify with a meat thermometer)
- Remove from the heat and scoop the mixture into your favorite serving dish. Let the chicken rest for a few minutes before serving and enjoy!
- Serve hot for dinner and any leftovers can be enjoyed chilled the next day.

Nutrition

- Calories: 262
- Total Fat: 9g
- Sat Fat: 4.9g
- Cholesterol: 109mg
- Sodium: 95mg
- Carbohydrates: 6.4g

- Fiber: 2.9g
- Sugar: 3.3g
- Protein: 37.5g
- Calcium: 25mg
- Iron: 1mg
- Potassium: 952mg

162. Summer Shrimp Primavera

Prep Time: 10 Minutes

Cook Time: 10-15 Minutes

Total Time: 20-25 Minutes

Servings: 4 Servings

Ingredients

- 4 teaspoons Luscious Lemon or Roasted Garlic Oil
- 2 pounds wild-caught shrimp, raw, peeled & deveined
- 1 Tablespoon of sea salt, scallions, fresh garlic, lemon & parsley)
- 1/2 C low sodium chicken broth
- 6 C vegetable noodles
- 1 scallion, green tops only, sliced for garnish if desired
- 8 T fresh grated Parmesan cheese for garnish

Instructions

- Make the vegetable noodles by spiralizing or using a vegetable peeler like I did to make big, wide noodles. Place noodles in a bowl and set aside.
- Place the oil in the pan over medium-high heat and let it get hot.
- Add the shrimp to the pan and cook for 3-4 minutes on one side before turning to cook on the other side. Sprinkle with seasoning and continue to cook for an additional 3 minutes. Add the broth to deglaze the pan and cook 1-2 minutes more, until shrimp are fully cooked.
- Using a slotted spoon, remove the shrimp from the pan and set it aside in a bowl.
- Put the pan back over heat and heat until the liquid is bubbling. Add the veggie noodles and saute for 1-2 minutes, until crisp-tender.
- Add the veggie noodles to a serving bowl. Top with the shrimp and sprinkle with scallions and Parmesan cheese before serving.

- Divide everything into 4 equal portions and serve hot.

Nutrition

- Calories: 281
- Total Fat: 9g
- Sat Fat: 2.4g
- Cholesterol: 392mg
- Sodium: 535mg
- Carbohydrates: 3.4g
- Fiber: 0.2g
- Sugar: 0.1g
- Protein: 44g
- Calcium: 234mg
- Iron: 1mg
- Potassium: 334mg

163. Thai Cashew Chicken

Prep Time: 10 Minutes

Cook Time: 20 Minutes

Total Time: 30 Minutes

Servings: 4 Serving

Ingredients

- 4 tsp Luscious Lemon Oil or Roasted Garlic Oil or oil of your choice
- 1 1/2 lbs boneless, skinless chicken breast cut into thin strips
- 1 T or garlic, onion, lemongrass, salt, red bell pepper, black pepper, lime zest, and chiles
- 2 C green bell pepper, cut into thin strips
- 2 C red bell pepper, cut into thin strips
- 3 scallions sliced- separate whites and greens
- 24 cashews chopped into small pieces

Instructions

- Heat oil in a large frying pan over medium-high heat.
- Add chicken to the pan and cook for 3-5 minutes on each side until opaque.
- Add peppers and whites of scallions to the pan and sprinkle with seasoning. Stir to combine.
- Cover and cook over high heat for an additional 5-7 minutes, stirring occasionally until vegetables are crisp-tender and chicken is fully cooked.
- Remove lid and sprinkle with nuts and scallion greens. Serve hot.

Nutrition

- Calories: 323
- Total Fat: 13.1g
- Sat Fat: 1.4g
- Cholesterol: 109mg
- Sodium: 92mg
- Carbohydrates: 12.3g
- Fiber: 2g
- Sugar: 6.6g
- Protein: 38.7g
- Calcium: 27mg
- Iron: 2mg
- Potassium: 919mg

164. Authentic New Orleans Seafood Gumbo

Prep Time: 30 Minutes

Cook Time: 2 Hours

Rest Time: 30 Minutes

Servings: 6 Servings

Ingredients

- ½ cup all-purpose flour
- ¼ cup vegetable oil
- ¼ cup butter
- 12 ounces fresh or frozen okra chopped
- 2 tablespoons white vinegar
- 2 cups dry long grain rice
- 12 ounces andouille sausage, sliced
- 1 large sweet onion peeled and chopped
- 1 large green bell pepper
- 1 cup chopped celery
- 4-5 cloves garlic minced
- 1 habanero pepper seeded and minced (or serrano)
- 8 cups seafood stock
- 1 tablespoon Worcestershire sauce
- 2 teaspoons dried thyme
- 2 teaspoons Cajun seasoning
- 1 bay leaf
- 1 pound crawfish
- 1 pound small "gumbo crabs" or blue crabs or crab meat
- 1 pound large raw shrimp cleaned
- 1 pint shucked oysters optionally
- 1 cup chopped parsley and/or chopped scallions for garnish

Instructions

- Make The Roux: Set a large 7-8 quart saucepot over medium-high heat. Add the flour, oil, and butter. Whisk well to break up any clumps. Cook the roux for 30-40 minutes, whisking regularly until it is the color of milk chocolate.
- Prep: Meanwhile, chop the sausages, all the vegetables, and herbs.
- De-Slime the Okra: Set a smaller sauce pot filled with water and over high heat. Add the vinegar. Once boiling, add the chopped okra. Boil for 3-4 minutes to reduce the slime. Then drain and set aside.
- Build The Base: Once the roux is a dark rich brown color, add in the andouille sausages. Fry it in the roux for 1-2 minutes, then add in the chopped onion, bell pepper, celery, garlic, and habanero. Stir and sauté for 8-10 minutes.
- Slow Simmer: Add in the seafood broth, Worcestershire sauce, thyme, Cajun seasoning, bay leaf. Stir well. Then mix in the crawfish and whole crabs. Simmer on low for 1 hour.
- Cook The Rice: Use the same smaller pot you used for the okra to cook the rice. Cook according to the package instructions. Once cooked, fluff the rice, and cover until ready to use.
- Finish: Now add the shrimp, oysters (plus crabmeat if using), and okra. Simmer another 5 minutes.
- Rest: Cover the gumbo pot and turn off the heat. Let the gumbo rest for at least 30 minutes, so all the flavors have longer to mix and mingle, without overcooking the seafood.
- To Serve: Rewarm the gumbo, if needed, for 2-3 minutes. Then serve it in large bowls with a heaping scoop of rice, and a sprinkling of parsley and/or scallions.

Nutrition

Calories: 865kcal, carbohydrates: 72g, protein: 57g, fat: 38g, saturatedfat: 18g, cholesterol: 306mg, sodium: 2905mg, potassium: 1215mg, fiber: 5g, sugar: 6g, vitamin a: 2827iu, vitamin c: 77mg, calcium: 371mg, iron: 7mg

165. Oven Roasted Cod With Poblano Pepper Garlic Cream Sauce

Prep Time: 15 Minutes

Cook Time: 20 Minutes

Total Time: 35 Minutes

Servings: 4 Servings

Ingredients

- 5.5 ounces poblano peppers, seeded & sliced (2 Green)
- 1 C sour cream (8 Healthy Fat)
- 1 Tablespoon of sea salt, scallions, fresh garlic & parsley) (6 condiments)
- 5 C riced cauliflower, uncooked (10 Green)
- 1/4 C water
- 2 pounds flaky white fish, such as cod, flounder or halibut (4 Lean)

Instructions

- preheat oven to 375 degrees.
- Place peppers, sour cream, and seasoning into a food processor. Pulse until fully blended.
- Add the cauliflower to the bottom of a 9x12 baking dish. Place the fish on top of the cauliflower in a single layer. Season with a little Salt & Pepper or a pinch of Dash of Desperation.
- Dollop the pepper mixture over the fish equally, spreading evenly over the fish with the back of a spoon.
- Pour the water into the cauliflower (pour in a corner of the dish as to not disturb the sauce.)
- Bake for 25-35 minutes until fish is fully cooked, opaque, and flaky. May take longer for fish over 1/2" thickness.
- Divide everything into 4 equal portions and serve hot.

Nutrition

- Calories: 314
- Total Fat: 11.2g
- Sat Fat: 6.3g
- Cholesterol: 102mg
- Sodium: 180mg
- Carbohydrates: 12.6g
- Fiber: 4.6g
- Sugar: 4.8g
- Protein: 41g

- Calcium: 132mg
- Iron: 2mg
- Potassium: 610mg

166. Ginger Lime Chicken And Noodles

Prep Time: 5 Minutes

Cook Time: 15-20 Minutes

Total Time: 25 (plus marinade time) Minutes

Servings: 4 Serving

Ingredients

- 4 tsp Valencia Orange Oil
- 1 Tablespoon Tasty Thai Seasoning (or garlic, lemongrass, lime, ginger, orange zest, red pepper, onion, salt, and pepper)
- Juice of one lime
- 1 1/2 lbs boneless, skinless chicken breasts (cut in half if large)
- 4 C prepared zucchini noodles

Instructions

- Add the first three ingredients to a large zipper-style plastic bag.
- Massage the plastic bag to combine the ingredients to make the marinade. Place chicken in the bag, squeeze out all the air, seal the bag, and store in the refrigerator for 4 hours, up to overnight.
- When ready to cook the chicken, preheat outdoor grill (or indoor grill pan or frying pan). Cook chicken on both sides for 12-15 minutes over medium-high heat, until chicken is fully cooked. Verify temperature with a meat thermometer.
- While chicken is cooking, prepare zucchini noodles. (Here's an easy recipe for zoodles)
- Serve chicken over zoodles, or with your favorite side dish, and enjoy!

Nutrition

- Calories: 252
- Total Fat: 9g
- Sat Fat: 0.6g
- Cholesterol: 109mg
- Sodium: 98mg
- Carbohydrates: 3.8g
- Fiber: 1.2g

- Sugar: 2g
- Protein: 37.4g
- Calcium: 25mg
- Iron: 1mg
- Potassium: 925mg

167. Crispy Kohlrabi Slaw

Prep Time: 25 Minutes

Cook Time: 0 Minutes

Total Time: 25 Minutes

Servings: 8 Serving

Ingredients

- 4 C kohlrabi, sliced into matchsticks
- 1/4 C cilantro, chopped
- 1 teaspoons Phoenix Sunrise Seasoning (or your favorite no-salt taco-style seasoning)
- 1 teaspoons Kickin' Cajun Seasoning* (or garlic, salt, black pepper, cumin, cayenne pepper, and onion)
- Zest of 1 lime
- Zest of 1 orange
- juice of 1 lime
- 4 teaspoons Valencia Orange Oil (or your favorite oil and fresh-squeezed orange juice)

Instructions

- Place all ingredients, except the kohlrabi & cilantro into a large salad bowl. Whisk to combine.
- Add the kohlrabi to the bowl, sprinkle with cilantro.
- Using two large spoons, pull the dressing up through the salad by placing the spoons at the bottom of the bowl and scooping the kohlrabi mixture upward. Keep tossing until fully coated.
- Set aside for 15 minutes up to a day ahead of time and serve chilled.

Nutrition

- Calories: 38
- Total Fat: 2.3g
- Sat Fat: 0.3g
- Cholesterol: 0mg
- Sodium: 14mg
- Carbohydrates: 4.2g
- Fiber: 2.5g

- Sugar: 1.8g
- Protein: 1.2g
- Calcium: 17mg
- Iron: 0mg
- Potassium: 237mg

168. Cashew Chicken & Cauliflower Rice

Prep Time: 15 Minutes

Cook Time: 15-20 Minutes

Total Time: 35 Minutes

Servings: 4 Serving

Ingredients

- 4 tsp Valencia Orange Oil or unrefined coconut oil
- 3 scallions sliced into thin medallions
- 1 1/2 lbs boneless skinless chicken breast cut into a thin strip
- 1 C green bell pepper cut into thin strips
- 1 C red bell pepper cut into thin strips
- 2 C additional vegetables of your choice (broccoli, snow peas, zucchini, etc.)
- 1 T (or fresh garlic, chives, salt, pepper, onion, and parsley)
- 1/2 C low sodium chicken broth (if needed)
- 2 C prepared cauliflower rice
- ❖ 24 cashews, chopped into small pieces

Instructions

- Add oil to a large frying pan over medium-high heat.
- When hot, add scallion and cook for 1 minute until fragrant.
- Add chicken and cook for 5-7 minutes until opaque.
- Add all the vegetables and sprinkle with seasoning. If you are using thicker, heavier vegetables like broccoli, add the broth to help steam/cook them a little faster. Cover with a lid and allow to cook for 5 more minutes until veggies are crisp-tender, but not overdone.
- While chicken is cooking, prepare cauliflower rice.
- Remove chicken mixture from heat. Divide cauliflower rice into 4 equal portions. Do the same with the chicken mixture.

- Place the chicken over the rice and sprinkle with 1/4 of the crushed cashews. Serve hot and enjoy!

Nutrition

- Calories: 337
- Total Fat: 13.2g
- Sat Fat: 1.4g
- Cholesterol: 109mg
- Sodium: 122mg
- Carbohydrates: 14.2g
- Fiber: 3.7g
- Sugar: 5.3g
- Protein: 40.8g
- Calcium: 69mg
- Iron: 2mg
- Potassium: 1111mg

169. Lemon Dill Roasted Radishes

Prep Time: 5 Minutes

Cook Time: 30 Minutes

Total Time: 35 Minutes

Servings: 4 Serving

Ingredients

- 4 C red radish halves, greens, and stems removed
- 2 teaspoons high quality cooking oil of your choice
- 1/2 T Citrus Dill Seasoning
- 1/2 T Brightening Blend (or freshly squeezed lemon)

Instructions

- preheat oven to 350 degrees
- Trim ends and tops of radishes, cut in half (all radish pieces should be about the same size- if you have small ones, leave them whole, big ones should be cut in 1/4, etc)
- Add all ingredients to a large bowl and toss to coat.
- Place radishes in an oven-safe roasting dish and place in oven, center rack, for 30 minutes. If you have a cast-iron skillet, this is the PERFECT time to use it!
- Serve hot

Nutrition

- Calories: 39
- Total Fat: 2.4g
- Sat Fat: 0.3g
- Cholesterol: 0mg
- Sodium: 45mg
- Carbohydrates: 3.9g
- Fiber: 1.9g
- Sugar: 2.2g
- Protein: 0.8g
- Calcium: 29mg
- Iron: 0mg
- Potassium: 270mg

170. Mediterranean Roasted Chicken With Lemon Dill Radishes

Prep Time: 5 Minutes

Cook Time: 30 Minutes

Total Time: 35 Minutes

Servings: 4 Serving

Ingredients

- 2 lbs chicken thighs (Remove skin if on Lean and Green. If using bone-in chicken, add additional cooking time)
- Pinch of Desperation Seasoning (or garlic, salt, black pepper, onion, and parsley)
- 1 Tablespoon
- Mediterranean Seasoning (or garlic, marjoram, basil, rosemary, and onion)

Instructions

- Preheat oven (or outdoor BBQ Grill) to 375 degrees.
- Season the chicken with just a pinch of Dash of Desperation Seasoning
- Place the chicken in a baking dish large enough to hold them without touching one another (this speeds up the cooking process.)
- Sprinkle chicken with Mediterranean seasoning.
- Bake in preheated oven for 30 minutes, or until chicken reaches 165 degrees F.
- Remove from oven and serve hot, or chilled over greens for a salad.

Nutrition

- Calories: 269

- Total Fat: 10.5g
- Sat Fat: 2.9g
- Cholesterol: 126mg
- Sodium: 122mg
- Carbohydrates: 0g
- Fiber: 0g
- Sugar: 0g
- Protein: 41g
- Calcium: 21mg
- Iron: 2mg
- Potassium: 344mg

171. Garlic Shrimp & Broccoli

Prep Time: 15 Minutes

Cook Time: 10 Minutes

Total Time: 25 Minutes

Servings: 4 Serving

Ingredients

- 4 teaspoons Roasted Garlic Oil (or fresh garlic and oil of your choice)
- 1 3/4 lbs wild-caught shrimp, thawed and shells removed
- 2 C fresh broccoli florets
- 2 teaspoon Rockin' Ranch Seasoning (or tarragon, black pepper, salt, lemon, parsley, chives, garlic, and onion)
- 1 teaspoon Garlic Gusto, Garlic & Spring Onion or Simply Brilliant Seasoning (or fresh garlic, lemon, and onion)
- 1/3 C low sodium chicken broth
- 4 C alternative "noodles" of your choice
- 2 Tablespoons butter

Instructions

- Add oil to a large frying pan (with a lid) over medium-high heat.
- When the oil is hot, add shrimp and cook for 1 minute on each side until slightly pink.
- Add seasonings and broth to the shrimp. Stir to combine.
- Add broccoli and place the cover on the pan. Bring to a boil and reduce heat to medium. Cook until broccoli is bright green (about 2 minutes).

- Remove the cover and add the butter. Stir to combine and then add the noodles. Toss the noodles in the liquid and cook until hot. Serve immediately.

Nutrition

- Calories: 340
- Total Fat: 12g
- Sat Fat: 4g
- Cholesterol: 398mg
- Sodium: 511mg
- Carbohydrates: 12.4g
- Fiber: 3.3g
- Sugar: 4.2g
- Protein: 41g
- Calcium: 219mg
- Iron: 2mg
- Potassium: 971mg

172. Make Crispy Croutons With This Lean and Green Biscuit Hack

Prep Time: 2 Minutes

Cook Time: 2 Minutes

Total Time: 4 Minutes

Servings: 1-2 Servings

Ingredients

- Packet Lean and Green Cheddar Herb Biscuits
- 2 Tablespoons water
- 1 Tablespoon lemon juice

Instructions

- Pour the contents of the packet into a small bowl.
- Add the water and juice and stir well with a small spatula.
- Spray a medium-sized, flat dish (or use a large bowl with a flat bottom) with nonstick cooking spray.
- Pour the mixture into the dish and carefully spread it into a thin layer. It should be about 1/4 inch thick.
- Microwave on high for 2 minutes.
- Carefully remove from the microwave, let cool, and then break into pieces. Serve cool.

Nutrition

- Calories: 110

- Total Fat: 2.5g
- Sat Fat: 1g
- Cholesterol: 20mg
- Sodium: 280mg
- Carbohydrates: 14g
- Fiber: 4g
- Sugar: 2g
- Protein: 11g
- Calcium: 219mg

173. Chicken With Garlic And Spring Onion Cream

Prep Time: 10 Minutes

Cook Time: 20 Minutes

Total Time: 30 Minutes

Servings: 4 Serving

Ingredients

- Nonstick cooking spray
- 1 1/2 lbs boneless, skinless chicken breasts, pounded to 3/8" thickness
- 1 teaspoons Dash of Desperation Seasoning (or natural sea salt and black pepper)
- 1 C low sodium chicken broth
- 2 teaspoons fresh lemon juice
- 1 Tablespoon (1 capful)
- Garlic and Spring Onion Seasoning (or fresh garlic, chives, salt, pepper, and lemon)
- 4 Tablespoons low-fat cream cheese
- 2 Tablespoons butter
- Fresh basil, parsley, and/or lemon wedges for garnish if desired

Instructions

- Pound chicken into 3/8" thickness. The easiest way to do this is to place one breast in a large plastic bag and hit it with the back of a small frying pan. Be careful to do this on a cutting board, or another safe surface. You do not want to crack your countertops!
- Spray a large, nonstick pan with cooking spray and place the pan over medium-high heat.
- Season each chicken breast with a pinch of Dash of Desperation Seasoning. When the pan is hot, place chicken in the pan.
- Cook chicken for 5-7 minutes on one side then flip to the other side. Cook an additional 5 minutes more.

- Add the broth, lemon juice, and Garlic and Spring Onion to the pan. Stir well to combine. Using a spatula, scrape all the yummy brown bits off the bottom of the pan.
- Let the mixture come to a simmer and continue to cook for 10-12 minutes until the sauce is reduced to only about 1/3 of a cup.
- Add the cream cheese and butter to the pan and whisk to combine.
- Remove from stove and sprinkle with fresh basil or other herbs and fresh lemon wedges or slices if desired. Serve hot with your favorite side dish.

Nutrition

- Calories: 285
- Total Fat: 13.5g
- Sat Fat: 5.9g
- Cholesterol: 135mg
- Sodium: 158mg
- Carbohydrates: 1.3g
- Fiber: 0.1g
- Sugar: 0.1g
- Protein: 37.1g
- Calcium: 23mg
- Iron: 1mg
- Potassium: 657mg

174. Turmeric Ginger Spiced Cauliflower

Prep Time: 10 Minutes

Cook Time: 25 Minutes

Total Time: 35 Minutes

Servings: 4 Serving

Ingredients

- 4 C cauliflower florets, larger sized
- 2 C carrots or yellow/orange/red bell pepper cut into strips
- 4 teaspoons oil
- 1/2 teaspoons Dash of Desperation or Salt and pepper to taste
- 1/4 C low sodium chicken broth
- 1 teaspoons Garlic Gusto Seasoning (or fresh garlic, parsley, and lemon spritz)
- 1/2 teaspoons Spices of India (or curry powder)

Instructions

- Set oven to broil and place the rack on the second shelf down in the oven. Veggies should cook 6-8" away from the heat source if possible.
- Toss vegetables with oil (* if you do not have room for a Healthy Fat in your meal, substitute 1/4 C of chicken broth instead) and season with Dash of Desperation Seasoning.
- Spread veggie mixture evenly on a cookie sheet and broil for 12-15 minutes until slightly charred. At the 6 minute mark, using tongs or a spatula turn the veggies over to promote browning on all sides.
- Place a large, nonstick pan over medium-high heat on the stovetop. When veggies have finished broiling, add broth and Garlic Gusto to the pan. Once bubbling, add veggies and cook for 5 minutes until the liquid has evaporated.
- Sprinkle with Spices of India and toss to coat. Cook one-2 additional minutes to toast the spices and then serve hot. Season with additional salt and pepper if desired.

Nutrition

- Calories: 32
- Total Fat: 0.2g
- Sat Fat: 0g
- Cholesterol: 0mg
- Sodium: 17mg
- Carbohydrates: 7.2g
- Fiber: 2.1g
- Sugar: 4.2g
- Protein: 1.6g
- Calcium: 16mg
- Iron: 0mg
- Potassium: 264mg

175. Middle Eastern Meatballs With Dill Sauce

Prep Time: 10 Minutes

Cook Time: 20 Minutes

Total Time: 35 Minutes

Servings: 4 Serving

Ingredients

- 1 1/2 lbs lean ground beef (or ground chicken, lamb, turkey or pork or a combination)
- 2 teaspoons Stacey Hawkins Spices of India (or curry powder)
- 1/4 teaspoon Stacey Hawkins Sinful Cinnamon or ground cinnamon & a pinch of nutmeg
- Salt and pepper to taste
- 1/2 C plain, low-fat Greek yogurt
- 11/2 teaspoons Stacey Hawkins Citrus Dill or fresh dill, onion, chives, and lemon)

Instructions

- Add seasoning to beef and mix well to combine.
- Divide mixture into 20 even portions and roll into balls.
- Place a nonstick pan over medium-high heat and add the meatballs once the pan has come to temperature.
- Cook for 15-20 minutes, turning meatballs every 2-3 minutes so they brown equally on all sides.
- While beef is cooking, make the sauce by combining the yogurt and Citrus Dill seasoning. Stir well & keep in the fridge until ready to eat.
- When meatballs are finished (internal temperature of 160 F) place on a plate and serve hot with sauce.
- Nutrition
- Calories: 208
- Total Fat: 6.9g
- Sat Fat: 2.6g
- Cholesterol: 97mg
- Sodium: 76mg
- Carbohydrates: 0.5g
- Sugar: 0.4g
- Protein: 33.8g
- Calcium: 14mg
- Iron: 20mg
- Potassium: 444mg

176. Creamy Skillet Chicken And Asparagus

Prep Time: 10 Minutes

Cook Time: 15 Minutes

Total Time: 25 Minutes

Servings: 4 Serving

Ingredients

- 4 teaspoons Stacey Hawkins Roasted Garlic Oil (or oil of your choice and fresh garlic)
- 1 3/4 lbs boneless, skinless chicken breast, cut into 1" chunks
- 1/2 C low sodium chicken broth

- 1 Tablespoon (one capful) Stacey Hawkins Garlic and Spring Onion or Garlic Gusto Seasoning or fresh chopped garlic, parsley, and chives
- 8 T (4 oz or half an 8 oz block) light cream cheese
- 4 C fresh asparagus, cut into 2" pieces
- Pinch of salt and pepper and garlic)

Instructions

- Add oil to a large skillet and heat over medium-high heat.
- When hot, add chicken breasts and cook for 7-10 minutes, stirring occasionally. The chicken should be slightly browned.
- Pour the broth into the pan and, using a spatula, scrape all the browned bits (fond) off the bottom of the pan.
- Add garlic seasoning, cream cheese, and asparagus. Turn the heat to high
- Stir the ingredients continually, allowing the cream cheese to melt evenly into the sauce. Bring to a boil and simmer until a thick, rich sauce has formed. Divide into 4 equal portions, sprinkle with a little Dash of Desperation and serve hot.

Nutrition

- Calories: 302
- Total Fat: 12.8g
- Sat Fat: 3.5g
- Cholesterol: 114mg
- Sodium: 223mg
- Carbohydrates: 7.1g
- Fiber: 2.8g
- Sugar: 4.4g
- Protein: 39g
- Calcium: 134mg
- Iron: 3mg
- ❖ Potassium: 851mg

177. Toasted Sesame Ginger Chicken

Prep Time: 10 Minutes

Cook Time: 15 Minutes

Total Time: 25 Minutes

Servings: 4 Serving

Ingredients

- 4 teaspoons oil of your choice and orange zest

- 1 1/2 lbs boneless, skinless chicken breast
- 1 Tablespoon of toasted sesame seeds, garlic, onion powder, red pepper, ground ginger, salt, pepper, and lemon)

Instructions

- Place chicken breasts on a clean, dry cutting board.
- Using a meat mallet or backside of a frying pan, gently flatten the chicken breasts to approx. 3/8" thickness.
- Sprinkle with seasoning.
- Heat Valencia Orange Oil in a large, nonstick frying pan over medium-high heat.
- Add chicken and cook for 7-8 minutes on one side, until a lovely crust has formed- it will be slightly brown.
- Gently flip chicken and cook on the other side for an additional 5-6 minutes until the chicken is fully cooked.
- Serve warm with your favorite side dish, or chilled over salad. Makes about 4 servings.

Nutrition

- Calories: 247
- Total Fat: 9.9g
- Sat Fat: 0.8g
- Cholesterol: 109mg
- Sodium: 87mg
- Carbohydrates: 0.5g
- Fiber: 0.3g
- Sugar: 0g
- Protein: 36.5g
- Calcium: 30mg
- Iron: 1mg
- Potassium: 640mg

178. Tender And Tasty Fish Tacos

Prep Time: 15 Minutes

Cook Time: 15 Minutes

Total Time: 30 Minutes

Servings: 4 Serving

Ingredients

- 1 3/4 lbs cod or haddock (wild-caught)
- 1 capful (1 tablespoon)

- Phoenix sunrise seasoning or cumin, cilantro, garlic, onion, red pepper, paprika, parsley, salt & pepper (or low sodium taco seasoning)
- 4 teaspoons of oil of your choice and fresh garlic
- Your favorite taco condiments (for a list of quantities and Lean and Green approved condiments.

Instructions

- Pat fish dry and cut into 1" chunks
- Sprinkle seasoning over fish and toss to coat.
- Heat Roasted Garlic Oil in a large, nonstick frying pan over medium-high heat.
- Add fish and cook for 10 - 12 minutes, until fish is opaque and breaks apart into flakes. Be careful not to overcook or the fish will be dry and chewy.
- Serve hot with your favorite condiments.
- Makes about 4 servings.

Nutrition

- Calories: 151
- Total Fat: 1.3g
- Sat Fat: 0.3g
- Cholesterol: 78mg
- Sodium: 111mg
- Carbohydrates: 0.2g
- Fiber: 0.1g
- Sugar: 0g
- Protein: 32.5g
- Calcium: 25mg
- Iron: 1mg
- Potassium: 355mg

179. Sausage Stuffed Mushrooms - A LBD LG Recipe

Prep Time: 5 Minutes

Cook Time: 25 Minutes

Total Time: 30 Minutes

Servings: 4 Serving

Ingredients

- 4 large portobello mushrooms (caps and stems)
- 1 1/2 pounds lean Italian sausage (85-94% lean)
- 1 capful (1 Tablespoon)

Instructions

- preheat oven to 350 degrees.

- Gently remove the mushroom stems & wash both the caps and stems
- Chop the stems into small pieces and place in a bowl. Add the meat and seasoning to the bowl and using your hands, combine all ingredients well.
- Place the mushroom caps smooth side down on a large cookie sheet or baking tray.
- Divide the meat mixture into 4 equal parts and gently press one portion into each mushroom cap.
- Bake for approximately 25 minutes & serve hot with your favorite side dishes.
- Makes about 4 servings.

Nutrition

- Calories: 244
- Total Fat: 12.7g
- Sat Fat: 0g
- Cholesterol: 0mg
- Sodium: 0mg
- Carbohydrates: 8g
- Fiber: 0g
- Sugar: 0g
- Protein: 23.1g
- Calcium: 0mg
- Iron: 0mg
- Potassium: 130mg

180. Smoky Shrimp Chipotle

Prep Time: 5 Minutes

Cook Time: 15 Minutes

Total Time: 20 Minutes

Servings: 4 Serving

Ingredients

- 4 teaspoons of oil of your choice and fresh garlic
- 1 C chopped chives or scallions (greens only)
- 2 lbs wild-caught, raw shrimp, shelled, deveined & tails removed
- 1 can (~16 oz) diced tomatoes (unflavored, no sugar added)
- 1 capful (1 Tablespoon)
- 4 lime wedges (optional)
- 4 T fresh cilantro (optional)

Instructions

- Heat oil in a medium-sized frying pan over medium-high heat.
- Add the scallions and cook for one minute, until slightly wilted and glistening.
- Add the shrimp and cook for 1 minute on each side.
- Add the tomatoes and Cinnamon Chipotle seasoning. Cook an additional 3-5 minutes, stirring occasionally until the tomatoes are hot and shrimp is opaque & fully cooked. Be careful not to overcook as it will make the shrimp tough and dry.
- Sprinkle with cilantro if desired and spritz with a wedge of lime (or serve the lime wedge on the plate for a pretty and functional garnish.
- Serve warm.
- Makes about 4 servings.

Nutrition

- Calories: 250
- Total Fat: 3.6g
- Sat Fat: 1.1g
- Cholesterol: 418mg
- Sodium: 487mg
- Carbohydrates: 6.2g
- Fiber: 1.5g
- Sugar: 1.4g
- Protein: 46.1g
- Calcium: 207g
- Iron: 1mg
- Potassium: 485mg

181. Pan Seared Balsamic Chicken And Vegetables

Prep Time: 5 Minutes

Cook Time: 25 Minutes

Total Time: 25 plus marinade time Minutes

Servings: 4 Serving

Ingredients

- 1 1/2 pounds boneless, skinless chicken thighs
- 1 Tablespoon (one Capful) of salt, pepper, garlic, red pepper, parsley, garlic powder, and onion to taste
- 4 Tablespoon of balsamic reduction
- 1 Tablespoon Dijon Mustard
- 2 C cherry or grape tomatoes, halved
- 2 C zucchini sliced into 3/8" slices (try to have the zucchini around 1" in diameter - smaller ones cook faster and have fewer seeds)
- 1/3 C water

Instructions

- Whisk together balsamic, mustard and seasoning in a bowl large enough to hold the chicken.
- Add the chicken and toss to coat. Place in the refrigerator for 20 minutes, up to 8 hours to marinate.
- When ready to cook, preheat the oven to 425 degrees.
- Place a well-seasoned cast-iron skillet (large enough to hold all the chicken without crowding) over medium-high heat.
- Shake off the excess marinade (reserving it in the bowl for later) and place the chicken in the pan. Cook until seared and slightly browned for about 5 minutes. Flip chicken and cook an additional 5 minutes on the other side.
- While chicken is cooking, prepare the vegetables.
- Add water to the remaining marinade in the bowl and whisk to combine.
- Scatter the vegetables around the pan. Season with a pinch of salt and pepper.
- Pour the marinade mixture over the veggies & chicken. Toss to combine. Place in the preheated oven for 15 minutes additional.
- Remove from oven and serve hot.

Nutrition

- Calories: 280
- Total Fat: 9.9g
- Sat Fat: 2.7g
- Cholesterol: 114mg
- Sodium: 179mg
- Carbohydrates: 7.5g
- Fiber: 1.9g
- Sugar: 5g
- Protein: 38.7g
- Calcium: 42g
- Iron: 2mg
- Potassium: 690mg

182. Low Carb Sloppy Joes

Prep Time: 5 Minutes

Cook Time: 25 Minutes

Total Time: 30 Minutes

Ingredients

- 1 1/2 pounds lean ground beef
- 1/2 C diced green bell pepper
- 2 Tablespoons tomato paste
- 1 teaspoon (one packet) powdered stevia
- 1 Tablespoon yellow mustard
- 1 Tablespoon of salt, pepper, crushed garlic, garlic powder, and onion to taste
- 1/2 Tablespoon
- 1 Tablespoon red wine vinegar
- 1 C low sodium beef broth
- Salt and Pepper to taste

Instructions

- Place the ground beef in a frying pan and place on the stove over medium heat. Break up the larger pieces of meat as it is cooking.
- Let the meat cook for about 7 minutes and then add the remaining ingredients (EXCEPT the broth) and stir to combine. Once mixed, add the water and turn up the heat to medium-high.
- Once the liquid is boiling, reduce the heat to low and let it simmer, uncovered for about 10-15 minutes until the liquid is somewhat reduced & you have a lovely sauce.
- Serve hot & enjoy!

Nutrition

- Calories: 302
- Total Fat: 11.5g
- Sat Fat: 5.2g
- Cholesterol: 132mg
- Sodium: 189mg
- Carbohydrates: 2.7g
- Fiber: 0.6g
- Sugar: 1g
- Protein: 44.1g
- Calcium: 25g
- Iron: 5mg
- Potassium: 776mg

183. Fresh Lime Crema

Prep Time: 10 Minutes

Cook Time: 0 Minutes

Total Time: 10 Minutes

Servings: 4+ Serving

Ingredients

- 1 Cup sour cream
- 1 teaspoon salt, pepper, garlic, and onion to taste
- Zest from one lime
- Juice from one lime
- 1/4 C fresh cilantro, finely shredded if desired

Instructions

- Place all ingredients in a mixing bowl and stir vigorously to combine.
- Let rest for 15 minutes before serving to allow flavors to develop. May be stored in an airtight container, refrigerated for up to one week.

Nutrition

- Calories: 27
- Total Fat: 2.5g
- Sat Fat: 1.6g
- Cholesterol: 5mg
- Sodium: 7mg
- Carbohydrates: 1g
- Fiber: 0.1g
- Sugar: 0.1g
- Protein: 0.4g
- Calcium: 15g
- Iron: 0mg
- Potassium: 24mg

184. Fresh Pico De Gallo

Prep Time: 15 Minutes

Cook Time: 0 Minutes

Total Time: 15 Minutes

Servings: 2+ Serving

Ingredients

- 1 C diced tomatoes (fresh or canned and well-drained)

- 1/4 C (4 Tablespoons) fresh onion, finely chopped
- 1teaspoon of salt, pepper, garlic, and onion to taste
- 2 T finely chopped cilantro
- Juice of one fresh lime

Instructions

- Place all ingredients in a bowl and toss gently to combine.
- For best flavor, let sit for 15 minutes before serving.

Nutrition

- Calories: 20
- Total Fat: 0.2g
- Sat Fat: 0g
- Cholesterol: 0mg
- Sodium: 7mg
- Carbohydrates: 4.6g
- Fiber: 1.2g
- Sugar: 2.6g
- Protein: 0.8g
- Calcium: 11g
- Iron: 0mg
- Potassium: 225mg

185. Tex-Mex Seared Salmon

Prep Time: 5 Minutes

Cook Time: 15 Minutes

Total Time: 20 Minutes

Servings: 4 Serving

Ingredients

- 1 1/2 pounds wild-caught salmon filet (will cook best if you have it at room temp)
- 1Tablespoon (one Capful) of salt, pepper, garlic, cumin, paprika, cayenne, and onion to taste

Instructions

- Preheat a nonstick pan over high heat for 1 minute.
- While heating, sprinkle seasoning over the salmon (NOT on the skin side)
- Reduce heat to medium-high.

- Place the fish, seasoning side down in the pan and let it cook for 4-6 minutes depending on thickness. You'll know it's ready to flip when a "crust" has formed from the seasoning and the fish releases from the pan easily.
- Reduce heat to medium-low. Flip the fish over to the skin side down and cook an additional 4-6 minutes.
- Remove from heat and serve. Fish should slide right off the skin and onto the plate. The serving size is 5 ounces of salmon

Nutrition

- Calories: 192
- Total Fat: 8.8g
- Sat Fat: 1.3g
- Cholesterol: 63mg
- Sodium: 147mg
- Carbohydrates: 0.8g
- Fiber: 0g
- Sugar: 0.2g
- Protein: 22.5g
- Calcium: 50mg
- Iron: 1mg
- Potassium: 544mg

186. Heavenly Green Beans And Garlic

Prep Time: 5 Minutes

Cook Time: 10 Minutes

Total Time: 15 Minutes

Servings: 4 Serving

Ingredients

- 1 1/2 pounds green beans (about 4 cups) ends trimmed
- 1/2 capful (1/2 Tablespoon) fresh chopped garlic, salt, and pepper
- 1Tablespoon of other fat of your choice
- 4 Tablespoons freshly grated Parmesan cheese

Instructions

- Place green beans in a pot with a lid and add 1" of water to the bottom.
- Sprinkle seasoning over the top of the beans, trying to keep most of the seasoning on the beans and out of the water.

- Place the covered pot on the stove over high heat. Bring water to a boil and let the beans steam for 5-7 minutes, until bright green and crisp-tender. Be careful not to overcook.
- Carefully drain all the water out of the pot.
- Drizzle with Roasted Garlic Oil and a pinch of salt and pepper (or Dash of Desperation Seasoning for more pop!) Sprinkle with cheese and serve hot.

Nutrition

- Calories: 84
- Total Fat: 5g
- Sat Fat: 1.5g
- Cholesterol: 5mg
- Sodium: 127mg
- Carbohydrates: 7.8g
- Fiber: 3.7g
- Sugar: 1.5g
- Protein: 4g
- Calcium: 81mg
- Iron: 1mg
- Potassium: 230mg

187. Roasted Garlic Zoodles

Prep Time: 5 Minutes

Cook Time: 5 Minutes

Total Time: 10 Minutes

Servings: 4 Serving

Ingredients

- 1Tablespoon Garlic Oil) or other fat of your choice
- 6 Cups zucchini noodles
- 1/2 capful (1/2 Tablespoon) of fresh chopped garlic, salt, and pepper
- Pinch of salt and pepper or Dash of Desperation Seasoning to taste

Instructions

- Add the oil/spray to a larger sized frying pan and heat over medium-high heat.
- Add the zucchini noodles to the pan and sprinkle with seasoning.
- Cook for just 2-3 minutes, tossing occasionally with a pair of tongs.

- Season with a pinch of salt and pepper (or Dash of Desperation Seasoning for more pop!) and serve hot.

Nutrition

- Calories: 57
- Total Fat: 3.7g
- Sat Fat: 0.5g
- Cholesterol: 0mg
- Sodium: 17mg
- Carbohydrates: 5.7g
- Fiber: 1.9g
- Sugar: 2.9g
- Protein: 2.1g
- Calcium: 25mg
- Iron: 1mg
- Potassium: 444mg

188. Charred Sirloin With Creamy Horseradish Sauce

Prep Time: 5 Minutes

Cook Time: 15 Minutes

Total Time: 20 Minutes

Servings: 4 Serving

Ingredients

- 1 1/2 pounds sirloin steaks, trimmed & visible fat removed
- 1/2 capful (1/2 Tablespoon) or salt, pepper, garlic, and onion to taste
- 6 Tablespoons low-fat sour cream
- 1-3 T horseradish (from the jar)

Instructions

- Preheat grill to medium-high heat.
- Season the steak on both sides with Dash of Desperation Seasoning
- Place on the grill and cook for 5-7 minutes on each side, depending on how thick the steak is and the way you like your meat cooked. You'll leave it on less for rare and more for medium-well. The BEST way to cook the steak is by using a meat thermometer.
- While meat is cooking, make the sauce by combining sour cream and horseradish. Add water, one Tablespoon at a time to thin the mixture to make a sauce. Set aside when done.

- When the meat is finished cooking, let it rest on a cutting board for 5 minutes, then slice thin.
- Serve drizzled with 1-2 T of sauce.

Nutrition

- Calories: 291
- Total Fat: 11.4g
- Sat Fat: 4.9g
- Cholesterol: 132mg
- Sodium: 115mg
- Carbohydrates: 1.1g
- Fiber: 0.2g
- Sugar: 0.4g
- Protein: 43.4g
- Calcium: 18mg
- Iron: 27mg
- Potassium: 601mg

189. Low Carb Taco Bowls

Prep Time: 5 Minutes

Cook Time: 15-20 Minutes

Total Time: 20-30 Minutes

Servings: 4 Serving

Ingredients

- 1 large head cauliflower, steamed until soft or frozen ready-to-cook cauliflower rice
- 1 1/2 pounds lean ground beef
- 1-2 capfuls of Southwestern Seasoning (or a combination of both!) or low salt taco seasoning
- 2 C canned, diced tomatoes (no sugar added, no flavor added)

Instructions

- Place a large frying pan over medium-high heat. Add ground beef to a large (preferably nonstick) pan and saute for 8-12 minutes until slightly browned. Break up the larger chunks into smaller pieces using a spatula or a chopping tool.
- Add tomatoes and seasoning. Stir to combine. Reduce the heat to low and allow the mixture to cook for 5 minutes until the liquid is reduced by 1/2 and nice & thick.
- While the meat is cooking, use a food processor or chopping tool to chop steamed cauliflower up into rice-sized bits. If using ready-to-cook cauli

rice, prepare it according to package instructions.
- Place 1/2 C cauliflower rice into a bowl and top with 1/4 of the meat mixture. Top with your favorite condiments and serve hot.

Nutrition

- Calories: 275
- Total Fat: 9.9g
- Sat Fat: 4.4g
- Cholesterol: 113mg
- Sodium: 128mg
- Carbohydrates: 6.2g
- Fiber: 2.3g
- Sugar: 3.6g
- Protein: 39g
- Calcium: 32mg
- Iron: 5mg
- Potassium: 950mg

190. Surf And Turk Burgers- So Easy!

Prep Time: 5 Minutes

Cook Time: 20 Minutes

Total Time: 25 Minutes

Servings: 4 Serving

Ingredients

- 1 1/4 pounds (20 oz) ground turkey
- 8 medium raw shrimp, peeled, deveined and tails removed (each shrimp should be about 1 oz each)
- 1 Tablespoon of garlic, lemon, parsley, onion, salt, pepper, and celery

Instructions

- Preheat the outdoor grill to 350 degrees.
- Place the turkey in a large bowl, sprinkle with seasoning and using your hands, combine well.
- Form turkey mixture into 4 individual patties.
- Gently press two raw shrimp into the top of the burger in a heart shape.
- Place on the grill and cook for 5-7 minutes on both sides until done. Turkey must be an internal temperature of 165 degrees F.
- Remove from the grill and serve with a great side dish!

Nutrition

- Calories: 191
- Total Fat: 9.7g
- Sat Fat: 1.7g
- Cholesterol: 132mg
- Sodium: 216mg
- Carbohydrates: 0.3g
- Fiber: 0g
- Sugar: 0g
- Protein: 28.1g
- Calcium: 41mg
- Iron: 2mg
- Potassium: 266mg

191. Stuffed Eggplant (or Zucchini) Provencale

Prep Time: 15 Minutes

Cook Time: 40 Minutes

Total Time: 55 Minutes

Servings: 4 Serving

Ingredients

- 2 small eggplants (about 6-7" each) can also use zucchini
- Natural sea salt
- 4 tsp Stacey Hawkins Roasted Garlic Oil (or fresh garlic and oil of your choice)
- 2 lb lean ground turkey
- 1 T (one capful) Simply Brilliant Seasoning (or garlic, onion, parsley, lemon, and paprika)
- 1 C fresh tomatoes, diced (or canned, drained well)
- ½ C zucchini, cut into ½ inch cubes
- ½ C mushrooms, sliced
- 1 C chicken stock, preferably low sodium

Instructions

- preheat oven to 350 degrees.
- Cut eggplants into halves, lengthwise. Using a small spoon, scoop out the seeds and throw them away.
- Scoop out the zucchini flesh, leaving ¾ inch of thickness around the inside to make a shell.
- Dice the scooped flesh & set it aside. Sprinkle a little salt over the shell halves and set aside.
- Heat Garlic Oil in a large skillet until sizzling.

- Add turkey and diced eggplant. Cook for 3-5 minutes, stirring occasionally until turkey is opaque. Stir in Garlic Gusto seasoning and remaining vegetables and cook for an additional minute.
- Rinse eggplant halves to remove the salt. Pat them dry and place hollow side up in a baking dis big enough to hold all 4 halves (or use 2 baking dishes.)
- Scoop turkey mixture equally into eggplant shells. Pour the stock into the bottom of the pan (use an additional cup if using 2 baking dishes) and place it on the middle rack in the oven.
- Bake for 30-40 minutes until eggplant is fork-tender.

Nutrition

- Calories: 180
- Total Fat: 9.7g
- Sat Fat: 1.7g
- Cholesterol: 132mg
- Sodium: 36mg
- Carbohydrates: 0.3g
- Protein: 28.1g
- Calcium: 21mg
- Iron: 2mg
- Potassium: 216mg

192. Seared Scallops in Creamy Garlic Sauce

Prep Time: 5 Minutes

Cook Time: 15 Minutes

Total Time: 20 Minutes

Servings: 4 Serving

Ingredients

- Nonstick cooking spray
- 2 lbs dry sea scallops
- 1 tsp of salt pepper garlic onion and parsley)
- 3/4 C chicken stock, vegetable stock, fish stock, or dry white wine
- 2 T butter
- 3/4 C Half and Half

Instructions

- Spray a large nonstick pan with nonstick cooking spray and place on the stove over high heat.

- When the pan is hot, add scallops, leaving space in between them, don't crowd or they will not cook evenly. Sprinkle with a little light dusting of Dash of Desperation.
- Cook on high heat for about 7-8 minutes, until they have a lovely brown coating on them.
- Flip each scallop over using tongs and cook an additional minute or two on the opposite side. Scallops will be done when they turn opaque. Remove the scallops from the pan and place them in a dish to the side. Return the pan to the stove.
- Stir in the butter until melted to make a quick pan sauce. Be sure to scrape any "bits" from the bottom of the pan for additional flavor.
- Add the stock, half and half, and Garlic Seasoning. Heat on high until boiling then reduce heat to medium-high and let simmer until liquid is reduced by half.
- Add scallops back to the pan and toss to coat with the sauce and reheat. Divide into four equal portions and serve immediately with your favorite side dish.

Nutrition

- Calories: 320
- Total Fat: 5.3g
- Sat Fat: 1.3g
- Cholesterol: 143mg
- Sodium: 137mg
- Carbohydrates: 7.3g
- Fiber: 3.7g
- Sugar: 4g
- Protein: 68g
- Calcium: 21mg
- Iron: 3mg
- Potassium: 1118mg

193. Tex Mex Turkey Stuffed Poblanos

Prep Time: 15 Minutes

Cook Time: 20 Minutes

Total Time: 35 Minutes

Servings: 4 Serving

Ingredients

- 2 large poblano peppers (or bell peppers) cut in half lengthwise and seeds removed
- 4 tsp (or fresh garlic and oil of your choice)
- 2 pounds ground turkey, 98% lean
- 1 T (one capful) or Phoenix Sunrise Seasoning (or garlic, onion, cilantro, cumin, and black pepper)
- 1 C reduced-fat extra sharp cheddar cheese, shredded (divided)
- 8 T sour cream
- Fresh cilantro and/or sliced jalapenos for garnish

Instructions

- Preheat the oven to 350 degrees. Spray a casserole dish large enough to hold the pepper halves with nonstick cooking spray and place the peppers, cut side up into the dish. Bake for 15 minutes.
- While peppers are cooking, add the Roasted Garlic Oil to a large skillet and heat over medium-high heat.
- Add turkey to the pan and sprinkle with the seasoning. Cook for 10 minutes, stirring occasionally until turkey is browned.
- Remove meat from the heat and stir in 1/2 C of the cheddar cheese.
- Remove the peppers from the oven and place equal portions of the meat into the pepper halves. Sprinkle with remaining cheese and bake until poblanos are tender and cheese is melted for about 5-7 additional minutes.
- Drizzle 2 T of sour cream over each pepper and sprinkle with cilantro and/or jalapenos if desired.

Nutrition

- Calories: 357
- Total Fat: 14.4g
- Sat Fat: 7.3g
- Cholesterol: 140mg
- Sodium: 324mg
- Carbohydrates: 4.1g
- Fiber: 0.3g
- Sugar: 1.2g
- Protein: 55g
- Calcium: 397mg
- Iron: 2mg
- Potassium: 705mg

194. Lean Green Chicken Soup

Prep Time: 15 Minutes

Cook Time: 25 Minutes

Total Time: 40 Minutes

Servings: 12

Ingredients

- 2 quarts chicken broth or stock
- 1 1/2 pounds boneless, skinless chicken breast
- 2 celery stalks, chopped
- 2 cups green beans, cut into 1-inch pieces
- 1 1/2 cups peas, fresh or frozen
- 2 cups asparagus, cut into 1-inch pieces, tops, and middles (avoid tough ends)
- 1 cup diced green onions
- 4-6 cloves garlic, minced
- 2 cups fresh spinach leaves, chopped and packed
- 1 bunch watercress, chopped with large stems removed
- 1/2 cup fresh parsley leaves, chopped
- 1/3 cup fresh basil leaves, chopped
- 1 teaspoon salt
- 1/2 teaspoon ground black pepper

Instructions

- Pour the chicken broth into a large pot, and set over medium-high heat. Add the chicken breasts and bring to a simmer. Cook for 15 minutes.
- Add the celery, green beans, peas, asparagus, onions, garlic, salt, and pepper. Simmer for 5-10 minutes until tender, then remove from heat.
- Remove the chicken breasts and shred with two forks or chop into bite-sized pieces. Return to the pot.
- Stir in the spinach, watercress, parsley, and basil. Taste, then salt and pepper as needed.

Nutrition

Calories: 105kcal, Carbohydrates: 7g, Protein: 15g, Fat: 2g, Saturated Fat: 0g, Cholesterol: 36mg, Sodium: 852mg, Potassium: 556mg, Fiber: 2g, Sugar: 2g, Vitamin A: 1345iu, Vitamin C: 30.3mg, Calcium: 52mg, Iron: 1.9mg

195. Lean & Green Smoothie

Active: 5 mins

Total: 10 mins

Servings: 4

Ingredients

- 2 ½ cups stemmed kale leaves
- 1 cup cubed pineapple
- ¾ cup apple juice, chilled
- ½ cup seedless green grapes, frozen
- ½ cup chopped Granny Smith apple
- 1 cup Halved green grapes

Instructions

- Place kale, pineapple, apple juice, frozen grapes, and apple in a blender. Cover and blend until smooth, about 3 minutes. If desired, garnish smoothies with halved grapes.

Nutrition

Per Serving: 81 calories; protein 2g; carbohydrates 19g; dietary fiber 2g; sugars 14g; fat 1g; sodium 19mg.

196. 10 Minute Lean & Green Tofu Stir-Fry

Cook Time: 10 mins

Total Time: 10 mins

Yield: 2

Ingredients

- 1/4 cup chopped onion
- 1/4 cup chopped button mushrooms
- 8 oz extra-firm tofu, pressed and chopped into bite-size cubes
- 3 teaspoons nutritional yeast
- 1 teaspoon braggs liquid aminos or coconut aminos
- 4 cups baby spinach
- 4–5 grape tomatoes, chopped
- Cooking spray
- Sriracha or another hot sauce, for topping (optional)

Instructions

- Spray a non-stick skillet with cooking spray and heat over medium heat. Add onion and mushrooms and sauté until onions are translucent and mushrooms have softened (about 2-3 minutes).

- Add tofu to the skillet. Toss to combine and cook for 1-2 minutes more.
- Add your nutritional yeast and liquid aminos to the pan. Stir until everything is well coated.
- Add spinach and tomatoes. Cook for 3-4 minutes longer, until spinach, is starting to wilt a tiny bit. Plate, top with sriracha, and serve.

Nutrition

- Serving Size: 1/2 recipe
- Calories: 202
- Sugar: 2
- Fat: 11
- Carbohydrates: 7
- Fiber: 5
- Protein: 18

197. Keto Taco Stuffed Peppers Recipe

Prep Time: 10 Minutes

Cook Time: 38 Minutes

Total Time: 48 Minutes

Servings: 4 Servings

Ingredients

- 1 tablespoon butter
- ½ cup chopped onion
- 1 pound ground beef
- 1 taco seasoning packet look for one without fillers
- 10 ounce Rotel diced tomatoes and green chiles
- 2 cups shredded Mexican cheese blend divided
- 2 extra-large bell peppers any color (or 3 large peppers)
- Optional Toppings: Pico de gallo cilantro, sour cream, lime wedges, shredded lettuce

Instructions

- Preheat the oven to 400 degrees F. Cut the bell peppers in half and remove the seeds. Place the pepper halves, cut side up, in a rimmed baking dish.
- Set a large skillet over medium heat. Add the butter and onions. Sauté for 2-3 minutes to soften. Then add in the ground beef. Break the meat apart with a wooden spoon and brown for 4-5 minutes.

- Mix in the taco seasoning, Rotel, and 1 ¼ cups shredded cheese. Stir well. Scoop the meat filling into the empty bell pepper halves.
- Cover the dish with foil and bake for 30 minutes, or until the peppers are soft. Remove the foil for the last 5 minutes, and sprinkle the remaining cheese over the tops.
- Serve warm, as-is, or topped with sour cream, pico de gallo, cilantro, lime wedges, or shredded lettuce.

Nutrition

Calories: 553kcal, Carbohydrates: 9g, Protein: 34g, Fat: 42g, Saturatedfat: 20g, Cholesterol: 141mg, Sodium: 521mg, Potassium: 642mg, Fiber: 2g, Sugar: 6g, Vitamin A: 2426iu, Vitamin C: 84mg, Calcium: 420mg, Iron: 3mg

198. Slow Cooker Buffalo Chicken Soup

Prep Time: 15 Minutes

Cook Time: 2 Hours

Total Time: 2 Hours 15 Minutes

Servings: 6

Ingredients

- 1 tablespoon butter
- 1/2 large onion peeled and chopped
- 2 cloves garlic minced
- 3 large carrots sliced
- 3 celery stalks sliced
- 1 pound boneless skinless chicken breast
- 1/4 cup Frank's Red Hot cayenne sauce
- 1/4 cup good blue cheese dressing could also use the low-cal dressing
- 4 cups chicken stock
- 1/2 cup crispy tortilla chip strips
- 1/4 cup crumbled blue cheese
- 1/4 cup chopped green onions

Instructions

Place a skillet over medium heat and add the butter. Once the butter has melted add the onions, garlic, carrots, and celery. Saute for 5 minutes to soften.

Slow Cooker Method:

- Place the sautéed garlic and onions, carrots, celery, chicken breasts, Franks hot sauce, blue cheese dressing, and chicken stock in a crockpot. Cover and turn on. Cook on high for 2-3 hours, or low for 4-5 hours.

- Once the chicken has cooked through, take the chicken breasts out. Using two forks, shred the chicken and place it back in the soup.

Stovetop Method:

- Place the sautéed garlic and onions, carrots, celery, chicken breasts, Franks hot sauce, blue cheese dressing, and chicken stock in a stockpot. Cover and bring to a boil. Then lower the heat and simmer for 15 minutes.
- Once the soup has cooked, take the chicken breasts out. Using two forks, shred the chicken and place it back in the soup.

To Serve:

- Scoop the Buffalo Chicken Soup into bowls and sprinkle with crunchy tortilla strips, crumbled blue cheese, and green onions.

Nutrition

Calories: 223kcal, Carbohydrates: 12g, Protein: 22g, Fat: 9g, Saturatedfat: 3g, Cholesterol: 63mg, Sodium: 861mg, Potassium: 637mg, Fiber: 1g, Sugar: 5g, Vitamin C: 5.4mg, Calcium: 72mg, Iron: 0.9mg

199. Crockpot Buffalo Chicken Dip

Prep Time: 10 Minutes

Cook Time: 2 Hours

Total Time: 2 Hours 10 Minutes

Servings: 16 Servings

Ingredients

- 16 ounces cream cheese softened
- 2 ½ cups chopped cooked chicken leftover or rotisserie
- 2 cups shredded cheddar cheese divided
- 1 cup sour cream
- 1 cup Frank's RedHot
- 1 cup chopped scallions divided
- ½ cup crumbled blue cheese
- 1 ranch dip mix packet
- Dippers: crackers, chips, fresh-cut vegetables

Instructions

- Set out a large 6-quart slow cooker. Add in the cream cheese, chopped chicken, 1 cup cheddar, sour cream, Frank's RedHot, ½ cup scallions, crumbled blue cheese, and ranch dip packet. (Reserve the remaining cheddar and scallions for later.)
- Mix well, then spread the dip out evenly in the crock. If needed, wipe the sides of the crockpot with a wet paper towel. Cover and set on LOW for 2-4 hours.
- When ready to serve, sprinkle the top with the remaining cheddar cheese and scallions. Serve warm with chips, crackers, or fresh cut veggies!

Nutrition

Calories: 159kcal, carbohydrates: 3g, protein: 7g, fat: 13g, saturatedfat: 8g, cholesterol: 41mg, sodium: 757mg, potassium: 132mg, fiber: 1g, sugar: 2g, vitamin a: 482iu, vitamin c: 1mg, calcium: 186mg, iron: 1mg

200. Calabacitas Recipe (Con Queso)

Prep Time: 15 Minutes

Cook Time: 10 Minutes

Total Time: 25 Minutes

Servings: 6

Ingredients

- 4 tablespoons butter, or oil
- 1 small sweet onion, peeled and chopped
- 3 cloves garlic, minced
- 2-3 corn cobs, corn cut off the cob
- 1-2 zucchini, cut into ½ inch cubes
- 1-2 yellow squash, cut into ½ inch cubes
- 1 large poblano pepper, seeded and chopped
- 1 red bell pepper, seeded and chopped
- 1 orange bell pepper, seeded and chopped
- ¼ cup chopped cilantro
- ½ lime, juiced
- 1 teaspoon ground cumin
- 1 teaspoon dried oregano
- Salt and pepper

Instructions

- Set an extra-large cast iron cast over medium-high heat. Add the butter, onion, garlic, and poblano pepper. Saute and soften for 3-5 minutes, stirring occasionally.

- Add the ground cumin and oregano to the skillet. Stir and push the onions to the sides of the skillet.
- Add about a third of the chopped squash and bell peppers. Brown for 1 minute. Then push them to the sides of the pan and add another third of the veggies. Cook for 1 more minute. Then push the veggies to the sides and add the remaining squash and peppers.
- Season with 1 teaspoon salt and ¼ teaspoon ground black pepper. Brown another minute, then stir in the corn, cilantro, and juice of ½ a lime.
- Stir to warm the corn, then turn off the heat. The veggies should be just barely cooked and still firm
- Serve warm with a generous sprinkling of crumbled queso fresco, a dollop of pico de gallo, avocado slices, and extra lime wedges.

Nutrition

Calories: 222kcal, carbohydrates: 23g, protein: 7g, fat: 13g, saturatedfat: 8g, cholesterol: 34mg, sodium: 501mg, potassium: 474mg, fiber: 3g, sugar: 12g, vitamin c: 87mg, calcium: 153mg, iron: 1mg

5. Lean and Green "Chicken And Poultry Recipes

201. Baked Chicken Breast {Extra Juicy Healthy Recipe}

Prep Time: 5 minutes

Cook Time: 35 minutes

Total Time: 40 minutes

Servings: 8 servings

Ingredients

- 2 lbs boneless & skinless chicken breasts
- 1 tbsp avocado or olive oil
- 1 tsp smoked paprika
- 1 tsp garlic powder
- 1 tsp oregano
- 1/2 tsp salt
- Ground black pepper to taste

Instructions

- Preheat oven to 450 degrees F.
- In a medium baking dish, place chicken, drizzle with oil and sprinkle with smoked paprika, garlic powder, oregano, salt, and pepper. Using tongs or hands, move the chicken around to coat on all sides evenly (I place the bottom of the breast on top of the seasoned one and then swoosh around).
- Bake for 25 minutes (thinner) to 35 minutes (2"+) or until 150 degrees F internal temperature. Remove from the oven, cover with foil or lid, and let rest for 10 minutes for the juices to settle (don't skip!).
- ❖ Slice against the grain and serve along any side with a salad. Meal prep for the week, use in salads and casseroles.

Nutrition

Calories: 147kcal | Carbohydrates: 1g | Protein: 24g | Fat: 5g | SaturatedFat: 1g | Cholesterol: 73mg | Sodium: 277mg | Potassium: 430mg | Fiber: 1g | Sugar: 1g | Vitamin C: 1mg | Calcium: 8mg | Iron: 1mg

202. Greek Marinated Chicken

Prep Time: 5 minutes

Cook Time: 30 minutes

Total Time: 35 minutes

Servings: 8 people

Ingredients

- ounce tube of plain Greek Yogurt, (I use Chobani)
- 2 Tablespoons extra virgin olive oil (if you have flavored olive oil, use it!)
- 6 cloves fresh garlic, minced
- Half Tablespoon dried oregano
- 1 lemon, (juice and zest)
- 1/2 teaspoon salt
- 1/4 teaspoon pepper
- 1/4 cup fresh chopped parsley
- 4 lbs boneless and skinless chicken thighs and drumsticks

Instructions

- To make the marinade, combine the yogurt, olive oil, minced garlic, oregano, lemon juice, parsley, salt, and pepper in a bowl. Stir well.
- Use a cheese grater or zester to scrape a thin layer of lemon zest from half the lemon. Add lemon zest to the bowl of marinade ingredients.
- Grab a gallon-sized Ziplock bag and add the chicken pieces and marinade to the bag. Move the chicken around to ensure each piece is well coated.
- Refrigerate the chicken in the marinade for at least 1 hour. I like to marinate mine overnight! The longer the marinade, the more flavorful!
- After marinating, you can choose to grill the chicken or bake in the oven. If you bake in the oven, preheat the oven to 350 and bake for the breasts for 30 minutes. If you are making thighs and drumsticks, I like to cook them for 35-40 minutes to ensure done.
- If you choose to grill the chicken, grill for a total of 30-35 minutes or until the juices run clear and the chicken is done all the way through. Your chicken regardless of the cut needs to reach an internal temperature of 165 degrees Fahrenheit before it is considered done.
- Top with freshly grated lemon zest and serve.

Nutrition

Calories: 301kcal | Protein: 43g | Fat: 12g | Saturated Fat: 2g | Cholesterol: 215mg | Sodium: 347mg | Potassium: 555mg | Vitamin A: 55IU | Calcium: 20mg | Iron: 1.8mg

203. Chicken Piccata

Prep Time: 10 Minutes

Cook Time: 20 Minutes

Total Time: 30 Minutes

Ingredients

- 4 boneless skinless chicken breast halves
- salt and black pepper, to taste
- 1/3 cup flour, (I used gluten-free flour)
- 4 Tbsp butter
- 4 Tbsp olive oil
- 1/2 cup chicken stock or dry white wine
- 2 Tbsp lemon juice
- 2 Tbsp shallots, chopped
- 3 cloves garlic, minced
- 2 Tbsp drained capers
- 2 Tbsp chopped fresh parsley

Instructions

- Place each chicken breast between a plastic wrap and lightly pound it to 1/4-inch thickness. Season both sides of chicken breasts with salt and black pepper. Place flour in a shallow dish, and dip chicken breasts into flour to coat, shake off excess.
- Heat 2 Tbsp butter and 2 Tbsp olive oil in a large skillet over medium-high heat. Add chicken (in batches if necessary) to the skillet and cook until golden and cooked through, about 3 minutes per side. Transfer chicken to a platter; cover with foil to keep warm.
- Add the remaining 2 Tbsp olive oil, chicken stock (or white wine), lemon juice, shallots, and minced garlic to the skillet. Boil until the sauce thickens slightly, about 2 minutes. Stir in capers and the remaining 2 Tbsp butter.
- Plate the chicken and pour the lemon piccata sauce over the chicken. Sprinkle with parsley.

Nutrition

Calories: 410kcal | Carbohydrates: 10g | Protein: 38g | Fat: 23g | Saturated Fat: 9g | Cholesterol: 139mg | Sodium: 429mg | Potassium: 702mg | Vitamin A: 565IU | Vitamin C: 8.6mg | Calcium: 19mg | Iron: 1.4mg

204. Baked Chicken Cordon Bleu

Prep Time: 10 Mins

Cook Time: 25 Mins

Total Time: 35 Mins

Yield: 6 Servings

Ingredients

- Cooking spray
- 12 thin-sliced, 36 oz total skinless boneless chicken breasts, 3 oz each
- Salt and fresh cracked pepper
- 1 large egg
- 2 large egg whites
- 1 tbsp water
- 1/2 cup seasoned breadcrumbs

- 1/4 cup grated parmesan cheese
- 5 oz 6 slices thinly sliced lean deli ham, sliced in half
- 6 slices 4.4 oz sargento reduced-fat swiss cheese, cut in half

Instructions

- Preheat oven to 450°F. Spray a large non-stick baking sheet with cooking spray.
- Wash and dry the chicken cutlets; lightly pound the chicken to make thinner and lightly season with salt and black pepper.
- Lay the chicken on a working surface and place a slice of ham on top of the chicken, then the cheese and roll, setting them aside seam side down.
- In a medium bowl, whisk eggs and egg whites along with water to make an egg wash.
- In another medium bowl, combine breadcrumbs and parmesan cheese.
- Dip the chicken into the egg wash, then into the breadcrumbs.
- Place chicken onto the baking sheet seam side down. Spray the top of the chicken with more cooking spray and bake for about 25 minutes.

Nutrition

Calories: 378kcal, Carbohydrates: 8g, Protein: 55g, Fat: 10g, Sodium: 813mg, Fiber: 0.5g, Sugar: 1g

205. Perfect Grilled Chicken Breasts

Prep time: 2 minutes

Cook time: 20 minutes

Additional time: 10 minutes

Ingredients

- 6 chicken breasts
- 12 oz Italian dressing
- 1 tbsp garlic powder
- 3 tbsp soy sauce
- 1 tsp salt
- 1 tsp black pepper

Instructions

- Put chicken breasts in a large zip bag and cover with Italian dressing, garlic powder, and soy sauce.
- Gently squeeze the air out of the bag.
- Shake the bag so all the chicken is covered with a dressing.
- Place the bag in a bowl and refrigerate overnight.
- Pre-heat and clean grill- rubbing ½ an onion on the hot grill cleans and flavors the grates.
- Remove chicken from the bag with marinade.
- Season with salt and pepper.
- Cook chicken on medium-high heat until 165 internal temperature, about 15 minutes.
- Enjoy when hot, or refrigerate and use for s sack-lunch.

Nutrition

- Calories 345
- Total Fat 16g
- Saturated Fat 3g
- Trans Fat 0g
- Unsaturated Fat 12g
- Cholesterol 102mg
- Sodium 1480mg
- Carbohydrates 7g
- Fiber 0g
- Sugar 6g
- Protein 38g

206. Healthy Chicken Piccata

Prep Time: 30 Minutes

Cook Time: 25 Minutes

Total Time: 30 Minutes

Yield: 4 Servings

Ingredients

- 1 lemon
- 1 pound boneless skinless chicken breasts
- ¼ cup all-purpose flour
- ½ teaspoon salt
- ½ teaspoon ground pepper
- 1 tablespoon plus 4 teaspoons extra-virgin olive oil, divided
- 1 large sweet onion, sliced
- 1 clove garlic, minced
- 1 cup reduced-sodium chicken broth
- ¼ cup dry white wine
- 4 teaspoons drained capers
- ¼ cup chopped parsley

Instructions

- Prepare Lemon And Chicken: Cut lemon in half. Juice half of it, and cut the remaining half into thin slices. Cut chicken breasts into 8 thin cutlets.
- Dredge Chicken: Whisk flour, salt, and pepper in a shallow dish or pie plate. Dredge chicken in the flour mixture, turning to coat. Discard 2 teaspoons dredging flour and reserve the rest to thicken the sauce in step 5.
- Brown Chicken: Heat 2 teaspoons oil in a large non-stick skillet over medium-high heat. Add half the chicken and cook until the bottom is browned, 2 to 4 minutes. Turn over and continue cooking until browned on the bottom, 2 to 3 minutes. Set aside on a plate. Repeat with 2 teaspoons oil and the remaining 4 pieces of dredged chicken, adjusting the heat to medium-low to prevent the chicken from burning. Transfer the second batch of chicken to the plate.
- Cook Onions And Garlic: Wipe out the skillet with a clean paper towel. Add the remaining 1 tablespoon oil and place the skillet over medium-high heat. Add onion, and cook, stirring often until soft and browned 5 to 7 minutes. Add garlic, and cook, stirring constantly until the garlic is fragrant and just starting to brown, 30 to 90 seconds.
- Make Sauce: Sprinkle the remaining dredging flour over the onion mixture and stir to coat. Stir in broth, white wine, capers, lemon slices, and the lemon juice, increase heat to high and bring to a simmer, stirring constantly.
- Finish Dish: Add the chicken and any accumulated juices from the plate to the skillet and turn to coat in the sauce. Bring to a simmer while turning the chicken in the sauce until the sauce is thickened, and the chicken is completely cooked through and hot, 3 to 4 minutes. Stir in parsley, remove from the heat and serve.

Nutrition

- Calories: 264
- Sugar: 2 G
- Sodium: 550 Mg
- Fat: 9 G

- Saturated Fat: 1 G
- Carbohydrates: 14 G
- Fiber: 1 G
- Protein: 28 G

207. One Pan Parmesan Tuscan Chicken

Prep Time: 5 Minutes

Cook Time: 30 Minutes

Total Time: 35 Minutes

Ingredients

- 1 lb chicken breasts
- 1 tbs vegetable oil spread
- 8 oz sliced baby bella mushrooms
- 4 cloves garlic, minced
- 1 ½ cups almond milk
- ½ cup nonfat greek yogurt
- 1 tbs cornstarch + 2 tbs water
- ¼ cup shaved parmesan cheese
- ¼ cup sun-dried tomatoes
- Salt and pepper to taste
- Parsley (optional garnish)

Instructions

- Spray medium nonstick skillet and turn on the heat to medium-high. Add the chicken breasts to the skillet, season with salt and pepper, and cook all the way through, approx 8-10 minutes on each side. Transfer the chicken breasts to a plate.
- Melt the vegetable oil spread in the skillet and then add the garlic and mushrooms. Cook until the mushrooms are browned and tender. Add the almond milk, Greek yogurt, garlic powder, and Parmesan cheese. Whisk occasionally until the cheese has fully melted and the sauce begins to boil. Mix the cornstarch with the water to create a slurry and whisk into the sauce. Once the sauce begins to boil and thicken, reduce the heat to low and add the chicken back to the skillet along with the sun-dried tomatoes. Simmer until the chicken is warm, approx 5 minutes.

Nutrition

- Calories: 304
- Total Fat: 9g
- Saturated Fat: 5g

- Trans Fat: 0g
- UnsaturatedFat: 7g
- Cholesterol: 105mg
- Sodium: 473mg
- Carbohydrates: 8g
- Fiber: 2g
- Sugar: 6g
- Protein: 44g

208. Skinny Orange Chicken

Prep Time: 10 Minutes

Cook Time: 10 Minutes

Total Time: 20 Minutes

Yield: About 4-6 Servings

Orange Chicken Ingredients:

- 2 Lb. Boneless, Skinless Chicken Breasts, Cut Into Bite-Sized Pieces
- Salt And Pepper
- 2 Tbsp. Olive Oil
- Orange Chicken Sauce (Ingredients Below)
- Toppings: Thinly-Sliced Green Onions, Toasted Sesame Seeds, Orange Zest

Orange Chicken Sauce Ingredients:

- 3 cloves garlic, minced
- 1/2 cup orange juice
- 1/2 cup honey
- 1/3 cup soy sauce
- 1/4 cup rice wine vinegar
- 3 tbsp. Cornstarch
- 1/2 tsp. Ground ginger
- 1/2 tsp. White pepper
- Zest of one orange
- Pinch of crushed red pepper flakes

Instructions

To Make The Orange Chicken:

- Season chicken generously with salt and pepper.
- Heat oil in a large saute pan over medium-high heat. Add chicken and saute for about 4-6 minutes, stirring occasionally, until the chicken is browned and nearly cooked through.
- Pour in the orange chicken sauce, and stir to combine. Let the sauce come to a boil, then boil for an additional minute or two until thickened. Remove from heat and serve immediately over

quinoa or rice. Garnish with green onions, sesame seeds, and additional orange zest.

To Make The Orange Chicken Sauce:

- Whisk all ingredients together until combined. If you would like the sauce to be even sweeter, add an extra 2-4 tablespoons of honey.

209. Blackened Chicken

Prep: 10 mins

Cook: 10 mins

Total: 20 mins

Servings: 2

Ingredients

- ½ Teaspoon paprika
- ⅛ teaspoon salt
- ¼ teaspoon cayenne pepper
- ¼ teaspoon ground cumin
- ¼ teaspoon dried thyme
- ⅛ teaspoon ground white pepper
- ⅛ teaspoon onion powder
- 2 skinless, boneless chicken breast halves

Directions

- Preheat oven to 350 degrees F (175 degrees C). Lightly grease a baking sheet. Heat a cast-iron skillet over high heat for 5 minutes until it is smoking hot.
- Mix the paprika, salt, cayenne, cumin, thyme, white pepper, and onion powder. Oil the chicken breasts with cooking spray on both sides, then coat the chicken breasts evenly with the spice mixture.
- Place the chicken in the hot pan, and cook for 1 minute. Turn, and cook for 1 minute on another side. Place the breasts on the prepared baking sheet.
- Bake in the preheated oven until no longer pink in the center and the juices run clear for about 5 minutes.

Nutrition

- Calories: 135.1
- Protein: 24.7g
- Carbohydrates: 0.9g
- Dietary Fiber: 0.4g
- Sugars: 0.1g

- Fat: 3g
- Saturated Fat: 0.8g
- Cholesterol: 67.2mg
- Vitamin A Iu: 421.1IU
- Niacin Equivalents: 15.7mg
- Vitamin B6: 0.5mg
- Vitamin C: 0.7mg
- Folate: 4.8mcg
- Calcium: 20mg
- Iron: 1.4mg
- Magnesium: 26mg
- Potassium: 227.7mg
- Sodium: 204.7mg
- Thiamin: 0.1mg
- Calories From Fat: 27.1

210. Slow Cooker Buffalo Chicken Soup

Prep Time: 15 MINUTES

Cook Time: 2 HOURS

Total Time: 2 HOURS 15 MINUTES

Servings: 6

Ingredients

- 1 tablespoon butter
- 1/2 large onion peeled and chopped
- 2 cloves garlic minced
- 3 large carrots sliced
- 3 celery stalks sliced
- 1 pound boneless skinless chicken breast
- 1/4 cup Frank's Red Hot cayenne sauce
- 1/4 cup good blue cheese dressing could also use the low-cal dressing
- 4 cups chicken stock
- 1/2 cup crispy tortilla chip strips
- 1/4 cup crumbled blue cheese
- 1/4 cup chopped green onions

Instructions

- Place a skillet over medium heat and add the butter. Once the butter has melted add the onions, garlic, carrots, and celery. Saute for 5 minutes to soften.

Slow Cooker Method:

- Place the sautéed garlic and onions, carrots, celery, chicken breasts, Franks hot sauce, blue cheese dressing, and chicken stock in a

crockpot. Cover and turn on. Cook on high for 2-3 hours, or low for 4-5 hours.
- Once the chicken has cooked through, take the chicken breasts out. Using two forks, shred the chicken and place it back in the soup.

Stovetop Method:

- Place the sautéed garlic and onions, carrots, celery, chicken breasts, Franks hot sauce, blue cheese dressing, and chicken stock in a stockpot. Cover and bring to a boil. Then lower the heat and simmer for 15 minutes.
- ❖ Once the soup has cooked, take the chicken breasts out. Using two forks, shred the chicken and place it back in the soup.

To serve:

- Scoop the Buffalo Chicken Soup into bowls and sprinkle with crunchy tortilla strips, crumbled blue cheese, and green onions.

Nutrition

- Calories: 223kcal, Carbohydrates: 12g, Protein: 22g, Fat: 9g, Saturated Fat: 3g, Cholesterol: 63mg, Sodium: 861mg, Potassium: 637mg, Fiber: 1g, Sugar: 5g, Vitamin C: 5.4mg, Calcium: 72mg, Iron: 0.9mg

211. Buffalo Chicken Casserole (Chicken And Rice Recipe)

Prep Time: 10 Minutes

Cook Time: 25 Minutes

Total Time: 35 Minutes

Servings: 8

Ingredients

- 1 1/2 pound boneless chicken breast, cut into bite-size pieces
- 2 tablespoons butter
- 1 cup chopped onions
- 1 cup chopped celery
- 1 1/2 cups long-grain rice
- 1/2 cup Frank's RedHot Sauce
- 2 1/2 cups water or chicken broth
- 1 cup shredded cheddar cheese
- 1/2 cup crumbled blue cheese
- 1/4 cup chopped green onions

Instructions

- Cut the chicken into 1-inch bite-size pieces. Chop all the vegetables.
- Place the butter in a large skillet or sauté pan, with a lid. Set over medium heat. Add the chopped onions and celery. Sauté for 3-5 minutes to soften.
- Add the chicken pieces, rice, hot sauce, broth, and 1/4 teaspoon salt. Stir, then cover the skillet. Bring to a boil. Lower the heat and simmer for 15 minutes, or until the broth has absorbed and there are air vent holes in the top of the rice.
- Fluff the rice with a fork. Stir in the cheddar, blue cheese, and green onions. Taste, then salt and pepper as needed.

Nutrition

Calories: 346kcal, carbohydrates: 30g, protein: 26g, fat: 12g, saturatedfat: 6g, cholesterol: 83mg, sodium: 806mg, potassium: 460mg, fiber: 1g, sugar: 1g, vitamin a: 405iu, vitamin c: 3.5mg, calcium: 175mg, iron: 0.8mg

212. Buffalo Chicken Chili (Stovetop, Crockpot, And Instant Pot)

Prep Time: 10 Minutes

Cook Time: 45 Minutes

Total Time: 55 Minutes

Servings: 8 Servings

Ingredients

- 2 tablespoons olive oil or butter
- 1 large onion peeled and chopped
- 4-6 cloves garlic minced
- 1 cup diced celery
- 1 cup diced carrots
- 1 ½ pound boneless chicken thighs or breasts
- 30 ounces canned red kidney beans rinsed and drained
- 28 ounces crushed tomatoes
- 8 ounces chopped green chiles mild or hot
- ½ – 1 cup Frank's RedHot cayenne pepper sauce
- Optional Toppings: sour cream, cheddar, blue cheese, scallions

Instructions

Stovetop:

- Set a large 6-quart pot over medium heat. Add the olive oil, onions, and garlic. Salt and pepper generously. Then sauté for 2-3 minutes. Next, add the celery and carrots. Stir and sauté another 3-5 minutes to soften.
- Place the whole chicken pieces in the pot. Add in the beans, crushed tomatoes, green chiles, and cayenne pepper sauce. If you like a lot of spice, use 1 cup of sauce. If you are nervous about the heat level, start with ½ cup, and use mild green chiles as well.
- Cover and simmer for 20-25 minutes, stirring every 5 minutes, so the beans don't stick to the bottom.
- Once the chicken is cooked through, remove the chicken pieces with tongs and use two forks to shred them into bite-size chunks. Place the shredded chicken back into the chili. Stir to combine.
- Simmer another 10-15 minutes, stirring regularly. Serve warm, with sour cream, cheese, and scallions.

Crockpot:

- Set a large skillet over medium heat. Add the olive oil, onions, and garlic. Salt and pepper generously. Then sauté for 2-3 minutes. Next, add the celery and carrots. Stir and sauté another 3-5 minutes to soften.
- Move the veggies to a large 6-quart slow cooker. Place the whole chicken pieces in the crock. Add in the beans, crushed tomatoes, green chiles, and cayenne pepper sauce. If you like a lot of spice, use 1 cup sauce. If you are nervous about the heat level, start with ½ cup, and use mild green chiles as well.
- Cover the crockpot and set on LOW for 5-6 hours, or on HIGH for 2-3 hours.
- Once the chicken is cooked through, remove the chicken pieces with tongs and use two forks to shred them into bite-size chunks. Place the shredded chicken back into the slow cooker. Stir to combine.
- Simmer another 10-15 minutes. Serve warm, with sour cream, cheese, and scallions.

Instant Pot:

- Pull out a large 6 quart Instant Pot and set to Sauté. Add the olive oil, onions, and garlic. Salt and pepper generously. Then sauté for 2-3 minutes. Next, add the celery and carrots. Stir and sauté another 3-5 minutes to soften.

- Place the whole chicken pieces in the pot. Add in the beans, crushed tomatoes, green chiles, and cayenne pepper sauce. If you like a lot of spice, use 1 cup sauce. If you are nervous about the heat level, start with ½ cup, and use mild green chiles as well.
- Lock the lid into place and set on Pressure Cook High for 15 minutes Then perform a Quick Release. Once the valve button drops it is safe to open the pot.
- Remove the chicken pieces with tongs and use two forks to shred them into bite-size chunks. Place the shredded chicken back into the slow cooker. Stir to combine.
- Simmer another 10-15 minutes on the Sauté setting. Serve warm, with sour cream, cheese, and scallions.

Nutrition

Calories: 411kcal, Carbohydrates: 37g, Protein: 26g, Fat: 19g, Saturatedfat: 4g, Cholesterol: 83mg, Sodium: 1523mg, Potassium: 1100mg, Fiber: 11g, Sugar: 7g, Vitamin A: 3118iu, Vitamin C: 57mg, Calcium: 100mg, Iron: 6mg

213. Buffalo Chicken Salad

Prep Time: 10 Minutes

Total Time: 10 Minutes

Servings: 8

Ingredients

- 4 cups chopped cooked chicken (leftover or rotisserie)
- 1 cup finely chopped celery
- 3/4 cup finely chopped carrots
- 3/4 cup mayonnaise (Paleo version below)
- 1/2 cup cayenne pepper sauce (like Frank's RedHot)
- 1/4 cup crumbled blue cheese (omit for paleo version)
- 2 tablespoons chopped parsley
- 2 tablespoon chopped chive
- 1 tablespoon chopped dill

Instructions

- Set out a large mixing bowl. Chop the chicken, vegetables, and herbs. Place them all in the bowl. Add in the mayonnaise, cayenne pepper sauce, and crumbled blue cheese. Mix well. Cover and refrigerate until ready to serve.

Nutrition

Calories: 168kcal, Carbohydrates: 2g, Protein: 2g, Fat: 17g, Saturatedfat: 3g, Cholesterol: 12mg, Sodium: 674mg, Potassium: 127mg, Fiber: 1g, Sugar: 1g, Vitamin A: 2722iu, Vitamin C: 10mg, Calcium: 45mg, Iron: 1mg

214. Perfect Baked Chicken Thighs

Prep Time: 5 Minutes

Cook Time: 25 Minutes

Total Time: 30 Minutes

Servings: 6

Ingredients

- 2 Tablespoons Olive Oil
- 6 Large, Bone-In Chicken Thighs, Or 8-10 Small
- 3-5 Sprigs Of Fresh Thyme
- 3-5 Sprigs Of Fresh Rosemary
- 1 Lemon, Sliced Into Rounds
- 1/2 Teaspoon Garlic Powder
- Salt And Pepper

Instructions

- Preheat the oven to 450 degrees F. Set a 12- to 14-inch cast-iron skillet on the stovetop over medium-high heat. Add the olive oil.
- Pat the skin on the chicken thighs dry with paper towels. Sprinkle the thighs with garlic powder. Then sprinkle generously with salt and ground black pepper.
- Once the oil is smoking hot, place the thighs in the skillet, skin side down. Sear for 5-7 minutes until the skin is golden-brown.
- Flip the chicken thighs over and add the fresh herb sprigs and the lemon slices.
- Place the entire skillet in the oven and roast for 15-18 minutes. Serve warm.

Nutrition

Calories: 290kcal, Carbohydrates: 0g, Protein: 18g, Fat: 23g, Saturated Fat: 5g, Cholesterol:

110mg, Sodium: 87mg, Potassium: 231mg, Fiber: 0g, Sugar: 0gvitamin C: 2.1mg, Calcium: 11mg, Iron: 0.8mg

215. Pozole Verde De Pollo (Chicken Pozole)

Prep Time: 15 Minutes

Cook Time: 1 Hour 10 Minutes

Total Time: 1 Hour 25 Minutes

Servings: 8 Servings

Ingredients

- 2 tablespoons olive oil
- 1 large sweet onion peeled and chopped
- 6-8 cloves garlic minced
- 6 poblano peppers seeded and chopped
- 2-3 jalapeno peppers seeded and chopped (optional for heat)
- ½ cup chopped cilantro
- 3 pounds boneless chicken thighs
- 1 ½ pounds tomatillos peeled and quartered
- 2 bay leaves
- 1 tablespoon dried oregano
- 6 cups chicken broth or water
- 2 – 15 ounce cans white hominy drained and rinsed
- Salt and pepper
- Garnishes: tortilla chips, shredded cabbage, lime wedges, sliced avocado, sliced radishes, chopped cilantro

Instructions

- Set a heavy 6-8 quart dutch oven over medium heat. Add the oil to the pot. Add in the chopped onion and garlic. Sauté for 2 minutes, then add in the chopped poblanos, jalapenos, and cilantro. Sauté another 8 minutes, stirring regularly.
- Place the chicken thighs, tomatillos, bay leaves, oregano, chicken broth, and 1 teaspoon salt.
- Cover the pot with a heavy lid and bring to a boil. Then lower the heat and simmer for 50-60 minutes, until the chicken is soft enough to shred. (Keep the pot covered.)
- Remove the chicken thighs, and bay leaves. Use tongs or forks to shred the chicken into small chunks.

- Add the shredded chicken back to the pot, along with the rinsed hominy. Stir to combine. Simmer another 2-3 minutes to warm the hominy. Taste, then season with salt and pepper as needed. Keep warm until ready to serve.
- To serve: Ladle the posole into bowls. Garnish the top with tortilla chips, shredded cabbage, sliced avocado, radishes, lime wedges, and cilantro.

Nutrition

Calories: 477kcal, Carbohydrates: 15g, Protein: 31g, Fat: 33g, Saturatedfat: 8g, Cholesterol: 167mg, Sodium: 785mg, Potassium: 954mg, Fiber: 4g, Sugar: 8g, Vitamin A: 676iu, Vitamin C: 101mg, Calcium: 61mg, Iron: 3mg

216. Creamy Parmesan Chicken And Rice Soup

Prep Time: 15 Minutes

Cook Time: 30 Minutes

Total Time: 45 Minutes

Servings: 8 People

Ingredients

- 2 Tablespoons Butter
- 1 Large Sweet Onion, Peeled And Chopped
- 1 Cup Chopped Carrots
- 1 Cup Chopped Celery
- 4 Cloves Garlic, Minced
- 1 Tablespoon Fresh Thyme Leaves, 1 Tsp Dried Thyme
- 1 Bay Leaf
- 1 Pound Boneless Chicken Thighs, Or Breasts
- 10 Cups Chicken Broth, Or Water + 10 Tsp Chicken Bouillon
- 1 Cup Dried Long-Grain Rice
- 2/3 Cup Grated Parmesan Cheese
- 3 Tablespoons Cornstarch
- 3 Tablespoons Chopped Parsley
- Salt And Pepper

Instructions

- Place a large 6-8 quart pot over medium heat. Add the butter. Once melted add in the onions, carrots, celery, and garlic. Sauté for 3-5 minutes, stirring to soften.

- Add in the thyme, bay leaf, chicken thighs, and chicken broth. Bring to a boil. Once boiling, stir in the dried rice.
- Cover and simmer for 12 minutes. Then use tongs to remove the chicken thighs. Use two forks to shred the chicken into bite-size pieces. Continue to simmer the soup uncovered, while you shred the chicken.
- Mix the grated parmesan cheese with the cornstarch. Stir the chicken back into the soup. Continue stirring as you add the parmesan mixture into the soup. Simmer another 2-4 minutes to thicken the soup base.
- Taste. Then salt and pepper as needed. Remove the bay leaf and stir in the fresh parsley. Serve warm.

Nutrition

Calories: 321kcal, Carbohydrates: 29g, Protein: 16g, Fat: 16g, Saturatedfat: 6g, Cholesterol: 70mg, Sodium: 1298mg, Potassium: 541mg, Fiber: 2g, Sugar: 3g, Vitamin A: 3101iu, Vitamin C: 28mg, Calcium: 148mg, Iron: 2mg

217. Creamy White Chicken Chili (3 Ways!)

Prep Time: 15 Minutes

Cook Time: 25 Minutes

Total Time: 40 Minutes

Servings: 8 Servings

Ingredients

- 2 tablespoons butter
- 1 large sweet onion peeled and chopped
- 3-4 cloves garlic minced
- ¼ cup chopped cilantro
- 1 tablespoon ground cumin
- 1 teaspoon dried oregano
- 1 ½ pound boneless chicken breast
- 30 ounces canned cannellini beans drained
- 7 ounces chopped green chiles mild or hot
- 1 cup frozen corn
- 4 cups chicken broth
- 8 ounces cream cheese cut into cubes (could be low fat)
- Possible Garnishes: cilantro scallions, tortilla chips, lime wedges, shredded pepper jack cheese, avocado

Instructions

On The Stovetop:

- Set a large 6+ quart saucepot over medium heat. Add the butter, chopped onion, minced garlic, cilantro, cumin, and oregano. Stir and sauté for 3-5 minutes.
- Add the whole chicken breasts, beans, green chiles, corn, chicken broth, and ½ teaspoon salt. Bring to a simmer. Lower the heat, cover, and simmer for 20-30 minutes. Meanwhile, cut the cream cheese into cubes.
- Use tongs to remove the chicken breasts. Stir the cream cheese cubes into the chili base. Use two forks to shred the chicken into bite-size chunks. Then stir the shredded chicken back into the pot.
- Taste, then salt and pepper as needed. Garnish with your favorite toppings.

Crockpot Instructions:

- Set a large skillet over medium heat. Add the butter, chopped onion, minced garlic, cilantro, cumin, and oregano. Sauté for 3-5 minutes.
- Pour the sautéed veggies into a large 6+ quart slow cooker. Add the whole chicken breasts, beans, green chiles, corn, chicken broth, cream cheese, and ½ teaspoon salt. Cover and set on LOW for 7-8 hours or on HIGH for 3-4 hours.
- Use tongs to remove the chicken breasts. Use two forks to shred the chicken into bite-size chunks. Then stir the shredded chicken back into the crock.
- Taste, then salt and pepper as needed. Garnish with your favorite toppings.

Instant Pot Instructions:

- Set a large 6+ Instant Pot on Sauté. Add the butter, chopped onion, minced garlic, cilantro, cumin, and oregano. Sauté for 3-5 minutes.
- Add the whole chicken breasts, beans, green chiles, corn, chicken broth, and ½ teaspoon salt. Lock the lid into place and set the Instant Pot on Pressure Cook High for 20 minutes. Meanwhile, cut the cream cheese into cubes.
- Perform a Quick Release. Once the steam button drops, it's safe to open the lid.
- Use tongs to remove the chicken breasts. Stir the cream cheese cubes into the chili base. Use

two forks to shred the chicken into bite-size chunks. Then stir the shredded chicken back into the pot. If the chili seems thin, set the IP back on sauté and simmer for 3-5 minutes to thicken.

- Taste, then salt and pepper to taste. Garnish with your favorite toppings.

Nutrition

Calories: 229kcal, Carbohydrates: 13g, Protein: 22g, Fat: 10g, Saturatedfat: 5g, Cholesterol: 77mg, Sodium: 792mg, Potassium: 635mg, Fiber: 2g, Sugar: 4g, Vitamin A: 344iu, Vitamin C: 22mg, Calcium: 83mg, Iron: 2mg

218. Homemade Chicken Noodle Soup Recipe

Prep Time: 10 Minutes

Cook Time: 50 Minutes

Total Time: 1 Hour

Servings: 10

Ingredients

- 1 teaspoon oil or butter
- 2 1/2 pounds bone-in chicken thighs (or a mix of thighs and breasts)
- 1 large sweet onion, peeled and chopped
- 2-4 cloves garlic, minced
- 1 1/2 cups sliced celery
- 1 1/2 cups sliced carrots
- 1 tablespoon fresh thyme leaves (1 teaspoon dried)
- 12 cups chicken broth
- 2 bay leaves
- 1/4 teaspoon turmeric
- 8-ounce Kluski egg noodles
- 1/4 cup chopped parsley
- 2 tablespoons fresh lemon juice
- 1 1/2 teaspoons cornstarch
- Salt and pepper

Instructions

- Set a large 6-8 quart soup pot over medium heat. Add the oil. Generously salt and pepper the chicken thighs on both sides. Place them skin-side down in the pot. Brown the chicken skin, then flip and cook the chicken for another 3 minutes. Remove the chicken from the pot and set it aside.

- Place the onions and garlic in the chicken fat. Stir and saute for 3-4 minutes. Then stir in the celery, carrots, and thyme and saute for another 2 minutes.
- Add the chicken broth, bay leaves, and turmeric to the pot. Then place the chicken thighs in the broth. Season with 3/4 teaspoon salt, and 1/4 teaspoon black pepper. Stir well. Cover and simmer for 30 minutes. (Turn the heat down a little, if needed.)
- Use tongs to pull out the bay leaves, and chicken thighs. Place the chicken on a cutting board. Then stir the egg noodles into the soup and simmer another 6-9 minutes, until the pasta is cooked.
- Meanwhile, remove the chicken skins and bones. Shred the chicken with a fork. Then stir the chicken back into the soup.
- When the noodles are almost cooked, measure the cornstarch and lemon juice into a small bowl. Whisk well. Then stir the mixture into the soup to thicken the base a little. Finally, stir in the chopped parsley. Taste, then salt and pepper as needed.

Nutrition

Calories: 279kcal, Carbohydrates: 23g, Protein: 16g, Fat: 13g, Saturatedfat: 4g, Cholesterol: 87mg, Sodium: 1122mg, Potassium: 573mg, Fiber: 2g, Sugar: 3g, Vitamin A: 3520iu, Vitamin C: 27mg, Calcium: 55mg, Iron: 2mg

219. Cheesy Chicken Alfredo Pasta Bake

Prep Time: 10 Minutes

Cook Time: 35 Minutes

Total Time: 45 Minutes

Servings: 12 Servings

Ingredients

- 1 pound dried penne or another similar shape
- 1 pound cooked chicken chopped (leftover or rotisserie)
- ¼ cup butter
- ¼ cup all-purpose flour
- 5-6 cloves garlic minced
- 4 cups half & half
- 2 teaspoons Italian seasoning

- 2 teaspoons chicken bouillon
- 3 cups shredded mozzarella cheese divided
- 1 cup grated parmesan
- Parsley for garnish

Instructions

- Preheat the oven to 350 degrees F. Set out a 9X13 inch baking dish.
- Set a large pot of salted water over high heat. Once boiling, stir in the penne and cook according to the package instructions. Then drain the pasta, reserving 1 cup of pasta water for later use.
- Meanwhile, set a second large saucepot over medium heat. Add the butter. Once melted, whisk in the flour. Then whisk in the minced garlic. Continue to whisk for 1-2 minutes until the roux is golden in color.
- Stir in the half & half, Italian seasoning, and bouillon. Once the mixture is hot, stir in 1 cup shredded mozzarella, and 1 cup parmesan cheese. Stir and simmer until the cheese is well incorporated.
- The sauce should be thick, but still saucy, not like gravy. If it seems too thick, mix in ½ to 1 cup pasta water. Then mix in the cooked pasta and chicken pieces.
- Pour the pasta mix into the baking dish. Spread out evenly. Then sprinkle the remaining 2 cups of mozzarella cheese over the top.
- Bake for 20-25 minutes, until the sides are bubbling and the cheese on top is melted with crispy edges. Serve warm.

Nutrition

Calories: 450kcal, Carbohydrates: 35g, Protein: 21g, Fat: 25g, Saturatedfat: 14g, Cholesterol: 83mg, Sodium: 388mg, Potassium: 264mg, Fiber: 1g, Sugar: 2g, Vitamin A: 696iu, Vitamin C: 1mg, Calcium: 337mg, Iron: 1mg

220. Chicken Bog (Rice Pilaf Recipe)

Prep Time: 15 Minutes

Cook Time: 50 Minutes

Total Time: 1 Hour 5 Minutes

Servings: 8 Servings

Ingredients

- 1 tablespoon butter
- 1 pound kielbasa sausage sliced and halved
- 1 cup diced sweet onion
- 1 cup diced carrots
- 1 cup diced celery
- 2-3 cloves garlic minced
- 2 teaspoons dried thyme
- ¼ – ½ teaspoon crushed red pepper
- 2 pounds bone-in chicken thighs
- 4 cups chicken broth
- 2 cups long-grain white rice
- 1 cup frozen peas
- Salt and pepper
- Hot sauce for serving

Instructions

- Set a large 6+ quart saucepot over medium heat. Add the butter. Once melted, stir in the sliced kielbasa. Brown the sausage for 2 minutes.
- Then stir in the diced onions, carrots, celery, garlic, thyme, and crushed red pepper. Sauté for 3-5 minutes.
- Meanwhile, liberally salt and pepper the chicken pieces. Once the veggies have softened, push them to the sides and move the chicken pieces to the bottom of the pot, skin-side-down. Brown for 2-3 minutes. Flip the chicken over and add the broth, 1 teaspoon salt, and ½ teaspoon black pepper.
- Cover and simmer on medium to medium-low for 25 minutes. Remove the chicken pieces with tongs. Discard the skins and bones. Break the chicken meat up a little bit, then stir the chicken chunks back into the broth.
- Use a wooden spoon to clear any stuck-on debris from the bottom of the pot. Stir in the rice. Then cover and cook the rice for 15 minutes.
- Once the rice is soft and you see vent holes in the top layer of rice, turn off the heat.
- Stir in the frozen peas to warm. Taste, then add salt and pepper as needed. Serve with hot sauce on the side.

Nutrition

Calories: 652kcal, Carbohydrates: 45g, Protein: 32g, Fat: 37g, Saturated Fat: 12g, Cholesterol:

155mg, Sodium: 1054mg, Potassium: 666mg, Fiber: 2g, Sugar: 3g, Vitamin A: 3029iu, Vitamin C: 19mg, Calcium: 61mg, Iron: 3mg

221. Low Carb Creamy Chicken Mushroom Soup

Prep Time: 10 Minutes

Cook Time: 23 Minutes

Total Time: 33 Minutes

Servings: 8

Ingredients

- 2 tablespoons unsalted butter
- 1 large sweet onion, peeled and chopped
- 1 cup chopped celery
- 5-6 cloves garlic, peeled and minced
- 18 ounces sliced mushrooms, mixed varieties
- 1 teaspoon fresh chopped rosemary
- 1 teaspoon dried thyme
- 1/3 cup dry sherry
- 1 pound boneless chicken breast
- 8 cups chicken broth
- 2/3 cup heavy cream
- 1 tablespoon cornstarch (or arrowroot for ketogenic)
- 1/4 cup chopped parsley
- ❖ Salt and pepper

Instructions

- Add the butter to a large 6-8 quart soup pot and set over medium heat. Once melted add the onions, celery, and garlic.
- Sauté for 2-3 minutes, then add in the mushrooms, rosemary, and thyme. Sauté until the mushrooms soften and cook down.
- Deglaze the pot with dry sherry. Then add in the whole chicken breasts, chicken broth, 1 teaspoon salt, and 1/4 teaspoon black pepper. Bring to a boil. Then lower the heat and simmer for 15 minutes, or until the chicken breasts have cooked through.
- When the chicken is fully cooked, remove the breasts with tongs, and chop into bite-size pieces.
- Whisk the cornstarch into the heavy cream, making sure there are no clumps. Then whisk the heavy cream into the soup pot and allow it to simmer and thicken. Stir the chopped chicken

back into the soup and add the parsley. Taste, then salt and pepper as needed.

Nutrition

Calories: 215kcal, Carbohydrates: 9g, Protein: 16g, Fat: 12g, Saturatedfat: 6g, Cholesterol: 70mg, Sodium: 952mg, Potassium: 722mg, Fiber: 1g, Sugar: 3g, Vitamin A: 610iu, Vitamin C: 24mg, Calcium: 53mg, Iron: 1.5mg

222. Easy Chicken Kiev Recipe

Prep Time: 15 Minutes

Cook Time: 10 Minutes

Total Time: 25 Minutes

Servings: 4 Servings

Ingredients

- 4 small boneless chicken breasts
- 6 tablespoons butter
- 4 teaspoons parsley chopped
- 1 clove garlic minced
- 1 teaspoon lemon pepper seasoning
- 2 large eggs
- 1 ½ cups panko breadcrumbs
- ½ cup all-purpose flour
- 2 teaspoons salt
- Oil for frying

Instructions

- Lay the chicken breasts out on a cutting board. With a knife parallel to the board, "butterfly" each breast by cutting it through the middle, leaving one long edge intact, so you can open it like a book.
- Open the breasts. In the center of each breast place: 1 ½ tablespoons butter, 1 teaspoon chopped parsley, a scant sprinkle of fresh minced garlic, and a generous sprinkle of lemon pepper seasoning.
- Close the chicken breast over the filling pressing around the edges.
- Set out three shallow pans. Place the eggs in one, then beat the eggs. Place the panko breadcrumbs in the second pan. Place the flour and salt in the third pan. Toss to mix the salt into the flour.
- Set a large skillet over medium heat. Add approximately ¾ inch of oil.

- One at a time, dunk the closed chicken breasts in flour, then in egg mixture, then in the panko breadcrumbs to create a crust. (It's important that the eggs thoroughly coat the entire surface of the breasts, as to "glue" the breasts shut so the butter doesn't seep out while cooking.)
- Once the oil is hot, carefully place the chicken breasts in the skillet. Cook for 4-5 minutes per side, gently flipping once, so the oil doesn't splatter.
- Remove from the pan and rest on a paper towel-lined plate to absorb the excess oil. Serve warm.

Nutrition

Calories: 459kcal, carbohydrates: 29g, protein: 32g, fat: 23g, saturated fat: 12g, cholesterol: 199mg, sodium: 1640mg, potassium: 509mg, fiber: 2g, sugar: 2g, vitamin a: 677iu, vitamin c: 2mg, calcium: 64mg, iron: 3mg

223. Parmesan Pesto Chicken Recipe

Prep Time: 3 Minutes

Cook Time: 20 Minutes

Total Time: 23 Minutes

Servings: 4

Ingredients

- 1 1/4 pounds boneless skinless chicken breast 2 large or 3-4 average breasts
- 1/4 cup DeLallo Traditional Basil Simply Pesto
- 3 tablespoons shaved Parmesan cheese
- Salt and pepper

Instructions

- Preheat the oven to 400 degrees F. Place the chicken breasts in a rimmed baking dish and pat dry with a paper towel.
- Scoop 1/4 cup DeLallo Simply Pesto on the chicken and rub to coat the chicken on both sides. Sprinkle with salt and pepper, then top each chicken breast with shaved parmesan cheese.
- Bake for 15-20 minutes, until the chicken, is just cooked through. Allow the chicken to rest for at least five minutes. Then slice and serve over Italian Pasta Salad with Sweet Oranges, Basil, and Golden Tomatoes.

Nutrition

Calories: 236kcal, Carbohydrates: 1g, Protein: 32g, Fat: 10g, Saturatedfat: 2g, Cholesterol: 95mg, Sodium: 369mg, Potassium: 524mg, Fiber: 1g, Sugar: 1g, Vitamin A: 385iu, Vitamin C: 1.7mg, Calcium: 76mg, Iron: 0.6mg

224. Instant Pot Italian Chicken Orzo

Prep Time: 10 Minutes

Cook Time: 16 Minutes

Total Time: 26 Minutes

Servings: 4 +

Ingredients

- 2-2 1/2 pounds bone-in chicken thighs (4-6 thighs)
- 1 tablespoon olive oil
- 3/4 cup chopped onion
- 2 cloves garlic, minced
- 3 cups water
- 28 ounces fire-roasted diced tomatoes
- 1-2 sprigs of fresh rosemary
- 3-5 sprigs of fresh thyme
- 12 ounces dry orzo pasta
- 1/3 cup fresh basil leaves, torn
- Salt and pepper

Instructions

- Place the oil in the Instant Pot and set it on Sauté. Salt and pepper the chicken pieces on both sides. Then place them skin-side-down in the Instant Pot. Sauté for 5 minutes per side, then remove from the pot. Scrape the bottom of the pot with a metal spatula to loosen any chicken skin.
- Next, add the onions and garlic to the pan juices. Sauté for 1-2 minutes. Then pour in the water and use a metal spatula to thoroughly deglaze the bottom of the pot. (Any skin or debris stuck to the bottom of the pot could later result in a "burn" notice.)
- Add the fresh herbs and diced tomatoes. Season with 1 1/2 teaspoons salt and stir well. Set the chicken thighs back in the pot. Then pour the orzo on top. Lock the lid into place and set the Instant Pot on Pressure Cook High for 4 minutes.

(The orzo must go in last so it doesn't stick to the bottom of the pot.)

- Once the timer goes off, turn off the Instant Pot and perform a Quick Release. When the steam valve button drops, it's safe to open the top. Remove all herb stems. Taste the orzo, and season with salt and pepper as needed. Stir in the fresh basil and serve.

Nutrition

Calories: 407kcal, Carbohydrates: 76g, Protein: 13g, Fat: 4g, Saturated Fat: 0g, Cholesterol: 0mg, Sodium: 324mg, Potassium: 233mg, Fiber: 4g, Sugar: 8g, Vitamin A: 935iu, Vitamin C: 7.8mg, Calcium: 101mg, Iron: 2.4mg

225. Basil Pesto Chicken Pasta

Prep Time: 15 Minutes

Cook Time: 10 Minutes

Total Time: 25 Minutes

Servings: 6 Servings

Ingredients

For The Homemade Pesto:

- 2 cups fresh basil leaves packed
- ½ cup pine nuts
- ½ cup grated pecorino cheese or parmesan
- 1 clove garlic peeled
- 2 teaspoons lemon juice
- 2/3 cup extra-virgin olive oil
- salt and pepper

For The Basil Pesto Chicken Pasta:

- 1 pound small pasta ziti, fusilli, or Gemelli
- 2 cups shredded cooked chicken

Instructions

For The Basil Pesto:

- Set out a food processor. Place the basil leaves, pine nuts, pecorino cheese, garlic clove, and lemon juice in the food processor. Cover and pulse until finely ground.
- Then add in the olive oil, ½ teaspoon salt, and ¼ teaspoon ground pepper. Pulse again until a smooth, thick pesto sauce is formed. Taste, then salt and pepper as needed.

For The Pesto Chicken Pasta:

- Set a large pot of salted water over high heat, and set out a mixing bowl. Once the water is boiling, stir the pasta into the water. Cook to al dente, according to the package instructions. Drain the pasta and place it in the bowl.
- Stir in the shredded cooked chicken. Allow the temperature of the pasta to come down a little, as to not cook the pesto. Once the pasta is warm (not hot) stir in the pesto, one-half cup at a time, until it is as saucy as you like.
- Serve at room temperature or cold. Cover and chill until ready to serve.

Nutrition

Calories: 551kcal, Carbohydrates: 59g, Protein: 15g, Fat: 29g, Saturatedfat: 5g, Cholesterol: 6mg, Sodium: 139mg, Potassium: 267mg, Fiber: 3g, Sugar: 3g, Vitamin A: 487iu, Vitamin C: 2mg, Calcium: 131mg, Iron: 2mg

226. Crispy Baked Chicken

Prep Time: 10 Minutes

Cook Time: 15 Minutes

Total Time: 25 Minutes

Servings: 8

Ingredients

- 2 pounds chicken cutlets usually 8 cutlets
- 1 1/2 cups panko bread crumbs
- 3/4 cup shredded Parmesan cheese
- 1 tablespoon fresh thyme leaves or 1 teaspoon dried thyme
- 1/3 cup light mayonnaise
- 1 tablespoon Dijon mustard
- Salt and pepper

Instructions

- Move one oven rack to a low position. Preheat the oven to 400 degrees F and line and baking sheet with foil. Spray the foil liberally with non-stick cooking spray and set aside.
- Set out two medium bowls. In one bowl, mix the mayo, mustard, 1/2 teaspoon salt, and 1/4 teaspoon pepper. In the other bowl, mix the panko, parmesan cheese, and thyme.
- Place the chicken cutlets in the mayo mixture and toss to coat. Then one at a time, press each

cutlet into the panko mixture on both sides to coat. Lay on the baking sheet.

- Bake in the lower part of the oven for 15 minutes. (Cooking low in the oven helps the bottoms to crisp up.)
- If the tops haven't browned, move the baking sheet to a higher rack and turn on the broiler for 1 minute. Watch to make sure they don't burn. Serve warm.

Nutrition

Calories: 235kcal, Carbohydrates: 10g, Protein: 29g, Fat: 8g, Saturatedfat: 3g, Cholesterol: 80mg, Sodium: 455mg, Potassium: 456mg, Fiber: 1g, Sugar: 1g, Vitamin A: 155iu, Vitamin C: 2.7mg, Calcium: 141mg, Iron: 1.2mg

227. Pressure-Cooker Chicken Enchilada Soup

Active: 20 mins

Total: 45 mins

Servings: 6

Ingredient

- 1 tablespoon olive oil
- 1 medium onion, chopped
- 1 poblano pepper, seeded and chopped
- 1 pound boneless, skinless chicken breast, cut into 1/2-inch pieces
- 3 cloves garlic, minced
- 2 tablespoons chili powder
- 1 teaspoon salt
- 4 cups low-sodium chicken broth
- 1 (15 ounces) can low-sodium black beans, rinsed
- 1 (14 ounces) can no-salt-added fire-roasted diced tomatoes
- Juice of 1 lime
- ½ cup chopped fresh cilantro, plus more for garnish
- ¾ cup shredded Mexican-style cheese blend
- Tortilla chips for garnish

Instructions

- Add onion, poblano, chicken, garlic, chili powder, and salt. Cook, stirring occasionally until the vegetables have softened and the chicken is no longer pink on the outside, about 5 minutes. Turn off the heat. Stir in broth, beans,

and tomatoes. Close and lock the lid. Cook at high pressure for 10 minutes.

- Release the pressure carefully. Stir in lime juice and cilantro. Top each serving with 2 tablespoons cheese and more cilantro if desired. Garnish with tortilla chips, if desired.

Nutrition

Calories: 269; Protein 26.4g; Carbohydrates 19.7g; Dietary Fiber 5.2g; Sugars 5.3g; Fat 9.6g; Saturated Fat 3.6g; Cholesterol 55.1mg; Vitamin A Iu 1340IU; Vitamin C 25mg; Folate 43.9mcg; Calcium 167.2mg; Iron 3mg; Magnesium 27.9mg; Potassium 564.5mg; Sodium 661.8mg; Thiamin 0.1mg.

228. Chicken Potpie Soup With Tater Tot Topping

Active: 40 mins

Total: 1 hr 10 mins

Servings: 6

Ingredients

- 3 cups frozen potato tots
- 2 tablespoons canola oil
- 2 tablespoons unsalted butter
- 1 cup chopped carrot
- 1 cup chopped parsnip
- ½ cup chopped celery
- ½ cup chopped onion
- ½ cup all-purpose flour
- 6 cups low-sodium chicken broth
- 3 cups diced cooked chicken or turkey
- 1 teaspoon garlic powder
- 1 teaspoon onion powder
- 1 teaspoon dried marjoram
- ½ teaspoon dried sage
- 1 cup frozen peas
- ½ cup half-and-half
- 3 tablespoons chopped fresh parsley

Instructions

- Preheat oven to 450 degrees F. Coat a large baking sheet with cooking spray.
- Place potato tots on the prepared baking sheet. Bake until golden and crispy, 20 to 25 minutes.
- Meanwhile, heat oil and butter in a large pot over medium heat. Add carrot, parsnip, celery, and onion. Cook, stirring occasionally until the

vegetables start to soften, about 5 minutes. Stir in flour and cook, stirring, for 1 minute. Stir in broth, chicken (or turkey), garlic powder, onion powder, marjoram, and sage. Bring to a boil over medium-high heat, stirring occasionally. Reduce heat and simmer until thickened and bubbly, about 2 minutes. Remove from heat. Stir in peas and half-and-half.

- Arrange the potato tots over the surface of the soup. Serve topped with parsley.

Nutrition

Calories: 461; Protein 31.7g; Carbohydrates 37.6g; Dietary Fiber 5g; Sugars 5.8g; Fat 20.7g; Saturated Fat 6.4g; Cholesterol 76.7mg; Vitamin A Iu 4436.5IU; Vitamin C 13.1mg; Folate 73.8mcg; Calcium 78.5mg; Iron 2.8mg; Magnesium 46.6mg; Potassium 854.3mg; Sodium 489.6mg.

229. Mediterranean Slow-Cooker Chicken Noodle Soup

Active: 15 mins

Total: 3 hrs 50 mins

Servings: 6

Ingredients

- 1 pound boneless, skinless chicken breast
- 1 (14 ounces) can no-salt-added fire-roasted diced tomatoes
- 4 cups low-sodium chicken broth
- 1 ½ cups chopped yellow onion
- 1 cup chopped orange bell pepper
- 4 cloves garlic, minced
- 1 tablespoon Italian seasoning
- ½ teaspoon ground pepper
- ¼ teaspoon salt
- ¼ teaspoon crushed red pepper
- 1 bay leaf
- 6 ounces whole-wheat rotini pasta
- 2 tablespoons chopped fresh basil
- 2 tablespoons chopped fresh flat-leaf parsley, plus more for garnish
- ½ cup grated Parmesan cheese

Instructions

- Combine chicken, tomatoes, broth, onion, bell pepper, garlic, Italian seasoning, pepper, salt,

crushed red pepper, and bay leaf in a 4-quart slow cooker. Cover and cook on High until the chicken is tender and an instant-read thermometer inserted into the thickest part of the chicken registers 165 degrees F, about 3 hours. Remove and discard the bay leaf. Transfer the chicken to a plate; let rest for 10 minutes.

- Meanwhile, stir pasta into the mixture in the slow cooker; cover and cook on High until the pasta is tender for about 30 minutes.
- Coarsely shred the chicken and stir it back into the soup, along with basil and parsley. Ladle the soup evenly into 6 bowls; sprinkle with Parmesan and garnish with parsley, if desired.

Nutrition

Calories: 256; Protein 23.7g; Carbohydrates 29g; Dietary Fiber 3.8g; Sugars 4.1g; Fat 4.8g; Saturated Fat 1.5g; Cholesterol 47.5mg; Vitamin A Iu 1037.9IU; Vitamin C 37.8mg; Folate 26.9mcg; Calcium 93.1mg; Iron 2mg; Magnesium 27.2mg; Potassium 516.2mg; Sodium 662.7mg; Thiamin 0.1mg.

30. Lemon Chicken Orzo Soup with Kale

Active: 40 mins

Total: 40 mins

Servings: 6

Ingredients

- 2 tablespoons extra-virgin olive oil, divided
- 1 pound boneless, skinless chicken breasts, trimmed and cut into 1-inch pieces
- 1 teaspoon dried oregano and/or thyme, divided
- 1 ¼ teaspoons salt, divided
- ¾ teaspoon ground pepper, divided
- 2 cups chopped onions
- 1 cup chopped carrots
- 1 cup chopped celery
- 2 cloves garlic, minced
- 1 bay leaf
- 4 cups unsalted chicken broth
- ⅔ cup orzo pasta, preferably whole-wheat
- 4 cups chopped kale
- 1 lemon, zested and juiced

Instructions

- Heat 1 tablespoon oil in a large pot over medium-high heat. Add chicken and sprinkle with 1/2 teaspoon each oregano (and/or thyme), salt, and pepper. Cook, stirring occasionally until lightly browned, 3 to 5 minutes. Using a slotted spoon, transfer the chicken to a plate.
- Add the remaining 1 tablespoon oil, onions, carrots, and celery to the pan. Cook, scraping up any browned bits until the vegetables are soft and lightly browned, 3 to 5 minutes. Add garlic, bay leaf, and the remaining 1/2 teaspoon oregano (and/or thyme). Cook, stirring, until fragrant, 30 to 60 seconds.
- Add broth and bring to a boil over high heat. Add orzo. Reduce heat to maintain a simmer, cover, and cook for 5 minutes. Add kale and the chicken, along with any accumulated juices. Continue cooking until the orzo is tender and the chicken is cooked through, 5 to 8 minutes more.
- Remove from heat. Discard bay leaf. Stir in lemon zest, lemon juice, and the remaining 3/4 teaspoon salt and 1/4 teaspoon pepper.

Nutrition

Calories: 245; Protein 21.1g; Carbohydrates 24.2g; Dietary Fiber 5.4g; Sugars 4.6g; Fat 7g; Saturated Fat 1.2g; Cholesterol 41.8mg; Vitamin A Iu 4723.8IU; Vitamin C 22.2mg; Folate 39.4mcg; Calcium 56.7mg; Iron 1mg; Magnesium 30.8mg; Potassium 480mg; Sodium 638.9mg.

231. Thai Grilled Chicken With Sweet & Spicy Dipping Sauce

Total: 1 hr 30 mins

Servings: 6

- Ingredients
- Chicken
- 3 medium cloves garlic
- 2 teaspoons whole black peppercorns, coarsely ground
- 2 tablespoons minced cilantro stems
- Pinch of salt
- 2 tablespoons fish sauce
- 4 pounds bone-in chicken drumsticks and thighs (about 12 pieces), skin removed, trimmed
- Dipping Sauce
- 1/2 cup rice vinegar or cider vinegar
- ½ cup sugar
- 1 teaspoon crushed red pepper
- 1 teaspoon minced garlic
- ¼ teaspoon salt

Instructions

- To prepare chicken: Combine garlic cloves, pepper, cilantro stems, and a pinch of salt in a large mortar or food processor or food mill and mash or pulse to a coarse paste. Transfer to a large bowl; stir in fish sauce and coconut milk. Add chicken and stir to coat with the marinade. Refrigerate, loosely covered, for at least 30 minutes and up to 1 hour.
- Preheat grill to medium.
- To prepare sauce: Heat vinegar to a boil in a small nonreactive pan. Add sugar, stir to dissolve it, then reduce heat and simmer for 3 to 4 minutes. Add crushed red pepper and minced garlic; simmer for 1 minute more. Remove from the heat and stir in salt. Pour into a serving bowl and let cool to room temperature before serving.
- Remove the chicken from the marinade. (Discard marinade.) Oil the grill rack. Grill, turning occasionally, until golden brown and an instant-read thermometer inserted into the thickest part without touching bone registers 165 degrees F, 15 to 20 minutes.
- Serve the chicken with the dipping sauce.

Nutrition

Calories: 443; Protein 53.1g; Carbohydrates 18.9g; Dietary Fiber 0.3g; Sugars 17g; Fat 15.9g; Saturated Fat 4.8g; Cholesterol 280.4mg; Vitamin C 0.8mg; Folate 10.3mcg; Calcium 26.9mg; Iron 2.5mg; Magnesium 50.9mg; Potassium 580.6mg; Sodium 628.7mg; Thiamin 0.2mg;

232. Butterflied Grilled Chicken With A Chile-Lime Rub

Total: 1 hr 25 mins

Servings: 6

Ingredients

- 3 tablespoons chile powder, preferably New Mexico chile, or Hungarian paprika
- 2 tablespoons extra-virgin olive oil
- 2 teaspoons freshly grated lime zest
- 3 tablespoons lime juice
- 1 tablespoon minced garlic
- 1 teaspoon ground coriander
- 1 teaspoon ground cumin
- 1 teaspoon dried oregano, preferably Mexican
- 1 ½ teaspoon kosher salt
- 1 teaspoon freshly ground pepper
- Pinch of ground cinnamon
- 1 3 1/2- to 4-pound chicken

Instructions

- Combine chile powder (or paprika) and oil in a small bowl with lime zest and juice, garlic, coriander, cumin, oregano, salt, pepper, and cinnamon to form a wet paste.
- Using kitchen shears, cut the chicken down one side of the backbone, through the ribs. Make an identical cut on the opposite side to remove the backbone completely; discard (or reserve it for the stock). Place the chicken cut-side down and flatten with the heel of your hand. Generously smear the spice rub under and over the skin and on the interior of the bird. Place in a nonreactive baking dish. Cover with plastic wrap and refrigerate overnight or up to 24 hours.
- Preheat half the grill to medium-high (or build a medium-high heat fire on one side of a charcoal grill); leave the other half unheated. Have a squirt bottle of water ready by the grill.
- Leave all the spice rub on the chicken. Place the chicken skin-side down over the heat and grill until the skin begins to color and char marks form, about 5 minutes. (Extinguish any flare-ups with the squirt bottle.) Flip over and grill 5 minutes more. Move the chicken to the unheated side. Close the lid and cook, making sure the chicken is flat against the grate until an instant-read thermometer inserted into the thickest part of a thigh without touching bone

registers 165 degrees F, 30 to 40 minutes. Transfer to a platter and let rest for 5 to 10 minutes before carving.

Nutrition

Calories: 212; Protein 28.3g; Carbohydrates 4g; Dietary Fiber 2g; Sugars 0.5g; Fat 9g; Saturated Fat 1.7g; Cholesterol 87.7mg; Vitamin A Iu 1274.5IU; Vitamin C 3.6mg; Folate 12.3mcg; Calcium 42.5mg; Iron 2.4mg; Magnesium 39.7mg; Potassium 425.2mg; Sodium 498.5mg; Thiamin 0.1mg.

233. Grilled Chicken Tenders With Cilantro Pesto

Total: 35 mins

Servings: 4

Ingredients

- ¼ cup lime juice
- ¼ cup reduced-sodium soy sauce
- 1 tablespoon canola oil
- 1 teaspoon chili powder
- 1 pound chicken tenders
- 2 cups loosely packed fresh cilantro leaves, (1-2 bunches)
- 2 scallions, sliced
- 2 tablespoons toasted sesame seeds,

Instructions

- Whisk lime juice, soy sauce, oil, and chili powder in a large bowl. Reserve 2 tablespoons of the marinade in a small bowl. Add chicken to the remaining marinade; toss to coat. Marinate in the refrigerator for 20 minutes or up to 1 hour.
- Preheat grill to medium-high.
- Meanwhile, place cilantro, scallions, sesame seeds, and the reserved marinade in a food processor and process until fairly smooth.
- Oil the grill rack. Remove the chicken from the marinade (discard marinade) and grill until cooked through and no longer pink in the middle, about 2 minutes per side. Serve the chicken with the cilantro-sesame pesto.
- Ingredient Note: Sesame seeds can be purchased already toasted. Look for them near other Asian ingredients. Or toast your own in a

small dry skillet over low heat, stirring constantly, until golden and fragrant, about 2 minutes.

- Tip: To oil, the grill rack, oil a folded paper towel, hold it with tongs, and rub it over the rack. (Do not use cooking spray on a hot grill.) When grilling delicate foods like tofu and fish, it is helpful to spray the food with cooking spray.
- People with celiac disease or gluten-sensitivity should use soy sauces that are labeled "gluten-free," as soy sauce may contain wheat or other gluten-containing sweeteners and flavors.

Nutrition

Calories: 168; Protein 24.3g; Carbohydrates 3.2g; Dietary Fiber 1.3g; Sugars 0.4g; Fat 6.2g; Saturated Fat 1.1g; Cholesterol 62.7mg; Vitamin A Iu 723.6IU; Vitamin C 5.6mg; Folate 17.3mcg; Calcium 30.1mg; Iron 1.5mg; Magnesium 42.1mg; Potassium 293.4mg; Sodium 302.9mg; Thiamin 0.1mg.

234. Grilled Chicken Taco Salad

Total: 35 mins

Servings: 4

Ingredients

- 2 tablespoons lime juice
- 2 tablespoons white-wine vinegar
- ¾ teaspoon salt, divided
- ¾ teaspoon ground pepper, divided
- ¼ cup extra-virgin olive oil
- 1 cup cherry tomatoes, halved
- ¾ cup diced zucchini
- 1 firm-ripe avocado, diced
- ¼ cup thinly sliced red onion
- 1 jalapeño, minced (Optional)
- 2 pounds boneless, skinless chicken breast
- 1 large ear corn, husked
- 5 cups arugula (about 3 ounces)
- 1 cup coarsely broken tortilla chips
- 2 tablespoons chopped fresh cilantro

Instructions

- Preheat grill to medium-high.
- Combine lime juice, vinegar, and 1/2 teaspoon each salt and pepper in a large bowl; whisk in oil.

Add tomatoes, zucchini, avocado, onion, and jalapeño, if using; gently toss to coat. Set aside.

- Sprinkle chicken with the remaining 1/4 teaspoon each salt and pepper.
- Oil the grill rack. Grill the chicken until an instant-read thermometer inserted into the thickest part registers 165 degrees F, 4 to 5 minutes per side. Grill corn until lightly charred on all sides, 2 to 4 minutes total. Transfer to a clean cutting board. Cut the chicken into bite-size pieces; cut corn kernels from the cob.
- Add the chicken and corn to the tomato mixture; stir in arugula, tortilla chips, and cilantro and gently toss to combine.

Nutrition

Calories: 447; Protein 27.2g; Carbohydrates 24.5g; Dietary Fiber 6g; Sugars 5.1g; Fat 27.8g; Saturated Fat 4.3g; Cholesterol 62.7mg; Vitamin A Iu 1078.1IU; Vitamin C 22.9mg; Folate 95.9mcg; Calcium 78.3mg; Iron 2mg; Magnesium 80.8mg; Potassium 811.5mg; Sodium 550.9mg; Thiamin 0.2mg.

235. Apple & Grilled Chicken Salad With Cheddar Toasts

Total: 50 mins

Servings: 4

Ingredients

- 1 pound boneless, skinless chicken breasts, trimmed
- ¾ teaspoon kosher salt, divided
- ½ teaspoon ground pepper, divided
- 4 diagonal slices baguette (1 inch thick)
- ½ cup shredded aged Cheddar cheese
- 3 tablespoons grapeseed oil or canola oil
- 2 tablespoons cider vinegar
- 1 tablespoon whole-grain mustard
- 1 head escarole (about 1 pound), torn into bite-size pieces
- 3 cups sliced sweet, crunchy apples (about 2 medium), Honeycrisp
- ¼ cup slivered red onion

Instructions

- Preheat grill to medium-high.

- Sprinkle chicken with 1/2 teaspoon salt and 1/4 teaspoon pepper.
- Oil the grill rack. Grill the chicken, turning occasionally until an instant-read thermometer inserted into the thickest part registers 165 degrees F, about 15 minutes total. Grill baguette slices over the coolest part of the grill until toasted on the bottom, 1 to 3 minutes. Turn over, sprinkle with cheese and cook until the cheese melts, 1 to 3 minutes.
- Meanwhile, whisk oil, vinegar, mustard, and the remaining 1/4 teaspoon each salt and pepper in a large bowl. Add escarole, apples, and onion; toss to coat.
- Slice the chicken. Divide the salad among 4 plates, top each with some chicken and serve with the cheese toasts.

Nutrition

Calories: 398; Protein 30.7g; Carbohydrates 28.2g; Dietary Fiber 7.7g; Sugars 10.3g; Fat 18.7g; Saturated Fat 4.6g; Cholesterol 77.1mg; Vitamin A Iu 2664.1IU; Vitamin C 12.1mg; Folate 171.8mcg; Calcium 174.3mg; Iron 1.9mg; Magnesium 48.3mg; Potassium 672.6mg; Sodium 553.1mg; Thiamin 0.2mg.

236. Greek Cauliflower Rice Bowls With Grilled Chicken

Active: 30 mins

Total: 30 mins

Servings: 4

Ingredients

- 6 tablespoons plus 1 teaspoon extra-virgin olive oil, divided
- 4 cups cauliflower rice (see Tip)
- ⅓ cup chopped red onion
- ¾ teaspoon salt, divided
- ½ cup chopped fresh dill, divided
- 1 pound boneless, skinless chicken breasts
- ½ teaspoon ground pepper, divided
- 3 tablespoons lemon juice
- 1 teaspoon dried oregano
- 1 cup halved cherry tomatoes
- 1 cup chopped cucumber
- 2 tablespoons chopped Kalamata olives
- 2 tablespoons crumbled feta cheese

- 4 wedges lemon wedges for serving

Instructions

- Preheat grill to medium.
- Heat 2 tablespoons oil in a large skillet over medium-high heat. Add cauliflower, onion, and 1/4 teaspoon salt. Cook, stirring occasionally until the cauliflower is softened, about 5 minutes. Remove from heat and stir in 1/4 cup dill.
- Meanwhile, rub 1 teaspoon of oil all over the chicken. Sprinkle with 1/4 teaspoon salt and 1/4 teaspoon pepper. Grill, turning once until an instant-read thermometer inserted into the thickest part of the breast reads 165 degrees F, about 15 minutes total. Slice crosswise.
- Meanwhile, whisk the remaining 4 tablespoons oil, lemon juice, oregano, and the remaining 1/4 teaspoon each salt and pepper in a small bowl.
- Divide the cauliflower rice between 4 bowls. Top with the chicken, tomatoes, cucumber, olives, and feta. Sprinkle with the remaining 1/4 cup dill. Drizzle with the vinaigrette. Serve with lemon wedges, if desired.

Nutrition

Calories: 117; Protein 29g; Carbohydrates 9.5g; Dietary Fiber 3.1g; Sugars 4.5g; Fat 27.5g; Saturated Fat 4.5g; Cholesterol 86.9mg; Vitamin A Iu 488IU; Vitamin C 54.3mg; Folate 26.5mcg; Calcium 68.9mg; Iron 1.2mg; Magnesium 44.5mg; Potassium 560.4mg; Sodium 629.8mg; Thiamin 0.2mg.

237. Balsamic-Dijon Chicken

Active: 15 mins

Total: 4 hrs 30 mins

Servings: 4

Ingredients

- 4 skinless, boneless chicken breast halves (1-pound total)
- ⅓ cup Dijon-style mustard
- 3 tablespoons balsamic vinegar
- 2 cloves garlic, minced
- 2 teaspoons snipped fresh thyme or basil or 1/2 teaspoon dried thyme or basil, crushed
- 1 Fresh thyme sprigs

Instructions

- Place chicken in a large resealable plastic bag in a shallow dish; set aside.
- For the marinade: In a small bowl, stir together mustard, balsamic vinegar, garlic, and thyme until smooth. Pour marinade over the chicken. Seal bag; turn to coat chicken. Marinate in the refrigerator for 4 to 24 hours, turning bag occasionally.
- Drain the chicken, reserving marinade. Place chicken on the rack of an uncovered grill directly over medium coals. Grill for 7 minutes, brushing occasionally with reserved marinade. Turn chicken; brush again with marinade. Discard any remaining marinade. Grill for 5 to 8 minutes more or until chicken is tender and no longer pink (165 degrees F). If desired, garnish with thyme sprigs.

Nutrition

Calories: 161; Protein 26.3g; Carbohydrates 3.3g; Dietary Fiber 0.1g; Sugars 2.7g; Fat 1.3g; Saturated Fat 0.3g; Cholesterol 65.7mg; Vitamin A Iu 36.9IU; Vitamin C 2.3mg; Folate 4.8mcg; Calcium 17.5mg; Iron 0.9mg; Magnesium 27.3mg; Potassium 247.6mg; Sodium 536.7mg.

238. Chicken Satay Bowls With Spicy Peanut Sauce

Active: 35 mins

Total: 35 mins

Servings: 4

Ingredients

- 1 recipe Thai Chicken Satay with Spicy Peanut Sauce
- 6 cups thinly sliced Savoy or green cabbage
- ½ cup thinly sliced red bell pepper
- ½ cup matchstick-cut carrots
- ¼ cup finely chopped green onion
- 2 tablespoons toasted sesame seeds

Instructions

- Prepare Thai Chicken Satay with Spicy Peanut Sauce as directed. Remove the chicken from the skewers and cut into strips. Divide the sauce among 4 small condiment containers with lids and refrigerate until ready to use.

- To prepare slaw: Toss cabbage, bell pepper, carrots, and green onion in a large bowl.
- Divide the slaw among 4 single-serving containers with lids. Top each with one-fourth of the chicken and 1/2 tablespoon sesame seeds. Dress with the reserved sauce just before serving.

Nutrition

Calories: 351; Protein 28.1g; Carbohydrates 14.4g; Dietary Fiber 4.6g; Sugars 6.3g; Fat 20g; Saturated Fat 2.6g; Cholesterol 62.7mg; Vitamin A Iu 3033.4IU; Vitamin C 60mg; Folate 62mcg; Calcium 81mg; Iron 2mg; Magnesium 42mg; Potassium 489.1mg; Sodium 497.5mg; Thiamin 0.1mg;

239. Greek Chicken & Cucumber Pita Sandwiches With Yogurt Sauce

Active: 45 mins

Total: 1 hr 45 mins

Servings: 4

Ingredient

- 1 teaspoon lemon zest
- 2 tablespoons fresh lemon juice
- 5 teaspoons olive oil, divided
- 1 tablespoon chopped fresh oregano or 1 teaspoon dried
- 2 ¾ teaspoons minced garlic, divided
- ¼ teaspoon crushed red pepper
- 1 pound chicken tenders
- 1 English cucumber, halved, seeded, and grated, plus 1/2 English cucumber, halved and sliced
- ½ teaspoon salt, divided
- ¾ cup nonfat plain Greek yogurt
- 2 teaspoons chopped fresh mint
- 2 teaspoons chopped fresh dill
- 1 teaspoon ground pepper
- 2 (6 1/2 inch) whole-wheat pita bread, halved
- 4 lettuce leaves
- ½ cup sliced red onion
- 1 cup chopped plum tomatoes

Instructions

- Combine lemon zest, lemon juice, 3 tsp. oil, oregano, 2 tsp. garlic, and crushed red pepper in a large bowl. Add chicken and toss to coat.

Marinate in the refrigerator for at least 1 hour or up to 4 hours.

- Meanwhile, toss grated cucumber with 1/4 tsp. salt in a fine-mesh sieve. Let drain for 15 minutes, then squeeze to release more liquid. Transfer to a medium bowl. Stir in yogurt, mint, dill, ground pepper, and the remaining 2 tsp. oil, 3/4 tsp. garlic, and 1/4 tsp. salt. Refrigerate until ready to serve.
- Preheat grill to medium-high.
- Oil the grill rack (see Tip). Grill the chicken until an instant-read thermometer inserted in the center registers 165 degrees F, 3 to 4 minutes per side.
- To serve, spread some of the sauce inside each pita half. Tuck in the chicken, lettuce, red onion, tomatoes, and sliced cucumber.

Nutrition

Serving Size: 1 Stuffed Pita Half Per Serving: 353 calories; protein 37.5g; carbohydrates 33.3g; dietary fiber 5.8g; sugars 6.3g; fat 8.6g; saturated fat 0.9g; cholesterol 57.7mg; vitamin a iu 1139.3IU; vitamin c 15.1mg; folate 31.4mcg; calcium 85.4mg; iron 1.6mg; magnesium 53.9mg; potassium 458.6mg; sodium 558.8mg.

240. Chicken Souvlaki Kebabs With Mediterranean Couscous

Active: 45 mins

Total: 2 hrs 20 mins

Servings: 4

Ingredients

- Chicken Souvlaki Kabobs
- 1 pound skinless, boneless chicken breast halves, cut into 1/2-inch strips
- 1 cup sliced fennel (reserve leaves, if desired)
- ⅓ cup dry white wine
- ¼ cup lemon juice
- 3 tablespoons canola oil
- 4 cloves garlic, minced
- 2 teaspoons dried oregano, crushed
- ½ teaspoon salt
- ¼ teaspoon black pepper
- Lemon wedges
- Mediterranean Couscous
- 1 teaspoon olive oil
- ½ cup Israeli (large pearl) couscous

- 1 cup water
- ½ cup snipped dried tomatoes (not oil-packed)
- ¾ cup chopped red sweet pepper
- ½ cup chopped cucumber
- ½ cup chopped red onion
- ⅓ cup plain fat-free Greek yogurt
- ¼ cup thinly sliced fresh basil leaves
- ¼ cup snipped fresh parsley
- 1 tablespoon lemon juice
- ¼ teaspoon salt
- ¼ teaspoon black pepper

Instructions

- Prepare kabobs: Place chicken and sliced fennel in a resealable plastic bag set in a shallow dish. For marinade, in a small bowl combine the white wine, lemon juice, oil, garlic, oregano, salt, and pepper. Remove 1/4 cup of the marinade and set aside.
- Pour the remaining marinade over the chicken mixture. Seal bag; turn to coat chicken mixture. Marinate in the refrigerator for 1 1/2 hours, turning bag once.
- Meanwhile, if using wooden skewers, soak eight 10- to 12-inch skewers in water for 30 minutes. Drain chicken, discarding marinade and fennel. Thread chicken, accordion-style, onto skewers.
- Grill chicken skewers, covered, over medium-high heat 6 to 8 minutes or until chicken is no longer pink, turning once. Remove from grill and brush with the reserved 1/4 cup marinade.
- Prepare couscous: In a small saucepan heat 1 teaspoon olive oil over medium heat. Add 1/2 cup Israeli (large pearl) couscous. Cook and stir for 4 minutes or until light brown. Add 1 cup water. Bring to boiling; reduce heat. Simmer, covered, 10 minutes or until couscous is tender and liquid is absorbed, adding 1/2 cup snipped dried tomatoes (not oil-packed) the last 5 minutes; cool. Transfer couscous to a large bowl. Stir in 3/4 cup chopped red sweet pepper, 1/2 cup each chopped cucumber and chopped red onion, 1/3 cup plain fat-free Greek yogurt, 1/4 cup each thinly sliced fresh basil leaves and snipped fresh parsley, 1 tablespoon lemon juice, and 1/4 teaspoon each salt and black pepper.
- Serve kabobs with couscous, lemon wedges, and, if desired, reserved fennel leaves.

Nutrition

Serving Size: 2 Kabobs And 3/4 Cup Couscous Per Serving: 332 Calories; Protein 32.1g; Carbohydrates 27.7g; Dietary Fiber 2.3g; Sugars 6.4g; Fat 9.4g; Saturated Fat 1.2g; Cholesterol 82.8mg; Vitamin A Iu 1502.3IU; Vitamin C 57.1mg; Folate 46.4mcg; Calcium 66.4mg; Iron 1.8mg; Magnesium 59.7mg; Potassium 792.8mg; Sodium 360mg.

241. Sheet-Pan Mediterranean Chicken, Brussels Sprouts & Gnocchi

Active: 20 mins

Total: 40 mins

Servings: 4

Ingredient

- 4 tablespoons extra-virgin olive oil, divided
- 2 tablespoons chopped fresh oregano, divided
- 2 large cloves garlic, minced, divided
- ½ teaspoon ground pepper, divided
- ¼ teaspoon salt, divided
- 1 pound Brussels sprouts, trimmed and quartered
- 1 (16 ounces) package shelf-stable gnocchi
- 1 cup sliced red onion
- 4 boneless, skinless chicken thighs, trimmed
- 1 cup halved cherry tomatoes
- 1 tablespoon red-wine vinegar

Instructions

- Preheat oven to 450 degrees F.
- Stir 2 tablespoons oil, 1 tablespoon oregano, half the garlic, 1/4 teaspoon pepper, and 1/8 teaspoon salt together in a large bowl. Add Brussels sprouts, gnocchi, and onion; toss to coat. Spread on a large rimmed baking sheet.
- Stir 1 tablespoon oil, the remaining 1 tablespoon oregano, the remaining garlic, and the remaining 1/4 teaspoon pepper and 1/8 teaspoon salt in the large bowl. Add chicken and toss to coat. Nestle the chicken into the vegetable mixture. Roast for 10 minutes.
- Remove from the oven and add the tomatoes; stir to combine. Continue roasting until the Brussels sprouts are tender and the chicken is just cooked through, about 10 minutes more.

Stir vinegar and the remaining 1 tablespoon oil into the vegetable mixture.

Nutrition

Serving Size: 1 Chicken Thigh & 1 1/2 Cups Vegetables Each Per Serving: 604 Calories; Protein 39.1g; Carbohydrates 60.6g; Dietary Fiber 6.8g; Sugars 4.8g; Fat 23.9g; Saturated Fat 4.7g; Cholesterol 154.3mg; Vitamin A Iu 1224.4IU; Vitamin C 104.1mg; Folate 89.7mcg; Calcium 96.8mg; Iron 3.8mg; Magnesium 66mg; Potassium 913.8mg; Sodium 657.3mg; Thiamin 0.3mg.

242. Avocado Ranch Chicken Salad

Active: 20 mins

Total: 20 mins

Servings: 6

Ingredients

- 1 ripe avocado, halved and pitted
- ⅓ cup ranch dressing
- 2 tablespoons chopped pickled jalapeño
- 1 tablespoon white-wine vinegar
- ¼ teaspoon salt
- ¼ teaspoon ground pepper
- 3 cups shredded or chopped cooked chicken
- ½ cup diced celery
- ¼ cup diced red onion

Instructions

Scoop avocado into a food processor. Add ranch dressing, pickled jalapeño, vinegar, salt, and pepper. Pulse until smooth. Transfer to a medium bowl. Add chicken, celery, and red onion; mix with a rubber spatula. Serve at room temperature or refrigerate until cold, about 2 hours.

Nutrition

Calories: 361; protein 32.5g; carbohydrates 4.7g; dietary fiber 2.5g; sugars 1.2g; fat 23.1g; saturated fat 5.1g; cholesterol 116.7mg; vitamin c 4.1mg; folate 40.8mcg; calcium 27mg; iron 2mg; magnesium 38.6mg; potassium 434.2mg; sodium 349.6mg; thiamin 0.1mg.

243. Buffalo Chicken Cauliflower Pizza

Active: 30 mins

Total: 1 hr 10 mins

Servings: 6

Ingredients

- 5 cups cauliflower florets
- 1 clove garlic
- 2 large eggs, lightly beaten
- 1 cup shredded part-skim mozzarella cheese
- ¼ cup shredded carrot
- 3 tablespoons chopped fresh chives, divided
- ¼ teaspoon salt
- 1 ½ cups shredded cooked chicken
- 2 tablespoons hot sauce, such as Frank's RedHot, divided
- 1 tablespoon white vinegar
- ¼ teaspoon cayenne pepper, or to taste
- ¼ cup crumbled blue cheese
- 1 stalk celery, thinly sliced

Instructions

- Preheat oven to 425 degrees F. Line a large baking sheet with parchment paper.
- Place cauliflower and garlic in a food processor; process until finely chopped. Transfer to a microwave-safe bowl and microwave on High for 3 minutes. Let cool slightly. Stir in eggs, mozzarella, carrot, 2 tablespoons chives, and salt. Spread the mixture into a 12-inch circle, 1/4 inch thick, on the prepared baking sheet.
- Bake the cauliflower crust until brown and crispy around the edges, 35 to 40 minutes.
- ❖ Combine chicken, 1 tablespoon hot sauce, vinegar, and cayenne in a small bowl. Remove the crust from the oven and top with the chicken and blue cheese. Return to the oven and bake until the chicken is warm and the cheese is starting to melt, about 5 minutes more. Top with celery and the remaining 1 tablespoon each chive and hot sauce.

Nutrition

- Calories 189; Protein 21.4g; Carbohydrates 6.7g; Dietary Fiber 2.1g; Sugars 2.6g; Fat 8.6g; Saturated Fat 4.2g; Cholesterol 110.4mg; Vitamin A Iu 1194.4IU; Vitamin C 48.1mg; Folate 72.5mcg; Calcium 202.6mg; Iron 1.2mg;

Magnesium 35.1mg; Potassium 482.9mg; Sodium 498mg; Thiamin 0.1mg.

244. Sheet-Pan Chicken Fajitas

Active: 20 mins

Total: 40 mins

Servings: 4

Ingredients

- 1 pound boneless, skinless chicken breasts
- 2 tablespoons extra-virgin olive oil
- 1 tablespoon chili powder
- 2 teaspoons ground cumin
- 1 teaspoon garlic powder
- ¾ teaspoon salt
- 1 large red bell pepper, sliced
- 1 large yellow bell pepper, sliced
- 2 cups sliced red or yellow onion (about 1 large)
- 1 tablespoon lime juice
- 8 corn tortillas, warmed

Instructions

- Preheat oven to 400 degrees F. Coat a large rimmed baking sheet with cooking spray.
- Cut chicken breasts in half horizontally, then slice crosswise into strips. Combine oil, chili powder, cumin, garlic powder, and salt in a large bowl. Add the chicken and stir to coat with the spice mixture. Add bell peppers and onion and stir to combine. Transfer the chicken and vegetables to the prepared baking sheet and spread in an even layer.
- Roast on the middle rack for 15 minutes. Leave the pan there and turn the broiler too high. Broil until the chicken is cooked through and the vegetables are browning in spots, about 5 minutes more. Remove from oven. Stir in lime juice.
- Serve the chicken and vegetables in warmed tortillas accompanied by lime wedges and topped with cilantro, sour cream, avocado, and/or pico de gallo, if desired.

Nutrition

Calories: 357; Protein 30.1g; Carbohydrates 32.5g; Dietary Fiber 6g; Sugars 5.1g; Fat 12.1g; Saturated Fat 1.9g; Cholesterol 82.8mg; Vitamin A Iu 2012.7IU; Vitamin C 141.6mg; Folate

52mcg; Calcium 75.9mg; Iron 2.2mg; Magnesium 84.5mg; Potassium 761.1mg; Sodium 572.9mg.

245. 20-Minute Creamy Italian Chicken Skillet

Active: 20 mins

Total: 20 mins

Servings: 4

Ingredient

- 1 pound chicken cutlets
- ¼ teaspoon salt, divided
- ¼ teaspoon ground pepper, divided
- 2 tablespoons extra-virgin olive oil, divided
- 1 medium zucchini, halved lengthwise and thinly sliced
- ½ cup chopped onion
- ⅓ cup dry white wine
- 1 (15-ounce) can no-salt-added diced tomatoes
- 2 ounces cream cheese, cut into cubes
- 1 teaspoon Italian seasoning
- ½ teaspoon garlic powder
- ¼ cup chopped fresh basil

Instructions

- Sprinkle chicken with 1/8 teaspoon each salt and pepper. Heat 1 tablespoon oil in a large skillet over medium heat. Add the chicken and cook, turning once, until browned and an instant-read thermometer inserted into the thickest part registers 165 degrees F. Transfer to a plate.
- Add the remaining 1 tablespoon oil, zucchini, and onion to the pan. Cook, stirring, until starting to soften, about 2 minutes. Increase heat to medium-high and add wine. Cook, scraping up any browned bits until the liquid has mostly evaporated, about 2 minutes. Add tomatoes, cream cheese, Italian seasoning, garlic powder, and the remaining 1/8 teaspoon each salt and pepper. Bring to a simmer and cook, stirring to melt the cream cheese, for 5 minutes. Return the chicken to the pan and turn to coat with the sauce. Serve topped with basil.

Nutrition

Calories: 301; Protein 27.4g; Carbohydrates 8.9g; Dietary Fiber 1.8g; Sugars 5.4g; Fat 14.8g; Saturated Fat 4.5g; Cholesterol 97.1mg; Vitamin A Iu 693IU; Vitamin C 23.9mg; Folate 29.3mcg; Calcium 57.8mg; Iron 1.2mg; Magnesium 49mg; Potassium 748.6mg; Sodium 251.9mg.

246. Sweet & Sour Chicken

Active: 20 mins

Total: 20 mins

Servings: 4

Ingredients

- ¼ cup no-salt-added ketchup
- ¼ cup pineapple juice
- 3 tablespoons reduced-sodium soy sauce
- 1 tablespoon rice vinegar
- 2 teaspoons honey
- ¼ teaspoon salt
- ½ teaspoon ground pepper
- 2 tablespoons toasted sesame oil, divided
- 1 pound boneless, skinless chicken breasts, cut into bite-size pieces
- 8 ounces small broccoli florets
- 2 cups chopped red bell pepper
- 1 cup diagonally sliced scallions (1-inch)
- 3 cups cooked brown rice

Instructions

- Whisk ketchup, pineapple juice, soy sauce, vinegar, honey, salt, and pepper in a small bowl.
- Heat 1 tablespoon oil in a large skillet over high heat. Add chicken and cook, turning occasionally, until browned on all sides, 4 to 5 minutes. Transfer to a plate.
- Wipe the pan clean; return to high heat and add the remaining 1 tablespoon oil. Add broccoli and bell pepper; cook until charred, about 5 minutes. Add scallions and cook for 1 minute. Return the chicken to the pan and add the ketchup mixture. Cook until bubbly and the sauce coats the chicken. Serve in shallow bowls over rice.

Nutrition

Calories: 444; Protein 29.9g; Carbohydrates 55.7g; Dietary Fiber 6.3g; Sugars 12.9g; Fat 11.1g; Saturated Fat 2g; Cholesterol 62.7mg;

Vitamin C 154.3mg; Folate 102.3mcg; Calcium 81.8mg; Iron 3.1mg; Magnesium 120.4mg; Potassium 762.3mg; Sodium 624.1mg; Thiamin 0.3mg;

247. Baked Lemon-Pepper Chicken

Active: 10 mins

Total: 20 mins

Servings: 4

Ingredient

- 4 (6 ounces) boneless, skinless chicken breasts
- ½ teaspoon salt, plus 1/8 teaspoon, divided
- 1 tablespoon extra-virgin olive oil
- 1 medium lemon, thinly sliced
- 2 tablespoons lemon juice
- 1 tablespoon pure maple syrup
- 2 tablespoons unsalted butter, cut into pieces
- 1 teaspoon cracked pepper

Instructions

- Preheat oven to 425 degrees F.
- Sprinkle chicken evenly with 1/2 teaspoon salt. Heat oil in a large ovenproof skillet over medium-high heat. Add the chicken; cook, undisturbed, until the underside is golden brown, about 4 minutes. Flip the chicken; arrange lemon slices around the chicken in the pan.
- Transfer the skillet to the oven; bake until an instant-read thermometer inserted into the thickest portion of meat registers 165 degrees F, about 10 minutes.
- Transfer the chicken to a platter. Add lemon juice and maple syrup to the pan. Add butter, 1 piece at a time, stirring until it melts into the sauce. Stir in pepper and the remaining 1/8 teaspoon salt. Drizzle the sauce over the chicken.

Nutrition

Calories: 286; Protein 34.8g; Carbohydrates 7.1g; Dietary Fiber 1.4g; Sugars 3.2g; Fat 13.3g; Saturated Fat 5.2g; Cholesterol 109.2mg; Vitamin C 23.7mg; Folate 8.1mcg; Calcium 43.1mg; Iron 1.4mg; Magnesium 38mg; Potassium 350.1mg; Sodium 447.6mg; Thiamin 0.1mg.

248. Chicken Parmesan Casserole

Active: 25 mins

Total: 50 mins

Servings: 6

Ingredients

- 8 ounces whole-wheat rotini
- 4 tablespoons extra-virgin olive oil, divided
- 1 cup chopped onion
- 1 (28 ounces) can no-salt-added crushed tomatoes
- 1 teaspoon garlic powder
- ½ teaspoon dried basil
- ½ teaspoon dried oregano
- ½ teaspoon salt
- ¼ teaspoon crushed red pepper
- 2 cups shredded cooked chicken
- 1 cup shredded mozzarella cheese
- ½ cup panko breadcrumbs
- ¼ cup grated Parmesan cheese
- 2 tablespoons chopped parsley

Instructions

- Preheat oven to 400 degrees F. Lightly coats an 8-inch-square baking dish with cooking spray.
- Bring a large saucepan of water to a boil. Add rotini and cook according to package directions. Drain.
- Meanwhile, heat 2 tablespoons of oil in a large skillet over medium heat. Add onion and cook, stirring, until starting to soften, about 3 minutes. Add tomatoes, garlic powder, basil, oregano, salt, and crushed red pepper; bring to a simmer. Cook, stirring, until thickened, about 5 minutes. Stir in chicken and the cooked rotini. Transfer to the prepared baking dish and top with mozzarella.
- Stir panko, Parmesan, parsley, and the remaining 2 tablespoons oil together in a small bowl. Sprinkle over the casserole. Bake until hot and the topping is golden, 25 to 30 minutes.

Nutrition

Calories: 442; Protein 25.5g; Carbohydrates 50.1g; Dietary Fiber 8.6g; Sugars 5.8g; Fat 16.8g; Saturated Fat 4.5g; Cholesterol 43mg; Vitamin A Iu 338.6IU; Vitamin C 3.7mg; Folate 36mcg; Calcium 189.3mg; Iron 2.7mg; Magnesium

76mg; Potassium 281.4mg; Sodium 461.7mg; Thiamin 0.2mg.

249. Oven-Roasted Whole Chicken

Active: 30 mins

Total: 10 hrs 15 mins

Servings: 6

Ingredients

- 2 cups water
- 2 tablespoons kosher salt plus 1/2 teaspoon, divided
- 2 tablespoons granulated sugar
- 1 tablespoon whole black peppercorns
- 1 ½ teaspoon fennel seed
- 2 lemons (1 quartered, 1 zested, and juiced), divided
- 3 cloves garlic, crushed
- 6 fresh thyme sprigs plus 1 teaspoon thyme leaves, divided
- 2 fresh bay leaves
- 6 cups ice
- 1 (4 to 5 pound) whole chicken
- 2 teaspoons extra-virgin olive oil
- 1 teaspoon ground pepper

Instructions

- Combine water, 2 tablespoons salt, sugar, peppercorns, fennel seed, lemon wedges, garlic, thyme sprigs, and bay leaves in a small saucepan. Bring to a boil over medium-high heat and stir until the salt is dissolved for about 2 minutes. Remove from heat.
- Place ice in a 5-quart bowl or pot and pour the brine over it. Let cool, stirring occasionally, about 5 minutes. Add chicken, making sure it is completely submerged in the brine. (Add more cold water and use a plate to weigh it down if necessary.) Refrigerate overnight or up to 24 hours.
- To roast chicken, preheat the oven to 375 degrees F. Line a rimmed baking sheet with foil and place a wire rack on top. Coat the rack with cooking spray.
- Remove the chicken from the brine and place it on the prepared rack. Pat it dry with a paper towel.

- Zest the remaining lemon and juice it to get 2 teaspoons. Combine the zest and juice with oil, pepper, and the remaining 1 teaspoon thyme and 1/2 teaspoon salt. Loosen and lift the skin from the breast and legs with your fingers and rub the paste under and over the skin. Truss the chicken with kitchen string (see Tip).
- Roast the chicken for 1 hour. Rotate the pan, and increase the heat to 400 degrees F. Cook until an instant-read thermometer registers 160 degrees F in the thickest part of the breast, 25 to 30 minutes more. Let the chicken rest for 10 minutes before carving.

Nutrition

Calories: 204; Protein 28g; Carbohydrates 1g; Sugars 1g; Fat 9g; Saturated Fat 2g; Cholesterol 87mg; Vitamin A Iu 55IU; Vitamin C 1mg; Folate 6mcg; Calcium 19mg; Iron 1mg; Magnesium 26mg; Potassium 247mg; Sodium 326mg.

250. Chicken Breasts With Mushroom Cream Sauce

Total: 30 mins

Servings: 2

Ingredient

- 2 5-ounce boneless, skinless chicken breasts, trimmed and tenders removed
- ½ teaspoon freshly ground pepper
- ¼ teaspoon salt
- 1 tablespoon canola oil
- 1 medium shallot, minced
- 1 cup thinly sliced shiitake mushroom caps
- 2 tablespoons dry vermouth, or dry white wine
- ¼ cup reduced-sodium chicken broth
- 2 tablespoons heavy cream
- 2 tablespoons minced fresh chives, or scallion greens

Instructions

- Season chicken with pepper and salt on both sides.
- Heat oil in a medium skillet over medium heat. Add the chicken and cook, turning once or twice and adjusting the heat to prevent burning, until brown and an instant-read thermometer inserted into the thickest part registers 165

degrees F, 12 to 16 minutes. Transfer to a plate and tent with foil to keep warm.

- Add shallot to the pan and cook, stirring, until fragrant, about 30 seconds. Add mushrooms; cook, stirring occasionally, until tender, about 2 minutes. Pour in vermouth (or wine); simmer until almost evaporated, scraping up any browned bits, about 1 minute. Pour in broth and cook until reduced by half, 1 to 2 minutes. Stir in cream and chives (or scallions); return to a simmer. Return the chicken to the pan, turn to coat with sauce and cook until heated through about 1 minute.

Nutrition

Calories: 274; Protein 25.2g; Carbohydrates 4.8g; Dietary Fiber 0.7g; Sugars 1.7g; Fat 15.4g; Saturated Fat 4.8g; Cholesterol 83.2mg; Vitamin A Iu 548.2IU; Vitamin C 3.9mg; Folate 18.8mcg; Calcium 32.9mg; Iron 1.3mg; Magnesium 31.3mg; Potassium 403.4mg; Sodium 425mg; Thiamin 0.1mg.

251. Thai Red Curry Grilled Chicken Salad

Prep Time: 15 Minutes

Cook Time: 10 Minutes

Total Time: 25 Minutes

Servings: 4

Ingredients

For The Thai Red Curry Grilled Chicken:

- 2 pounds boneless skinless chicken breast
- 4 ounces Panang Red Curry Paste
- For the Peanut Dressing:
- 1/3 cup creamy peanut butter
- 1/3 cup rice vinegar
- 1 tablespoon sesame oil
- 1 teaspoon honey
- 1 clove garlic

For The Thai Red Curry Grilled Chicken Salad:

- 8 cups chopped napa cabbage (from one big cabbage)
- 1 mango, peeled and sliced thin
- 1 cup radishes, sliced
- 1 cup mini bell peppers, sliced
- 1/2 cup red onion, sliced
- 1/2 cup fresh cilantro leaves

- 1/4 cup roasted peanuts

Instructions

- Preheat the grill. Place the chicken in a baking dish. Rub the pieces of chicken on all sides with Panang red curry paste. Do not salt and pepper. Let the chicken marinate for at least 20 minutes.
- Place the ingredients for the dressing in a blender. Puree until smooth.
- Prep all the produce. Once the grill reaches 350-400 degrees F, grill the chicken for 5 minutes per side. Allow the chicken to rest another 5 minutes, before slicing into thin strips.
- Arrange the napa cabbage, mangos, and vegetables on salad plates. Top with sliced grilled chicken, cilantro, and peanuts. Serve each salad plate with a side of peanut dressing.

Nutrition

Calories: 575kcal, Carbohydrates: 24g, Protein: 59g, Fat: 27g, Saturatedfat: 5g, Cholesterol: 145mg, Sodium: 429mg, Potassium: 1602mg, Fiber: 6g, Sugar: 14g, Vitamin A: 5815iu, Vitamin C: 76.6mg, Calcium: 203mg, Iron: 2.8mg

252. Summer Cobb Salad Recipe

Prep Time: 20 Minutes

Cook Time: 10 Minutes

Total Time: 30 Minutes

Servings: 6

Ingredients

- 2 large boneless, skinless chicken breasts
- 1 tablespoon olive oil
- Salt and pepper
- 2 romaine hearts, chopped
- 3 hardboiled eggs, peeled and chopped
- 2/3 cup crumbled blue cheese
- 2 avocados, chopped
- 1 cup blackberries
- 1 cup raspberries
- 1 cup toasted almonds
- Creamy Garlic Lime Dressing Recipe

Instructions

- Preheat the grill. Then rub the chicken breasts with oil, and salt, and pepper liberally. Grill for 5 minutes per side over medium heat. Allow the chicken to rest for at least 5 minutes before chopping. Then cut into bite-sized pieces.

- Meanwhile chop the romaine lettuce, eggs, and avocados. Place the lettuce on a large serving platter or bowl.
- Arrange all the toppings over the bed of lettuce and serve with Creamy Garlic Lime Vinaigrette.

Nutrition

Calories: 426kcal, Carbohydrates: 17g, Protein: 21g, Fat: 32g, Saturated Fat: 6g, Cholesterol: 128mg, Sodium: 292mg, Potassium: 864mg, Fiber: 10g, Sugar: 4g, Vitamin A: 3685iu, Vitamin C: 19mg, Calcium: 189mg, Iron: 2.4mg

253. Sun-Dried Tomato Chicken Pasta Salad

Prep Time: 15 Minutes

Cook Time: 8 Minutes

Total Time: 23 Minutes

Servings: 10

Ingredients

- 1 pound small dried pasta (any variety)
- 2 cups chopped leftover cooked chicken or rotisserie chicken
- 1 cup fresh baby spinach, packed
- 7 ounces sun-dried tomatoes in oil, drained
- 5 ounces pitted green olives, halved
- 1/3 cup chopped red onion
- 3/4 cup light mayonnaise
- 1/4 cup red wine vinegar
- 1 tablespoon dried Italian seasoning
- 1 clove garlic, peeled
- 1/4 teaspoon crushed red pepper

Instructions

- Place a large pot of salted water on the stovetop and bring to a boil. Cook the pasta according to package instructions. Drain the pasta in a colander and rinse with cold water to cool. Allow the paste to drain while you prep the remaining ingredients.
- Chop the sun-dried tomatoes into bite-sized pieces. Place the mayonnaise, red wine vinegar, Italian seasoning, garlic, crushed red pepper, and 1/4 cup chopped sun-dried tomatoes in the blender jar. Cover and puree.

- Place the cooled pasta, chopped chicken, spinach, remaining chopped sun-dried tomatoes, olives, and onions in a large salad bowl. Add the creamy dressing and toss to coat. Cover the bowl with plastic wrap and refrigerate until ready to serve.

Nutrition

Calories: 285kcal, Carbohydrates: 48g, Protein: 9g, Fat: 7g, Saturated Fat: 1g, Cholesterol: 2mg, Sodium: 401mg, Potassium: 823mg, Fiber: 4g, Sugar: 9g, Vitamin C: 9.1mg, Calcium: 52mg, Iron: 2.8mg

254. Instant Pot Sweet Soy Chicken Thighs

Prep Time: 5 Minutes

Cook Time: 35 Minutes

Total Time: 45 Minutes

Servings: 6

Ingredients

- 4 pounds bone-in chicken thighs (10-12 thighs)
- 1 cup low-sodium soy sauce (I bought gluten-free)
- 3/4 cup brown sugar, packed
- 1/4 cup ketchup
- 4 cloves garlic, minced
- 2 tablespoons fresh grated ginger
- 1 tablespoon sesame oil
- 1 tablespoon cornstarch or arrowroot
- Garnishes: sesame seeds and chopped scallions

Instructions

- Turn the Instant Pot on the Sauté setting and add the sesame oil. Add several of the chicken thighs, skin-side-down. Brown the skin for 2-3 minutes, until golden brown. Then remove the chicken thighs and repeat with the remaining thighs until all have been browned on the skin side. Place all the chicken thighs back in the Instant Pot, skin-side-up. This first step is optional. Then the skin will not stay crisp once pressure-cooked, but the browning process gives the skin a much richer color once finished. If skipping the browning, pile the raw thighs in the Instant Pot and move onto step 2.

- Pour the soy sauce, brown sugar, ketchup, garlic, and ginger into a bowl. Whisk well, then pour the glaze over the top of the chicken.
- Lock the lid into place. Set the Instant Pot on Pressure Cook High for 20 minutes. Then turn the Instant Pot Off and perform a Quick Release. Once the pressure valve button drops, it's safe to open the lid.
- Scoop 1/4 cup of the glaze out of the pot. Whisk 1 tablespoon cornstarch into the glaze. Then turn the Instant Pot back on Sauté and stir the cornstarch slurry back into the pot. Let it simmer for 2-4 minutes to thicken the glaze. Turn off the pot. Sprinkle with sesame seeds and chopped scallions before servings.

Nutrition

Calories: 831kcal, Carbohydrates: 36g, Protein: 51g, Fat: 52g, Saturated Fat: 13g, Cholesterol: 296mg, Sodium: 1748mg, Potassium: 782mg, Fiber: 0g, Sugar: 29g, Vitamin C: 1.1mg, Calcium: 58mg, Iron: 3.2mg

255. Pesto Chicken Baked Tortellini

Prep Time: 10 Minutes

Cook Time: 40 Minutes

Total Time: 50 Minutes

Servings: 10

Ingredients

- 40 ounces cheese tortellini, refrigerated or frozen and thawed
- 1 pound boneless, skinless chicken breasts, chopped into 1 inch cubes
- 1 tablespoon butter
- 1 red bell pepper, seeded and chopped
- 1/2 red onion, peeled and chopped
- 6 ounces basil pesto or homemade pesto
- 2 cups fresh baby spinach
- 2 cups chicken broth
- 1 cup heavy cream
- 2 cups shredded fontina cheese
- 1/2 cup shaved Parmesan cheese
- Salt and pepper

Instructions

- Preheat the oven to 400 degrees F. Place the butter in a medium-sized skillet and set it on the stovetop over medium heat. Add the onions and sauté for 2 minutes. Then stir in the chopped red pepper and sauté for another 2 minutes. Turn off the heat.
- Pour the tortellini into a large 3-quart (9x13-inch) baking dish. Place the chopped chicken, fresh spinach, and sautéed onions and peppers in the dish. Toss to mix evenly and spread out in the pan.
- Mix the pesto, chicken broth, heavy cream, 1 teaspoon salt, and 1/2 teaspoon ground black pepper in a bowl or measuring pitcher. Whisk well, then pour the mixture over the tortellini.
- Cover the pan with foil and bake for 20 minutes. Then gently stir the pasta to make sure the tortellini on top is covered in sauce. Sprinkle the top with both kinds of cheese and bake, uncovered, for another 15-20 minutes. Serve warm.

Nutrition

Calories: 694kcal, Carbohydrates: 53g, Protein: 37g, Fat: 36g, Saturated Fat: 16g, Cholesterol: 143mg, Sodium: 1191mg, Potassium: 311mg, Fiber: 5g, Sugar: 4g, Vitamin C: 21.3mg, Calcium: 420mg, Iron: 3.6mg

256. Grilled Tex Mex Stuffed Avocado Recipe

Prep Time: 5 Minutes

Cook Time: 5 Minutes

Total Time: 10 Minutes

Servings: 8 Halves

Ingredients

- 4 ripe avocados
- 16 ounces Old El Paso Refried Beans
- 10 ounces Old El Paso Red Enchilada Sauce
- 1 cup shredded cooked chicken (use leftovers or a rotisserie chicken)
- 1 cup shredded Mexican blend cheese (could be reduced fat)
- 1/4 cup crumbled queso fresco
- 1/4 cup chopped green onions

Instructions

- Preheat the grill to high heat. Slice the avocados in half, lengthwise, and remove the pits. Lay the avocados on the grill(cut side down) and grill for 2 minutes.

- Take the avocados off the grill and turn them over. Dollop 1-2 tablespoons of refried beans in the center of each avocado. Then top with shredded chicken, a generous spoonful of enchilada sauce, and shredded cheese.
- Grill the avocados with the fillings up, for another 2-3 minutes, until the fillings are warm and the cheese has melted.
- Sprinkle with crumbled queso fresco and chopped green onions. Serve warm.

Nutrition

Calories: 305kcal, Carbohydrates: 18g, Protein: 11g, Fat: 21g, Saturated Fat: 5g, Cholesterol: 26mg, Sodium: 776mg, Potassium: 539mg, Fiber: 9g, Sugar: 4g, Vitamin C: 11.6mg, Calcium: 148mg, Iron: 1.5mg

257. Peruvian Baked Chicken And Vegetable Roll-Ups

Prep Time: 15 Minutes

Cook Time: 30 Minutes

Total Time: 45 Minutes

Servings: 8 Rolls

Ingredients

- 2 pounds chicken breast cutlets (8 cutlets)
- 1 teaspoon ground cumin
- 1 teaspoon smoked paprika
- 1 teaspoon dried oregano
- 1/4 teaspoon garlic powder
- 2 plantains
- 2 bell peppers, any color
- 1 bunch scallions
- 2 tablespoons olive oil
- Salt and pepper
- Aji Verde Sauce

Instructions

- Preheat the oven to 425 degrees F. Line a large rimmed baking sheet with parchment paper.
- Trim the ends off the plantains and score a shallow line from end to end, to open the peel. Gently pull off the peel in sections. Then cut the plantains in half, and cut each half into quarters lengthwise, creating 8 french fry-shaped strips per plantain.

- Cut the bell peppers in half. Remove the seeds, then cut the peppers into strips, 1/2-inch inch wide. Trim the root ends off the scallions, then cut them in half, so that all the produce is about the same length.
- Place the plantains and peppers on the baking sheet. Sprinkle with salt and roast in the oven for 15 minutes.
- Meanwhile, mix the cumin, paprika, oregano, garlic powder, 1 teaspoon salt, and 1/4 teaspoon ground black pepper in a small bowl. Sprinkle the spice mix over the chicken cutlets, coating both sides.
- After the plantains and peppers are partially cooked, lay 2-4 pieces of each across each chicken cutlet. (Larger cutlets will hold more.) Fold the ends of the chicken over the produce and fasten tightly with a toothpick. Lay the finished rolls on the baking sheet.
- Bake for 15-20 minutes until the thickest part of the chicken is cooked through. Serve warm, topped with fresh zesty Aji Verde sauce.

Nutrition

Calories: 195kcal, Carbohydrates: 8g, Protein: 24g, Fat: 6g, Saturated Fat: 1g, Cholesterol: 72mg, Sodium: 133mg, Potassium: 595mg, Fiber: 1g, Sugar: 4g, Vitamin A: 315iu, Vitamin C: 28.4mg, Calcium: 19mg, Iron: 1mg

258. Chicken Minestrone Soup

Prep Time: 10 Minutes

Cook Time: 35 Minutes

Total Time: 45 Minutes

Servings: 8

Ingredients

- 1 1/4 pounds boneless, skinless chicken breast
- 2 tablespoons olive oil
- 1 large onion, peeled and chopped
- 6 cloves garlic, minced
- 8 ounces button mushrooms, sliced
- 2 carrots, sliced
- 6 cups chicken broth
- 6 cups water
- 2 cans fire-roasted diced tomatoes (15-ounce cans)

- 1/2 cup red wine
- 2 tablespoons dried Italian seasoning
- 1 small zucchini, quartered and sliced
- 1 small summer squash, quartered and sliced
- 15 ounces kidney beans, drained (1 can)
- 15 ounces cannellini beans, drained (1 can)
- 8 ounce dried macaroni noodles (could be gluten-free)
- 1 cup frozen cut green beans
- 1/2 cup chopped roasted red peppers
- Salt and pepper

Instructions

- Set a large 6-8 quart soup pot over medium heat. Add the olive oil, onions, garlic, mushrooms, and carrots. Sauté for 5-8 minutes to soften the vegetables, stirring regularly.
- Place the whole chicken breasts down in the sautéed veggies at the bottom of the pot. Add in the chicken broth, water, canned tomatoes, red wine, Italian seasoning, 1 teaspoon salt, and 1/4 teaspoon ground black pepper. Bring to a boil and simmer for 15-20 minutes, until the chicken breasts are cooked through.
- Remove the chicken breasts with tongs and set them on a cutting board. Add the zucchini, summer squash, canned beans, macaroni, green beans, and roasted red peppers to the pot. Stir well. Bring to a simmer and cook for another 5-8 minutes, until the pasta is cooked through.
- Meanwhile, chop the chicken into bite-size pieces. Stir the chicken back into the soup. Taste, then salt and pepper as needed.

Nutrition

Calories: 338kcal, Carbohydrates: 43g, Protein: 25g, Fat: 6g, Saturatedfat: 1g, Cholesterol: 45mg, Sodium: 1147mg, Potassium: 839mg, Fiber: 6g, Sugar: 6g, Vitamin A: 3240iu, Vitamin C: 32.6mg, Calcium: 137mg, Iron: 3.9mg

---

259. Honey Orange Roasted Chicken Recipe

Prep Time: 10 Minutes

Cook Time: 2 Hours

Total Time: 2 Hours 10 Minutes

Servings: 6

Ingredients

For The Honey Orange Roast Chicken:

- 7-8 pound chicken, whole
- 1/2 cup unsalted butter, softened
- 1/4 cup honey
- 1 small orange, such as a clementine
- Salt and pepper
- For the Honey Orange Gravy:
- Pan juices from the chicken
- 3 tablespoons flour
- 2 cups chicken stock
- Salt and pepper

For The Grilled Spring Veggies:

- 12 ounces thin french green beans (haricot vert) trimmed
- 12 ounces thin baby asparagus, trimmed
- Salt and pepper

Instructions

- Preheat the oven to 450 degrees F. Remove the neck and gizzards from inside the chicken. Place the chicken in a small dry skillet and pat the skin dry with paper towels. Slide a regular tablespoon, curved side down, underneath the skin of the chicken. Run the spoon along the breast to loosen the skin on both sides, and down over the drumsticks. Then mix the butter, honey, and the zest of one orange with 3/4 teaspoon salt and 1/4 teaspoon black pepper. Mash the ingredients in a small bowl until well combined. Use the spoon to deposit the butter mixture underneath the skin of the chicken. Place as much of the butter as possible over the breast meat and drumsticks. Then press the skin to smooth. Rub any remaining butter over the outside of the skin and sprinkle with salt and pepper. Slice the orange and place it inside the chicken.
- Roast the chicken for 45 minutes to crisp up the skin, then lower the heat to 350 degrees F. If the skin is brown, cover the chicken loosely with foil and continue roasting for another 75 - 90 minutes. (My chicken was exactly 8 pounds and it was finished in 2 hours total.) To test the chicken for doneness, stick a knife down between the drumstick and the breast. If the juices run out clear, the chicken is ready.

- Remove the chicken from the oven and carefully lift it out of the juices. Place it on a platter and cover with foil to keep it warm.
- While the chicken is roasting, place a large grill pan over two burners and turn them both on medium heat. Lay the asparagus and green beans on the grill pan and sear until the color has intensified and grill marks have formed. Flip once and salt and pepper. Cook the veggies until just cooked through, so they are bright green and firm. Approximately 6-10 minutes.
- Place the sauté pan with the chicken juices over another burner. Heat the burner to medium heat and whisk in the flour. Add the chicken stock, then salt and pepper to taste. (You may need as much as 3/4 teaspoon salt, depending on how salty the juices and stock are. Start with a little salt and add more.) Bring the gravy to a boil and whisk. Continue simmering and stirring until the gravy is thick enough to coat a spoon.
- To Serve: Cut the chicken into pieces and distribute it onto plates. Spoon the grilled veggies next to the chicken and drizzle honey orange gravy over both the chicken and veggies.

Nutrition

Calories: 806kcal, Carbohydrates: 26g, Protein: 52g, Fat: 54g, Saturated Fat: 20g, Cholesterol: 233mg, Sodium: 299mg, Potassium: 845mg, Fiber: 3g, Sugar: 17g, Vitamin A: 1695iu, Vitamin C: 25.9mg, Calcium: 78mg, Iron: 4.5mg

---

260. Pollo Rojo (Red Pepper Chicken)

Prep Time: 25 Minutes

Cook Time: 10 Minutes

Total Time: 35 Minutes

Servings: 4

Ingredients

For The Red Pepper Mole:

- 14-15 dried New Mexico chiles, Anaheims or California
- 2 cloves garlic
- 1 cup chicken stock (any stock would work)
- 1 tablespoon ground cumin
- 2 tablespoons honey
- 3 tablespoons rice vinegar

- 1/2 teaspoon salt
- For the Red Pepper Chicken:
- 2 pounds chicken cutlets (thinly sliced breast meat)
- 1 tablespoon oil
- 1 tablespoon butter
- Salt and pepper

Instructions

- Prepare a bowl of boiling water. Place the chiles in the water and allow them to soak for 10-15 minutes, until soft to the touch.
- Remove the stems, seeds, and membranes, rinsing each pepper in the bowl. Then place in a food processor.
- Add the garlic cloves and half the chicken stock. Puree until smooth. Then add the cumin, honey, vinegar, salt, and remaining stock. Puree again until smooth. Taste and salt again if needed. The sauce should have a very intense flavor, but not be overly spicy if the seeds and membranes are properly removed.
- Heat a large to medium-high heat. Pat the chicken cutlets dry and salt the pepper on both sides.
- Add the oil and butter to the skillet. Once melted, place half the cutlets in the pan. Saute for 2-3 minutes per side. Repeat with the remaining cutlets.
- To Serve: Warm the red pepper sauce and pour over the chicken. Garnish with cilantro leaves or queso fresco.

Nutrition

Calories: 441kcal, Carbohydrates: 25g, Protein: 53g, Fat: 13g, Saturated Fat: 3g, Cholesterol: 154mg, Sodium: 682mg, Potassium: 1436mg, Fiber: 2g, Sugar: 17g, Vitamin C: 229.5mg, Calcium: 50mg, Iron: 3.6mg

---

261. Healthy Chicken Cacciatore Soup

Prep Time: 15 Minutes

Cook Time: 30 Minutes

Total Time: 45 Minutes

Servings: 10

Ingredients

- 2 boneless, skinless chicken breasts, cubed

- 1 tablespoon olive oil
- 1 tablespoon butter
- 4-6 cloves garlic, minced
- 1 large onion, chopped
- 1 cup celery, chopped
- 1 cup carrots, chopped
- 1 medium zucchini, chopped
- 8 ounces mushrooms (cremini or button), sliced
- 2 cans diced tomatoes, (2 cans) with garlic and herbs for added flavor
- 28 ounces tomato sauce
- 6 cups chicken stock
- 1 cup wine, white or red
- 1/8-1/4 teaspoon crushed red pepper flakes
- 1 tablespoon Italian seasonings
- 1 bunch fresh basil leaves
- 2 cups small dried pasta
- 1 cup shredded Parmesan cheese
- Salt and pepper

Instructions

- In a large stock, pot browns the chicken in oil and butter over medium heat.
- Add the garlic, onions, celery, and carrots. Sauté for 3-5 minutes, then and 1 cup of the stock simmering for 3 minutes.
- Add everything except the fresh basil, Parmesan cheese, and pasta. Stir in 1 teaspoon salt and 1/2 teaspoon ground black pepper. Simmer for 10 minutes.
- Add the pasta and half of the fresh basil. Simmer for 8-10 more minutes until the pasta is al dente. At this point add 1-2 cups of water if needed. Stir in Parmesan cheese.
- Garnish with a sprinkle of Parmesan cheese and more fresh basil.

Nutrition

Calories: 259kcal, Carbohydrates: 27g, Protein: 16g, Fat: 8g, Saturatedfat: 3g, Cholesterol: 28mg, Sodium: 849mg, Potassium: 929mg, Fiber: 3g, Sugar: 10g, Vitamin A: 2840iu, Vitamin C: 20.1mg, Calcium: 190mg, Iron: 2.8mg

262. Skillet Chicken Puttanesca

Prep Time: 5 Minutes

Cook Time: 18 Minutes

Total Time: 23 Minutes

Servings: 4

Ingredients

- 4 boneless skinless chicken breasts
- 2 tablespoons olive oil
- 3 cloves garlic, minced
- 8 anchovy fillets, minced (from a small can)
- 28 ounces crushed tomatoes
- 1/4 cup chopped parsley
- 1 1/2 teaspoon dried oregano
- 1/2 teaspoon crushed red pepper
- 6 ounces pitted kalamata olives, drained
- 3 ounces pitted green olives, drained
- 3 ounces capers, drained
- Salt and pepper

Instructions

- Set a large sauté pan over medium-high heat. Season the chicken on both sides with salt and pepper. Add the oil to the pan and cook the chicken breasts for 4-5 minutes per side. Remove the chicken from the skillet and set it aside.
- Next, add the garlic and anchovies to the skillet. Sauté for 2 minutes, then pour in the tomatoes, parsley, oregano, and crushed red pepper. Stir well, and add in the olives and capers. Simmer 8-10 minutes.
- Place the chicken back into the sauce. Simmer the chicken for 3-4 minutes to heat through. Serve warm as a low carb meal, or serve with pasta.

Nutrition

Calories: 369kcal, Carbohydrates: 19g, Protein: 30g, Fat: 20g, Saturated Fat: 3g, Cholesterol: 77mg, Sodium: 1989mg, Potassium: 1096mg, Fiber: 7g, Sugar: 9g, Vitamin A: 1145iu, Vitamin C: 26.2mg, Calcium: 148mg, Iron: 4.4mg

263. Skinny Creamy Chimichurri Chicken Skillet

Prep Time: 5 Minutes

Cook Time: 13 Minutes

Total Time: 18 Minutes

Servings: 4

Ingredients

- 4 boneless skinless chicken breasts
- 1 tablespoon olive oil
- 1 bunch parsley, stems removed
- 1/2 onion, cut into wedges
- 2 cloves garlic
- 3 ounces fat-free cream cheese
- 3 tablespoons red wine vinegar
- 1 tablespoon dried oregano
- 1 1/2 teaspoons ground cumin
- 1/4 teaspoon crushed red pepper
- 1 cup water
- Salt and pepper

Instructions

- Place a large deep skillet over medium heat and add the oil. Season the chicken breasts with salt and pepper. Once the skillet is hot add the chicken breasts and cook 4 minutes per side.
- Meanwhile, peel the onion and garlic cloves. Place the parsley, onion, garlic, vinegar, oregano, cumin, crushed red pepper, and 1/2 teaspoon salt in the food processor. Pulse until the mixture is well chopped. Then add in the cream cheese and water. Turn on and puree until very smooth.
- Once the chicken has seared for 4 minutes per side, pour the sauce over the chicken. Simmer for 3-5 minutes to let the chicken finish cooking and the sauce thicken. Taste, then salt and pepper as needed.

Nutrition

Calories: 253kcal, Carbohydrates: 4g, Protein: 26g, Fat: 14g, Saturated Fat: 5g, Cholesterol: 95mg, Sodium: 215mg, Potassium: 575mg, Fiber: 1g, Sugar: 1g, Vitamin C: 21.8mg, Calcium: 79mg, Iron: 2.4mg

264. Skinny Creamy Chicken Broccoli Soup

Prep Time: 10 Minutes

Cook Time: 25 Minutes

Total Time: 35 Minutes

Servings: 6

Ingredients

- ❖ 1 large onion, chopped
- 3 cloves garlic, minced
- 1 tablespoon butter

- 1 pound boneless skinless chicken breast
- 8 cups low-sodium chicken broth
- 3 tablespoons dry sherry
- 2 tablespoons Dijon mustard
- 1 teaspoon cornstarch
- 1/2 teaspoons smoked paprika
- 1/4 teaspoon crushed red pepper
- 4 ounces fat-free cream cheese, cut into cubes
- 3 cups small fresh broccoli florets
- Salt and pepper
- Possible Garnishes: Low fat shredded cheese, chopped scallions, fresh parsley

Instructions

- Place the butter in a 4-quart soup pot and set over medium heat. Once the butter has melted, add the onions and garlic. Sauté for 3-4 minutes, stirring to make sure the garlic doesn't burn.
- Place the whole chicken breasts at the bottom of the pot. Add the broth, sherry, Dijon mustard, corn starch, smoked paprika, crushed red pepper, 1 teaspoon salt, and 1/2 teaspoon ground black pepper.
- Bring the broth to a boil. Lower the heat, cover, and simmer for 15-20 minutes to cook the chicken.
- Remove the chicken breast with tongs. Then add in the cream cheese. Whisk to melt the cream cheese into the broth. Then use two forks to shred the chicken.
- Add the broccoli florets and the shredded chicken to the soup. Stir well and turn off the heat. The small broccoli florets will cook quickly in the hot broth.
- Taste, then salt and pepper as needed. Serve warm.

Nutrition

Calories: 254kcal, Carbohydrates: 10g, Protein: 25g, Fat: 12g, Saturated Fat: 5g, Cholesterol: 74mg, Sodium: 334mg, Potassium: 759mg, Fiber: 1g, Sugar: 2g, Vitamin C: 43.3mg, Calcium: 66mg, Iron: 1.5mg

265. Low Carb Green Curry Chicken Noodle Soup

Prep Time: 10 Minutes

Cook Time: 25 Minutes

Total Time: 35 Minutes

Servings: 8

Ingredients

- 1 teaspoon coconut oil
- 1 onion, peeled and chopped
- 3 cloves garlic, minced
- 1 tablespoon fresh grated ginger
- 1 red bell pepper, seeded and chopped
- 3 carrots, sliced
- 1 1/4 pounds whole boneless skinless chicken breast
- 13.5 ounces thick unsweetened coconut milk (1 can)
- 3-6 tablespoons green curry paste
- 9 cups chicken broth
- 3 tablespoons fish sauce
- 14 ounces konnyaku noodles
- 2 cups small broccoli florets
- 1/2 cup fresh Thai basil leaves
- Salt and pepper

Instructions

- Place the oil in a large 6-8 quart saucepot over medium heat. Once the oil is hot, sauté the onions, minced garlic, and ginger for 3 minutes to soften. Stir in the chopped bell pepper and carrots.
- Add the chicken breasts, coconut milk, 3 tablespoons green curry paste, chicken broth, and fish sauce to the pot. Raise the heat to high and bring to a boil. Once boiling, reduce the heat back to medium, then simmer for 15 minutes.
- Meanwhile, drain and rinse the konnyaku noodles.
- Using tongs, remove the chicken breasts from the pot. Use a fork and tongs to shred the chicken. Then place it back in the pot. Stir in the konnyaku noodles and the broccoli florets. Taste, then add 1-3 more tablespoons green curry paste if desired. Taste again, then salt and pepper as needed.
- Garnish with fresh basil leaves and serve warm.

Nutrition

Calories: 231kcal, Carbohydrates: 9g, Protein: 18g, Fat: 13g, Saturated Fat: 10g, Cholesterol: 45mg, Sodium: 1610mg, Potassium: 803mg, Fiber: 1g, Sugar: 3g, Vitamin C: 62.6mg, Calcium: 65mg, Iron: 3mg

266. The Best Thai Panang Chicken Curry

Prep Time: 10 Minutes

Cook Time: 22 Minutes

Total Time: 32 Minutes

Servings: 6

Ingredients

- 1 1/2 pounds boneless skinless chicken thighs chopped
- 1 small onion, peeled and chopped
- 1 red bell pepper, seeded and chopped
- 1 orange bell pepper, seeded and chopped
- 2 cloves garlic, minced
- 1 tablespoon coconut oil
- 4 ounces Panang red curry paste (1 can)
- 1 tablespoon peanut butter
- 12 kaffir lime leaves, crushed
- 13.5 ounces thick coconut milk, unsweetened (1 can)
- 3 tablespoons fish sauce
- 1/4 cup Thai basil leaves or sweet basil

Instructions

- Cut the chicken into bite-size pieces. Chop the onions and peppers into roughly 1-inch pieces. Mince the garlic. Then crush the kaffir lime leaves to help release their oils.
- Place a 14-inch skillet (or wok) over medium-high heat. Add the coconut oil. Once the oil melts, add the onions. Sauté for 1 minute, then add the peppers and garlic. Sauté another 2-3 minutes.
- Move the veggies to the sides of the skillet and add the Panang red curry paste and peanut butter to the center of the pan. Sauté the curry for 2-3 minutes to intensify the flavor, moving around the pan. Then add the kaffir lime leaves, coconut milk, and fish sauce. Stir to blend.
- Stir in the chopped chicken and bring to a boil. Lower the heat and simmer for 10-15 minutes,

until the chicken is cooked through and the sauce thickens. Stir occasionally. Remove from heat and stir in the basil leaves. Serve with rice, quinoa, or noodles.

Nutrition

Calories: 340kcal, Carbohydrates: 8g, Protein: 24g, Fat: 23g, Saturated Fat: 16g, Cholesterol: 107mg, Sodium: 163mg, Potassium: 545mg, Fiber: 2g, Sugar: 4g, Vitamin C: 54.7mg, Calcium: 56mg, Iron: 3.8mg

267. Spicy Thai Chicken Soup

Prep Time: 10 Minutes

Cook Time: 25 Minutes

Total Time: 35 Minutes

Servings: 6 Servings

Ingredients

- 1 1/2 pounds boneless skinless chicken breast, sliced thin
- 1 large onion, peeled and sliced thin
- 1 red bell pepper, quartered and sliced thin
- 1 cup shredded carrots
- 1 cup thinly sliced snap peas
- 1/2 cup roughly chopped Thai basil
- 2 tablespoons vegetable oil
- 1 teaspoon sesame oil
- 1/4 - 1/2 teaspoon crushed red pepper
- 2 tablespoons freshly grated ginger, grated
- 4 cloves garlic, minced
- 64 ounces chicken stock
- 1 1/2 cups unsweetened coconut milk
- 1/4 cup fish sauce
- 1/2 cup chopped green onions for garnish

Instructions

- Place a large saucepot over medium-high heat. Add both oils to the pot, followed by the onions. Saute the onions for 2-3 minutes, stirring regularly. Then add the garlic and ginger and saute for 1 more minute.
- Add the stock, coconut milk, fish sauce, and crushed red pepper. Bring to a boil. Simmer for 10 minutes. Then add the sliced chicken. Stir to separate, then simmer another 5-8 minutes until the chicken is cooked through.

- Turn off the heat and add the red bell peppers, carrots, snap peas, and basil. Cover the pot and steep the vegetable for 5 minutes, until barely cooked through, but still firm. Taste, then salt and pepper as needed. Serve warm with a sprinkle of chopped green onions.

Nutrition

- Calories: 462kcal, Carbohydrates: 22g, Protein: 34g, Fat: 26g, Saturated Fat: 18g, Cholesterol: 81mg, Sodium: 1350mg, Potassium: 1138mg, Fiber: 3g, Sugar: 10g, Vitamin A: 4595iu, Vitamin C: 44mg, Calcium: 60mg, Iron: 2.9mg

268. Skinny Creamy Chimichurri Chicken Skillet

Prep Time: 5 Minutes

Cook Time: 13 Minutes

Total Time: 18 Minutes

Servings: 4

Ingredients

- 4 boneless skinless chicken breasts
- 1 tablespoon olive oil
- 1 bunch parsley, stems removed
- 1/2 onion, cut into wedges
- 2 cloves garlic
- 3 ounces fat-free cream cheese
- 3 tablespoons red wine vinegar
- 1 tablespoon dried oregano
- 1 1/2 teaspoons ground cumin
- 1/4 teaspoon crushed red pepper
- 1 cup water
- Salt and pepper

Instructions

- Place a large deep skillet over medium heat and add the oil. Season the chicken breasts with salt and pepper. Once the skillet is hot add the chicken breasts and cook 4 minutes per side.
- Meanwhile, peel the onion and garlic cloves. Place the parsley, onion, garlic, vinegar, oregano, cumin, crushed red pepper, and 1/2 teaspoon salt in the food processor. Pulse until the mixture is well chopped. Then add in the cream cheese and water. Turn on and puree until very smooth.
- Once the chicken has seared for 4 minutes per side, pour the sauce over the chicken. Simmer

for 3-5 minutes to let the chicken finish cooking and the sauce thicken. Taste, then salt and pepper as needed.

Nutrition

Calories: 253kcal, Carbohydrates: 4g, Protein: 26g, Fat: 14g, Saturatedfat: 5g, Cholesterol: 95mg, Sodium: 215mg, Potassium: 575mg, Fiber: 1g, Sugar: 1g, Vitamin C: 21.8mg, Calcium: 79mg, Iron: 2.4mg

269. Skinny Creamy Chicken Broccoli Soup

Prep Time: 10 Minutes

Cook Time: 25 Minutes

Total Time: 35 Minutes

Servings: 6

Ingredients

- 1 large onion, chopped
- 3 cloves garlic, minced
- 1 tablespoon butter
- 1 pound boneless skinless chicken breast
- 8 cups low-sodium chicken broth
- 3 tablespoons dry sherry
- ❖ 2 tablespoons Dijon mustard
- 1 teaspoon cornstarch
- 1/2 teaspoons smoked paprika
- 1/4 teaspoon crushed red pepper
- 4 ounces fat-free cream cheese, cut into cubes
- 3 cups small fresh broccoli florets
- Salt and pepper
- Possible garnishes: Low fat shredded cheese, chopped scallions, fresh parsley

Instructions

- Place the butter in a 4-quart soup pot and set over medium heat. Once the butter has melted, add the onions and garlic. Sauté for 3-4 minutes, stirring to make sure the garlic doesn't burn.
- Place the whole chicken breasts at the bottom of the pot. Add the broth, sherry, Dijon mustard, corn starch, smoked paprika, crushed red pepper, 1 teaspoon salt, and 1/2 teaspoon ground black pepper.
- Bring the broth to a boil. Lower the heat, cover, and simmer for 15-20 minutes to cook the chicken.

- Remove the chicken breast with tongs. Then add in the cream cheese. Whisk to melt the cream cheese into the broth. Then use two forks to shred the chicken.
- Add the broccoli florets and the shredded chicken to the soup. Stir well and turn off the heat. The small broccoli florets will cook quickly in the hot broth.
- Taste, then salt and pepper as needed. Serve warm.

Nutrition

Calories: 254kcal, Carbohydrates: 10g, Protein: 25g, Fat: 12g, Saturated Fat: 5g, Cholesterol: 74mg, Sodium: 334mg, Potassium: 759mg, Fiber: 1g, Sugar: 2g, Vitamin C: 43.3mg, Calcium: 66mg, Iron: 1.5mg

270. Chicken Caesar Pasta Salad

Prep Time: 20 Minutes

Cook Time: 15 Minutes

Total Time: 35 Minutes

Servings: 12

Ingredients

For The Chicken Caesar Pasta Salad:

- 1 1/2 pounds boneless skinless chicken breasts
- 1 pound fusilli pasta
- 1-pint grape tomatoes
- 1 cup pitted black olives
- 1 cup chopped green onions
- 1 head romaine lettuce
- 3/4 cup shredded Parmesan cheese
- 2 cups croutons, store-bought or homemade
- Homemade Caesar Dressing
- Salt and pepper

For The Homemade Caesar Dressing:

- 1 cup low-fat buttermilk
- 1/2 cup light mayonnaise
- 1 1/2 tablespoons lemon juice
- 1 tablespoon Dijon mustard
- 7 whole anchovies from a can
- 2 cloves garlic, peeled

Instructions

- Preheat the grill to medium heat. Place a large pot of salted water over high heat and bring to a boil. Salt and pepper the chicken breasts.
- Once the grill is hot, grill the chicken for 5-6 minutes per side. Then remove from heat and allow it to rest. Meanwhile, drop the pasta in the boiling water. Cook for 6-8 minutes, then drain and cool.
- Place all the ingredients for the homemade Caesar dressing in the blender. Puree until smooth. Chop the chicken breasts into bite-size pieces and roughly chop the romaine lettuce.
- To assemble, place the pasta, tomatoes, black olives, and chopped green onions in a large bowl. Top with the chopped grilled chicken Then pour the dressing over the pasta salad and toss to coat. If making ahead, cover the Chicken Caesar Pasta Salad and refrigerate until ready to serve.
- Right before serving, toss in the chopped romaine, shredded Parmesan cheese, and croutons. Salt and pepper to taste. Serve cold or at room temperature.

Nutrition

Calories: 320kcal, Carbohydrates: 39g, Protein: 22g, Fat: 8g, Saturated Fat: 2g, Cholesterol: 44mg, Sodium: 493mg, Potassium: 595mg, Fiber: 4g, Sugar: 4g, Vitamin C: 10.8mg, Calcium: 149mg, Iron: 1.8mg

271. Bistro Slow Cooker Chicken And Rice

Prep Time: 10 Minutes

Cook Time: 2 Hours

Total Time: 2 Hours 10 Minutes

Servings: 8

Ingredients

- 1 onion, peeled and diced
- 6 cloves garlic, peeled and minced
- 1/4 cup unsalted butter
- 4 boneless skinless chicken breast
- 2 1/2 cups jasmine rice
- Bouquet de garni (bundle of herbs with 2 sprigs of rosemary and 4 sprigs thyme)
- 1 lemon sliced and seeds removed
- 1/2 teaspoon paprika
- 5 cups chicken broth
- Salt
- Pepper

Instructions

- Place the butter in a medium skillet and set over medium heat. Add the chopped onion and garlic. Saute for 3-5 minutes to soften, then pour the onions and butter into the crock of a large slow cooker.
- Add the bouquet de Garni and the chicken to the slow cooker. Sprinkle the chicken with 1 teaspoon salt, 1/2 teaspoon ground pepper, and 1/2 teaspoon paprika. Pour the rice over the top and lay the lemon slices over it. Then pour the chicken broth over the rice.
- Cover and cook on high for 2-3 hours, or on low for 3-5 hours. (The first time you make this dish, be watchful of the rice. All slow cookers are slightly different, and you do not want the rice to cook to mush. Turn the slow cooker off when the rice is firm and fluffy. My slow cooker takes 2 hours on high.)
- Pull the chicken breast and the bouquet de garni out of the crock and cut into bite-size chunks. Add the chicken back to the crock and toss. Serve warm.

Nutrition

Calories: 343kcal, Carbohydrates: 49g, Protein: 17g, Fat: 8g, Saturated Fat: 4g, Cholesterol: 51mg, Sodium: 608mg, Potassium: 422mg, Fiber: 1g, Sugar: 1g, Vitamin C: 13.6mg, Calcium: 37mg, Iron: 1.1mg

272. Sweet and Tangy Chicken Quesadillas

Prep Time: 5 Minutes

Cook Time: 20 Minutes

Total Time: 25 Minutes

Servings: 4 Large Quesadillas

Ingredients

- 1 1/4 pound chicken breast or tenders
- 1 red onion sliced
- 1 orange bell pepper seeded and sliced
- 1 tablespoon butter
- 1/2 cup Musselman's Apple Butter

- 2 tablespoons cayenne pepper sauce
- 4 teaspoons Musselman's Apple Cider Vinegar
- 8 large wheat tortillas
- 3 cups shredded Mexican blend cheese at room temperature
- 1/4 cup chopped cilantro

Instructions

- Preheat a large nonstick skillet to medium-high heat. Chop the chicken into bite-size pieces and set aside. When the skillet is hot, add the sliced onions and sear for 2 minutes to soften and char the edges, flipping once. Move the onions to a plate and sear the sliced peppers for 2 minutes until slightly charred. Move the peppers to the plate as well.
- Add the butter to the skillet. Once melted, add the chicken pieces. Salt and pepper liberally, then brown for 2 minutes per side. Add the apple butter, cayenne pepper sauce, and vinegar. Stir to combine and let the mixture simmer for another 2 minutes. Then turn off the heat and stir to coat the chicken in the sauce. Move the chicken to the holding plate as well.
- Lower the heat to medium-low and add the first tortilla to a clean nonstick skillet. Sprinkle it with a heaping 1/4 cup cheese. Spread one-quarter of the onions, peppers, and chicken over the top. Then sprinkle with fresh cilantro. Sprinkle another 1/4 cup cheese over the top and cover with a second tortilla.
- Wait to flip the quesadilla until the bottom tortilla is golden brown, and the cheese has started to melt to hold everything together. Place a flat spatula under the bottom tortilla, and another on the top tortilla. Then quickly flip the quesadilla. Brown the bottom tortilla, then move to a warming drawer or warm oven to keep crisp. Repeat with the remaining ingredients. Once all 4 quesadillas of cooked, cut them into wedges and serve warm!

Nutrition

Calories: 1170kcal, Carbohydrates: 67g, Protein: 81g, Fat: 63g, Saturatedfat: 35g, Cholesterol: 267mg, Sodium: 2235mg, Potassium: 810mg, Fiber: 8g, Sugar: 21g, Vitamin C: 42.2mg, Calcium: 1351mg, Iron: 4.1mg

273. Korean Fried Chicken Recipe

Prep Time: 10 Minutes

Cook Time: 30 Minutes

Resting Time: 4 Hours

Total Time: 4 Hours 40 Minutes

Servings: 12

Ingredients

- For the Fried Chicken Recipe
- 4 pounds whole chicken, wings, and drumsticks about 12 pieces
- 1/2 cup salt + 1-quart warm water
- 1 1/4 cup corn starch divided
- 1 tablespoon baking powder divided
- 3/4 cup all-purpose flour
- 12-ounce light beer or club soda
- 2 quarts fry oil peanut, canola, grape seed
- For the Korean Dunking Sauce
- 1/2 cup gochujang sauce
- 1/4 cup low-sodium soy sauce
- 1/4 cup rice vinegar
- 1/4 cup brown sugar
- 3 tablespoons sesame oil
- 5 cloves garlic smashed
- 1 tablespoon fresh grated ginger
- 1-2 tablespoons Sriracha optional for extra heat

Instructions

- Place the salt and warm water in a large bowl and swirl to dissolve the salt. Then add the chicken pieces to the brine. Cover and refrigerate for 4 hours (or up to 12 hours.) Take the chicken out of the brine and dry with paper towels. Set out to allow the skin to continue drying.
- Pour the oil into a large heavy-bottomed stockpot and set over medium heat. Attach a deep-fry thermometer if you have one. Mix 3/4 cup of cornstarch and 2 teaspoons of baking powder in a bowl. Move the chicken to the bowl and toss to coat well.
- Then place the remaining 1/2 cup of cornstarch, 1 teaspoon baking powder, and 3/4 cup of flour in a separate bowl. Whisk in the beer to create the tempura batter.

- Turn the oven on warm (175-200 degrees F) and set out an oven-safe plate lined with paper towels. Check the temperature of the frying oil. It should be at 350 degrees F. Drop a little batter into the oil to check. If the batter turns brown right away the oil is too hot. Turn off the heat and wait for it to cool, before continuing. One-piece at a time, tap the excess cornstarch off the chicken and dunk it in the tempura batter. Dunk a couple of times to make sure there are no air pockets. Shake the chicken a little to allow the excess batter to drip back into the bowl then slowly swirl the chicken as you place it in the oil. Continue... frying 4-6 pieces at a time, until golden brown and crispy. Flip the chicken with tongs as needed and cover with a splatter screen if you have one. The wings should be golden and cooked for around 10 minutes, and the drumsticks will take between 12-15 minutes. Check the interior temperature with a meat thermometer - it should be 165 degrees F. Using the tongs, move the chicken to the plate and place it in the oven while you repeat with the remaining chicken. This will take 2-3 batches, depending on the width of your pot.
- While the chicken is frying, place the first seven ingredients for the Korean dunking sauce in a medium saucepot. Set over medium heat, stir, and bring to a boil. Once the sauce reaches a boil, turn the heat on low and let it simmer for 2 minutes. Then remove from heat. Taste for spice. If you want your chicken to be extra spicy stir in sriracha to taste.
- Once all the chicken is fried, and you are ready to eat, dunk each piece of chicken in the sauce, one at a time to coat well. Serve immediately.

Nutrition

Calories: 315kcal, Carbohydrates: 28g, Protein: 15g, Fat: 15g, Saturated Fat: 4g, Cholesterol: 54mg, Sodium: 5163mg, Potassium: 279mg, Fiber: 1g, Sugar: 7g, Vitamin C: 2.4mg, Calcium: 63mg, Iron: 1.4mg

274. One Pot Chicken Pasta With Light Basil Cream Sauce

Prep Time: 5 Minutes

Cook Time: 20 Minutes

Total Time: 25 Minutes

Servings: 6

Ingredients

- 1 1/4 pounds boneless skinless chicken breast
- 1 tablespoons butter
- 1 pound DeLallo whole wheat Gemelli pasta
- 1 1/2 cups low-fat sour cream
- 1 cup low-fat milk
- 1 bunch fresh basil about 1 cup packed leaves
- 2-3 cloves garlic
- 1 cup grape tomatoes halved
- Salt and pepper

Instructions

- Heat a large deep sauté pan over medium heat. Cut the chicken into bite-size pieces. When the skillet is hot add the butter, and the chicken. Salt and pepper liberally. Then sauté for 3-5 minutes until mostly cooked. Remove the chicken from the pan and set it aside. (Do not cook the chicken through yet.)
- Add the pasta to the skillet and cover with 3 cups of water. Place the lid on the pan and simmer until the pasta has absorbed all the water and is almost cooked through.
- Meanwhile, place the sour cream, milk, basil, and garlic in the blender. Cover and puree until very smooth. Once the pasta has absorbed all the water, add the cream sauce to the pasta and stir to coat. Simmer for 2 minutes, then add the chicken back to the skillet and simmer another 2-3 minutes, until the chicken and pasta are cooked through and the sauce has tightened a little. Salt and pepper to taste.
- Remove the skillet from heat. The sauce will continue to thicken as it cools. Toss well, then add the tomato halves to the pasta. Serve immediately.

Nutrition

Calories: 320kcal, Carbohydrates: 27g, Protein: 28g, Fat: 11g, Saturated Fat: 6g, Cholesterol: 88mg, Sodium: 188mg, Potassium: 623mg, Fiber: 4g, Sugar: 3g, Vitamin C: 5.6mg, Calcium: 153mg, Iron: 1.3mg

275. Vietnamese Banh Mi Street Tacos

Prep Time: 20 Minutes

Cook Time: 10 Minutes

Resting Time: 1 Hour

Total Time: 30 Minutes

Servings: 20 Tacos

Ingredients

For The Vietnamese Banh Mi Chicken

- 2 tablespoons coconut oil
- 2 pounds boneless skinless chicken thighs
- 1/2 cup fresh lime juice
- 1/3 cup fish sauce
- 1/4 cup granulated sugar
- 1 jalapeno
- 4 cloves garlic minced

- For The Spicy Mayo

- 3/4 cup mayonnaise
- 1-2 tablespoons Sriracha
- 1 tablespoon rice vinegar
- 1 tablespoon granulated sugar
- For the Street Tacos
- 2 packages Old El Paso Flour Tortillas taco size
- 3 carrots shredded
- 1 English cucumber sliced thin
- 2 bunches radishes sliced thin
- 4 jalapenos sliced
- 1 bunch fresh mint or cilantro
- 2 limes cut into wedges

Instructions

For The Vietnamese Banh Mi Chicken:

- Pour the fish sauce, lime juice, and sugar into a medium microwave-safe bowl. Microwave for 1-2 minutes, until the sugar dissolves. Cut the chicken thighs into very small (1/-inch) pieces. Place in a bowl along with jalapeno slices and minced garlic. Stir and refrigerate for at least 1 hour. (3 hours is best!)

For The Spicy Mayo:

- Place the rice vinegar and sugar in a small microwave-safe bowl. Microwave for 1 minute to dissolve the sugar. Then mix in the mayo and

Sriracha. Add more Sriracha for an extra kick. Refrigerate until ready to serve.

- Prep all the veggies. Once the chicken has marinated, drain off the marinade. Then heat a large skillet to medium-high heat. Once hot, add 1 tablespoon coconut oil to the skillet. Then add half the chicken to the skillet. Sear for 4-5 minutes, stirring to caramelize on all sides. Remove and repeat with the remaining chicken.

To Serve:

- Place a scoop of chicken in Old El Paso flour tortillas. Top with shredded carrots, cucumber slices, radishes, fresh mint leaves, and jalapeno slices. Drizzle with spicy mayo and serve with fresh lime wedges.

Nutrition

Calories: 234kcal, Carbohydrates: 21g, Protein: 12g, Fat: 12g, Saturated Fat: 3g, Cholesterol: 47mg, Sodium: 618mg, Potassium: 250mg, Fiber: 1g, Sugar: 6g, Vitamin C: 10.4mg, Calcium: 47mg, Iron: 1.5mg

276. Asian Chicken Sliders With Slaw

Prep Time: 15 Minutes

Cook Time: 6 Minutes

Total Time: 21 Minutes

Servings: 12

Ingredients

For The Asian Chicken Sliders:

- 1 pound ground chicken, or ground white meat turkey
- 1/2 cup jasmine rice, cooked
- 1/4 cup panko bread crumbs
- 1/4 cup chopped green onions
- 1 jalapeno, seeded and diced
- 1 tablespoon grated ginger
- 1 large egg
- 4 tablespoons Bertolli 100% Pure Olive Oil, divided
- 2 tablespoons soy sauce
- 12 small yeast buns, dinner rolls
- 1/2 cup wasabi mayonnaise (1/2 cup mayo + 1 teaspoon wasabi paste)

For The Asian Slaw:

- 2 cups shredded napa cabbage
- 1/2 cup shredded carrots
- 1/2 cup mung bean sprouts
- 1/2 ripe mango, cut julienne
- 1/4 cup chopped cilantro
- 3 tablespoons rice vinegar
- 2 tablespoon Bertolli Extra Virgin Olive Oil
- Salt and pepper

Instructions

- Preheat the grill to medium heat, approximately 350 degrees F. Place the ground chicken, jasmine rice, panko, green onions, jalapeno, and ginger in a large bowl. Crack the egg into the bowl and add 1 tablespoon Bertolli® 100% Pure Olive Oil, and soy sauce. Mix the ingredients by hand until well combined.
- Scoop 3 tablespoon portions of chicken mixture and roll into tight balls. Place on a foil-lined baking sheet. Press the balls flat with the back of a spatula, to 1/2 inch thick. Brush the tops with olive oil.
- Cut the rolls in half and brush the insides with Bertolli 100% Pure Olive Oil.

For The Asian Slaw:

- Mix the napa cabbage, carrots, mung bean sprouts, mango, and cilantro in a medium bowl. Drizzle with rice vinegar and Bertolli® Extra Virgin Olive Oil. Toss to coat, then season with salt and pepper to taste.
- Grill the buns for 1 minute. Remove from the grill. Then place the chicken patties on the grill top-side-down and grill for 2 minutes. Brush the tops of the patties with oil. Flip, and grill another 2-3 minutes.

To Assemble:

- Smear the buns with wasabi mayo. Then add the chicken patties, and top with Asian slaw. Place the bun topper on the slaw and serve!

Nutrition

Calories: 356kcal, Carbohydrates: 45g, Protein: 14g, Fat: 12g, Saturated Fat: 2g, Cholesterol: 46mg, Sodium: 506mg, Potassium: 345mg, Fiber: 2g, Sugar: 7g, Vitamin C: 16.2mg, Calcium: 37mg, Iron: 11.5mg

277. Jamaican Jerk Chicken Thighs

Prep Time: 10 Minutes

Cook Time: 15 Minutes

Total Time: 25 Minutes

Servings: 8

Ingredients

- 4-4.5 pounds boneless skinless chicken thighs
- 1 bunch scallions, trimmed and cut into chunks
- 6 garlic cloves, peeled
- 3-4 habanero peppers, stemmed and seeded
- 1 piece fresh ginger (2-inch piece)
- 1/4 cup fresh lime juice + zest of 3 limes
- 1/4 cup olive oil
- 3 tablespoons soy sauce
- 3 tablespoons brown sugar
- 1 tablespoon salt
- 1 tablespoon dried thyme
- 1 tablespoon allspice
- 1 teaspoon ground black pepper
- 1 teaspoon ground nutmeg
- 1 teaspoon ground cinnamon

Instructions

- Place the chicken thighs in a large gallon zip bag. Place all remaining ingredients in the food processor. Puree on high until well-combined and pasty.
- Pour the jerk marinade over the chicken in the zip bag. Close the bag tightly and gently massage the bag to ensure all the chicken thighs are coated in marinade. Refrigerate for 3 to 48 hours. (The longer the marinade time, the more complex and spicy the chicken will taste.)
- Preheat the grill to medium heat, approximately 350-400 degrees F. Once hot, carefully brush the grates with oil. Take the chicken out of the bag with tongs and grill for 5-7 minutes per side. Serve warm!

Nutrition

Calories: 168kcal, Carbohydrates: 9g, Protein: 12g, Fat: 9g, Saturated Fat: 1g, Cholesterol: 53mg, Sodium: 1303mg, Potassium: 260mg, Fiber: 1g, Sugar: 5g, Vitamin C: 37.4mg, Calcium: 36mg, Iron: 1.6mg

278. Thai Chicken Noodle Bowl With Peanut Sauce

Prep Time: 15 Minutes

Cook Time: 20 Minutes

Total Time: 35 Minutes

Servings: 6

Ingredients

For The Thai Chicken Noodle Bowl:

- 1 pound boneless skinless chicken breast 2 large
- 1 tablespoon fresh grated ginger
- 2 cloves garlic minced
- 1/4 cup fish sauce
- 1/4 cup soy sauce
- 1 tablespoon sesame oil
- 1 tablespoon chile-garlic sauce
- 1 pound DeLallo Whole Wheat Capellini Pasta
- 6 ounces mung bean sprouts
- 1 cup fresh basil leaves use Thai Basil if you can find it
- 3/4 cup sliced green onions
- 1 cup sliced cucumber
- 1/2 cup roasted peanuts
- 2 limes cut into wedges

For The Peanut Sauce:

- 1/2 cup peanut butter
- 1 tablespoon fresh grated ginger
- 1/3 cup chicken broth
- 1 tablespoon honey
- 1/4 cup soy sauce
- 3 tablespoons rice vinegar
- 3 tablespoons sesame oil
- 2 cloves garlic
- 1 tablespoon chile-garlic sauce optional

Instructions

- Place the chicken in a baking dish and top with grated ginger, garlic, fish sauce, soy sauce, sesame oil, and chile-garlic sauce. Allow the chicken to soak while you prep the rest of the ingredients.
- Preheat the grill to medium heat and bring a large pot of water to boil. Meanwhile, place all the ingredients for the peanut sauce in the blender. Puree until smooth.

- Grill the chicken for approximately 5 minutes per side, then place on a plate and cover with foil to keep warm.
- Drop the pasta in the boiling water, cook according to package instructions (about 2-3 minutes) then drain.
- After the chicken has rested for at least 5 minutes, slice it into pieces. Then toss the pasta with the peanut sauce and divide into bowls. Top each bowl with chicken slices, bean sprouts, basil leaves, green onion, cucumber slices, peanuts, and a couple of lime wedges.

Nutrition

Calories: 691kcal, Carbohydrates: 75g, Protein: 40g, Fat: 29g, Saturated Fat: 5g, Cholesterol: 48mg, Sodium: 2416mg, Potassium: 897mg, Fiber: 4g, Sugar: 9g, Vitamin C: 16.5mg, Calcium: 97mg, Iron: 5mg

279. Chicken Marsala Recipe With Tomatoes And Basil

Prep Time: 15 Minutes

Cook Time: 25 Minutes

Total Time: 40 Minutes

Servings: 4

Ingredients

- 2 large boneless skinless chicken breasts or 6 chicken cutlets
- 1/4 cup all-purpose flour could be a gluten-free baking mix
- 1 tablespoon butter
- 1 tablespoon olive oil
- 1-pint cherry tomatoes
- 1 shallot peeled and sliced
- 3 cloves garlic peeled and minced
- 1 pound cremini mushrooms sliced thin
- 1/2 cup marsala wine
- 1/4 cup chicken broth
- 1/4 cup fresh chopped parsley
- 1/4 cup fresh basil leaves
- Parmesan cheese for garnish

Instructions

- If working with whole chicken breasts, slice each one into 3 flat cutlets. Place them on a cutting board and cover with plastic wrap. Use a meat tenderizer (or rolling pin) to beat the chicken cutlets into thin even pieces. Place the flour in a shallow dish and season with 1 teaspoon salt and 1/2 teaspoon ground pepper. Then coat the chicken cutlets in flour and dust off.

- Heat a large skillet over medium-high heat. Add 1/2 tablespoon butter and 1/2 tablespoon oil to the skillet. Once melted, add 3 cutlets to the skillet at a time, cooking for 2-3 minutes per side. Remove and cover with foil. Then repeat with the remaining cutlets.
- Add the tomatoes to the skillet and let them blister on several sides, swirling the pan a few times. Once the first tomato pops, remove it from the skillet and cover it with foil.
- Add the remaining butter and oil to the skillet. Then add the mushrooms, shallots, and garlic. Saute the mushrooms until they are soft. Then add the marsala wine and broth. Cook until most of the liquid is absorbed. Add the chicken and tomatoes back to the skillet and toss. Turn off the heat and toss in the fresh basil leaves and parsley. Serve warm with parmesan cheese, if desired.

Nutrition

Calories: 253kcal, Carbohydrates: 22g, Protein: 17g, Fat: 8g, Saturated Fat: 3g, Cholesterol: 44mg, Sodium: 170mg, Potassium: 1065mg, Fiber: 2g, Sugar: 8g, Vitamin C: 35.1mg, Calcium: 48mg, Iron: 2.3mg

---

280. Chicken Broccoli Slow Cooker Lasagna

Prep Time: 15 Minutes

Cook Time: 3 Hours

Total Time: 3 Hours 15 Minutes

Servings: 8

Ingredients

- 1 box DeLallo No-Boil Lasagna Noodles
- 2 packages of cream cheese (8-ounce packages) could be low fat
- 1/2 cup diced onion
- 2 cloves garlic minced
- 1 cup milk
- 4 cups small broccoli florets
- 1 1/4 pounds boneless skinless chicken breast

- 4 cups shredded sharp cheddar cheese
- Salt and pepper

Instructions

- Spray a large slow cooker with nonstick cooking spray. Place the cream cheese, onions, and garlic in a microwave-safe bowl with 1 teaspoon salt, and 1/4 teaspoon ground pepper. Microwave on high for 1-2 minutes, until the cream cheese, is molten and the onions are soft. Pour in the milk and whisk until smooth.
- Cut the broccoli into small florets and slice the chicken into small bite-size pieces.
- Spread a small amount of the cream cheese sauce in the bottom of the slow cooker. Then cover it with a single layer of dried lasagna sheets. Break the noodles to fit into the slow cooker along the round edges. Sprinkle the pasta sheets with 1 cup of broccoli, one-quarter of the chopped chicken, and 1 cup of shredded cheese. Drizzle one-quarter of the remaining cream cheese sauce over the ingredients. Repeat the lasagna sheet, chicken, broccoli, cheese, and sauce layering until you have 4 full layers.
- Place the crock in the slow cooker and cover with the lid. Slow cooker for 2-3 hours on high, or 4-6 hours on low. Cut and serve warm.

Nutrition

Calories: 670kcal, Carbohydrates: 53g, Protein: 43g, Fat: 31g, Saturated Fat: 18g, Cholesterol: 138mg, Sodium: 731mg, Potassium: 781mg, Fiber: 3g, Sugar: 8g, Vitamin C: 42.4mg, Calcium: 566mg, Iron: 1.8mg

---

281. Nam Sod Lettuce Wraps

Prep Time: 20 Minutes

Cook Time: 8 Minutes

Total Time: 28 Minutes

Servings: 4

Ingredients

- 1 teaspoon peanut oil
- 1 pound ground pork
- 2 cloves garlic minced
- 1 tablespoon fresh ginger grated
- 1 tablespoon fresh mint chopped

- 2 teaspoons low sodium soy sauce
- 1 tablespoon fish sauce
- 2 tablespoon lime juice
- 1/4 teaspoon crushed red pepper
- 1 head butter lettuce leaves separated
- 1 cup shredded carrot
- 1 cup sliced red onion
- 1 cup chopped green onions scallions
- 1 cup chopped cilantro
- 1 cup dry roasted peanuts
- 1 cup sliced red bell pepper optional

Instructions

- Place a large skillet over medium heat. Add the oil, ground pork, garlic, and ginger. Brown for 5 minutes, breaking into small pieces with a wooden spoon. Then add the mint, soy sauce, fish sauce, lime juice, and crushed red pepper Stir and cook for another 3 minutes until the liquid absorbs.
- For Lettuce Wraps: Place a spoonful of the Nam sod meat filling in lettuce leaves, then top with veggies and peanuts.
- For The Salad: Arrange the lettuce leaves in 4 serving bowls, then divide the nam sod between the bowls and top with veggies and peanuts.

Nutrition

Calories: 591kcal, Carbohydrates: 22g, Protein: 31g, Fat: 44g, Saturated Fat: 12g, Cholesterol: 82mg, Sodium: 791mg, Potassium: 1011mg, Fiber: 7g, Sugar: 8g, Vitamin C: 63.6mg, Calcium: 99mg, Iron: 3.2mg

282. Southwest Chicken Caesar Salad

Prep Time: 20 Minutes

Cook Time: 30 Minutes

Total Time: 50 Minutes

Servings: 6

Ingredients

- 1 1/2 pounds new small potatoes halved
- 1 1/2 pounds chicken tenders
- 5-6 ounces fresh chopped romaine or green leaf lettuce
- 2 avocados sliced
- 3 corn cobs corn cut off
- 1 poblano pepper seeded and chopped
- 1 cup dried cherries
- 1 shallot peeled and diced
- 1 clove garlic minced
- 1 tablespoon butter
- 2 tablespoons olive oil divided
- Newman's Own Creamy Caesar Dressing
- Salt and pepper

Instructions

- Preheat the oven to 450 degrees F. Cut the potatoes in half, lengthwise, and place on a rimmed baking sheet. Drizzle with 1 tablespoon olive oil, toss, and sprinkle with salt and pepper. Bake for 30 minutes, flipping once.
- Preheat the grill (or a grill pan) to medium heat. Drizzle the remaining olive oil over the chicken tenders. Salt and pepper and toss to coat. Grill the chicken for 4-5 minutes per side, then set aside.
- Place the butter in a large skillet. Once melted, add the chopped shallots, garlic, and poblano peppers. Saute for 2-3 minutes, then add the corn. Saute another 4-5 minutes, then toss in the cherries and salt and pepper to taste. Remove from heat.
- To serve, pile the lettuce in a large serving bowl (or on individual dinner plates.) Cut the chicken into bite-size pieces. Then top the greens with roasted potatoes, sliced avocado, and grilled chicken. Spoon the corn salsa over the top, and drizzle with Newman's Own Creamy Caesar Dressing.

Nutrition

Calories: 523kcal, Carbohydrates: 51g, Protein: 31g, Fat: 23g, Saturated Fat: 5g, Cholesterol: 80mg, Sodium: 232mg, Potassium: 1450mg, Fiber: 11g, Sugar: 16g, Vitamin C: 50.8mg, Calcium: 58mg, Iron: 2.6mg

283. Best Chicken Pot Pie Recipe

Prep Time: 20 Minutes

Cook Time: 40 Minutes

Total Time: 1 Hour

Servings: 4 Mini Pot Pies

Ingredients

- 1 cup all-purpose flour
- 1 teaspoon sugar
- 1/2 teaspoon salt
- 1/2 cup Land O Lakes Unsalted Butter COLD
- 3 tablespoons ice-cold water more as needed
- For the Pot Pie Recipe:
- 8 ounces chicken tenders cut into bite-size pieces
- 1/4 cup chopped onion
- 1 garlic clove minced
- 1 tablespoon Land O Lakes® Unsalted Butter
- 2 teaspoons all-purpose flour
- 1 teaspoon fresh thyme leaves
- 2 teaspoons chopped parsley
- 1-2 dashes of cayenne pepper
- 3/4 teaspoon chicken base or 1 bouillon cube
- 3/4 cup water
- 3 tablespoon heavy cream
- 3/4 cup frozen peas and carrots mix
- Egg wash 1 egg + 1 tablespoon water, whisked
- Salt and pepper

Instructions

- For the pastry dough, place the flour, sugar, and salt in the food processor and pulse a few times. Pour water over a cup of ice to chill. Then cut the cold butter into cubes and add to the flour. Pulse several times until the butter is cut into the size of peas. Add 3 tablespoons of ice water (without the ice) and pulse again until the dough absorbs the flour and looks like soft pebbles.
- Flour a work surface and dump the crumbly dough out onto the surface. Press together into a flat square, then fold toward the center into a 3-section fold. Roll the dough down to 3/4 inch and fold again in the same manner. If the dough is not coming together, sprinkle 1 teaspoon of ice water over the top and keep folding. Fold and roll the dough 3-4 times, until it is smooth. Then fold into a rectangle, wrap in plastic, and chill.
- Preheat the oven to 400o F and spray a muffin tin (or four 6-ounce ramekins) with non-stick cooking spray. Place a large skillet over medium heat and add the butter and onions. Sauté 2 minutes, then add the chicken pieces and garlic. Sauté for another 2-3 minutes, then add the flour, herbs, and chicken base. Stir to coat. Pour

in the water and cream, then stir well. Allow the mixture to come to a simmer to thicken, then add the frozen veggies. Taste for salt and pepper and add a couple of dashes of cayenne for a little kick. Remove from heat.

- Now take the pastry dough out of the fridge and roll it out into a 12-inch circle/square. Cut it into 4 equal triangular pieces. Then fit each piece down into the prepared muffin tin. Spread them apart—they grow! Fill the pastry dough with chicken filling, spooning in the creamy base. Then loosely fold the flaps over the top. It's okay if there are gaps in the top as long as the pastry dough sides come up high. Brush the egg wash over the top of the pastry dough. Bake for 20-25 minutes on the bottom rack, until golden brown. Allow them to cool for 10 minutes.
- To serve, run a butter knife around the inside edge of the muffin tins. Tip the knife down and carefully lift each pot pie out. If you accidentally poke a hole in the pot pie, serve it in a bowl.

Nutrition

Calories: 475kcal, Carbohydrates: 30g, Protein: 17g, Fat: 32g, Saturated Fat: 19g, Cholesterol: 120mg, Sodium: 479mg, Potassium: 309mg, Fiber: 2g, Sugar: 2g, Vitamin C: 5.4mg, Calcium: 29mg, Iron: 2.1mg

---

284. Chicken Salad Recipe With Berries

Prep Time: 15 Minutes

Total Time: 15 Minutes

Servings: 6

Ingredients

- 1 whole rotisserie or baked chicken boned and shredded into chunks
- 1/2 cup light mayonnaise
- 1 teaspoon Dijon mustard
- 4 ounces NatureBox Cherry Berry Bonanza dried cherries, blueberries, and cranberries
- 1/2 cup toasted sliced almonds
- 3/4 cup chopped celery
- 1/2 cup chopped green onion
- Salt and pepper to taste

Instructions

- Chop the celery and green onions and add all the ingredients to a large bowl.
- Stir to thoroughly coat, then salt and pepper to taste. Keep in an air-tight container in the fridge until ready to serve.

Nutrition

Calories: 451kcal, Carbohydrates: 19g, Protein: 28g, Fat: 29g, Saturated Fat: 7g, Cholesterol: 98mg, Sodium: 252mg, Potassium: 380mg, Fiber: 4g, Sugar: 11g, Vitamin C: 4mg, Calcium: 74mg, Iron: 2mg

285. Spicy Oven Chicken Wings With Apple Onion Dip

Prep Time: 10 Minutes

Cook Time: 50 Minutes

Total Time: 1 Hour

Servings: 6

Ingredients

For The Spicy Oven Chicken Wings:

- 3 pounds chicken wings or drumettes
- 3 tablespoons vegetable oil
- 1 teaspoon garlic powder
- 1/4 cup Dijon mustard
- 1/4 cup spicy whole-grain mustard-like Lusty Monk
- 1/4 cup maple syrup or honey
- 1 tablespoon Sriracha chili sauce

For The Apple Onion Dip:

- 1 tablespoon butter
- 1 small onion diced
- 3 tablespoons Musselman's Apple Butter
- 1 cup plain Greek yogurt
- 1 tablespoon Dijon mustard
- 1 teaspoon Musselman's Apple Cider Vinegar
- Salt and pepper

Instructions

- Preheat the oven to 450 degrees F and line a large rimmed baking sheet with foil. Dry the chicken wings thoroughly with paper towels, then toss with oil, garlic powder, 1 1/2 teaspoons salt, and 1/2 teaspoon pepper. Spread evenly over the baking sheet. Bake the

wings for 20 minutes. Flip, then bake another 15-20 minutes until the skin is crisp.

- Meanwhile, whisk the mustards, maple syrup, and Sriracha together. Once the chicken has cooked through and the skin is crispy, pour the sauce over the chicken and toss to coat. Spread the wings back out and bake another 10 minutes.

For The Apple Onion Dip:

- While the chicken is baking, place a small skillet of medium-low heat. Add the butter and onions and saute for 10-15 minutes until the onions are caramelized.
- Mix the onions with the Musselman's apple butter, Greek yogurt, dijon, and Musselman's apple cider vinegar. Salt and pepper to taste. Serve the spicy chicken wings warm, with the apple onion dip.

Nutrition

Calories: 445kcal, Carbohydrates: 17g, Protein: 27g, Fat: 30g, Saturated Fat: 13g, Cholesterol: 101mg, Sodium: 443mg, Potassium: 337mg, Fiber: 1g, Sugar: 13g, Vitamin C: 4.1mg, Calcium: 82mg, Iron: 1.5mg

286. Chai Pani's Malabar Chicken Curry

Prep Time: 15 Minutes

Cook Time: 1 Hour

Total Time: 1 Hour 15 Minutes

Servings: 4

Ingredients

- 2 pounds chicken breast cut into bite-size pieces
- 1/2 cup vegetable oil + 1 tablespoon
- 1 1/2 teaspoons mustard seeds
- 1/2 teaspoon fenugreek seeds
- 12-15 curry leaves finely chopped
- 2-3 small dried red chiles cayenne, bird...
- 4 cups chopped red onion about 2 large onions
- 2 1/2 tablespoons grated ginger
- 1 teaspoon chili powder
- 1 1/2 tablespoons ground coriander
- 1 teaspoon turmeric
- 1/2 cup chopped cilantro leaves and/or stems
- 3 cups chopped tomatoes
- 2 tablespoons fresh lime juice

- 1 teaspoon salt
- 1 cup unsweetened coconut milk

Instructions

- Pour 1/2 cup oil in a large saucepot over medium heat. When the oil is hot, add the mustard seeds, fenugreek seeds, curry leaves, and red chiles.
- Sauté for 1-2 minutes, then add the ginger and onions. Reduce the heat to medium-low and allow the onions to brown until they are dark and soft enough the smash with a spatula about 25-30 minutes.
- Add the chili powder, coriander, turmeric, and cilantro mix.
- Raise the heat back to medium and add the tomatoes, salt, and lime juice. Simmer, stirring occasionally, until the tomatoes have disintegrated and the oil separates 15-20 minutes.
- Add 1/2 cup of water and 1 cup coconut milk. Bring to a boil, then turn down the heat.
- In a separate skillet, heat 1 tablespoon of oil over high. Add the chicken to the skillet and brown on all sides, leaving the centers pink 2-4 minutes.
- Add the chicken to the curry and simmer for 5-7 minutes until the chicken has cooked through. Serve over basmati rice.

Nutrition

Calories: 750kcal, Carbohydrates: 30g, Protein: 54g, Fat: 49g, Saturated Fat: 36g, Cholesterol: 145mg, Sodium: 1129mg, Potassium: 1644mg, Fiber: 7g, Sugar: 14g, Vitamin A: 740iu, Vitamin C: 96.4mg, Calcium: 142mg, Iron: 4.8mg

287. Ethiopian Recipes: Doro Wat And Injera Recipe

Prep Time: 30 Minutes

Cook Time: 6 Minutes

Total Time: 36 Minutes

Servings: 8

Ingredients

For The Doro Wat:

- 3 pounds boneless chicken breasts and thighs, cut into 1-inch cubes
- 2 large onions chopped
- 4 cloves garlic minced
- 1 cup butter
- 1 cup red wine
- 2 cups water
- 2 teaspoons salt
- 1 teaspoon ground cardamom
- 2 tablespoons garam masala
- 1/3 cup hot smoked paprika
- 1 tablespoon crushed red pepper
- 2 teaspoons fenugreek seeds
- 1 tablespoon dried thyme
- 3 tablespoons tomato paste
- 1 tablespoon sugar
- 1 lime juiced
- For the Injera Recipe:
- 3 cups all-purpose flour
- 1 cup buckwheat flour
- 2 tablespoons baking soda
- 1 teaspoon salt
- 4 cups club soda
- 1 cup white vinegar or rice vinegar
- Oil for pan

Instructions

For The Doro Wat:

- Place all the ingredients, minus the lime juice, in a slow cooker and cover. Cook for 4-6 hours depending on your slow cooker settings until the chicken is tender. Then mash the chicken to shreds with a potato masher (or the bottom of a ladle.) Stir in the lime juice and keep warm.
- For the Injera Recipe:
- In a large bowl, mix both flours, salt, and baking soda. Whisk in the club soda until smooth. Then add the vinegar and whisk.
- Heat a large skillet over medium heat. Pour oil on a paper towel and wipe the skillet with the oiled paper towel.
- Using a scoop, pour batter into the skillet creating a 6-inch circle. Carefully swirl the pan around to thin out the batter until it measures 8- to 9-inches across.
- Cook for 1 minute, then using a large spatula, flip the Injera over and cook another minute. Remove from the skillet and stack on a plate. Repeat with the remaining batter. The Injera will

seem slightly crisp in the pan but will soften immediately when placed on the plate.

- Once finished cooking the Injera. Cut the circles in half with a pizza cutter, roll into tubes, and stack. Keep warm until ready to serve. Serve the Doro Wat and Injera together, tearing a piece of Injera and using it to pick up the Doro Wat.

Nutrition

Calories: 705kcal, Carbohydrates: 59g, Protein: 45g, Fat: 30g, Saturated Fat: 16g, Cholesterol: 170mg, Sodium: 2233mg, Potassium: 1078mg, Fiber: 7g, Sugar: 5g, Vitamin A: 3635iu, Vitamin C: 8.6mg, Calcium: 88mg, Iron: 6.1mg

288. Cool Chicken Taco Pasta Salad

Prep Time: 15 Minutes

Cook Time: 10 Minutes

Total Time: 25 Minutes

Servings: 8

Ingredients

- 1 pound fusilli pasta
- 3 cups chopped cooked chicken, leftover or rotisserie
- 1-pint cherry tomatoes halved
- 1 cup chopped scallions
- 3.8 ounces sliced black olives (1 can)
- 1/4 cup chopped cilantro
- 8 ounces French or Catalina Dressing (1 bottle)
- 1/2 cup sour cream
- 1 packet Old El Paso Taco Seasoning
- 4.5 ounce Old El Paso Chopped Green Chiles (1 can)
- 1/2 cup shredded Mexican blend cheese (optional)

Instructions

- Boil a large pot of water and cook the fusilli pasta according to package instructions. Drain and rinse under cold water to cook the pasta. Shake off excess water and pour the pasta into a large salad bowl.
- Add the chopped chicken, tomatoes, scallions, black olives, and cilantro to the pasta.
- In a separate bowl, combine the French dressing with sour cream, Old El Paso Taco Seasoning, and Chopped Green Chiles. Stir until smooth.

- Pour the dressing over the pasta salad and toss well to coat. Toss in the shredded cheese if desired. Cover and chill until ready to serve.

Nutrition

Calories: 529kcal, Carbohydrates: 54g, Protein: 18g, Fat: 26g, Saturated Fat: 6g, Cholesterol: 45mg, Sodium: 964mg, Potassium: 438mg, Fiber: 4g, Sugar: 9g, Vitamin C: 25.2mg, Calcium: 114mg, Iron: 2.6mg

289. Bruschetta Chicken Sheet Pan Dinner

Prep Time: 12 Minutes

Cook Time: 18 Minutes

Total Time: 30 Minutes

Servings: 4

Ingredients

- 2 large boneless skinless chicken breasts
- 3 tablespoon olive oil, divided
- 3/4 teaspoon dried Italian seasoning, divided
- 1 pound asparagus, trimmed
- 8-ounce fresh mozzarella ball
- 12 ounces grape tomatoes, mixed colors
- 2 cloves garlic minced
- 8-10 leaves fresh basil, chopped
- 2 teaspoon balsamic vinegar, divided
- Salt and pepper

Instructions

- Preheat the oven to 400 degrees F. Line a large rimmed sheet pan with parchment paper. Lay each chicken breast flat and cut in half, parallel to the cutting board, to make four thinner chicken breasts. Rub each piece with olive oil and sprinkle both sides with 1/2 teaspoon Italian seasoning. Then salt and pepper liberally. Place the chicken breasts in a line down one long edge of the sheet pan. Bake for 10 minutes.
- Meanwhile, slice the mozzarella ball into four equal rounds. Then cut the grape tomatoes into quarters and place them in a bowl. Add the garlic, chopped basil, 2 tablespoons olive oil, and 1 teaspoon balsamic vinegar. Toss well, then season with salt and pepper to taste.
- After 10 minutes, take the sheet pan out of the oven. Flip the chicken breasts over and place one slice of mozzarella over each chicken breast.

Then spread the asparagus out on the empty side of the sheet pan. Drizzle the asparagus with 1/2 tablespoon olive oil, 1 teaspoon balsamic vinegar, 1/4 teaspoon Italian seasoning, salt, and pepper.

- Place the sheet pan back in the oven and bake for another 8-10 minutes. Remove from the oven and top the chicken with the tomatoes bruschetta salad. Serve the bruschetta chicken with a side of roasted asparagus.

Nutrition

Calories: 370kcal, Carbohydrates: 10g, Protein: 27g, Fat: 24g, Saturated Fat: 9g, Cholesterol: 80mg, Sodium: 428mg, Potassium: 682mg, Fiber: 3g, Sugar: 5g, Vitamin A: 2020iu, Vitamin C: 19.1mg, Calcium: 334mg, Iron: 3.3mg

290. Yakhni Pulao

Prep Time: 10 Minutes

Cook Time: 30 Minutes

Total Time: 40 Minutes

Servings: 4

Ingredients

- 1 1/4 pounds chicken breast or lamb, cut into bite-size pieces
- 2 tablespoons olive oil
- 4 pods green cardamom
- 10 whole peppercorns
- 1 cinnamon stick
- 1 bay leaf
- 1-star anise
- 1 pinch saffron (small)
- 1 cup diced onion
- 2 tablespoons fresh grated ginger
- 2 cloves garlic, minced
- 1 cup basmati rice
- 1 1/4 cup stock, chicken or beef
- 1/3 cup sultanas (golden raisins)
- 1/3 cup chopped dried apricot
- 1/2 cup almonds or cashews
- Salt
- Chopped cilantro for garnish

Instructions

- In a large stockpot heat 2 tablespoons of oil over medium heat. Add the cardamom, peppercorns, cinnamon, bay leaf, anise, and saffron. Stir for 2-3 minutes, to allow the spices to release their flavor. Then add the onions.
- Sauté for 2-3 minutes. Add the ginger and garlic and sauté for another 2 minutes. Add the chicken to the pot. Salt liberally and cook for 1-2 minutes.
- Next, add the rice and stir to coat it in oil. Add the stock and bring to a boil. Once boiling pour the sultanas on top, cover, and reduce the heat to low.
- Cover and steam the rice for 15 minutes. Then remove from heat. Stir in the chopped apricots and nuts, then cover again.
- Allow the Yakhni Pulao to sit another 5 minutes, covered. Serve with cilantro sprinkled on top!

Nutrition

- Calories: 572kcal, Carbohydrates: 60g, Protein: 38g, Fat: 20g, Saturated Fat: 2g, Cholesterol: 90mg, Sodium: 465mg, Potassium: 922mg, Fiber: 5g, Sugar: 11g, Vitamin A: 450iu, Vitamin C: 7.3mg, Calcium: 102mg, Iron: 2.4mg

291. Pesto Chicken Kebabs With Cool Quinoa Pilaf

Prep Time: 15 Minutes

Cook Time: 30 Minutes

Total Time: 45 Minutes

Servings: 6

Ingredients

- 1 tablespoon SimpleNature Organic Coconut Oil, or olive oil
- 4 Kirkwood Never Any! Fresh Boneless Skinless Chicken Breasts
- 1/3 cup Priano Genovese Pesto Sauce
- 1 1/2 cups SimplyNature Organic Quinoa
- 1 1/2 cups chopped cucumber
- 1 1/2 cups chopped fresh strawberries
- 1 mango, peeled and chopped
- 3/4 cup Southern Grove Slivered Almonds
- 1/2 cup chopped red onion
- 1/4 cup chopped cilantro
- Salt and pepper, Stonemill Sea Salt Grinder, and Whole Black Pepper Grinder

- 12 wooden skewers

Instructions

- Preheat the grill to medium-low heat, about 300 degrees F. Soak wooden skewers in water for 20+ minutes so they don't burn up on the grill. Cut the chicken breasts into 1-inch cubes. Place them in a bowl and toss the chicken pieces with pesto sauce. Set aside.
- Place the slivered almonds in a medium saucepot and set over medium heat. Toast the almonds for 3-5 minutes, stirring every minute, until they are golden brown. Then pour the almonds onto a plate.
- Set the same saucepot back over medium heat. Add the oil and quinoa. Allow the quinoa to toast for 2-3 minutes. Then add 3 cups of water and 1 teaspoon salt. Cover the pot with a lid and bring to a boil. Simmer the quinoa for 15-20 minutes, until the water has absorbed and vent holes form on the surface of the quinoa. Remove from heat and let the quinoa rest for 10 minutes, covered. Then fluff with a fork and pour the quinoa into a large salad bowl to cool.
- Meanwhile, slide the chicken pieces onto 12 skewers. Grill the chicken kebabs for 5 minutes. Carefully flip them over and grill another 5-7 minutes. Move the kebabs to a platter and cover loosely with foil to keep warm.
- While the kebabs are grilling, add the chopped cucumber, red onion, strawberries, mango, toasted almonds, and cilantro to the cooled quinoa. Toss well. Taste, then salt and pepper as needed.
- Serve the pesto chicken kebabs warm over the cool quinoa pilaf.

Nutrition

Calories: 455kcal, Carbohydrates: 41g, Protein: 27g, Fat: 21g, Saturated Fat: 4g, Cholesterol: 49mg, Sodium: 220mg, Potassium: 809mg, Fiber: 6g, Sugar: 7g, Vitamin A: 665iu, Vitamin C: 34.3mg, Calcium: 110mg, Iron: 3.2mg

---

292. Caribbean Chicken Curry Sheet Pan Dinner

Prep Time: 15 Minutes

Cook Time: 30 Minutes

Total Time: 45 Minutes

Servings: 4

Ingredients

- 2 pounds boneless skinless chicken thighs (4-6 pieces)
- 1 red onion
- 1 red bell pepper
- 1 large sweet potato
- 1 tablespoon fresh thyme leaves (or 1 teaspoon dried)
- 1 1/2 teaspoon curry powder
- 1 teaspoon Chinese five-spice powder, or allspice
- 1/4 - 1/2 teaspoon cayenne pepper
- 13 ounces unsweetened coconut milk (1 can)
- 2-3 cloves garlic
- 2 tablespoons fresh grated ginger
- 2 tablespoons honey
- 1 1/2 teaspoons corn starch or arrowroot powder
- Salt and pepper

Instructions

- Preheat the oven to 425 degrees F. Lay a large rimmed 18x13 inch "half sheet" baking pan out and spray with nonstick cooking spray. Place the chicken thighs on the baking sheet.
- Peel the onion, and cut it into quarters. Then slice into 1/4 inch wedges. Seed the bell pepper, and slice into 1/4-inch strips. Then cut the strips in half. Peel the sweet potato, and cut into 1/4-inch rounds. Then cut all the rounds into quarters. Spread the vegetables out on the baking sheet in a single layer.
- Sprinkle the top of the chicken and vegetables with curry powder, Chinese five-spice, cayenne, thyme, 1 1/2 teaspoons salt, and black pepper to taste. Bake for 20 minutes.
- Meanwhile, place the coconut milk, peeled garlic cloves, ginger, honey, and cornstarch in the blender. Puree until smooth.
- After 20 minutes, remove the sheet pan from the oven. Pour the coconut mixture over the top of the chicken and veggies. Jiggle the pan a little to help mix the roasted spices into the coconut milk. Then place back in the oven for 10 minutes, or until the curry sauce simmers. Serve warm.

Nutrition

Calories: 288kcal, Carbohydrates: 13g, Protein: 23g, Fat: 15g, Saturated Fat: 10g, Cholesterol: 107mg, Sodium: 118mg, Potassium: 530mg, Fiber: 2g, Sugar: 7g, Vitamin C: 23.4mg, Calcium: 36mg, Iron: 2.3mg

293. Skinny Chicken Enchilada Dip

Prep Time: 8 Minutes

Cook Time: 30 Minutes

Total Time: 38 Minutes

Servings: 12

Ingredients

- 16 ounces Old El Paso Traditional Refried Beans (1 can) or fat-free
- 2 cans Old El Paso Red Enchilada Sauce (10-ounce cans) or one 19-ounce can
- 8 ounces light cream cheese
- 1 1/4 cups reduced-fat Mexican-style shredded cheese, separated
- 2 cups chopped cooked chicken
- Scallions or cilantro for garnish
- Baked veggie chips

Instructions

- Preheat the oven to 350 degrees F. Spread the Old El Paso Refried Beans in the bottom of an 8- or 9-inch baking dish. Cover the beans with chopped chicken. Then top the chicken with 1 cup shredded cheese.
- Place the cream cheese in a food processor (or blender.) Puree to soften. Then add in the Old El Paso Red Enchilada Sauce and puree until smooth.
- Pour the creamy enchilada sauce over the shredded cheese. Bake for 30 minutes. Then pull the dip out of the oven and sprinkle the top with the remaining 1/4 cup shredded cheese. Garnish with fresh chopped scallion or cilantro if desired. Serve warm with baked veggie chips or raw vegetables.

Nutrition

Calories: 177kcal, Carbohydrates: 5g, Protein: 9g, Fat: 13g, Saturated Fat: 6g, Cholesterol: 47mg, Sodium: 365mg, Potassium: 73mg, Fiber:

1g, Sugar: 1g, Vitamin C: 0.3mg, Calcium: 118mg, Iron: 0.7mg

294. Indian Grilled Chicken

Prep Time: 15 Minutes

Cook Time: 40 Minutes

Total Time: 55 Minutes

Servings: 8

Ingredients

- 3 1/2 pounds boneless chicken breast
- 1/4 cup oil
- 1 lemon, zested, and juice from half
- 2 tablespoons Garam Masala
- 2 tablespoons chopped cilantro
- 2 cloves garlic, minced
- 1 tablespoon freshly grated ginger
- 1 teaspoon cumin
- 2 teaspoons salt
- 1/2 teaspoon ground black pepper
- 1/2 teaspoon cayenne pepper

Instructions

- Preheat the grill to medium heat. Place the chicken in a large baking dish.
- In a separate bowl, combine all the remaining ingredients and mix well. Rub the mixture over the chicken, coating completely.
- Grill the chicken for approximately 5-6 minutes per side, turning once. (Grill 35-40 minute total for bone-in chicken.) Serve warm!

Nutrition

Calories: 297kcal, Carbohydrates: 1g, Protein: 42g, Fat: 12g, Saturated Fat: 1g, Cholesterol: 127mg, Sodium: 812mg, Potassium: 738mg, Fiber: 0g, Sugar: 0g, Vitamin A: 120iu, Vitamin C: 3.5mg, Calcium: 14mg, Iron: 0.9mg

295. Vietnamese Cold Chicken Salad (Goi Ga)

Prep Time: 10 Minutes

Total Time: 10 Minutes

Servings: 8

Ingredients

For The Vietnamese Cold Chicken Salad:

- 6 cups shredded napa cabbage
- 2 1/2 cups cooked shredded chicken, cold (use leftovers or a rotisserie chicken)
- 3/4 cup fresh mint, roughly chopped
- 3/4 cup shredded carrots
- 1/2 red onion, peeled and sliced thin
- 1/2 cup fresh cilantro, roughly chopped
- 1/2 cup chopped roasted peanuts (cashews for paleo-friendly)

For The Nuoc Cham Dressing:

- 1/4 cup fresh lime juice
- 1/4 cup water
- 3 tablespoons honey
- 2 tablespoons fish sauce
- 1 teaspoon chili garlic sauce

Instructions

- Place all the salad ingredients in a large bowl.
- In a small bowl, whisk together the lime juice, water, honey, fish sauce, and chili garlic sauce.
- When ready to serve, pour the dressing over the salad and toss well.

Nutrition

Calories: 167kcal, Carbohydrates: 14g, Protein: 13g, Fat: 7g, Saturated Fat: 1g, Cholesterol: 33mg, Sodium: 202mg, Potassium: 348mg, Fiber: 2g, Sugar: 9g, Vitamin A: 2315iu, Vitamin C: 25.2mg, Calcium: 51mg, Iron: 0.9mg

296. Chicken Broccoli Quinoa Skillet

Prep Time: 10 Minutes

Cook Time: 25 Minutes

Total Time: 35 Minutes

Servings: 8

Ingredients

- 1 1/2 pounds boneless skinless chicken breast
- 1 1/4 cups dried quinoa
- 3 1/2 - 4 cups chicken broth
- 2 cups small broccoli floret
- 1 bell pepper (yellow or orange), seeded and chopped
- 4 garlic cloves, minced
- 1 cup pecan pieces
- 3/4 cup dried cranberries

- 3/4 cup chopped scallions
- 1 tablespoon olive oil
- 1/2 teaspoon crushed red pepper
- Salt and pepper

Instructions

- Place a large skillet or saute pan over medium-high heat. Once hot, add the oil and chopped bell pepper. Saute for 2 minutes. Then add the broccoli florets. Stir and saute another 3-4 minutes, until the broccoli is partially softened. Remove all veggies from the skillet and set them aside.
- Next add the whole chicken breasts, garlic, quinoa, 3 1/2 cups chicken broth, 1/2 teaspoon salt, 1/2 teaspoon crushed red pepper, 1/4 teaspoon black pepper. Stir and bring to a simmer. Once the quinoa is boiling, lower the heat and simmer until the chicken is cooked through, the broth is evaporated, and the quinoa spirals have separated about 18-20 minutes. Add another 1/2 cup broth if needed.
- Remove the chicken from the skillet. Chop the chicken and add back to the skillet. Then toss in the sautéed vegetables, pecan pieces, cranberries, and scallions. Taste, then salt and pepper as needed. Serve warm!

Nutrition

Calories: 476kcal, Carbohydrates: 42g, Protein: 32g, Fat: 20g, Saturated Fat: 2g, Cholesterol: 72mg, Sodium: 151mg, Potassium: 879mg, Fiber: 6g, Sugar: 12g, Vitamin A: 1030iu, Vitamin C: 56.9mg, Calcium: 62mg, Iron: 3.1mg

297. Southwestern Vegetable & Chicken Soup

Total: 1 hr 30 mins

Servings: 8

Ingredients

- 2 medium poblano peppers
- 2 teaspoons canola oil
- 12 ounces boneless, skinless chicken thighs, trimmed, cut into bite-size pieces
- 1 1/2 cups chopped onion (1 large)
- 1 1/2 cups chopped red or green bell pepper (1 large)

- 1 ½ cups green beans, cut into 1/4-inch pieces, or frozen, thawed
- 4 cloves garlic, minced
- 1 tablespoon chili powder
- 1 ½ teaspoon ground cumin
- 6 cups reduced-sodium chicken broth
- 1 (15 ounces) can of black beans or pinto beans, rinsed
- 1 (14 ounces) can diced tomatoes
- 4 cups chopped chard or spinach
- 1 ½ cups corn kernels, fresh or frozen
- ½ cup chopped fresh cilantro
- ½ cup fresh lime juice, plus lime wedges for serving

Instructions

- To roast poblanos: Position oven rack about 5 inches from the heat source; preheat broiler. Line the broiler pan with foil. Broil whole poblanos, turning once, until starting to blacken, 8 to 12 minutes. Transfer to a paper bag and let steam to loosen skins, about 10 minutes. When the poblanos are cool enough to handle, peel, seed, stem, and coarsely chop; set aside.
- Meanwhile, heat oil in a large soup pot or Dutch oven over medium-high heat. Add chicken and cook, turning occasionally, until lightly browned, 3 to 5 minutes. Transfer to a plate and set aside.
- Reduce the heat to medium and add onion, bell pepper, green beans, and garlic. Cook, stirring, until beginning to soften, 5 to 7 minutes. Stir in chili powder and cumin and cook, stirring, until fragrant, about 30 seconds. Stir in broth, beans, tomatoes, and the chopped poblanos; bring to a boil. Reduce heat to maintain a simmer and cook, stirring occasionally, until the vegetables are tender, about 15 minutes.
- Add the reserved chicken and juices, chard (or spinach), and corn; return to a simmer and cook for 15 minutes more to heat through and blend flavors.
- Top each portion with 1 tablespoon each cilantro and lime juice; serve with lime wedges.

Nutrition

213 Calories; Protein 16.6g; Carbohydrates 24.9g; Dietary Fiber 5.9g; Sugars 6.7g; Fat 6.4g; Saturated Fat 1.3g; Cholesterol 39mg; Vitamin A Iu 2806.4IU; Vitamin C 72.3mg; Folate 44.5mcg; Calcium 79mg; Iron 2.8mg; Magnesium 72.2mg; Potassium 778.5mg; Sodium 385.5mg; Thiamin 0.5mg.

298. Chicken & Spinach Soup With Fresh Pesto

Total: 30 mins

Servings: 5

Ingredients

- 2 teaspoons plus 1 tablespoon extra-virgin olive oil, divided
- ½ cup carrot or diced red bell pepper
- 1 large boneless, skinless chicken breast (about 8 ounces), cut into quarters
- 1 large clove garlic, minced
- 5 cups reduced-sodium chicken broth
- 1 ½ teaspoons dried marjoram
- 6 ounces baby spinach, coarsely chopped
- 1 15-ounce can cannellini beans or great northern beans, rinsed
- ¼ cup grated Parmesan cheese
- ⅓ cup lightly packed fresh basil leaves
- Freshly ground pepper to taste
- ¾ cup plain or herbed multigrain croutons for garnish (optional)

Instructions

- Heat 2 teaspoons oil in a large saucepan or Dutch oven over medium-high heat. Add carrot (or bell pepper) and chicken; cook, turning the chicken and stirring frequently until the chicken begins to brown, 3 to 4 minutes. Add garlic and cook, stirring, for 1 minute more. Stir in broth and marjoram; bring to a boil over high heat. Reduce the heat and simmer, stirring occasionally, until the chicken is cooked through, about 5 minutes.
- With a slotted spoon, transfer the chicken pieces to a clean cutting board to cool. Add spinach and beans to the pot and bring to a gentle boil. Cook for 5 minutes to blend the flavors.
- Combine the remaining 1 tablespoon oil, Parmesan, and basil in a food processor (a mini processor works well). Process until coarse paste forms, adding a little water and scraping down the sides as necessary.

- Cut the chicken into bite-size pieces. Stir the chicken and pesto into the pot. Season with pepper. Heat until hot. Garnish with croutons, if desired.

Nutrition

Calories: 227; Protein 19.4g; Carbohydrates 18g; Dietary Fiber 6g; Sugars 1.7g; Fat 9.1g; Saturated Fat 2g; Cholesterol 28.5mg; Vitamin A Iu 3865.7IU; Vitamin C 29.4mg; Folate 76.7mcg; Calcium 92.8mg; Iron 2.1mg; Magnesium 43.7mg; Potassium 524.6mg; Sodium 211.4mg; Thiamin 0.1mg.

299. Lemon Chicken Orzo Soup With Kale

Active: 40 mins

Total: 40 mins

Servings: 6

Ingredient

- 2 tablespoons extra-virgin olive oil, divided
- 1 pound boneless, skinless chicken breasts, trimmed and cut into 1-inch pieces
- 1 teaspoon dried oregano and/or thyme, divided
- 1 ¼ teaspoons salt, divided
- ¾ teaspoon ground pepper, divided
- 2 cups chopped onions
- 1 cup chopped carrots
- 1 cup chopped celery
- 2 cloves garlic, minced
- 1 bay leaf
- 4 cups unsalted chicken broth
- ⅔ cup orzo pasta, preferably whole-wheat
- 4 cups chopped kale
- 1 lemon, zested and juiced

Instructions

- Heat 1 tablespoon oil in a large pot over medium-high heat. Add chicken and sprinkle with 1/2 teaspoon each oregano (and/or thyme), salt, and pepper. Cook, stirring occasionally until lightly browned, 3 to 5 minutes. Using a slotted spoon, transfer the chicken to a plate.
- Add the remaining 1 tablespoon oil, onions, carrots, and celery to the pan. Cook, scraping up any browned bits until the vegetables are soft

and lightly browned, 3 to 5 minutes. Add garlic, bay leaf, and the remaining 1/2 teaspoon oregano (and/or thyme). Cook, stirring, until fragrant, 30 to 60 seconds.
- Add broth and bring to a boil over high heat. Add orzo. Reduce heat to maintain a simmer, cover, and cook for 5 minutes. Add kale and the chicken, along with any accumulated juices. Continue cooking until the orzo is tender and the chicken is cooked through, 5 to 8 minutes more.
- Remove from heat. Discard bay leaf. Stir in lemon zest, lemon juice, and the remaining 3/4 teaspoon salt and 1/4 teaspoon pepper.

Nutrition

Calories: 245; Protein 21.1g; Carbohydrates 24.2g; Dietary Fiber 5.4g; Sugars 4.6g; Fat 7g; Saturated Fat 1.2g; Cholesterol 41.8mg; Vitamin A Iu 4723.8IU; Vitamin C 22.2mg; Folate 39.4mcg; Calcium 56.7mg; Iron 1mg; Magnesium 30.8mg; Potassium 480mg; Sodium 638.9mg.

300. Tinola (Filipino Ginger-Garlic Chicken Soup)

Active: 45 mins

Total: 45 mins

Servings: 4

Ingredients

- 3 tablespoons canola oil or avocado oil
- ½ cup chopped yellow onion
- ¼ cup thinly sliced fresh ginger
- 6 cloves garlic, minced
- 1 pound boneless, skinless chicken thighs, trimmed and cut into 1/2-inch pieces
- 4 cups low-sodium chicken broth
- 1 ½ cups peeled and cubed green papaya or chayote
- 2 cups chopped malunggay leaves or bok choy leaves
- 1 tablespoon fish sauce
- ¼ teaspoon salt
- ¼ teaspoon ground black pepper

Instructions

Heat oil in a large pot over medium heat. Add onion, ginger, and garlic; cook, stirring until the onion starts to turn translucent, about 3 minutes. Add chicken and broth; cook, stirring, until the chicken is just cooked through, about 5 minutes. Add papaya (or chayote), malunggay (or bok choy), fish sauce, salt, and pepper; continue simmering until the vegetables are tender and the flavors have melded, about 5 minutes more.

Nutrition

Calories: 344; Protein 27.4g; Carbohydrates 14.2g; Dietary Fiber 1.9g; Sugars 6.1g; Fat 20.5g; Saturated Fat 3.6g; Cholesterol 75.5mg; Vitamin A Iu 2134.5IU; Vitamin C 52.1mg; Folate 56mcg; Calcium 82.8mg; Iron 2.3mg; Magnesium 51.9mg; Potassium 634.2mg; Sodium 663mg; Thiamin 0.1mg.

6. Lean and Green "Soup And Salad Recipes

301. Cabbage Diet Soup

Active: 35 mins

Total: 55 mins

Servings: 6

Ingredients

- 2 tablespoons extra-virgin olive oil
- 1 medium onion, chopped
- 2 medium carrots, chopped
- 2 stalks celery, chopped
- 1 medium red bell pepper, chopped
- 2 cloves garlic, minced
- 1 ½ teaspoon Italian seasoning
- ½ teaspoon ground pepper
- ¼ teaspoon salt
- 8 cups low-sodium vegetable broth
- 1 medium head green cabbage, halved and sliced
- 1 large tomato, chopped
- 2 teaspoons white-wine vinegar

Instructions

- Heat oil in a large pot over medium heat. Add onion, carrots, and celery. Cook, stirring until the vegetables begin to soften, 6 to 8 minutes. Add bell pepper, garlic, Italian seasoning, pepper, and salt and cook, stirring, for 2 minutes.

- Add broth, cabbage, and tomato; increase the heat to medium-high and bring to a boil. Reduce heat to maintain a simmer, partially cover, and cook until all the vegetables are tender, 15 to 20 minutes more. Remove from heat and stir in vinegar.

Nutrition

- Calories: 133; Protein 3g; Carbohydrates 19.8g; Dietary Fiber 7g; Sugars 11g; Fat 5.2g; Saturated Fat 0.7g; Vitamin A Iu 4480.2IU; Vitamin C 88.2mg; Folate 91mcg; Calcium 110.7mg; Iron 1.5mg; Magnesium 30.2mg; Potassium 504.1mg; Sodium 451.1mg; Thiamin 0.1mg.

302. Vegetable Weight-Loss Soup

Active: 45 mins

Total: 1 hr

Servings: 8

Ingredient

- 2 tablespoons extra-virgin olive oil
- 1 medium onion, chopped
- 2 medium carrots, chopped
- 2 stalks celery, chopped
- 12 ounces fresh green beans, cut into 1/2-inch pieces
- 2 cloves garlic, minced
- 8 cups no-salt-added chicken broth or low-sodium vegetable broth
- 2 (15 ounces) cans of low-sodium cannellini or other white beans, rinsed
- 4 cups chopped kale
- 2 medium zucchini, chopped
- 4 Roma tomatoes, seeded and chopped
- 2 teaspoons red-wine vinegar
- ¾ teaspoon salt
- ½ teaspoon ground pepper
- 8 teaspoons prepared pesto

Instructions

- Heat oil in a large pot over medium-high heat. Add onion, carrot, celery, green beans, and garlic. Cook, stirring frequently until the vegetables begin to soften, about 10 minutes. Add broth and bring to a boil. Reduce heat to a simmer and cook, stirring occasionally, until the vegetables are soft, about 10 minutes more.

- Add white beans, kale, zucchini, tomatoes, vinegar, salt, and pepper. Increase heat to return to a simmer; cook until the zucchini and kale have softened, about 10 minutes. Top each serving of soup with 1 teaspoon pesto.

Nutrition

Calories: 225; Protein 12.7g; Carbohydrates 27.8g; Dietary Fiber 7.6g; Sugars 5.3g; Fat 8.4g; Saturated Fat 1.4g; Vitamin A Iu 4134.1IU; Vitamin C 30.3mg; Folate 52.3mcg; Calcium 106.4mg; Iron 3.1mg; Magnesium 88.6mg; Potassium 865.8mg; Sodium 406mg; Thiamin 0.7mg.

303. Italian Wedding Soup

Total: 1 hr 30 mins

Servings: 8

Ingredients

- Meatballs
- 1 pound ground turkey breast
- 1 cup fresh whole-wheat breadcrumbs
- 1 large egg, lightly beaten
- ¼ cup finely chopped fresh parsley
- 2 cloves garlic, minced
- 1 tablespoon Worcestershire sauce
- ½ teaspoon crushed fennel seeds
- ½ teaspoon freshly ground pepper
- ¼ teaspoon salt
- 2 teaspoons extra-virgin olive oil
- ½ cup dry white wine

Soup

- 1 tablespoon extra-virgin olive oil
- 1 cup chopped onion (1 medium)
- 1 cup chopped carrots (2 medium)
- 1 cup chopped celery (2 medium stalks)
- 4 cups chopped cabbage (about 1/2 small head)
- 8 cups low-sodium chicken broth
- 1 15-ounce can white beans, rinsed
- 8 cups coarsely chopped escarole or thinly sliced kale leaves (about 1 bunch)
- ½ cup freshly grated Romano cheese

Instructions

- To prepare meatballs: Combine turkey, breadcrumbs, egg, parsley, garlic,

Worcestershire, fennel seeds, pepper, and salt in a large bowl. Refrigerate for 10 minutes to firm up. With damp hands, shape the mixture into 32 (1-inch) meatballs (about 1 scant tablespoon each).
- Heat 2 teaspoons oil in a large nonstick skillet over medium heat. Add the meatballs and cook, turning occasionally, until browned on all sides, 7 to 9 minutes. Remove from the heat and add wine, stirring gently to loosen any browned bits.
- To prepare soup: Heat 1 tablespoon oil in a soup pot or Dutch oven over medium heat. Add onion, carrots, and celery and cook, stirring, until the onion is translucent, 7 to 9 minutes. Add cabbage and cook, stirring, 5 minutes more. Stir in broth, beans, escarole (or kale), and the meatballs, and any juice. Bring just to a boil, reduce heat to maintain a simmer, and cook, stirring occasionally, until the vegetables are tender, 20 to 25 minutes. Top each portion with 1 tablespoon grated cheese.

Nutrition

Calories: 284; Protein 23.9g; Carbohydrates 23.5g; Dietary Fiber 6.3g; Sugars 4.6g; Fat 11.1g; Saturated Fat 3.5g; Cholesterol 60.1mg; Vitamin A Iu 4130.1IU; Vitamin C 21.9mg; Folate 141.5mcg; Calcium 205.7mg; Iron 3.3mg; Magnesium 33.3mg; Potassium 869.9mg; Sodium 522.5mg; Thiamin 0.1mg.

304. Vegan Weight-Loss Lentil Soup

Active: 20 mins

Total: 1 hr

Servings: 6

Ingredients

- 2 tablespoons extra-virgin olive oil
- 1 cup chopped yellow onion
- 1 tablespoon minced garlic
- 2 teaspoons ground turmeric
- 1 teaspoon ground ginger
- ½ teaspoon ground cumin
- 4 cups lower-sodium vegetable broth
- 1 cup dry green lentils
- 1 (15 ounces) can no-salt-added chickpeas, rinsed
- ¾ teaspoon salt

- 1 cup chopped fresh spinach
- 1 cup frozen green beans
- 1 tablespoon fresh lemon juice
- 1 teaspoon crushed red pepper
- Cilantro sprigs for garnish

Instructions

- Heat oil in a medium saucepan over medium heat. Add onion and cook, stirring occasionally, until softened, about 3 minutes. Add garlic, turmeric, ginger, and cumin; cook, stirring constantly, until fragrant, about 1 minute. Stir in broth, lentils, chickpeas, and salt. Bring to a boil over medium-high heat. Reduce heat to medium-low to maintain a simmer; cover and cook, stirring occasionally, until the lentils are tender, 30 to 40 minutes.
- Remove from heat and stir in spinach, green beans, and lemon juice, stirring until the spinach wilts and the green beans are heated for about 1 minute. Ladle the soup into 6 bowls; sprinkle with crushed red pepper and garnish with a sprig of cilantro, if desired.

Nutrition

Calories: 253; Fat 7g; Sodium 479mg; Carbohydrates 37g; Dietary Fiber 9g; Protein 12g; Sugars 4g; Niacin Equivalents 1mg; Saturated Fat 1g; Vitamin A Is 1570IU.

305. Slow-Cooker Mediterranean Chicken & Chickpea Soup

Active: 20 mins

Total: 4 hrs 20 mins

Servings: 6

Ingredients

- 1 ½ cups dried chickpeas, soaked overnight
- 4 cups water
- 1 large yellow onion, finely chopped
- 1 (15 ounces) can no-salt-added diced tomatoes, preferably fire-roasted
- 2 tablespoons tomato paste
- 4 cloves garlic, finely chopped
- 1 bay leaf
- 4 teaspoons ground cumin
- 4 teaspoons paprika
- ¼ teaspoon cayenne pepper

- ¼ teaspoon ground pepper
- 2 pounds bone-in chicken thighs, skin removed, trimmed
- 1 (14 ounces) can artichoke hearts, drained and quartered
- ¼ cup halved pitted oil-cured olives
- ½ teaspoon salt
- ¼ cup chopped fresh parsley or cilantro

Instructions

- Drain chickpeas and place in a 6-quart or larger slow cooker. Add 4 cups water, onion, tomatoes and their juice, tomato paste, garlic, bay leaf, cumin, paprika, cayenne, and ground pepper; stir to combine. Add chicken.
- Cover and cook on Low for 8 hours or High for 4 hours.
- Transfer the chicken to a clean cutting board and let cool slightly. Discard bay leaf. Add artichokes, olives, and salt to the slow cooker and stir to combine. Shred the chicken, discarding bones. Stir the chicken into the soup. Serve topped with parsley (or cilantro).

Nutrition

Calories: 447; Protein 33.6g; Carbohydrates 43g; Dietary Fiber 11.6g; Sugars 8.5g; Fat 15.3g; Saturated Fat 3.3g; Cholesterol 76.5mg; Vitamin A Iu 1590IU; Vitamin C 15.1mg; Folate 194.1mcg; Calcium 114.7mg; Iron 5.7mg; Magnesium 78.7mg; Potassium 608.8mg; Sodium 761.8mg.

306. Mexican Cabbage Soup

Total: 20 mins

Servings: 8

Ingredient

- 2 tablespoons extra-virgin olive oil
- 2 cups chopped onions
- 1 cup chopped carrot
- 1 cup chopped celery
- 1 cup chopped poblano or green bell pepper
- 4 large cloves garlic, minced
- 8 cups sliced cabbage
- 1 tablespoon tomato paste
- 1 tablespoon minced chipotle chiles in adobo sauce

- 1 teaspoon ground cumin
- ½ teaspoon ground coriander
- 4 cups low-sodium vegetable broth or chicken broth
- 4 cups water
- 2 (15 ounces) cans of low-sodium pinto or black beans, rinsed
- ¾ teaspoon salt
- ½ cup chopped fresh cilantro, plus more for serving
- 2 tablespoons lime juice
- Crumbled queso fresco, nonfat plain Greek yogurt, and/or diced avocado for garnish

Instructions

- Heat oil in a large soup pot (8-quart or larger) over medium heat. Add onions, carrot, celery, poblano (or bell pepper), and garlic; cook, stirring frequently, until softened, 10 to 12 minutes. Add cabbage; cook, stirring occasionally until slightly softened, about 10 minutes more. Add tomato paste, chipotle, cumin, and coriander; cook, stirring, for 1 minute more.
- Add broth, water, beans, and salt. Cover and bring to a boil over high heat. Reduce heat and simmer, partially covered, until the vegetables are tender about 10 minutes. Remove from heat and stir in cilantro and lime juice. Serve garnished with cheese, yogurt, and/or avocado, if desired.

Nutrition

Calories: 167; Protein 6.5g; Carbohydrates 27.1g; Dietary Fiber 8.7g; Sugars 6.6g; Fat 3.8g; Saturated Fat 0.6g; Vitamin A Iu 2968.9IU; Vitamin C 47.2mg; Folate 48.4mcg; Calcium 115mg; Iron 2.3mg; Magnesium 50.5mg; Potassium 623.7mg; Sodium 408.1mg; Thiamin 0.1mg.

307. Roasted Cauliflower & Potato Curry Soup

Active: 50 mins

Total: 1 hr 30 mins

Servings: 8

Ingredients

- 2 teaspoons ground coriander
- 2 teaspoons ground cumin
- 1 ½ teaspoon ground cinnamon
- 1 ½ teaspoon ground turmeric
- 1 ¼ teaspoons salt
- ¾ teaspoon ground pepper
- ⅛ teaspoon cayenne pepper
- 1 small head cauliflower, cut into small florets (about 6 cups)
- 2 tablespoons extra-virgin olive oil, divided
- 1 large onion, chopped
- 1 cup diced carrot
- 3 large cloves garlic, minced
- 1 ½ teaspoons grated fresh ginger
- 1 fresh red chile pepper, such as serrano or jalapeño, minced, plus more for garnish
- 1 (14 ounces) can no-salt-added tomato sauce
- 4 cups low-sodium vegetable broth
- 3 cups diced peeled russet potatoes (1/2-inch)
- 3 cups diced peeled sweet potatoes (1/2-inch)
- 2 teaspoons lime zest
- 2 tablespoons lime juice
- 1 (14 ounces) can coconut milk
- Chopped fresh cilantro for garnish

Instructions

- Preheat oven to 450 degrees F.
- Combine coriander, cumin, cinnamon, turmeric, salt, pepper, and cayenne in a small bowl. Toss cauliflower with 1 tablespoon oil in a large bowl, sprinkle with 1 tablespoon of the spice mixture, and toss again. Spread in a single layer on a rimmed baking sheet. Roast the cauliflower until the edges are browned, 15 to 20 minutes. Set aside.
- Meanwhile, heat the remaining 1 tablespoon oil in a large pot over medium-high heat. Add onion and carrot and cook, stirring often, until starting to brown, 3 to 4 minutes. Reduce heat to medium and continue cooking, stirring often, until the onion is soft, 3 to 4 minutes. Add garlic, ginger, chile, and the remaining spice mixture. Cook, stirring, for 1 minute more.
- Stir in tomato sauce, scraping up any browned bits, and simmer for 1 minute. Add broth, potatoes, sweet potatoes, lime zest, and juice. Cover and bring to a boil over high heat. Reduce heat to maintain a gentle simmer and cook,

partially covered and stirring occasionally, until the vegetables are tender, 35 to 40 minutes.

- Stir in coconut milk and the roasted cauliflower. Return to a simmer to heat through. Serve garnished with cilantro and chiles, if desired.

Nutrition

Calories: 272; Protein 5.3g; Carbohydrates 33.4g; Dietary Fiber 7.2g; Sugars 8.3g; Fat 14.8g; Saturated Fat 10.1g; Vitamin A Iu 9200.1IU; Vitamin C 52.2mg; Folate 73.8mcg; Calcium 86.3mg; Iron 3.6mg; Magnesium 69.4mg; Potassium 910.5mg; Sodium 509.4mg.

308. Turkey & Squash Soup

Total: 45 mins

Servings: 6

Ingredients

- 2 teaspoons canola oil
- 2 leeks, trimmed, chopped, and rinsed
- 1 red bell pepper, chopped
- 3 cloves garlic, minced
- 4 cups reduced-sodium chicken broth
- 1 1/2 pounds butternut squash, (1 small to medium), peeled, seeded, and cut into 1-inch cubes
- 2 tablespoons minced fresh thyme, or 2 teaspoons dried thyme
- 1 ½ teaspoon ground cumin
- 1 pound turkey cutlets, cut into 1/2-by-2-inch strips
- 2 cups frozen corn kernels
- 2 tablespoons lime juice
- ½ teaspoon crushed red pepper
- ¼ teaspoon salt
- Freshly ground pepper, to taste

Instructions

- Heat oil in a Dutch oven over medium-high heat. Add leeks and bell pepper; cook, stirring often until the vegetables begin to soften, 3 to 4 minutes. Add garlic and cook, stirring, for 1 minute more. Stir in broth, squash, thyme, and cumin; cover and bring to a boil. Reduce heat to medium-low and cook until the vegetables are tender about 10 minutes.

- Add turkey and corn; return to a simmer and cook until the turkey is just cooked through 3 to 4 minutes. Add lime juice and crushed red pepper. Season with salt and pepper.

Nutrition

Calories: 231; Protein 24.3g; Carbohydrates 31.1g; Dietary Fiber 6.1g; Sugars 6.8g; Fat 2.7g; Saturated Fat 0.2g; Cholesterol 30mg; Vitamin A Iu 12451.7IU; Vitamin C 52mg; Folate 85.5mcg; Calcium 83.8mg; Iron 3.5mg; Magnesium 64.1mg; Potassium 692.2mg; Sodium 550mg; Thiamin 0.1mg.

309. Baked Vegetable Soup

Total: 1 hr 40 mins

Servings: 8

Ingredients

- 5 tablespoons extra-virgin olive oil
- 1 pound Yukon Gold potatoes, halved and sliced 1/4 inch thick
- 1 ½ teaspoons salt, divided
- 2 medium zucchini, halved and sliced 1/2 inch thick
- 2 medium leeks, white and light green parts only, thinly sliced (see Tip)
- 4 medium stalks celery, thinly sliced
- 10 ounces cremini (Baby Bella) mushrooms, quartered
- 4 cups frozen artichoke hearts (two 9-ounce boxes), thawed, or 10 fresh artichoke hearts, quartered
- ¼ cup chopped fresh parsley, plus more for garnish
- 1 (15 ounces) can no-salt-added diced tomatoes, with their juice
- 1 (2 inches) piece Parmesan cheese rind, plus finely shredded Parmesan for garnish
- 6 cups water
- ½ teaspoon ground pepper

Instructions

- Preheat oven to 350 degrees F.
- Pour oil into a large ovenproof pot (about 6-quart) and arrange potato slices in an even layer over the oil. Sprinkle with 3/4 teaspoon salt. Layer in zucchini, leeks, celery, mushrooms,

artichoke hearts, and 1/4 cup parsley; sprinkle with the remaining 3/4 teaspoon salt. Pour tomatoes over the vegetables and nestle Parmesan rind into them. Add water (the vegetables will not be completely submerged), cover, and bring to a boil over high heat.

- Once boiling, transfer the pot to the oven and bake, covered, until the vegetables are tender, but still firm, 1 to 1 1/4 hours. Season with pepper and serve garnished with parsley and Parmesan, if desired.

Nutrition

Calories: 204; Protein 5.2g; Carbohydrates 25.6g; Dietary Fiber 6.9g; Sugars 5.3g; Fat 9.6g; Saturated Fat 1.4g; Vitamin A Iu 1290.4IU; Vitamin C 26.8mg; Folate 148.6mcg; Calcium 97.5mg; Iron 1.7mg; Magnesium 58.4mg; Potassium 812.9mg; Sodium 529.2mg; Thiamin 0.2mg.

310. Slow-Cooker Vegetable Soup

Active: 35 mins

Total: 4 hrs 35 mins

Servings: 8

Ingredients

- 1 medium onion, chopped
- 2 medium carrots, chopped
- 2 stalks celery, chopped
- 12 ounces fresh green beans, cut into 1/2-inch pieces
- 4 cups chopped kale
- 2 medium zucchini, chopped
- 4 Roma tomatoes, seeded and chopped
- 2 cloves garlic, minced
- 2 (15 ounces) cans of no-salt-added cannellini or other white beans, rinsed
- 4 cups low-sodium chicken broth or low-sodium vegetable broth
- 2 teaspoons salt
- ½ teaspoon ground pepper
- 2 teaspoons red-wine vinegar
- 8 teaspoons prepared pesto

Instructions

- Combine onion, carrots, celery, green beans, kale, zucchini, tomatoes, garlic, white beans,

broth, salt, and pepper in a 6-quart or larger slow cooker. Cook on High for 4 hours or Low for 6 hours. Stir in vinegar and top each serving of soup with 1 teaspoon pesto.

Nutrition

Calories: 174; Protein 10.3g; Carbohydrates 26.4g; Dietary Fiber 7.6g; Sugars 5.2g; Fat 4.2g; Saturated Fat 0.7g; Vitamin A Iu 4134.1IU; Vitamin C 30.3mg; Folate 52.3mcg; Calcium 101.8mg; Iron 2.8mg; Magnesium 87.4mg; Potassium 762.7mg; Sodium 714.3mg; Thiamin 0.7mg.

311. Butternut Squash Soup With Apple Grilled Cheese Sandwiches

Active: 30 mins

Total: 45 mins

Servings: 4

Ingredient

- 2 tablespoons grapeseed oil or coconut oil, divided
- 1 cup chopped onion
- 2 tablespoons minced fresh ginger
- 1 teaspoon ground cumin
- 1 teaspoon ground turmeric
- ¼ teaspoon cayenne pepper, plus more for garnish
- 5 cups cubed (1-inch) peeled butternut squash
- 1 (15 ounces) can light coconut milk, divided
- 2 cups low-sodium no-chicken broth or chicken broth
- 1 small apple, thinly sliced, divided
- ¾ teaspoon salt
- 1 tablespoon lime juice
- 4 slices whole-wheat country bread
- 1 cup shredded smoked Gouda or Cheddar cheese
- Ground pepper for garnish

Instructions

- Heat 1 tablespoon oil in a large saucepan over medium heat. Add onion and ginger; cook, stirring, until starting to soften, about 3 minutes. Add cumin, turmeric, and cayenne; cook, stirring, for 30 seconds. Add squash, coconut milk (reserve 4 tablespoons for garnish, if desired), broth, half the apple slices, and salt. Bring to a boil. Reduce the heat to maintain a simmer and cook, stirring occasionally, until the squash is tender, about 20 minutes. Stir in lime juice. Remove from heat.

- Puree the soup in the pan using an immersion blender or in batches in a blender. (Use caution when blending hot liquids.)
- Divide 1/2 cup cheese between 2 slices of bread. Top with the remaining apple slices, cheese, and bread. Heat the remaining 1 tablespoon oil in a large nonstick skillet over medium heat. Add the sandwiches and cook until lightly browned on both sides and the cheese is melted, about 2 minutes per side. Cut in half. Garnish the soup with the reserved coconut milk, more cayenne, and ground pepper, if desired.

Nutrition

Calories: 419; Protein 13.5g; Carbohydrates 43.3g; Dietary Fiber 8.4g; Sugars 10.4g; Fat 23.1g; Saturated Fat 10.6g; Cholesterol 26.3mg; Vitamin A Iu 16927.8IU; Vitamin C 28.5mg; Folate 49.7mcg; Calcium 298.2mg; Iron 2.2mg; Magnesium 72.9mg; Potassium 622.5mg; Sodium 826.9mg.

312. Winter Minestrone

Active: 40 mins

Total: 4 hrs 45 mins

Servings: 8

Ingredient

- 1 pound uncooked Italian or pork sausage links, cut into 3/4-inch slices
- 2 ½ cups peeled winter squash, such as butternut squash, cut into 1-inch cubes
- 1 ½ cups cubed potatoes
- 2 medium fennel bulbs, trimmed and cut into 1-inch pieces
- 1 large onion, chopped
- 2 cloves garlic, minced
- 1 (15 ounces) can of red kidney beans, rinsed and drained
- ½ teaspoon dried sage, crushed
- 4 cups chicken broth or vegetable broth
- 1 cup dry white wine
- 4 cups chopped kale or fresh spinach

Instructions

- In a large skillet, cook the sausage until browned; drain well.
- In a 5- to the 6-quart slow cooker, place squash, potatoes, fennel, onion, garlic, beans, and sage. Top with sausage. Pour broth and wine overall.
- Cover and cook on Low for 8 to 10 hours or on High for 4 to 5 hours. Stir in kale (or spinach). Cover and cook 5 minutes more.

Nutrition

Calories: 315; Protein 16g; Carbohydrates 27g; Dietary Fiber 14g; Sugars 1g; Fat 14g; Saturated Fat 5g; Cholesterol 38mg; Sodium 933mg.

313. Garden-Fresh Asparagus Soup

Total: 50 mins

Servings: 6

Ingredient

- 2 tablespoons butter
- 2 tablespoons extra-virgin olive oil
- 1 medium onion, finely chopped
- ½ teaspoon salt
- ½ teaspoon curry powder
- ¼ teaspoon ground ginger
- Zest and juice of 1 lemon, divided
- 2 cups diced peeled red potatoes
- 3 cups vegetable broth, or reduced-sodium chicken broth
- 1 cup "lite" coconut milk
- 2 cups 1/2-inch pieces trimmed asparagus, (about 1 bunch)
- Freshly ground pepper to taste
- ¼ cup crème fraîche or reduced-fat sour cream
- 1/4 cup finely chopped scallion greens, or fresh chives

Instructions

- Melt butter and oil in a large saucepan over medium heat. Add onion and 1/4 teaspoon salt and cook, stirring often, until golden, about 5 minutes. Stir in curry powder, ginger, lemon zest, and potatoes and simmer, stirring occasionally, for 5 minutes. Stir in broth, coconut milk, and asparagus. Bring to a simmer over medium heat, partially cover, and continue to cook until

- The potatoes are tender, about 15 minutes.
- Puree the soup with an immersion blender or a regular blender (in batches) until smooth. (Use caution when pureeing hot liquids.) Season with the remaining 1/4 teaspoon salt and pepper.
- Whisk creme fraiche (or sour cream), lemon juice, and scallion greens (or chives) in a small bowl and garnish with a swirl of it.

Nutrition

Calories: 181; Protein 5.2g; Carbohydrates 15.1g; Dietary Fiber 2.3g; Sugars 2.6g; Fat 12.1g; Saturated Fat 5.3g; Cholesterol 10.2mg; Vitamin C 13.8mg; Folate 35.8mcg; Calcium 28.7mg; Iron 1.6mg; Magnesium 21.2mg; Potassium 455.9mg; Sodium 251.1mg; Thiamin 0.1mg.

314. Creamy Chopped Cauliflower Salad

Total: 15 mins

Servings: 6

Ingredients

- 5 tablespoons reduced-fat mayonnaise
- 2 tablespoons cider vinegar
- 1 small shallot, finely chopped
- 1/2 teaspoon caraway seeds, (optional)
- ¼ teaspoon freshly ground pepper
- 3 cups chopped cauliflower florets, (about 1/2 large head)
- 2 cups chopped heart of romaine
- 1 tart-sweet red apple, chopped

Instructions

- Whisk mayonnaise, vinegar, shallot, caraway seeds (if using), and pepper in a large bowl until smooth. Add cauliflower, romaine, and apple; toss to coat.

Nutrition

Calories: 68; Protein 1.5g; Carbohydrates 10.9g; Dietary Fiber 2.2g; Sugars 5.1g; Fat 2.6g; Saturated Fat 0.4g; Cholesterol 3.1mg; Vitamin A Iu 1437.8IU; Vitamin C 29.5mg; Folate 56.1mcg; Calcium 22.9mg; Iron 0.5mg; Magnesium 13.4mg; Potassium 256.8mg; Sodium 120.3mg; Thiamin 0.1mg.

315. Spinach & Warm Mushroom Salad

Total: 30 mins

Servings: 4

Ingredients

- 8 cups spinach, tough stems removed
- 2 cups coarsely chopped radicchio
- 2 tablespoons extra-virgin olive oil, divided
- 2 slices bacon, chopped
- 1 large shallot, halved and sliced (1/2 cup)
- 3 cups sliced mixed mushrooms, such as shiitake, oyster, and cremini
- ¼ teaspoon salt
- ¼ teaspoon ground pepper
- 2 tablespoons white balsamic vinegar
- ½ teaspoon honey

Instructions

- Combine spinach and radicchio in a large bowl.
- Heat 1 tablespoon oil in a large skillet over medium heat. Add bacon and shallot and cook, stirring, until the bacon is crisp, 4 to 5 minutes. Add mushrooms, salt, and pepper and cook, stirring, until the mushrooms are tender, 5 to 7 minutes. Remove from heat and stir in the remaining 1 tablespoon oil, vinegar, and honey, scraping up any browned bits. Immediately pour the warm vinaigrette over the spinach mixture and toss to coat.

Nutrition

Calories; Protein 4.7g; Carbohydrates 11.5g; Dietary Fiber 2.7g; Sugars 3.9g; Fat 8.8g; Saturated Fat 1.5g; Cholesterol 3.5mg; Vitamin A Iu 5871.6IU; Vitamin C 20.1mg; Folate 140.7mcg; Calcium 74.7mg; Iron 2.3mg; Magnesium 64.8mg; Potassium 617.8mg; Sodium 259.6mg; Thiamin 0.1mg; Added Sugar 1g.

316. Fattoush

Total: 40 mins

Servings: 8

Ingredients

- 2 6-inch whole-wheat pitas, split
- 3 tablespoons extra-virgin olive oil, divided

- 1 1/4 teaspoons ground sumac, (see note), divided
- ¼ cup lemon juice
- ½ teaspoon salt
- ¼ teaspoon freshly ground pepper
- 1 large head of romaine lettuce, coarsely chopped
- 2 large tomatoes, diced
- 2 small salad cucumbers, or 1 large cucumber, seeded and diced
- ½ cup thinly sliced red onion
- ⅓ cup thinly sliced fresh mint

Instructions

- Preheat oven to 350F.
- Place pita halves rough-side up on a large baking sheet. Brush with 1 tablespoon oil and sprinkle with 1 teaspoon sumac. Bake until the pita halves are golden and crisp, about 15 minutes. When cool, break into bite-size pieces.
- Whisk lemon juice, salt, pepper, and the remaining 2 tablespoons oil and 1/4 teaspoon sumac in a large bowl. Add lettuce, tomatoes, cucumber, onion, mint, and the pita pieces;
- Toss to coat. Let stand for 15 minutes before serving.

Nutrition

Calories: 117; Protein 2.9g; Carbohydrates 14.9g; Dietary Fiber 3.2g; Sugars 2.9g; Fat 6g; Saturated Fat 0.9g; Vitamin A Iu 3820.9IU; Vitamin C 12.7mg; Folate 70.1mcg; Calcium 35.5mg; Iron 1.6mg; Magnesium 30.2mg; Potassium 322.3mg; Sodium 224mg; Thiamin 0.1mg.

317. Mixed Green Salad With Grapefruit & Cranberries

Total: 25 mins

Servings:12

Ingredients

- 2 red grapefruit
- ¼ cup extra-virgin olive oil
- 2 tablespoons minced scallions
- 1 tablespoon white-wine vinegar
- ¼ teaspoon salt
- ¼ teaspoon freshly ground pepper
- 8 cups torn butter lettuce

- 6 cups baby spinach
- 1 14-ounce can hearts of palm (see Shopping Tip), drained and cut into bite-size pieces
- ⅓ cup dried cranberries
- 1/3 cup toasted pine nuts

Instructions

- Remove the skin and white pith from grapefruit with a sharp knife. Working over a bowl, cut the segments from their surrounding membranes. Cut the segments in half on a cutting board and transfer to a large salad bowl. Squeeze the grapefruit peel and membranes over the original bowl to extract 1/4 cup grapefruit juice.
- Whisk oil, scallions, vinegar, salt, and pepper into the bowl with the grapefruit juice.
- Add lettuce, spinach, and hearts of palm to the salad bowl with the grapefruit segments. Just before serving, toss the salad with the dressing until well coated. Sprinkle cranberries and pine nuts on top.

Nutrition

Calories: 162; Protein 3.3g; Carbohydrates 14.9g; Dietary Fiber 3.2g; Sugars 8.4g; Fat 11.3g; Saturated Fat 1.3g; Vitamin A Iu 4656.3IU; Vitamin C 30mg; Folate 104.9mcg; Calcium 72.7mg; Iron 2.5mg; Magnesium 55mg; Potassium 424.8mg; Sodium 205.3mg; Thiamin 0.1mg; Added Sugar 3g.

318. Melon, Tomato & Onion Salad With Goat Cheese

Total: 30 mins

Servings: 8

Ingredient

- 1 cup very thinly sliced sweet white onion, separated into rings
- 1 small firm-ripe melon
- 2 large tomatoes, very thinly sliced
- 1 small cucumber, very thinly sliced
- ½ teaspoon kosher salt
- ¼ teaspoon freshly ground pepper
- 1 cup crumbled goat cheese
- ¼ cup extra-virgin olive oil
- 4 teaspoons balsamic vinegar
- ⅓ cup very thinly sliced fresh basil

Instructions

- Place onion rings in a medium bowl, add cold water to cover and a handful of ice cubes. Set aside for about 20 minutes. Drain and pat dry.
- Meanwhile, cut melon in half lengthwise and scoop out the seeds. Remove the rind with a sharp knife. Place each melon half cut-side down and slice crosswise into 1/8-inch-thick slices.
- Make the salad on a large platter or 8 individual salad plates. Begin by arranging a ring of melon slices around the edge. Top with a layer of overlapping tomato slices. Arrange a second ring of melon slices toward the center. Top with the remaining tomato slices. Tuck cucumber slices between the layers of tomato and melon. Sprinkle with salt and pepper. Top with goat cheese and the onion rings. Drizzle with oil and vinegar. Sprinkle with basil.

Nutrition

Calories: 194; Protein 4.7g; Carbohydrates 19.4g; Dietary Fiber 2.3g; Sugars 16g; Fat 11.6g; Saturated Fat 4g; Cholesterol 11.2mg; Vitamin A Iu 774.7IU; Vitamin C 37.5mg; Folate 45.3mcg; Calcium 67.2mg; Iron 0.8mg; Magnesium 30.7mg; Potassium 570.6mg; Sodium 161.2mg; Thiamin 0.1mg.

319. Curried Carrot Soup

Total: 1 hr

Servings: 6

Ingredients

- 3 tablespoons canola oil
- 2 teaspoons curry powder
- 8 medium carrots, peeled and thinly sliced
- 4 medium stalks celery, thinly sliced
- 1 medium onion, coarsely chopped
- 5 cups reduced-sodium chicken broth
- 1 tablespoon lemon juice
- ½ teaspoon salt
- Freshly ground pepper, to taste

Instructions

- Cook oil and curry powder in a large saucepan over medium heat, stirring, until fragrant, 1 to 2 minutes. Stir in carrots, celery, and onion; toss

to coat in oil. Cook, stirring frequently, for 10 minutes. Stir in broth. Bring to a boil. Reduce heat and simmer until the vegetables are very tender about 10 minutes. Remove from the heat; let stand 10 minutes. Lay a paper towel over the surface of the soup to blot away the oil that has risen to the top. Discard the paper towel.
- Working in batches of no more than 2 cups at a time, transfer the soup to a blender and puree (use caution when pureeing hot liquids). Return the pureed soup to the pan, place over medium heat, and heat through. Season with lemon juice, salt, and pepper.

Nutrition

Calories: 122; Protein 4g; Carbohydrates 11.7g; Dietary Fiber 3.4g; Sugars 5.5g; Fat 7.4g; Saturated Fat 0.6g; Vitamin A Iu 13708.5IU; Vitamin C 8.8mg; Folate 35.4mcg; Calcium 45.9mg; Iron 0.7mg; Magnesium 18.5mg; Potassium 538.1mg; Sodium 637.5mg; Thiamin 0.1mg.

320. Clam Chowder

Total: 45 mins

Servings: 6

Ingredients

- 3 tablespoons extra-virgin olive oil
- 1 cup diced onion
- 1 cup diced celery
- ½ cup all-purpose flour
- ½ teaspoon dried thyme
- ¼ teaspoon salt
- ¼ teaspoon ground pepper
- 1 bay leaf
- 4 cups clam juice (see Tip) or seafood stock
- 1 cup whole milk
- 3 cups diced white potatoes
- 1 16-ounce container chopped fresh clams (plus their liquid), thawed if frozen
- Chopped cooked bacon for garnish
- Snipped chives for garnish

Instructions

- Heat oil in a large pot over medium heat. Add onion and celery; cook, stirring frequently until

softened and beginning to brown, 3 to 6 minutes. Sprinkle flour, thyme, salt, pepper, and bay leaf over the vegetables and cook, stirring, for 1 minute more. Add clam juice (or seafood stock) and milk; bring to a gentle boil, stirring constantly.
- Stir in potatoes and bring just to a simmer. Simmer, uncovered, stirring occasionally, until the potatoes are tender, 12 to 15 minutes.
- Add clams and cook, stirring frequently, until cooked through, 2 to 4 minutes. Serve topped with bacon and chives, if desired.

Nutrition

Calories: 229; Protein 12.2g; Carbohydrates 26.5g; Dietary Fiber 3.6g; Sugars 5g; Fat 9g; Saturated Fat 1.8g; Cholesterol 35.3mg; Folate 60.4mcg; Calcium 105.1mg; Iron 2.9mg; Magnesium 44.6mg; Potassium 693.2mg; Sodium 476.8mg; Thiamin 0.2mg.

321. New Mexico Chile Verde (Green Chili)

Prep Time: 30 Minutes

Cook Time: 3 Hours 30 Minutes

Total Time: 4 Hours

Ingredients

- 1/4 cup oil
- 4 pounds pork butt, trimmed and cut into 1 1/2-inch cube
- 2 large onions, peeled and chopped
- 1 tablespoon ground cumin
- 1 tablespoon ground coriander
- 1 tablespoon oregano
- 4 cloves garlic, minced
- 2 Hatch peppers, chopped (or Anaheims)
- 2 Poblano peppers, chopped
- 1-2 jalapeno peppers, seeded and diced
- 1 pound tomatillos (peeled and cleaned), chopped
- 2 bay leaves
- 1 bunch cilantro (large), chopped
- 3 tablespoons masa (corn flour)
- 4 cups water or chicken stock
- 1 tablespoon salt, divided
- Lime wedges for garnish

Instructions

- Heat the oil in a large pot over medium-high heat. Add the pork and 2 teaspoons of salt. Brown the pork on all sides, stirring regularly. Remove the pork from the pot and pour out all rendered fat, saving about 1 tablespoon.
- Add the onions, remaining salt, cumin, coriander, and oregano to the pot. Sauté for 3-5 minutes. Then add the garlic and peppers. Sauté another 3-5 minutes. Add the chopped tomatillos, bay leaves, and cilantro. Toss the pork with the masa and add back to the pot. Stir well.
- Finally, add the water. Bring to a boil, then reduce the heat to low. Cover and simmer for 3 hours, or until the pork is falling apart, stirring occasionally.
- Take 2 forks and break the pork up even more. Salt and pepper to taste.

Nutrition

Serving: 1cup, Calories: 626kcal, Carbohydrates: 23g, Protein: 63g, Fat: 30g, Saturatedfat: 7g, Cholesterol: 186mg, Sodium: 1657mg, Potassium: 1599mg, Fiber: 5g, Sugar: 8g, Vitamin C: 49.9mg, Calcium: 115mg, Iron: 6.4mg

322. Pozole Verde De Pollo (Chicken Pozole)

Prep Time: 15 Minutes

Cook Time: 1 Hour 10 Minutes

Total Time: 1 Hour 25 Minutes

Servings: 8 Servings

Ingredients

- 2 tablespoons olive oil
- 1 large sweet onion peeled and chopped
- 6-8 cloves garlic minced
- 6 poblano peppers seeded and chopped
- 2-3 jalapeno peppers seeded and chopped (optional for heat)
- ½ cup chopped cilantro
- 3 pounds boneless chicken thighs
- 1 ½ pounds tomatillos peeled and quartered
- 2 bay leaves
- 1 tablespoon dried oregano
- 6 cups chicken broth or water

- 2 – 15 ounce cans white hominy drained and rinsed
- Salt and pepper
- Garnishes: Tortilla chips, shredded cabbage, lime wedges, sliced avocado, sliced radishes, chopped cilantro

Instructions

- Set a heavy 6-8 quart dutch oven over medium heat. Add the oil to the pot. Add in the chopped onion and garlic. Sauté for 2 minutes, then add in the chopped poblanos, jalapenos, and cilantro. Sauté another 8 minutes, stirring regularly.
- Place the chicken thighs, tomatillos, bay leaves, oregano, chicken broth, and 1 teaspoon salt.
- Cover the pot with a heavy lid and bring to a boil. Then lower the heat and simmer for 50-60 minutes, until the chicken is soft enough to shred. (Keep the pot covered.)
- Remove the chicken thighs, and bay leaves. Use tongs or forks to shred the chicken into small chunks.
- Add the shredded chicken back to the pot, along with the rinsed hominy. Stir to combine. Simmer another 2-3 minutes to warm the hominy. Taste, then season with salt and pepper as needed. Keep warm until ready to serve.
- To Serve: Ladle the posole into bowls. Garnish the top with tortilla chips, shredded cabbage, sliced avocado, radishes, lime wedges, and cilantro.

Nutrition

Calories: 477kcal, Carbohydrates: 15g, Protein: 31g, Fat: 33g, Saturatedfat: 8g, Cholesterol: 167mg, Sodium: 785mg, Potassium: 954mg, Fiber: 4g, Sugar: 8g, Vitamin A: 676iu, Vitamin C: 101mg, Calcium: 61mg, Iron: 3mg

323. The Ultimate Wedge Salad Recipe

Prep Time: 15 Minutes

Cook Time: 5 Minutes

Total Time: 20 Minutes

Servings: 4 Servings

Ingredients

For The Blue Cheese Dressing:

- ½ cup sour cream
- ½ cup mayonnaise
- 1/3 cup buttermilk
- 1 tablespoon apple cider vinegar
- ½ teaspoon salt
- ¼ teaspoon cracked black pepper
- ¼ teaspoon garlic powder
- ½ cup crumbled blue cheese

For The Wedge Salad:

- 8 slices bacon chopped
- 1 head iceberg lettuce
- 1 cup cherry or grape tomatoes halved
- 1 cup blue cheese dressing
- ½ cup chopped scallions
- ½ cup crumbled blue cheese

Instructions

Make The Dressing: Set out a medium mixing bowl. Add the sour cream, mayonnaise, buttermilk, apple cider vinegar, salt, pepper, and garlic powder. Stir well. Then mix in the crumbled blue cheese. Cover and chill until ready to use. (If possible, make a day ahead, or early in the day, so the blue cheese has time to permeate the dressing.)

Cook The Bacon: Set a skillet over medium heat. Place the chopped bacon in the skillet. Brown the bacon for 4-6 minutes until crispy, stirring regularly. Then scoop the bacon out of the skillet onto a paper towel-lined plate to drain off the grease.

Prep The Veggies: Slice the tomatoes in half and chop the scallions. Then set the head of lettuce on the cutting board. Trim the root/core end a little. Cut the head in half, through the core. (This helps hold the wedges together.) Then cut each half in two, through the core.

Stack The Wedges: Set each lettuce wedge on a plate. Drizzle with a generous amount of blue cheese dressing. (At least ¼ cup per salad.) Then sprinkle the tops with halved tomatoes, scallions, bacon, and more blue cheese crumbles. Finish each salad plate off with a bit of fresh cracked pepper. Serve cold.

Nutrition

Calories: 653kcal, Carbohydrates: 12g, Protein: 19g, Fat: 59g, Saturatedfat: 21g, Cholesterol: 84mg, Sodium: 1870mg, Potassium: 547mg, Fiber: 2g, Sugar: 8g, Vitamin C: 15mg, Calcium: 325mg, Iron: 2mg

324. Crispy Brussel Sprouts Quinoa Salad Recipe

Prep Time: 15 Minutes

Cook Time: 30 Minutes

Total Time: 45 Minutes

Servings: 8

Ingredients

- 1 1/4 cup dried lentils, choose a more firm lentil type
- 2/3 cup dried quinoa
- 3 cups water
- 3/4 teaspoon curry powder
- 8 ounces Brussels sprouts
- 1 cup thinly sliced shallots, about 3-4
- 2 tablespoons olive oil
- 1/2 cup DeLallo Sun-Dried Peppers, chopped
- 1/2 cup scallions, chopped
- 1/2 lemon, juiced
- Salt and pepper

Instructions

- Preheat the oven to 400 degrees F. Place the quinoa and lentils in a medium stockpot with 3 cups of water, 1 teaspoon salt, and 3/4 teaspoon curry powder. Bring to a boil, then cover and reduce the heat to medium-low. Cook for 25-30 minutes until the quinoa is fluffy and the lentils are cooked, but firm. Remove from heat, but keep covered until ready to use.
- Meanwhile, cut the Brussels sprouts in half and slice thin. Place them on a rimmed baking sheet with the sliced shallots and drizzle with olive oil. Toss to coat then spread them out thin and salt and pepper. Bake for 20-25 minutes, until crispy.
- Fluff the quinoa and lentils and move to a large bowl. Add the crispy Brussels sprouts and shallots, chopped sweet peppers, chopped scallions, and the juice of half a lemon. Toss and salt and pepper to taste. Serve immediately.

Nutrition

Calories: 214kcal, Carbohydrates: 33g, Protein: 11g, Fat: 5g, Saturatedfat: 1g, Sodium: 18mg, Potassium: 546mg, Fiber: 12g, Sugar: 3g, Vitamin A: 900iu, Vitamin C: 30.9mg, Calcium: 44mg, Iron: 3.6mg

325. Hungarian Mushroom Soup (Vegan or Gluten-Free!)

Prep Time: 10 Minutes

Cook Time: 33 Minutes

Total Time: 43 Minutes

Servings: 6 Servings

Ingredients

- ¼ cups butter (or plant-based butter)
- 1 large onion peeled and chopped
- 1 cup chopped celery
- 1 pound button mushrooms sliced
- 3 tablespoons soy sauce (gluten-free)
- 2 tablespoons fresh chopped dill
- 1 tablespoon smoked paprika
- 1 tablespoon lemon juice
- 6 cups vegetable broth or mushroom broth
- ¾ cups sour cream (or Vegan Cashew Sour Cream)
- 3 tablespoons all-purpose flour (or GF baking mix)
- Salt and pepper
- Garnishes: Fresh chopped dill, scallions, and/or parsley, sour cream, or cashew cream

Instructions

- Set a large 6-quart saucepot over medium heat. Add the butter, onions, and celery. Sauté for 3-5 minutes to soften. Then move the veggies to the side of the pot and add in the mushrooms, 1 teaspoon salt, and ½ teaspoon pepper. Sauté another 8-10 minutes, stirring regularly.
- Stir in the soy sauce, dill, smoked paprika, lemon juice, and vegetable broth. Simmer for 10-15 minutes.
- Meanwhile, set out a medium bowl. Add the sour cream and flour. Stir until smooth.
- Ladle some of the soup broth into the sour cream mixture, stirring constantly so the sour cream doesn't curdle. Once the mixture is thin, whisk the sour cream mixture into the soup base, whisking continually.
- Simmer another 3-5 minutes to thicken. Taste, then add additional salt and lemon juice if needed.
- Serve warm with a sprinkling of fresh herbs and a dollop of sour cream on top.

Nutrition

Calories: 185kcal, Carbohydrates: 13g, Protein: 5g, Fat: 14g, Saturatedfat: 8g, Cholesterol: 35mg, Sodium: 1552mg, Potassium: 397mg, Fiber: 2g, Sugar: 6g, Vitamin A: 1577iu, Vitamin C: 5mg, Calcium: 52mg, Iron: 1mg

326. Zesty Wor Wonton Soup Recipe

Prep Time: 35 Minutes

Cook Time: 15 Minutes

Total Time: 50 Minutes

Servings: 8 Servings

Ingredients

For The Wontons:

- ½ pound ground pork or chicken
- ¼ cup chopped scallions
- 2 tablespoons soy sauce
- 2-3 cloves garlic minced
- 1 tablespoon fresh grated ginger
- 1 teaspoon sesame oil
- ½ teaspoon crushed red pepper
- 25 refrigerated wontons wrappers usually 2-inch squares

For The Wonton Soup:

- 1 tablespoon sesame oil
- 3-4 cloves garlic minced
- 1 tablespoon fresh grated ginger
- 8 cups chicken broth
- 2 tablespoons soy sauce
- 2 cups cooked shredded chicken use up leftovers
- 2 cups chopped bok choy
- 8 ounces sliced shiitake mushrooms
- ½ cup chopped scallions

Instructions

For The Wontons:

- Set out a medium mixing bowl. Add ground pork or chicken, scallions, soy sauce, garlic, ginger, sesame oil, and crushed red pepper. Mix until well combined.
- Layout several wontons wrappers. Set out a small dish of water to act as glue. Place 1 ½ teaspoon of the meat filling in the center of each

wonton. Use your finger to paint a line of water along two connected edges. Fold the wet corner up to meet the opposite corner. Use your fingers to close and seal the edges of the wonton wrapper, making a triangle shape.

- Now use your finger to dampen the two bottom corners. Bring them together and pinch to seal. Repeat with the remaining wonton wrappers and filling.

For The Wonton Soup:

- Set a large 6-8 quart saucepot over medium-high heat. Add the sesame oil, garlic, and ginger. Sauté for 2 minutes, to soften the aromatics, then pour in the chicken broth and soy sauce. Bring to a simmer. Simmer the soup base for 10 minutes.
- Meanwhile, load soup bowls with shredded chicken, bok choy, sliced mushrooms, and scallions. (These ingredients will steep in the hot broth, "Hot Pot" style!)
- Once the soup has simmered 10 minutes, reduce the heat, and gently lower the wontons into the soup. Simmer on medium-low for 2-3 minutes. (DO NOT over-cook the wontons or they will open up and disintegrate into the soup.) Then ladle the wonton soup broth into the bowls. Serve hot.

Nutrition

Calories: 165kcal, Carbohydrates: 19g, Protein: 10g, Fat: 6g, Saturatedfat: 1g, Cholesterol: 26mg, Sodium: 1532mg, Potassium: 535mg, Fiber: 2g, Sugar: 1g, Vitamin A: 912iu, Vitamin C: 27mg, Calcium: 55mg, Iron: 2mg

327. Creamy Parmesan Chicken And Rice Soup

Prep Time: 15 Minutes

Cook Time: 30 Minutes

Total Time: 45 Minutes

Servings: 8 People

Ingredients

- 2 tablespoons butter
- 1 large sweet onion, peeled and chopped
- 1 cup chopped carrots
- 1 cup chopped celery
- 4 cloves garlic, minced

- 1 tablespoon fresh thyme leaves, 1 tsp dried thyme
- 1 bay leaf
- 1 pound boneless chicken thighs, or breasts
- 10 cups chicken broth, or water + 10 tsp chicken bouillon
- 1 cup dried long-grain rice
- 2/3 cup grated parmesan cheese
- 3 tablespoons cornstarch
- 3 tablespoons chopped parsley
- Salt and pepper

Instructions

- Place a large 6-8 quart pot over medium heat. Add the butter. Once melted add in the onions, carrots, celery, and garlic. Sauté for 3-5 minutes, stirring to soften.
- Add in the thyme, bay leaf, chicken thighs, and chicken broth. Bring to a boil. Once boiling, stir in the dried rice.
- Cover and simmer for 12 minutes. Then use tongs to remove the chicken thighs. Use two forks to shred the chicken into bite-size pieces. Continue to simmer the soup uncovered, while you shred the chicken.
- Mix the grated parmesan cheese with the cornstarch. Stir the chicken back into the soup. Continue stirring as you add the parmesan mixture into the soup. Simmer another 2-4 minutes to thicken the soup base.
- Taste. Then salt and pepper as needed. Remove the bay leaf and stir in the fresh parsley. Serve warm.

Nutrition

Calories: 321kcal, Carbohydrates: 29g, Protein: 16g, Fat: 16g, Saturated fat: 6g, Cholesterol: 70mg, Sodium: 1298mg, Potassium: 541mg, Fiber: 2g, Sugar: 3g, Vitamin C: 28mg, Calcium: 148mg, Iron: 2mg

328. Nana's Epic Navy Bean Ham Bone Soup

Prep Time: 10 Minutes

Cook Time: 1 Hour 10 Minutes

Total Time: 1 Hour 20 Minutes

Servings: 8

Ingredients

- 1 pound dried navy beans
- 1 ham bone + ham scraps
- 1 tablespoon olive oil
- 1 large onion, peeled and chopped
- 6 cloves garlic, minced
- 1 tablespoon fresh thyme leaves
- 2 teaspoons ground cumin
- 1/2-1 teaspoon crushed red pepper
- 10 cups water
- Salt and pepper

Instructions

- The Night Before: Place the dried beans in a large bowl and cover with three inches of water. Soak the dried beans overnight (up to 24 hours) to soften. Drain when ready to use.
- Place a large 6-quart pot over medium heat. Add the oil, ham bone, onions, and garlic. Sauté for 3-5 minutes to soften the onions.
- Then add in the drained beans, thyme, ground cumin, crushed red pepper, 10 cups of water, and any remaining ham scraps. (Do not salt the soup until the end, because ham bones can be very salty.)
- Bring the soup to a boil. Lower the heat and simmer for 60-90 minutes, covered, until the beans are very soft. Uncover and stir occasionally, then place the lid back on top.
- Use a fork to pull any remaining ham off the bone and stir it into the soup. Discard the bone. Add 1-2 cups additional water if the soup is too thick. Taste, then salt and pepper as needed.

Nutrition

Calories: 218kcal, Carbohydrates: 36g, Protein: 13g, Fat: 2g, Saturated fat: 0g, Cholesterol: 0mg, Sodium: 22mg, Potassium: 715mg, Fiber: 14g, Sugar: 2g, Vitamin A: 85iu, Vitamin C: 3.1mg, Calcium: 108mg, Iron: 3.7mg

329. Best Turkey Chili (Leftover Turkey Recipe)

Prep Time: 15 Minutes

Cook Time: 30 Minutes

Total Time: 45 Minutes

Servings: 6

Ingredients

- 1 1/2 cup red bell pepper, diced

- 1 cup red onion, diced
- 1 cup celery, chopped
- 4 cloves garlic, minced
- 1/2 cup butter
- 6 tablespoons masa (corn flour)
- 2 tablespoons ground cumin
- 2 tablespoons ground coriander
- 1 1/2 tablespoons chili powder
- 1 tablespoon dried oregano
- 6 cups turkey stock or chicken stock
- 6 cups turkey meat, cooked and chopped
- 45 ounces canned black beans, drained and rinsed
- 1 1/2 cups frozen corn
- 2 tablespoon honey
- Salt and pepper to taste
- Possible Toppings: shredded cheese, sour cream, diced red onion, chopped scallions, salsa, corn chips

Instructions

- Place the butter in a large stockpot and set over medium heat. Add the bell pepper, onions, celery, and garlic. Sauté for 5-8 minutes, until softened. Stir to make sure the veggies don't burn.
- Mix in the masa, cumin, coriander, chili powder, and oregano. Stir to coat and sauté for another 2 minutes. Then pour in the turkey stock and scrape the bottom of the pot to loosen the veggies.
- Add the chopped turkey, beans, corn, and honey. Season with 1 1/2 teaspoons of salt and 1/2 teaspoon ground pepper. Bring the chili to a low boil and simmer for at least 20 minutes, stirring occasionally. Taste and season again if needed. Serve warm.

Nutrition

Calories: 674kcal, Carbohydrates: 37g, Protein: 95g, Fat: 16g, Saturatedfat: 6g, Cholesterol: 234mg, Sodium: 1476mg, Potassium: 1607mg, Fiber: 9g, Sugar: 6g, Vitamin C: 30.2mg, Calcium: 139mg, Iron: 6.2mg

---

330. Classic Beef Barley Soup

Prep Time: 15 Minutes

Cook Time: 45 Minutes

Total Time: 1 Hour

Servings: 8 Servings

Ingredients

- 1 tablespoon olive oil
- 2 1/2 - 3 pounds beef chuck roast
- 1 large sweet onion, peeled and chopped
- 2 cups sliced carrots
- 2 cups sliced celery
- 4 cloves garlic, minced
- 12 cups beef broth
- 15 ounces fire-roasted diced tomatoes (1 can)
- 1 cup dried barley
- 1 tablespoon fresh thyme leaves (1 teaspoon dried)
- 1 tablespoon freshly chopped rosemary leaves (1 teaspoon dried)
- 1/2 teaspoon crushed red pepper
- Salt and pepper

Instructions

- Place a large saucepot over medium heat and add the olive oil and onions. Saute the onions for 2-3 minutes. Then stir in the carrots, celery, and garlic. Cook for another 3-5 minutes.
- Meanwhile, cut the beef into small 1/2-inch chunks. Push the veggies to the side of the pot and add the meat. Brown for 5 minutes, stirring once or twice. Then add in the broth, tomatoes, barley, herbs, crushed red pepper, and 1/2 teaspoon salt. Stir well.
- Cover the pot and bring to a boil. Lower the heat if needed and simmer until the barley is cooked and the beef is tender, stirring occasionally. About 30 minutes.
- Taste. Then season with salt and pepper as needed.

Nutrition

Calories: 373kcal, Carbohydrates: 27g, Protein: 30g, Fat: 16g, Saturated Fat: 6g, Cholesterol: 78mg, Sodium: 1563mg, Potassium: 903mg, Fiber: 6g, Sugar: 5g, Vitamin C: 7.7mg, Calcium: 103mg, Iron: 4.6mg

---

331. The Perfect Greek Salad Dressing Recipe

Prep Time: 5 Minutes

Total Time: 5 Minutes

Servings: 12 Servings

Ingredients

- ¾ Cup Extra-Virgin Olive Oil
- 1 Large Juicy Lemon Zested And Juiced (About ¼ Cup)
- ¼ Cup Red Wine Vinegar
- 1 Teaspoon Dijon Mustard
- 1 Teaspoon Dried Oregano
- 1 Clove Garlic Minced
- ¼ Cup Crumbled Feta Optional
- Salt And Pepper

Instructions

- Set out a pint jar. Place the oil, lemon juice and zest, vinegar, Dijon mustard, oregano, and minced garlic in the jar.
- Cover and shake well to emulsify. Add the crumbled feta, if using, and shake again.
- Taste, then salt and pepper as needed. (I usually add about ½ teaspoon salt and ¼ teaspoon fresh cracked pepper.)

Nutrition

Calories: 132kcal, Carbohydrates: 1g, Protein: 1g, Fat: 14g, Saturatedfat: 2g, Cholesterol: 3mg, Sodium: 41mg, Potassium: 12mg, Fiber: 1g, Sugar: 1g, Vitamin A: 13iu, Vitamin C: 5mg, Calcium: 20mg, Iron: 1mg

332. Homemade Egg Drop Soup Recipe

Prep Time: 5 Minutes

Cook Time: 10 Minutes

Total Time: 15 Minutes

Servings: 8

Ingredients

- 8 cups chicken broth
- 1/4 cup cornstarch (1/4 cup arrowroot powder for paleo)
- 1 1/2 tablespoon soy sauce (coconut aminos for paleo)
- 2 teaspoons sesame oil
- 1 teaspoon grated ginger
- 3/4 teaspoon garlic powder
- 1/4 teaspoon ground turmeric
- 6 large eggs

Instructions

- Add the chicken broth, cornstarch, soy sauce, sesame oil, grated ginger, garlic powder, and turmeric in a large saucepot. Whisk well. Then turn the heat on high and bring to a boil.
- In a small bowl, whisk the eggs well. Then stir the soup base to get it swirling and slowly pour the eggs into the soup. The eggs swirling into the soup will create ribbons of egg. Turn off the heat.
- Taste the soup and add salt and pepper to taste. Serve as-is, or garnish with chopped green onions and crunchy Chinese noodles.

Nutrition

Calories: 121kcal, Carbohydrates: 5.5g, Protein: 9.8g, Fat: 6.3g, Saturatedfat: 1.7g, Cholesterol: 140mg, Sodium: 985mg, Fiber: 0.1g, Sugar: 1.1g

333. Crispy Brussel Sprouts Quinoa Salad Recipe

Prep Time: 15 Minutes

Cook Time: 30 Minutes

Total Time: 45 Minutes

Servings: 8

Ingredients

- 1 1/4 cup dried lentils, choose a more firm lentil type
- 2/3 cup dried quinoa
- 3 cups water
- 3/4 teaspoon curry powder
- 8 ounces Brussels sprouts
- 1 cup thinly sliced shallots, about 3-4
- 2 tablespoons olive oil
- 1/2 cup DeLallo Sun-Dried Peppers, chopped
- 1/2 cup scallions, chopped
- 1/2 lemon, juiced
- Salt and pepper

Instructions

- Preheat the oven to 400 degrees F. Place the quinoa and lentils in a medium stockpot with 3 cups of water, 1 teaspoon salt, and 3/4 teaspoon curry powder. Bring to a boil, then cover and reduce the heat to medium-low. Cook for 25-30 minutes until the quinoa is fluffy and the lentils are cooked, but firm. Remove from heat, but keep covered until ready to use.

- Meanwhile, cut the Brussels sprouts in half and slice thin. Place them on a rimmed baking sheet with the sliced shallots and drizzle with olive oil. Toss to coat then spread them out thin and salt and pepper. Bake for 20-25 minutes, until crispy.
- Fluff the quinoa and lentils and move to a large bowl. Add the crispy Brussels sprouts and shallots, chopped sweet peppers, chopped scallions, and the juice of half a lemon. Toss and salt and pepper to taste. Serve immediately.

Nutrition

Calories: 214kcal, Carbohydrates: 33g, Protein: 11g, Fat: 5g, Saturatedfat: 1g, Sodium: 18mg, Potassium: 546mg, Fiber: 12g, Sugar: 3g, Vitamin A: 900iu, Vitamin C: 30.9mg, Calcium: 44mg, Iron: 3.6mg

334. Harvest Salad (Cobb Style)

Prep Time: 20 Minutes

Cook Time: 2 Minutes

Total Time: 22 Minutes

Servings: 4

Ingredients

For The Cobb Salad:

- 2 romaine hearts roughly chopped
- 2 cups cooked chicken cut into cubes
- 2 cups roasted butternut squash cubes
- 6 slices thick-cut bacon cooked and crumbled
- 3 large hard-boiled eggs peeled and chopped
- 2 ripe avocadoes sliced
- 1 cup shelled pecans
- 1 tablespoon butter
- 1/4 teaspoon ground mustard
- 1/4 teaspoon garlic powder
- 1/4 teaspoon hot paprika
- 1/4 teaspoon salt

For The Creamy Corn And Poblano Dressing:

- 1 poblano pepper
- 1 clove garlic
- 2 ears corn on the cob cooked
- 2 limes juiced
- 1 teaspoon ground cumin

- 1 teaspoon salt
- 2/3 cup olive oil

Instructions

- Heat a skillet to medium-low heat. Melt the butter in the skillet, then add the pecans. Sprinkle the pecans with the ground mustard, garlic powder, paprika, and salt and toss to coat. Sauté for 3-5 minutes, stirring regularly to toast. Be careful not to burn the pecans.
- Pile the chopped romaine on a large platter. Arrange the chopped chicken, roasted butternut squash, bacon, pecans, eggs, and avocados in rows on top of the romaine.
- Preheat the oven to broil. Place the poblano pepper on a small baking sheet and set it on the top rack in the oven. Check the pepper every 1-2 minutes, turning when the skin is black and blistered. Remove the poblano from the oven when it's black on all sides. Place the pepper in a zip bag and allow it to steam for 10 minutes.
- Cut the corn off the cobs and place them in the blender. Add the garlic clove, lime juice, salt, and cumin. Once the pepper has steamed, removed the papery skin, stem, and seeds. Place the poblano flesh in the blender.
- Puree until smooth, then remove the ingredient cup from the lid and slowly pour in the olive oil to emulsify. Once the dressing is smooth and creamy, turn off the blender and pour the dressing into a serving bowl.

Nutrition

Calories: 860kcal, Carbohydrates: 20g, Protein: 16g, Fat: 83g, Saturatedfat: 17g, Cholesterol: 64mg, Sodium: 1139mg, Potassium: 741mg, Fiber: 6g, Sugar: 5g, Vitamin C: 52mg, Calcium: 94mg, Iron: 3mg

335. Greek Orzo Pasta Salad With Lemon Vinaigrette

Prep Time: 15 Minutes

Cook Time: 10 Minutes

Total Time: 25 Minutes

Servings: 8 Servings

Ingredients

- 1 pound dried orzo pasta
- 1 large red bell pepper seeded and diced

- 1 cup pitted olives (I used half kalamata and half green)
- 3 ounces sun-dried tomatoes chopped
- 1/3 cup diced red onion
- 1/3 cup chopped fresh basil
- 1/3 cup chopped fresh dill
- 1/3 cup chopped parsley
- For the Lemon Vinaigrette
- ½ cup fresh lemon juice
- ½ cup extra-virgin olive oil
- 1-2 teaspoons granulated sugar
- 1 clove garlic
- Salt and pepper

Instructions

- Set a large pot of salted water over high heat. Bring to a boil. Then cook the orzo as directed on the package. Drain.
- Meanwhile, set out a large salad bowl. Chop the bell pepper, onions, sun-dried tomatoes, and fresh herbs.
- In a small bowl (or measuring pitcher) whisk the lemon juice, olive oil, sugar, and garlic together. Set aside.
- Once the orzo is cooked and drained, place it in the salad bowl. Add in the bell peppers, olives, sun-dried tomatoes, onion, and all chopped herbs.
- Pour the lemon dressing over the salad and toss well. Cover and refrigerate until ready to serve.

Nutrition

Calories: 397kcal, Carbohydrates: 52g, Protein: 10g, Fat: 17g, Saturatedfat: 2g, Sodium: 296mg, Potassium: 583mg, Fiber: 4g, Sugar: 7g, Vitamin A: 1039iu, Vitamin C: 35mg, Calcium: 43mg, Iron: 2mg

336. Chunky Strawberry Salad With Poppyseed Dressing

Prep Time: 15 Minutes

Cook Time: 0 Minutes

Total Time: 15 Minutes

Servings: 8 Servings

Ingredients

- 2 cups fresh strawberries hulled and sliced

- 6 ounces fresh baby spinach
- 1 cup sliced radishes
- ¾ cup chopped roasted macadamia nuts
- 1/3 cup crumbled chevre goat cheese
- ¼ sliced red onion
- ¼ cup store-bought poppyseed dressing (or homemade)

Instructions

- Slice the strawberries, radishes, and onion. Chop the macadamia nuts.
- Set out a large salad bowl. Add the spinach leaves, sliced strawberries, radishes, chopped nuts, and onions. Pour the dressing over the top and toss to coat.
- Then sprinkle the top with crumbled goat cheese, and gently toss again.

Nutrition

Calories: 166kcal, carbohydrates: 8g, protein: 4g, fat: 14g, saturatedfat: 3g, cholesterol: 6mg, sodium: 114mg, potassium: 259mg, fiber: 3g, sugar: 4g, vitamin a: 2091iu, vitamin c: 30mg, calcium: 54mg, iron: 1mg

337. Wild Rice Salad With Blueberries And Herbs

Prep Time: 20 Minutes

Cook Time: 45 Minutes

Total Time: 1 Hour 5 Minutes

Servings: 12 Servings

Ingredients

- 2 cups dry wild rice
- 2 cups fresh blueberries
- 1 cup chopped scallions
- ½ cup shelled pistachios chopped
- ½ cup roughly chopped mint leaves
- ½ cup fresh chopped dill
- 1 large juicy orange zested and juiced
- 1 juicy lime zested and juiced
- ¼ cup olive oil
- 1 tablespoon honey or agave
- Salt and pepper

Instructions

- Cook the rice according to the package instructions. (For wild rice, usually, 2 cups of rice requires 6 cups of water and approximately 45-50 minutes of covered cook time.) Allow the rice to cool.
- Meanwhile, chop the herbs and pistachios. Then zest and juice the citrus.
- Move the cooled wild rice to a large salad bowl. Add the blueberries, scallions, chopped pistachios, mint, dill, orange zest, and lime zest.
- In a measuring pitcher, combine the orange juice, lime juice, olive oil, honey, 1 ¼ teaspoon salt, and ½ teaspoon ground black pepper. Whisk well then pour over the rice mixture. Toss to coat.
- Taste, then add additional salt and pepper if needed.
- Cover and refrigerate until ready to serve.

Nutrition

Calories: 126kcal, Carbohydrates: 15g, Protein: 3g, Fat: 7g, Saturated Fat: 1g, Sodium: 4mg, Potassium: 162mg, Fiber: 2g, Sugar: 6g, Vitamin A: 293iu, Vitamin C: 13mg, Calcium: 23mg, Iron: 1mg

338. Japanese Ginger Salad Dressing

Prep Time: 10 Minutes

Total Time: 10 Minutes

Servings: 8 Servings

Ingredients

- 1 cup carrots roughly chopped
- ½ cup onion peeled and roughly chopped
- ¼ cup celery roughly chopped
- ½ cup rice vinegar
- 1/3 cup canola oil
- 3 tablespoons fresh grated ginger
- 2 tablespoons granulated sugar or honey
- 1-2 tablespoons soy sauce (I always buy GF and low sodium.)
- 1 small garlic clove

Instructions

- Roughly chop all the produce. Place in the blender.

- Add all other ingredients to the blender. If you are sensitive to sodium, start with 1 tablespoon of soy sauce. You can always add more if needed.
- Cover the blender and turn on high. Puree until smooth.
- Taste, then add more soy sauce if desired.
- Refrigerate until ready to serve.

Nutrition

Calories: 111kcal, Carbohydrates: 6g, Protein: 1g, Fat: 9g, Saturated Fat: 1g, Sodium: 140mg, Potassium: 90mg, Fiber: 1g, Sugar: 4g, Vitamin A: 2687iu, Vitamin C: 2mg, Calcium: 9mg, Iron: 1mg

339. Bubbly Taco Salad Bowls Recipe

Prep Time: 5 Minutes

Cook Time: 13 Minutes

Total Time: 18 Minutes

Servings: 4

Ingredients

- 4 10-12 inch flour tortillas (XL burrito size)
- 4 tablespoons vegetable oil (or any flavorless oil)

Instructions

- Preheat the oven to 350 degrees F. Set 4 oven-safe cereal bowls on a large rimmed baking sheet. Then set a large 12-14 inch skillet on the stovetop over medium heat.
- Pour 1 tablespoon oil into the skillet. Once hot, place the tortilla in the skillet. Use tongs to swirl the tortilla to coat it in oil, flip it over, and swirl it again. It needs to be coated in oil, on both sides, right away.
- Pan-fry the tortilla for 30-45 seconds per side, allowing it to puff up with large bubbles. (The bigger the bubbles the better!) Flip and repeat. Make sure the tortilla isn't turning dark. It should be golden-brown.
- Use tongs to move the tortilla to one of the cereal bowls. Tuck it down into the bottom of the bowl, to create a bowl shape with the tortilla. Take care not to deflate the bubbles.
- Repeat with the remaining three tortillas. Once all the tortillas are flash-fried and shaped into

bowls, bake for 9-10 minutes until very crispy. Cool and fill.

Nutrition

Calories: 124kcal, Carbohydrates: 1g, Protein: 1g, Fat: 14g, Saturated Fat: 11g, Sodium: 7mg, Sugar: 1g

340. Hawaiian Macaroni Salad With Potatoes

Prep Time: 15 Minutes

Cook Time: 14 Minutes

Total Time: 29 Minutes

Servings: 16

Ingredients

- 3 pounds Russet potatoes, peeled and chopped into 1-inch cubes
- 12 ounces dried macaroni noodles
- 1/2 cup shredded onion
- 1 large carrot, shredded
- 10 ounces frozen peas
- 1/2 cup chopped scallions
- 2 1/2 cups low fat mayonnaise
- 1 cup sweet pickle relish
- 1 tablespoon apple cider vinegar
- 1 teaspoon yellow mustard
- 1 teaspoon ground allspice
- Salt and pepper

Instructions

- Cut the potatoes into 1-inch cubes and place them in a large stockpot. Fill the pot with cold water until it is one inch over the top of the potatoes. Set the pot over high heat and bring to a boil. Once boiling, add 1 tablespoon salt. Then set the timer and cook the potatoes for 5 minutes. After 5 minutes, stir in the macaroni noodles and continue boiling for 6-8 minutes, until the pasta is al dente.
- Meanwhile, in a medium bowl mix the mayonnaise, sweet pickle relish including juices, apple cider vinegar, mustard, allspice, 1/2 teaspoon salt, and pepper to taste. Stir until smooth. Then use a grater to shred the onions and carrot.

- Drain the potatoes and macaroni in a colander and place in a large salad bowl. Add in the onion, carrots, peas, and scallions. Pour the dressing over the top and mix until well combined.
- Cover the potato macaroni salad and refrigerate for at least 4 hours. If you have time to make it ahead, it tastes even better on day two! Keep refrigerated in an airtight container for up to one week.

Nutrition

Calories: 268kcal, Carbohydrates: 43g, Protein: 5g, Fat: 8g, Saturatedfat: 1g, Cholesterol: 5mg, Sodium: 398mg, Potassium: 488mg, Fiber: 3g, Sugar: 8g, Vitamin A: 1015iu, Vitamin C: 13.3mg, Calcium: 28mg, Iron: 1.5mg

341. The Ultimate Southern Chicken Salad Recipe

Prep Time: 20 Minutes

Cook Time: 3 Minutes

Total Time: 23 Minutes

Servings: 12 Servings

Ingredients

- 1 whole rotisserie chicken, about 5 cups chopped chicken
- 1 ¼ – 1 ½ cups mayonnaise
- 1 cup chopped celery
- 1 cup diced apple, a firm variety
- ½ cup sweet pickle relish
- ½ cup toasted almonds
- ½ cup chopped scallions
- 2 tablespoons dijon mustard
- 1 tablespoon fresh chopped dill
- Salt and pepper

Instructions

- Place the almonds in a small dry skillet. Set over medium heat. Toss and brown for 3-5 minutes, until golden. Turn off the heat. Meanwhile, chop all the produce.
- Remove the skin from the chicken and pull the cooked meat off the bones. Place all the chicken meat on a cutting board and roughly chop. Discard the skin and bones.
- Set out a large mixing bowl. Place the chicken in the bowl. Then add the mayonnaise, celery,

diced apple, sweet pickle relish, toasted almonds, scallions, Dijon mustard, and dill.

- Stir well to evenly mix all the ingredients. Taste, then salt and pepper as needed.
- Cover and chill until ready to serve. (Chicken salad always tastes better after it has time to rest and chill. If possible, make a day ahead.)

Nutrition

Calories: 268kcal, Carbohydrates: 4g, Protein: 18g, Fat: 20g, Saturatedfat: 3g, Cholesterol: 59mg, Sodium: 274mg, Potassium: 154mg, Fiber: 1g, Sugar: 3g, Vitamin C: 1mg, Calcium: 11mg, Iron: 1mg

342. Ahi Poke Bowl Recipe

Prep Time: 15 Minutes

Cook Time: 20 Minutes

Total Time: 35 Minutes

Servings: 6 Servings

Ingredients

- 2 cups dried jasmine rice
- 1 pound sashimi-grade ahi tuna
- 3 tablespoons gluten-free soy sauce
- 2 teaspoons honey
- 1 teaspoon sesame oil
- 1/2 – 1 teaspoon wasabi paste
- 3/4 cup chopped green onions (green and white ends)
- 1 1/2 teaspoons sesame seeds
- 1 ripe avocado
- 1 bunch radishes
- 1 cup sprouts (alfalfa, broccoli, bean)
- Furikake Rice Seasoning

Instructions

- Pour the rice into a medium saucepot. Add 4 cups of water. Cover and bring to a boil. Once boiling, stir well. Then cover and lower the heat to medium-low. Simmer for 15-20 minutes until all the water is absorbed and there are air holes in the top of the rice. Remove from heat, fluff the rice with a fork, then cover to keep warm and set aside.
- Meanwhile, cut the ahi tuna steaks into 1/4 to 1/3 inch cubes. Place them in a bowl and add the soy sauce, honey, sesame, oil, and wasabi paste.

Toss well to coat. Then stir in the chopped green onions and sesame seeds.

- Slice the avocado and radishes. Once the rice is cooked, assemble the bowls: Scoop a heaping portion of rice into 4-6 salad bowls. Spoon the ahi poke next to the rice and arrange sprouts and sliced radishes around the rice. Place several avocado slices over the top and sprinkle furikake on top.

Nutrition

Calories: 415kcal, Carbohydrates: 56g, Protein: 24g, Fat: 10g, Saturatedfat: 1g, Cholesterol: 28mg, Sodium: 543mg, Potassium: 496mg, Fiber: 3g, Sugar: 2g, Vitamin A: 1830iu, Vitamin C: 7.4mg, Calcium: 47mg, Iron: 2mg

343. Grandma's Best Ambrosia Salad Recipe

Prep Time: 15 Minutes

Cook Time: 0 Minutes

Total Time: 15 Minutes

Servings: 12

Ingredients

- 15 ounce can mandarin oranges
- 15 ounce can peach slices, drained
- 8 ounce can pineapple tidbits
- 5-ounce jar maraschino cherries stems removed
- ¾ cup fresh green grapes halved lengthwise
- ¾ cup sweetened coconut flakes
- ¾ cup mini marshmallows
- ½ cup chopped pecans, optional
- ¼ cup diced crystallized ginger, candied ginger
- 4 ounces sour cream
- 4 ounces cool whip
- Pinch of salt

Instructions

- Set a large colander in the sink. Pour the mandarin oranges, peaches, pineapple tidbits, and cherries into the colander.
- Once they are well-drained, chop each peach slice into 3-4 pieces. Remove all cherry stems, then cut the cherries in half.
- Cut the green grapes in half. Chop the pecans (if using) and dice the crystallized ginger pieces.
- Set out a large salad bowl. Pour the drained fruit into the bowl. Add the grapes, coconut,

marshmallows, pecans, crystallized ginger, sour cream, and cool whip. Add a good pinch of salt and gently mix the salad until everything is well incorporated.
- Cover and refrigerate until ready to serve. Can be made up to 7 days in advance.

Nutrition

Calories: 172kcal, Carbohydrates: 27g, Protein: 2g, Fat: 7g, Saturated Fat: 3g, Cholesterol: 6mg, Sodium: 35mg, Potassium: 218mg, Fiber: 3g, Sugar: 23g, Vitamin A: 675iu, Vitamin C: 16.5mg, Calcium: 40mg, Iron: 0.5mg

344. The Best Macaroni Salad Recipe

Prep Time: 15 Minutes

Cook Time: 10 Minutes

Total Time: 25 Minutes

Servings: 12 Servings

Ingredients

- 1 pound macaroni pasta
- 12 ounces roasted red pepper, (1 jar) drained and chopped
- 3/4 cup kale, finely chopped
- 1/2 cup cooked bacon, chopped
- 1/2 cup sweet pickle relish
- 1/2 cup scallions, chopped
- 1 1/2 cups mayonnaise, could be low fat
- 3 tablespoons apple cider vinegar
- 1 tablespoon granulated sugar
- 1 tablespoon hot sauce, i used frank's redhot
- 1 clove garlic, minced
- Salt and pepper

Instructions

- Bring a large pot of salted water to a boil. Cook the macaroni according to the package instructions, usually 7-10 minutes. Then drain and rinse with cold water.
- In a medium bowl mix the mayonnaise, apple cider vinegar, sugar, hot sauce, garlic, 1 teaspoon salt, and 1/2 teaspoon ground pepper.
- Pour the macaroni into a large bowl. Pour the dressing over the top. Then add the chopped roasted red peppers, kale, bacon, pickle relish, and scallions.

- Toss well to coat. Then refrigerate until ready to serve.

Nutrition

Calories: 362kcal, Carbohydrates: 34g, Protein: 5g, Fat: 22g, Saturated Fat: 3g, Cholesterol: 12mg, Sodium: 689mg, Potassium: 163mg, Fiber: 1g, Sugar: 5g, Vitamin A: 750iu, Vitamin C: 20mg, Calcium: 31mg, Iron: 1mg

345. Fresh Peach Salad Recipe With Basil

Prep Time: 10 Minutes

Total Time: 10 Minutes

Servings: 6

Ingredients

- 4-6 ripe peaches pitted and cut into bite-size pieces
- 1 tablespoon honey
- 6 basil leaves thinly sliced
- 1/2 cup lemon chevre or plain chevre with a little lemon zest
- Pinch of salt

Instructions

- Place the peaches in a bowl. Drizzle with honey and sprinkle with salt. Toss to coat.
- Gently fold in basil and chevre. Serve immediately.

Nutrition

Calories: 99kcal, Carbohydrates: 12g, Protein: 4g, Fat: 4g, Saturatedfat: 2g, Cholesterol: 8mg, Sodium: 69mg, Potassium: 190mg, Fiber: 1g, Sugar: 11g, Vitamin A: 540iu, Vitamin C: 6.6mg, Calcium: 32mg, Iron: 0.6mg

346. Spicy Kani Salad Recipe

Prep Time: 30 Minutes

Cook Time: 0 Minutes

Total Time: 30 Minutes

Servings: 4

Ingredients

For The Dressing:

- 1/4 cup mayonnaise
- 2 tablespoon rice vinegar

- 1/2 teaspoon sugar
- 1 teaspoon sriracha sauce (chile sauce)
- 1/2 teaspoon paprika
- 1/2 teaspoon freshly grated ginger
- Pinch salt

For The Salad:

- 4 Kani sticks (1/2 pound imitation crab)
- 1 mango peeled and shredded
- 1 large cucumber (or three baby cucumbers) peeled and shredded
- 3/4 cup panko bread crumbs

Instructions

- Whisk the first seven ingredients together for the dressing. Taste for seasoning and salt and pepper as needed. Set aside.
- Shred the crab sticks by hand and place them in a large bowl. Shred the cucumber and mango in a food processor (or julienne by hand) and place in the bowl.
- Toss with the dressing and top with panko immediately before serving.

Nutrition

Calories: 178kcal, Carbohydrates: 16g, Protein: 2g, Fat: 11g, Saturated Fat: 1g, Cholesterol: 6mg, Sodium: 208mg, Potassium: 193mg, Fiber: 1g, Sugar: 8g, Vitamin A: 625iu, Vitamin C: 18.2mg, Calcium: 36mg, Iron: 0.8mg

347. Cucumber Salad

Prep Time: 15 Minutes

Cook Time: 0 Minutes

Total Time: 15 Minutes

Servings: 6

Ingredients

- 3 English cucumbers
- 1 tablespoon fresh chopped dill
- 1 clove garlic, minced
- 1 lemon, zested and juiced
- 1/2 cup plain greek yogurt
- 2 teaspoons granulated sugar
- Salt and pepper

Instructions

- Peel the cucumbers. Cut in half lengthwise. Then slice into thin pieces. Place the sliced cucumbers into a large bowl.
- Add the chopped dill, minced garlic, the zest of one lemon, 1 tablespoon of lemon juice, 1/2 cup plain greek yogurt, sugar, 1/2 teaspoon salt, and 1/4 teaspoon ground black pepper.
- Toss until the yogurt blends into a thin dressing. Taste, then salt and pepper as needed. Serve cold.

Nutrition

Calories: 38kcal, Carbohydrates: 7g, Protein: 2g, Fat: 0g, Saturatedfat: 0g, Cholesterol: 0mg, Sodium: 9mg, Potassium: 244mg, Fiber: 0g, Sugar: 4g, Vitamin A: 155iu, Vitamin C: 5.6mg, Calcium: 42mg, Iron: 0.4mg

348. Mexican Salad With Chipotle Shrimp

Prep Time: 15 Minutes

Cook Time: 10 Minutes

Total Time: 25 Minutes

Servings: 8

Ingredients

- 2-pound raw jumbo shrimp, peeled and cleaned (tail on or off)
- 8 cups chopped kale
- 4 ears corn on the cob, shucked
- 15 ounce can of black beans, drained
- 1-pint grape or cherry tomatoes halved
- 1 whole ripe avocado, peeled and chopped
- 2-3 whole chipotle peppers in adobo sauce
- 7 tablespoons fresh lime juice, divided
- 1/4 cup olive oil
- 1/4 cup mayonnaise
- 2 tablespoons honey
- 3 cloves garlic
- 1/2 teaspoon salt

Instructions

- Preheat the grill to medium heat. To a blender jar, add the chipotle peppers, 4 tablespoons of lime juice, olive oil, garlic, and salt. Cover and puree until smooth.
- Measure out 3 tablespoons of the chipotle puree and save it for the dressing. In a medium

bowl, mix the shrimp and the remaining marinade, until well coated.

- In a separate small bowl, mix the 3 tablespoons of chipotle puree, 3 tablespoons lime juice, mayonnaise, and honey. Whisk until smooth. Then taste, and salt and pepper as needed.
- Prep all the veggies. Set out a large salad bowl. Add the kale. Then toss it with the dressing until well coated. (I like to massage the dressing into the kale by hand.) Then add in the black beans, tomatoes, and avocado.
- Place the shrimp and corn cobs on the grills. *If your shrimp are small they will fall through the grates. Either use a grill basket or place them on a piece of foil. Grill the shrimp for 3-5 minutes until pink. Grill the corn for 8-10 minutes rotating every 2 minutes.
- Once the corn is cool enough to handle, cut it off the cobs and add it to the salad. Then toss in the shrimp and serve.

Nutrition

Calories: 372kcal, Carbohydrates: 31g, Protein: 31g, Fat: 15g, Saturatedfat: 2g, Cholesterol: 288mg, Sodium: 1314mg, Potassium: 849mg, Fiber: 5g, Sugar: 9g, Vitamin C: 107.2mg, Calcium: 293mg, Iron: 5.1mg

349. Horiatiki (Greek Village Salad)

Prep Time: 10 Minutes

Cook Time: 0 Minutes

Total Time: 10 Minutes

Servings: 8

Ingredients

For The Greek Salad:

- 1 large English cucumber
- 1-pint grape tomatoes
- 1 bell pepper, any color
- 8-ounce feta cheese
- 1 cup pitted kalamata olives
- 1/2 cup fresh chopped mint leaves
- 1/4 cup sliced red onion
- For the Herb Vinaigrette:
- 4 tablespoons extra virgin olive oil
- 3 tablespoons red wine vinegar (or lemon juice)
- 1 clove garlic, minced

- 1 teaspoon dried oregano
- Salt and pepper

Instructions

- Set out a large salad bowl, and a small bowl for the vinaigrette. In the small bowl, whisk together the oil, vinegar, garlic, oregano, 1/2 teaspoon salt and 1/4 teaspoons ground black pepper. Set aside.
- Cut the cucumber into quarters, lengthwise. Then slice it into 1/2 inch chunks. Cut the grape tomatoes in half. Seed and chop the bell pepper into 1/2 pieces. Cut the feta into 1/2 inch cubes. Chop the mint and slice the red onion.
- Place all the fresh produce in the large bowl. Pour the vinaigrette over the top. Gently toss to coat all the chunks in dressing. Then cover and refrigerate until ready to serve.

Nutrition

Calories: 186kcal, Carbohydrates: 6g, Protein: 5g, Fat: 15g, Saturatedfat: 5g, Cholesterol: 25mg, Sodium: 584mg, Potassium: 267mg, Fiber: 2g, Sugar: 4g, Vitamin C: 29.6mg, Calcium: 170mg, Iron: 0.9mg

350. Market Bean Salad Recipe

Prep Time: 15 Minutes

Cook Time: 40 Minutes

Total Time: 55 Minutes

Servings: 8

Ingredients

- 1 pound black-eyed peas, raw or frozen
- 1/2 pound white acre peas (field peas), raw or frozen
- 1/2 pound mixed sprouted peas and lentils
- 1-pint ripe cherry tomatoes
- 1/2 small red onion, chopped
- 2 cloves garlic, minced
- 1/3 cup flat-leaf parsley, chopped
- 2 tablespoons apple cider vinegar
- 1/4 cup extra virgin olive oil
- Salt and pepper

Instructions

- Place a large pot of water over high heat and bring to a boil. Salt the water liberally, then add the black-eyed peas. Simmer for 10 minutes, then add the white acre peas and simmer another 20-30 minutes, until both are soft and tender. Drain the peas in a colander and rinse under cold water to bring the temperature down. Shake to remove excess water.

- Place the cooked peas (beans) in a large mixing bowl. Add the sprouted peas, red onion, garlic, parsley, vinegar, and oil. Toss, then salt and pepper to taste and toss again.
- Cut the large cherry tomatoes in half and leave the small tomatoes whole. When ready to serve, pour the bean salad out on a serving platter then top with the cherry tomatoes.

Nutrition

Calories: 264kcal, Carbohydrates: 36g, Protein: 13g, Fat: 7g, Saturatedfat: 1g, Cholesterol: 0mg, Sodium: 14mg, Potassium: 650mg, Fiber: 14g, Sugar: 5g, Vitamin A: 735iu, Vitamin C: 30.4mg, Calcium: 49mg, Iron: 4.6mg

351. Lieutenant Dan's Steakhouse Salad

Prep Time: 10 Minutes

Total Time: 10 Minutes

Servings: 6

Ingredients

- 8 ounces romaine lettuce hearts
- 3 tablespoons Worcestershire sauce
- 3 tablespoons extra virgin olive oil
- 2 tablespoons fresh lemon juice
- 1 teaspoon minced garlic, fresh or from the jar
- 1/2 cup shaved Parmesan cheese
- Salt and pepper

Instructions

- Chop the romaine lettuce and place in a large salad bowl.
- Pour the Worcestershire sauce, olive oil, and lemon juice into a small jar. Add in the minced garlic, 1/2 teaspoon salt, and 1/4 teaspoon cracked black pepper. Whisk well.
- Pour the dressing over the lettuce and toss well to coat.
- Sprinkle the Parmesan cheese over the top and lightly toss. Serve immediately!

Nutrition

Calories: 109kcal, Carbohydrates: 3g, Protein: 3g, Fat: 9g, Saturatedfat: 2g, Cholesterol: 5mg, Sodium: 220mg, Potassium: 169mg, Fiber: 0g, Sugar: 1g, Vitamin A: 3355iu, Vitamin C: 4.7mg, Calcium: 120mg, Iron: 0.9mg

352. 3-Ingredient Almond Butter Balsamic Vinaigrette

Prep Time: 1 Minute

Total Time: 1 Minute

Servings: 4 Ounces

Ingredients

- 3 tablespoons almond butter
- 3 tablespoons balsamic vinegar
- 3 tablespoons water

Instructions

- Slowly whisk all ingredients until well blended. That's it. You're done!

Nutrition

Carbohydrates: 4g, Protein: 2g, Fat: 6g, Saturatedfat: 0g, Cholesterol: 0mg, Sodium: 4mg, Potassium: 103mg, Fiber: 1g, Sugar: 2g, Calcium: 45mg, Iron: 0.5mg

353. Chicken Gyro Salad With Creamy Tzatziki Sauce

Prep Time: 30 Minutes

Cook Time: 10 Minutes

Total Time: 40 Minutes

Servings: 4

Ingredients

For The Tzatziki Sauce:

- 1 cup plain Greek yogurt
- 1 hothouse cucumber
- 1 lemon, zested + 1 tablespoon juice
- 1 tablespoon olive oil
- 1 clove garlic, minced
- 1 tablespoon fresh chopped dill
- 1/2 teaspoon salt
- 1/4 teaspoon pepper
- For the Chicken:
- 1 pound boneless skinless chicken breast
- 1 tablespoon red wine vinegar
- 2 tablespoons olive oil

- 1 clove garlic, minced (large)
- 1 teaspoon dried oregano
- 1/2 teaspoon crushed dried rosemary
- Salt and pepper

For The Salad:

- 2 pieces flatbread
- 1 cup fresh mint leaves
- 1 small red onion, sliced thin
- 1 cup sliced cucumber
- 1 cup sliced tomato wedges
- 6 cups chopped romaine lettuce (2 cups for classic gyros)

Instructions

- Preheat the grill to high heat. Place the chicken in a baking dish and top with vinegar, oil, herbs, 1/2 teaspoon salt, and pepper to taste. Mix to coat and allow the chicken to marinate for at least 15 minutes.
- For the Tzatziki Sauce: Cut the cucumber in half. Use half for the tzatziki sauce and slice the remaining half for the salad. Peel half of the cucumber for the tzatziki sauce and grate it with a cheese grater. Wrap the shredded cucumber in a paper towel and squeeze it firmly over the sink to extract extra moisture. Then place the cumber in a bowl. Add the yogurt, zest on 1 lemon, 1 tablespoon lemon juice, olive oil, garlic, dill, salt, and pepper. Mix well and refrigerate until ready to serve.
- Once the grill is hot, lower the heat to medium and grill the chicken for approximately 5 minutes per side. Remove the chicken and allow it to rest 5 minutes before cutting.
- For the Salad: Pile chopped romaine in 4 bowls. Cut the flatbread into wedges. Slice the chicken and layer on top of each salad. Then arrange mint, red onion, cucumbers, tomato, flatbread wedges, and tzatziki sauce all around the chicken.

Nutrition

12ounces, Calories: 311kcal, Carbohydrates: 14g, Protein: 31g, Fat: 14g, Saturatedfat: 2g, Cholesterol: 75mg, Sodium: 458mg, Potassium: 1012mg, Fiber: 4g, Sugar: 6g, Vitamin C: 20.5mg, Calcium: 146mg, Iron: 2.3mg

354. Brazilian Chopped Salad

Prep Time: 15 Minutes

Total Time: 15 Minutes

Servings: 8

Ingredients

For The Brazilian Chopped Salad:

- 14 ounces hearts of palm
- 12 ounces cherry or grape tomatoes
- 1 fennel bulb
- 1 ripe avocado
- 1/2 small red onion
- 1/4 cup chopped mint
- For the Lime Vinaigrette:
- 1/4 cup fresh squeezed lime juice
- 1/4 cup olive oil
- 1 clove garlic, minced
- 1 teaspoon honey or agave
- Salt and pepper

Instructions

For The Vinaigrette: For the vinaigrette: Pour all the ingredients into a jar. Add 1 teaspoon salt and 1/2 teaspoon ground black pepper. Screw the lid on tight and shake to combine.

To Assemble: Drain The can of hearts of palm, then chop into 1/4-inch rounds. Cut the tomatoes in half. Cut the stems off the fennel bulb. Then cut the bulb in half and remove the core. Lay the fennel bulb halves flat, and slice into thin "shaved" pieces. Cut the avocado into chunks. Cut the onion half, in half again, then slice into thin strips. Finally, chop the fresh mint.

Place the shaved fennel on a large platter (or in a salad bowl.) Top with tomatoes, hearts of palm, onion, avocado, and mint. Drizzle the salad dressing over the top and toss.

Nutrition

1cup, calories: 182kcal, carbohydrates: 21g, protein: 2g, fat: 10g, saturatedfat: 1g, cholesterol: 0mg, sodium: 29mg, potassium: 1258mg, fiber: 3g, sugar: 10g, vitamin a: 375iu, vitamin c: 23mg, calcium: 36mg, iron: 1.6mg

355. Sun-Dried Tomato Chicken Pasta Salad

Prep Time: 15 Minutes

Cook Time: 8 Minutes

Total Time: 23 Minutes

Servings: 10

Ingredients

- 1 pound small dried pasta (any variety)
- 2 cups chopped leftover cooked chicken or rotisserie chicken
- 1 cup fresh baby spinach, packed
- 7 ounces sun-dried tomatoes in oil, drained
- 5 ounces pitted green olives, halved
- 1/3 cup chopped red onion
- 3/4 cup light mayonnaise
- 1/4 cup red wine vinegar
- 1 tablespoon dried Italian seasoning
- 1 clove garlic, peeled
- 1/4 teaspoon crushed red pepper

Instructions

- Place a large pot of salted water on the stovetop and bring to a boil. Cook the pasta according to package instructions. Drain the pasta in a colander and rinse with cold water to cool. Allow the paste to drain while you prep the remaining ingredients.
- Chop the sun-dried tomatoes into bite-sized pieces. Place the mayonnaise, red wine vinegar, Italian seasoning, garlic, crushed red pepper, and 1/4 cup chopped sun-dried tomatoes in the blender jar. Cover and puree.
- Place the cooled pasta, chopped chicken, spinach, remaining chopped sun-dried tomatoes, olives, and onions in a large salad bowl. Add the creamy dressing and toss to coat. Cover the bowl with plastic wrap and refrigerate until ready to serve.

Nutrition

8ounces, Calories: 285kcal, Carbohydrates: 48g, Protein: 9g, Fat: 7g, Saturatedfat: 1g, Cholesterol: 2mg, Sodium: 401mg, Potassium: 823mg, Fiber: 4g, Sugar: 9g, Vitamin A: 545iu, Vitamin C: 9.1mg, Calcium: 52mg, Iron: 2.8mg

356. Tabouli With Feta And Endive

Prep Time: 20 Minutes

Cook Time: 5 Minutes

Total Time: 25mins

Servings: 12

Ingredients

- 1 cup bulgur wheat
- 1 1/2 cups boiling water
- 2 lemons, zested and juiced
- 1/3 cup extra virgin olive oil
- 1/4 teaspoon cayenne pepper
- 1 clove garlic (large), minced
- 2 1/2 teaspoon salt
- 1 bunch green onions, chopped (tops and bottoms)
- 1 bunch flat-leaf parsley, chopped
- 1 bunch mint leaves, chopped
- 1 English cucumber, chopped
- 2 pints cherry tomatoes, quartered (or 2 large tomatoes, diced)
- 1 cup crumbled feta cheese
- 8 heads endive (small)

Instructions

- In a large bowl, add the bulgur wheat, lemon zest and juice, oil, cayenne, garlic, and salt. Pour the boiling water over the top. Stir and allow it to sit for at least 1 hour.
- Wash the endive and cut off the bottoms. Carefully separate the leaves and set them aside.
- Chop all the herbs, cucumber, and tomatoes. Once the wheat has plumped up and absorbed the liquid, toss in the herbs, cumbers, and tomatoes. Then salt and pepper to taste.
- You can eat the tabouli immediately, but the flavor does develop if you give it a little time to sit. Scoop into endive leaves and sprinkle each with feta.

Nutrition

Calories: 202kcal, Carbohydrates: 25g, Protein: 8g, Fat: 9g, Saturatedfat: 2g, Cholesterol: 11mg, Sodium: 706mg, Potassium: 1260mg, Fiber: 12g, Sugar: 4g, Vitamin C: 54.7mg, Calcium: 248mg, Iron: 3.9mg

357. Raw Beet And Sweet Potato Salad

Prep Time: 10 Minutes

Total Time: 10 Minutes

Servings: 6

Ingredients

- 2 large sweet potatoes
- 1 bunch beets 3-4
- 4 scallions
- 1/2 cup toasted pepitas pumpkins seeds
- Garlic Lime Vinaigrette

Instructions

- Peel the sweet potatoes and beets. Then use a spiralizer to cut the veggies into long curly strips. Use a pair of kitchen shears to cut the pieces into manageable lengths.
- Mix the beet and sweet potato ribbons in a large bowl. Then cut the scallion tops on an angle to make long rings. Sprinkle the salad with scallions and pepitas. Serve with your favorite vinaigrette.

Nutrition

Calories: 169kcal, Carbohydrates: 11g, Protein: 2g, Fat: 13g, Saturatedfat: 2g, Cholesterol: 0mg, Sodium: 36mg, Potassium: 255mg, Fiber: 2g, Sugar: 3g, Vitamin A: 6225iu, Vitamin C: 3.2mg, Calcium: 23mg, Iron: 1mg

358. Healthy Rainbow Chopped Salad

Prep Time: 15 Minutes

Total Time: 15 Minutes

Servings: 4

Ingredients

For The Salad:

- 8-10 red radishes, chopped
- 1 orange bell pepper, seeded and chopped
- 1/2 pint yellow cherry tomatoes, quartered
- 2 small zucchini, chopped
- 1/4 small red cabbage, chopped
- 1 head romaine lettuce, chopped
- For the Avocado Chimichurri Vinaigrette:
- 1 soft avocado, peeled and pitted

- 1/2 cup chopped fresh parsley
- 1 tablespoon chopped fresh oregano
- 2-3 cloves garlic, minced
- 1/4 cup avocado oil or olive oil
- 2 tablespoons honey
- 2 tablespoons white wine vinegar
- 1/4 cup water, plus more as needed
- 1/2 teaspoon salt
- 1/4-1/2 teaspoon crushed red pepper

Instructions

- Place all the vinaigrette ingredients in a food processor or blender. Puree until smooth. Taste and salt as needed.
- Chop all vegetables and toss together in a large bowl. (Or you can lay them out in rainbow rows until just before serving.)
- Once ready to serve, pour the dressing over the salad and toss.

Nutrition

Calories: 321kcal, Carbohydrates: 30g, Protein: 6g, Fat: 22g, Saturatedfat: 2g, Cholesterol: 0mg, Sodium: 355mg, Potassium: 1304mg, Fiber: 10g, Sugar: 16g, Vitamin C: 113.7mg, Calcium: 137mg, Iron: 3.9mg

359. Thai Red Curry Grilled Chicken Salad

Prep Time: 15 Minutes

Cook Time: 10 Minutes

Total Time: 25 Minutes

Servings: 4

Ingredients

For The Thai Red Curry Grilled Chicken:

- 2 pounds boneless skinless chicken breast
- 4 ounces Panang Red Curry Paste
- For the Peanut Dressing:
- 1/3 cup creamy peanut butter
- 1/3 cup rice vinegar
- 1 tablespoon sesame oil
- 1 teaspoon honey
- 1 clove garlic
- For the Thai Red Curry Grilled Chicken Salad:
- 8 cups chopped napa cabbage (from one big cabbage)
- 1 mango, peeled and sliced thin

- 1 cup radishes, sliced
- 1 cup mini bell peppers, sliced
- 1/2 cup red onion, sliced
- 1/2 cup fresh cilantro leaves
- 1/4 cup roasted peanuts

Instructions

- Preheat the grill. Place the chicken in a baking dish. Rub the pieces of chicken on all sides with Panang red curry paste. Do not salt and pepper. Let the chicken marinate for at least 20 minutes.
- Place the ingredients for the dressing in a blender. Puree until smooth.
- Prep all the produce. Once the grill reaches 350-400 degrees F, grill the chicken for 5 minutes per side. Allow the chicken to rest another 5 minutes, before slicing into thin strips.
- Arrange the napa cabbage, mangos, and vegetables on salad plates. Top with sliced grilled chicken, cilantro, and peanuts. Serve each salad plate with a side of peanut dressing.

Nutrition

Calories: 575kcal, Carbohydrates: 24g, Protein: 59g, Fat: 27g, Saturatedfat: 5g, Cholesterol: 145mg, Sodium: 429mg, Potassium: 1602mg, Fiber: 6g, Sugar: 14g, Vitamin C: 76.6mg, Calcium: 203mg, Iron: 2.8mg

360. Garlic Lime Roasted Shrimp Salad

Prep Time: 10 Minutes

Cook Time: 5 Minutes

Total Time: 15 Minutes

Servings: 10

Ingredients

- 2 pounds raw jumbo shrimp, peeled and deveined
- 2 tablespoons olive oil, divided
- 1 large English cucumber, chopped
- 1 firm avocado, peeled and chopped
- 1 lime, juiced
- 1 clove garlic, minced
- 1/4 cup fresh chopped mint leaves
- 2 tablespoons fresh chopped cilantro
- Salt and pepper

Instructions

- Preheat the oven to 450 degrees F. Line a large rimmed baking sheet with parchment paper. Pour the shrimp onto the baking sheet and drizzle with 1 tablespoon olive oil. Toss the shrimp in the oil and spread them out on the baking sheet. Sprinkle generously with salt and pepper.
- Roast the shrimp in the oven for 5-7 minutes, until pink. They should still be in the shape of C's. If they shrink to O's, you've overcooked them. Cool the shrimp on the baking sheet.
- Meanwhile, chop the cucumber and avocado in 3/4-inch chunks. Place the cucumber, avocado, minced garlic, chopped mint leaves, and cilantro in a salad bowl. Pour the lime juice and 1 tablespoon olive oil over the salad and toss well to coat. Taste, then salt and pepper as needed.
- Once the shrimp have cooled to room temperature, toss them into the salad. Cover and chill until ready to serve.

Nutrition

Calories: 155kcal, Carbohydrates: 3g, Protein: 19g, Fat: 7g, Saturatedfat: 1g, Cholesterol: 228mg, Sodium: 707mg, Potassium: 227mg, Fiber: 1g, Sugar: 0g, Vitamin A: 115iu, Vitamin C: 9mg, Calcium: 144mg, Iron: 2.2mg

361. Summer Cobb Salad Recipe

Prep Time: 20 Minutes

Cook Time: 10 Minutes

Total Time: 30 Minutes

Servings: 6

Ingredients

- 2 large boneless, skinless chicken breasts
- 1 tablespoon olive oil
- Salt and pepper
- 2 romaine hearts, chopped
- 3 hardboiled eggs, peeled and chopped
- 2/3 cup crumbled blue cheese
- 2 avocados, chopped
- 1 cup blackberries
- 1 cup raspberries
- 1 cup toasted almonds
- Creamy Garlic Lime Dressing Recipe

Instructions

- Preheat the grill. Then rub the chicken breasts with oil, and salt, and pepper liberally. Grill for 5 minutes per side over medium heat. Allow the chicken to rest for at least 5 minutes before chopping. Then cut into bite-sized pieces.
- Meanwhile chop the romaine lettuce, eggs, and avocados. Place the lettuce on a large serving platter or bowl. Arrange all the toppings over the bed of lettuce and serve with Creamy Garlic Lime Vinaigrette.

Nutrition

calories: 426kcal, carbohydrates: 17g, protein: 21g, fat: 32g, saturatedfat: 6g, cholesterol: 128mg, sodium: 292mg, potassium: 864mg, fiber: 10g, sugar: 4g, 3685iu, vitamin c: 19mg, calcium: 189mg, iron: 2.4mg

362. Tortellini Salad With Basil Vinaigrette

Prep Time: 10 Minutes

Cook Time: 5 Minutes

Total Time: 15 Minutes

Servings: 12

Ingredients

- 20 ounces refrigerated tortellini, cheese, or spinach
- 3 cups small broccoli florets
- 1-pint grape and/or cherry tomatoes halved
- 3/4 cup jarred piquillo peppers, chopped (or roasted red peppers)
- 1/2 cup chopped scallions
- 1/2 cup crumbled feta cheese
- 1/2 cup olive oil
- 1/3 cup fresh basil leaves, packed
- 1/4 cup red wine vinegar
- 1 clove garlic
- Salt and pepper

Instructions

- Set a large pot of salted water on the stovetop. Bring to a boil. Stir in the tortellini and cook just under the set package instruction timeframe, about 5-6 minutes. Drain and rinse in cold water. Then toss with 1 teaspoon of olive oil so they don't stick together.

- Place the basil leaves, remaining olive oil, red wine vinegar, garlic, and 1/2 teaspoon salt in the blender. Cover and puree until smooth.
- Pour the tortellini, broccoli florets, tomato halves, chopped peppers, and scallions into a large salad bowl. Drizzle the dressing over the top and toss to coat. Then gently mix in the feta cheese. Taste, then salt and pepper as needed.

Nutrition

Calories: 269kcal, Carbohydrates: 26g, Protein: 9g, Fat: 14g, Saturatedfat: 3g, Cholesterol: 23mg, Sodium: 353mg, Potassium: 180mg, Fiber: 2g, Sugar: 3g, Vitamin A: 820iu, Vitamin C: 41.5mg, Calcium: 116mg, Iron: 2.1mg

363. Chopped Israeli Salad With Lemon Vinaigrette

Prep Time: 10 Minutes

Total Time: 10 Minutes

Servings: 8

Ingredients

- 2 1/2 cups chopped English cucumbers or Persian cucumbers, cut into 3/4-inch pieces
- 2 1/2 cups grape tomatoes and/or cherry tomatoes, halved
- 1 1/2 cup sliced radishes
- 1 yellow bell pepper, seeded and chopped in 3/4-inch pieces
- 1/3 cup diced onion
- 1/3 cup chopped fresh mint
- 1/4 cup chopped parsley
- 1/4 cup extra virgin olive oil
- 1 lemon, zested and juiced
- 1 teaspoon ground sumac, or substitute paprika
- Salt and pepper

Instructions

- Chop all the vegetables and herbs and place them in a large salad bowl, or on a platter.
- Sprinkle the top of the salad with lemon zest and ground sumac. Then drizzle with olive oil and lemon juice.
- Toss well. Taste, then salt and pepper as needed. Refrigerate until ready to serve.

Nutrition

Calories: 85kcal, Carbohydrates: 5g, Protein: 1g, Fat: 6g, Saturatedfat: 0g, Cholesterol: 0mg, Sodium: 13mg, Potassium: 271mg, Fiber: 1g, Sugar: 2g, Vitamin A: 690iu, Vitamin C: 42.3mg, Calcium: 26mg, Iron: 0.6mg

364. Watermelon Feta Salad With Golden Tomatoes And Tarragon

Prep Time: 15 Minutes

Total Time: 15 Minutes

Servings: 6

Ingredients

- 1/4 ripe seedless watermelon cut into 1/2 x 1 x 2-inch wedges
- 2 golden tomatoes cut into wedges
- 1/2 red onion sliced
- 8 ounces feta cut into 1/2 x 1-inch chunks
- 3 tablespoons roughly chopped tarragon leaves
- 2 tablespoons olive oil
- 1 tablespoon rice vinegar
- 1 tablespoon honey
- 1 teaspoon dry sherry
- Salt and pepper

Instructions

- Chop the watermelon, tomatoes, onion, feta, and tarragon and place in a large salad bowl.
- Whisk the olive oil, rice vinegar, honey, and sherry in a small bowl and season with salt and pepper to taste.
- Drizzle the vinaigrette over the top of the salad and gently toss.

Nutrition

Calories: 230kcal, Carbohydrates: 23g, Protein: 8g, Fat: 13g, Saturatedfat: 6g, Cholesterol: 34mg, Sodium: 429mg, Potassium: 450mg, Fiber: 2g, Sugar: 18g, Vitamin A: 1715iu, Vitamin C: 23.3mg, Calcium: 246mg, Iron: 1.9mg

365. Jamaican Jerk Chicken Salad

Prep Time: 20 Minutes

Cook Time: 10 Minutes

Resting Time: 1 Hour

Total Time: 30 Minutes

Servings: 4 large servings

Ingredients

For The Jamaican Jerk Chicken:

- 2 pounds boneless skinless chicken thighs
- 2-4 habanero peppers seeded
- 2 tablespoons fresh thyme leaves
- 1/2 small red onion
- 1 tablespoon fresh grated ginger
- 4 cloves garlic
- 3 tablespoons soy sauce
- 2 tablespoons lime juice
- 2 tablespoons brown sugar
- 2 teaspoons ground allspice
- 1 teaspoon cinnamon
- 1/2 teaspoon nutmeg
- 1 teaspoon salt
- 1/2 teaspoon black pepper

For The Salad:

- 2 heads romaine lettuce chopped
- 2 large red bell peppers seeded and cut into rings
- 2 ripe avocados peeled and sliced
- 1 English cucumber sliced
- 1/2 ripe pineapple cut into chunks
- 1 bottle Newman's Honey Mustard Lite Dressing

Instructions

- For the Jamaican Jerk Chicken: Place all the ingredients, except the chicken, in the food processor and puree until smooth. (If you are sensitive to spicy heat, use only 1-2 habanero peppers.) Pour the marinade into a large zip bag and add the chicken. Allow the chicken to marinate for at least one hour, but up to 16 hours.
- When the chicken is ready to grill, preheat the grill to medium heat. Once hot, remove the chicken from the marinade and place it on the

grill. Grill for 5 minutes per side. Then allow the chicken to rest 5 minutes before cutting.

- Meanwhile, grill the red pepper rings for 1-2 minutes per side to soften.
- Once the chicken has rested, cut into strips. Arrange the romaine lettuce on a large platter, topped with grilled peppers, cucumbers, pineapple, and avocado slices. Fan the chicken pieces over the top and drizzle with Newman's Honey Mustard Lite Dressing. Serve immediately.

Nutrition

Calories: 634kcal, Carbohydrates: 54g, Protein: 54g, Fat: 26g, Saturatedfat: 5g, Cholesterol: 216mg, Sodium: 1582mg, Potassium: 2364mg, Fiber: 19g, Sugar: 27g, 29830iu, Vitamin C: 213.1mg, Calcium: 213mg, Iron: 7.4mg

366. Kale Salad Recipe With Pecorino, Strawberries, Pine Nuts

Prep Time: 15 Minutes

Total Time: 15 Minutes

Servings: 6

Ingredients

- 1 bunch Tuscan kale
- 3 tablespoons bread crumbs
- 3 tablespoons fresh-squeezed lemon juice
- 3 tablespoons olive oil
- 1 tablespoon honey
- 1 1/2 cup fresh sliced strawberries
- 2 ounces toasted pine nuts about 1/3 cup
- 1 ounce shaved pecorino cheese
- Salt and pepper

Instructions

- Wash and dry the kale leaves. Fold each leaf in half, lengthwise, and cut out the stem. Then slice the kale into thin ribbons. Place in a large salad bowl.
- Sprinkle the kale with bread crumbs, lemon juice, olive oil, and honey. Toss well, then salt and pepper to taste. Cover and place in the refrigerator for at least 2 hours.
- Once the kale has wilted a little, toss in the sliced strawberries and toasted pine nuts. Use a veggie

peeler to shave bands of nutty pecorino cheese over the top. Enjoy!

Nutrition

- Calories: 198kcal, Carbohydrates: 13g, Protein: 5g, Fat: 15g, Saturatedfat: 2g, Cholesterol: 5mg, Sodium: 102mg, Potassium: 235mg, Fiber: 1g, Sugar: 6g, Vitamin A: 2185iu, Vitamin C: 50.1mg, Calcium: 98mg, Iron: 1.3mg

367. Smoked Trout Salad With Avocado Dressing

Prep Time: 10 Minutes

Total Time: 10 Minutes

Servings: 6

Ingredients

For The Smoked Trout Salad:

- 1 bunch radishes stem removed and sliced thin
- 2 large ripe peaches pitted and sliced thin
- 5 ounces spring salad greens
- 12 ounces smoked trout broken into chunks

For The Avocado Dressing:

- 1 ripe avocado
- 1/4 cup plain Greek yogurt
- 1/2 lemon juiced
- 1/2 cup water
- 3/4 teaspoon salt
- 2 tablespoons chive

Instructions

- Place all the ingredients for the avocado dressing in the food processor (or blender). Puree until smooth.
- Using a large spoon, pool the dressing on 4-6 salad plates, or streak across the plates like at a restaurant.
- Arrange the greens on the plates, followed by radishes, peach slices, and smoked trout chunks.

Nutrition

Calories: 161kcal, Carbohydrates: 10g, Protein: 15g, Fat: 8g, Saturatedfat: 1g, Cholesterol: 61mg, Sodium: 349mg, Potassium: 589mg, Fiber: 3g, Sugar: 5g, Vitamin C: 18.7mg, Calcium: 36mg, Iron: 0.7mg

368. Roasted Beet Chickpea Kale Salad

Prep Time: 20 Minutes

Cook Time: 20 Minutes

Total Time: 40 Minutes

Servings: 8

Ingredients

- 4 large beets (I used 2 red and 2 gold)
- 1 large sweet potato
- 4 tablespoons extra virgin olive oil, divided
- 1 bunch kale, stems removed and chopped (6 cups)
- 15 ounce can chickpeas, drained and rinsed
- ½ cup shelled pistachios, chopped
- ¾ cup plain greek yogurt
- 1 whole lemon, juiced
- 1 clove garlic, peeled
- 2 tablespoons fresh mint leaves
- 1 tablespoon fresh rosemary leaves
- 1 tablespoon honey
- Salt and pepper

Instructions

- Preheat the oven to 450 degrees Line 2 large rimmed baking sheets with parchment paper.
- Peel the beets and sweet potato. Cut them all in half, lengthwise. Then slice the halves into thin 1/8th slices.
- Pile the slices on one baking sheet. Drizzle with 3 tablespoons of olive oil. Toss them well to coat. Then spread the beets and sweet potato slices out in a single layer across two baking sheets. Salt and pepper generously.
- Roast the beets and sweet potatoes in the oven for 20-30 minutes, until soft, but crispy around the edges.
- Meanwhile, prep the chickpeas and pistachios.
- To a blender jar, add the yogurt, lemon juice, garlic, mint, rosemary, honey, remaining tablespoon olive oil, ½ teaspoon salt, and ¼ teaspoon ground black pepper. Cover and puree until smooth.
- Set out a large salad bowl. Add the chopped kale and chickpeas.
- Once the beets and sweet potatoes are out of the oven, allow them to cool for a few minutes. Then move them to the salad bowl.

- Pour ¾ of the dressing over the top of the salad and toss. Taste, and add more dressing if desired. Then toss in the chopped pistachios and serve.

Nutrition

Calories: 276kcal, Carbohydrates: 35g, Protein: 10g, Fat: 12g, Saturatedfat: 2g, Cholesterol: 1mg, Sodium: 291mg, Potassium: 854mg, Fiber: 8g, Sugar: 14g, Vitamin C: 28.1mg, Calcium: 109mg, Iron: 2.6mg

369. The Best Broccoli Salad Recipe

Prep Time: 15 Minutes

Total Time: 15 Minutes

Servings: 12 Servings

Ingredients

- 6 cups broccoli florets
- 3 cups kale finely chopped
- 1 cup red onion chopped
- 1 cup shredded carrots roughly chopped
- 1 apple chopped
- 3/4 cup dried cherries
- 3/4 cup cooked bacon chopped
- 3/4 cup sunflower seed kernels
- 1 cup mayonnaise could be low fat
- 1/4 cup apple cider vinegar
- 3 tablespoons honey
- 1/2-1 teaspoon crushed red pepper
- 1/2 teaspoon salt

Instructions

- Chop and prep all the ingredients. In a large bowl add the broccoli florets, chopped kale, red onion, shredded carrots, chopped apple, dried cherries, chopped bacon, and sunflower kernels.
- In a medium bowl, whisk the mayonnaise, apple cider vinegar, honey, crushed red pepper, and salt, until smooth.
- Pour the dressing over the salad and toss until thoroughly coated. Then cover and refrigerate until ready to serve. *Can be made up to 3 days ahead.

Nutrition

Calories: 265kcal, carbohydrates: 20g, protein: 4g, fat: 19g, saturatedfat: 2g, cholesterol: 8mg, sodium: 260mg, potassium: 360mg, fiber: 3g, sugar: 12g, vitamin a: 4055iu, vitamin c: 63.1mg, calcium: 69mg, iron: 1.3mg

370. Fried Oysters Salad

Prep Time: 30 Minutes

Cook Time: 10 Minutes

Total Time: 40 Minutes

Servings: 4

Ingredients

For The Almond Brittle:

- 1/2 cup sugar
- 1/4 cup corn syrup
- 1/2 teaspoon salt
- 3/4 cup chopped almonds
- 1/2 teaspoon almond extract
- 1/2 teaspoon baking soda

- For The Buttermilk Dressing:

- 1/2 cup buttermilk
- 3 tablespoons mayonnaise
- 1/4 teaspoon curry powder
- 1/8 teaspoon garlic powder
- 1/8 teaspoon salt
- Pinch cayenne pepper
- For the Fried Oysters:
- 1 pound fresh shucked oysters in the bucket
- 1/2 cup buttermilk
- 1/2 cup flour
- 1/2 cup cornmeal
- Salt and pepper
- Oil for frying

For The Salad:

- 2 romaine hearts chopped
- 2 Granny Smith apples sliced thin

Instructions

For The Almond Brittle:

- Place the sugar, corn syrup, and salt in a large microwave-safe bowl. Use the largest bowl that will fit in your microwave, because the mixture will boil and expand. Microwave on high for 4 minutes. Then stir in the almonds and

microwave again for 3 minutes. Lay a piece of parchment paper on a cookie sheet and spray with nonstick spray. When the brittle comes out of the microwave, quickly stir in the almond extract and baking soda. Pour the hot mixture out on the baking sheet and spread thin. Allow the brittle to cool and dry for 20 minutes before breaking into pieces.

- Pour all the ingredients for the buttermilk dressing in a jar. Place the lid on tight and shake until smooth. Refrigerate the dressing until ready to serve.

For The Fried Oysters: Pour 1 inch of oil in a large saucepot. Place over high heat. Then pour the buttermilk, flour, and cornmeal into three pie pans for easy dipping. Season the buttermilk with 1/4 tsp. salt and 1/8 tsp. pepper. Drain the oysters. Working in small batches, dip them in flour, then in buttermilk, and finally in cornmeal. Gently drop them in the hot oil and fry for 1-3 minutes. You want the exterior to be golden, but the oysters to be just slightly cooked. Remove from the oil and place on a paper towel-lined plate. Sprinkle with salt and repeat with the rest of the oysters.

For The Salad: Pile romaine lettuce on four plates. Top each pile with several fried oysters, sliced apples, and almond brittle. Drizzle with buttermilk dressing and serve immediately.

Nutrition

Calories: 618kcal, Carbohydrates: 92g, Protein: 13g, Fat: 25g, Saturatedfat: 4g, Cholesterol: 16mg, Sodium: 660mg, Potassium: 605mg, Fiber: 9g, Sugar: 56g, Vitamin C: 6.4mg, Calcium: 173mg, Iron: 3.5mg

7. Lean and Green Seafood Recipes

371. Salmon Pinwheels

Total: 30 mins

Servings: 4

Ingredients

- 1/2 cup coarse dry breadcrumbs, preferably whole-wheat (see Tip)
- 1 tablespoon extra-virgin olive oil
- 1 tablespoon whole-grain mustard
- 1 tablespoon chopped shallot

- 1 tablespoon lemon juice
- 1 teaspoon chopped rinsed capers
- 1 teaspoon chopped fresh thyme, or 1/2 teaspoon dried
- 1 ¼ pounds center-cut salmon fillet, skinned and cut lengthwise into 4 strips
- 4 teaspoons low-fat mayonnaise

Instructions

- Preheat oven to 400 degrees F. Coat a 9-by-13-inch baking dish with cooking spray.
- Mix breadcrumbs, oil, mustard, shallot, lemon juice, capers, and thyme in a small bowl until combined.
- Working with one at a time, spread each salmon strip with 1 teaspoon mayonnaise. Spread about 3 tablespoons of the breadcrumb mixture over the mayonnaise. Starting at one end, roll the salmon up tightly, tucking in any loose filling as you go. Insert a toothpick through the end to keep the pinwheel from unrolling. Place in the prepared dish. Repeat with the remaining salmon strips.
- Bake the pinwheels until just cooked through, 15 to 20 minutes. Remove the toothpicks before serving.

Nutrition

Calories: 257; protein 29.9g; carbohydrates 8.9g; dietary fiber 1.1g; sugars 0.6g; fat 10.3g; saturated fat 1.9g; cholesterol 67.5mg; vitamin a iu 254.7IU; vitamin c 3.7mg; folate 17.8mcg; calcium 57.2mg; iron 1.2mg; magnesium 41.2mg; potassium 537.8mg; sodium 204.6mg; thiamin 0.1mg.

372. Fish Amandine

Active: 15 mins

Total: 20 mins

Servings: 4

Ingredients

- 4 (4 ounces) fresh or frozen skinless tilapia, trout, or halibut fillets, 1/2- to 1-inch thick
- ¼ cup buttermilk
- ½ cup panko bread crumbs or fine dry bread crumbs

- 2 tablespoons chopped fresh parsley or 2 teaspoons dried parsley flakes
- ½ teaspoon dry mustard
- ¼ teaspoon salt
- ¼ cup sliced almonds, coarsely chopped
- 2 tablespoons grated Parmesan cheese
- 1 tablespoon butter, melted
- ⅛ teaspoon crushed red pepper

Instructions

- Thaw fish, if frozen. Preheat oven to 450 degrees F. Grease a shallow baking pan; set aside. Rinse fish; pat dry with paper towels. Measure the thickness of fish.
- Pour buttermilk into a shallow dish. In another shallow dish, combine bread crumbs, parsley, dry mustard, and salt. Dip fish into buttermilk, then into crumb mixture, turning to coat. Place coated fish in the prepared baking pan.
- Sprinkle fish with almonds and Parmesan cheese; drizzle with melted butter. Sprinkle with crushed red pepper. Bake 4 to 6 minutes per 1/2-inch thickness of fish or until fish flakes easily when tested with a fork.

Nutrition

Calories: 209; protein 26.2g; carbohydrates 6.7g; dietary fiber 0.9g; sugars 1g; fat 8.7g; saturated fat 3.2g; cholesterol 66.9mg; vitamin a iu 287.5IU; vitamin c 2.9mg; folate 34.2mcg; calcium 69.6mg; iron 1.1mg; magnesium 50mg; potassium 413.8mg; sodium 301.6mg.

373. Salmon & Asparagus with Lemon-Garlic Butter Sauce

Active: 10 mins

Total: 25 mins

Servings: 4

Ingredients

- 1 pound center-cut salmon fillet, preferably wild, cut into 4 portions
- 1 pound fresh asparagus, trimmed
- ½ teaspoon salt
- ½ teaspoon ground pepper
- 3 tablespoons butter
- 1 tablespoon extra-virgin olive oil
- ½ tablespoon grated garlic

- 1 teaspoon grated lemon zest
- 1 tablespoon lemon juice

Instructions

- Preheat oven to 375 degrees F. Coat a large rimmed baking sheet with cooking spray.
- Place salmon on one side of the prepared baking sheet and asparagus on the other. Sprinkle the salmon and asparagus with salt and pepper.
- Heat butter, oil, garlic, lemon zest, and lemon juice in a small skillet over medium heat until the butter is melted. Drizzle the butter mixture over the salmon and asparagus. Bake until the salmon is cooked through and the asparagus is just tender, 12 to 15 minutes.

Nutrition

Serving Size: 1 Piece, Salmon & About 5 Spears Asparagus Per Serving: 270 calories; protein 25.4g; carbohydrates 5.6g; dietary fiber 2.5g; sugars 2.2g; fat 16.5g; saturated fat 6.9g; cholesterol 75.9mg; vitamin a iu 1288.6IU; vitamin c 10.5mg; folate 72.8mcg; calcium 79.3mg; iron 3.1mg; magnesium 49.2mg; potassium 667.1mg; sodium 350.5mg; thiamin 0.2mg.

374. Roasted Salmon with Smoky Chickpeas & Greens

Active: 40 mins

Total: 40 mins

Servings: 4

Ingredients

- 2 tablespoons extra-virgin olive oil, divided
- 1 tablespoon smoked paprika
- ½ teaspoon salt, divided, plus a pinch
- 1 (15 ounces) can no-salt-added chickpeas, rinsed
- ⅓ cup buttermilk
- ¼ cup mayonnaise
- ¼ cup chopped fresh chives and/or dill, plus more for garnish
- ½ teaspoon ground pepper, divided
- ¼ teaspoon garlic powder
- 10 cups chopped kale
- ¼ cup water
- 1 ¼ pounds wild salmon, cut into 4 portions

Instructions

- Position racks in upper third and middle of oven; preheat to 425 degrees F.
- Combine 1 tablespoon oil, paprika, and 1/4 teaspoon salt in a medium bowl. Very thoroughly pat chickpeas dry, then toss with the paprika mixture. Spread on a rimmed baking sheet. Bake the chickpeas on the upper rack, stirring twice, for 30 minutes.
- Meanwhile, puree buttermilk, mayonnaise, herbs, 1/4 teaspoon pepper, and garlic powder in a blender until smooth. Set aside.
- Heat the remaining 1 tablespoon oil in a large skillet over medium heat. Add kale and cook, stirring occasionally, for 2 minutes. Add water and continue cooking until the kale is tender, about 5 minutes more. Remove from heat and stir in a pinch of salt.
- Remove the chickpeas from the oven and push them to one side of the pan. Place salmon on the other side and season with the remaining 1/4 teaspoon each salt and pepper. Bake until the salmon is just cooked through, 5 to 8 minutes.
- Drizzle the reserved dressing on the salmon, garnish with more herbs, if desired, and serve with the kale and chickpeas.

Nutrition

Serving Size: 4 Oz. Salmon, 3/4 Cup Greens, 1/4 Cup Chickpeas & 2 1/2 Tbsp. Dressing Per Serving: 447 calories; protein 37g; carbohydrates 23.4g; dietary fiber 6.4g; sugars 2.2g; fat 21.8g; saturated fat 3.7g; cholesterol 72.9mg; vitamin a iu 5200IU; vitamin c 51.7mg; folate 77.9mcg; calcium 197.8mg; iron 3mg; magnesium 99.4mg; potassium 990.8mg; sodium 556.7mg.

375. Seafood Chowder Casserole

Total: 1 hr 45 mins

Servings: 8

Ingredients

- 1 tablespoon plus 1 teaspoon canola oil, divided
- 2 cups sliced leeks, rinsed (about 2 small)
- 1 cup sliced celery
- 2 large white potatoes (about 1 3/4 pounds), peeled and cut into 3/4-inch pieces
- 2 cups seafood stock or clam juice (see Tips)

- 2 teaspoons Old Bay seasoning, divided
- ½ teaspoon freshly ground pepper
- 1 cup low-fat milk
- ¼ cup all-purpose flour
- 1 tablespoon Dijon mustard
- 1 pound raw shrimp (21-25 count), peeled, deveined, and chopped (about 2 cups; see Tips)
- 12 ounces diced cod (see Tips) or another firm white fish
- 8 ounces pasteurized crabmeat, preferably jumbo, drained
- 2 cups shredded Gruyère cheese, divided
- 2 tablespoons chopped fresh dill or 2 teaspoons dried, divided
- 1/2 cup coarse whole-wheat breadcrumbs.

Instructions

- Preheat oven to 400 degrees F. Coat a 9-by-13-inch (or similar 3-quart) baking dish with cooking spray.
- Heat 1 tablespoon oil in a Dutch oven over medium-high heat. Add leeks and celery and cook, stirring often, until the leeks are softened, 2 to 3 minutes. Stir in potatoes, stock (or clam juice), 1 teaspoon Old Bay and pepper. Cover and bring to a simmer over high heat. Reduce heat to medium-low and simmer, covered, until the potatoes are just tender, 6 to 8 minutes.
- Whisk milk, flour, and mustard in a measuring cup. Stir into the potato mixture, increase heat to medium-high and bring to a simmer, stirring constantly. Stir in shrimp and fish and return to a simmer, stirring often; cook until the seafood is just cooked through, about 3 minutes. Remove from the heat and stir in crab, 1 1/2 cups Gruyere, and half the dill.
- Transfer the seafood mixture to the prepared baking dish. Mix breadcrumbs with the remaining 1 teaspoon each oil and Old Bay. Stir in the remaining 1/2 cup Gruyere and the remaining dill. Sprinkle the breadcrumb mixture over the casserole.
- Bake the casserole until it is bubbling and golden brown, 20 to 30 minutes. Let stand 10 minutes before serving.

Nutrition

Per Serving: 380 calories; protein 34.7g; carbohydrates 31.5g; dietary fiber 2.9g; sugars 3.6g; fat 12.6g; saturated fat 5.8g; cholesterol 171.8mg; vitamin a iu 889.5IU; vitamin c 10.1mg; folate 55.7mcg; calcium 410.8mg; iron 2.8mg; magnesium 63.5mg; potassium 611.6mg; sodium 1066.8mg; thiamin 0.2mg.

376. Beer-Battered Fish Tacos with Tomato & Avocado Salsa

Total: 40 mins

Servings: 2

Ingredients

- Tomato & Avocado Salsa
- 1 large tomato, diced
- ¼ cup diced red onion
- ½ jalapeno, minced
- 2-3 tablespoons lime juice
- ¼ teaspoon kosher salt
- ⅛ teaspoon freshly ground pepper
- ½ avocado, diced
- ¼ cup chopped fresh cilantro
- Pinch of cayenne, if desired
- Fish Tacos
- 3 tablespoons all-purpose flour
- ⅛ teaspoon ground cumin
- ⅛ teaspoon salt
- ⅛ teaspoon cayenne pepper, or to taste
- ⅓ cup beer
- 8 ounces tilapia fillet, cut crosswise into 1-inch wide strips
- 2 teaspoons canola oil
- 4 corn tortillas, warmed

Instructions

- To prepare salsa: Combine tomato, onion, jalapeno, lime juice to taste, kosher salt, and pepper in a medium bowl. Stir in avocado and cilantro. Add cayenne (if using).
- To prepare tacos: Combine flour, cumin, salt, and cayenne in a medium bowl. Whisk in beer to create a batter.
- Coat tilapia pieces in the batter. Heat oil in a large nonstick skillet over medium-high heat. Letting excess batter drip back into the bowl, add the fish to the pan; cook until crispy and golden, 2 to 4 minutes per side. Serve the fish with tortillas and salsa.

Nutrition

Serving Size: 2 Tacos & About 3/4 Cup Salsa, Per Serving: calories: 401; protein 28.5g; carbohydrates 39g; dietary fiber 8.3g; sugars 4.4g; fat 15.7g; saturated fat 2.3g; cholesterol 56.7mg; vitamin a iu 1042.3IU; vitamin c 28.3mg; folate 113.4mcg; calcium 77.2mg; iron 2.2mg; magnesium 97.3mg; potassium 974.3mg; sodium 406.5mg; thiamin 0.2mg.

377. Seafood Couscous Paella

Total: 35 mins

Servings: 2

Ingredients

- 2 teaspoons extra-virgin olive oil
- 1 medium onion, chopped
- 1 clove garlic, minced
- ½ teaspoon dried thyme
- ½ teaspoon fennel seed
- ¼ teaspoon salt
- ¼ teaspoon freshly ground pepper
- Pinch of crumbled saffron threads
- 1 cup no-salt-added diced tomatoes, with juice
- ¼ cup vegetable broth
- 4 ounces bay scallops, tough muscle removed
- 4 ounces small shrimp, (41-50 per pound), peeled and deveined
- ½ cup whole-wheat couscous

Instructions

- Heat oil in a large saucepan over medium heat. Add onion; cook, stirring constantly, for 3 minutes. Add garlic, thyme, fennel seed, salt, pepper, and saffron; cook for 20 seconds.
- Stir in tomatoes and broth. Bring to a simmer. Cover, reduce heat, and simmer for 2 minutes.
- Increase heat to medium, stir in scallops, and cook, stirring occasionally, for 2 minutes. Add shrimp and cook, stirring occasionally, for 2 minutes more. Stir in couscous. Cover, remove from heat, and let stand for 5 minutes; fluff.

Nutrition

Serving Size: 1 1/2 Cups Per Serving: calories: 403; protein 26.6g; carbohydrates 60.3g; dietary fiber 9.6g; sugars 6.6g; fat 6.8g; saturated fat 1g; cholesterol 104.5mg; vitamin a iu 894.1IU; vitamin c 25.7mg; folate 30mcg; calcium 89.9mg; iron 1.6mg; magnesium 36.8mg; potassium 288.9mg; sodium 1019.2mg; thiamin 0.1mg.

378. Seared Salmon With Pesto Fettuccine For Two

Total: 20 mins

Servings: 2

Ingredients

- 4 ounces whole-wheat fettuccine
- ⅓ cup refrigerated prepared pesto
- 10 ounces wild Alaskan salmon (see Tip), skinned and cut into 2 portions
- ⅛ teaspoon salt
- ⅛ teaspoon ground pepper
- 1 ½ teaspoon extra-virgin olive oil

Instructions

- Bring a large saucepan of water to a boil. Add fettuccine and cook until just tender, about 9 minutes. Drain and transfer to a medium bowl. Toss with pesto.
- Meanwhile, season salmon with salt and pepper. Heat oil in a medium cast-iron or nonstick skillet over medium-high heat. Add salmon and cook, turning once, until just opaque in the middle, 2 to 4 minutes per side. Serve the salmon with the pasta.

Nutrition

Serving Size: 4 Oz. Salmon & 1 1/4 Cups Pasta Per Serving: Calories: 603; protein 44g; carbohydrates 45.3g; dietary fiber 8g; sugars 2.1g; fat 28.4g; saturated fat 7g; cholesterol 79.6mg; vitamin a iu 590.7IU; vitamin c 4.7mg; folate 48mcg; calcium 371.4mg; iron 4.2mg; magnesium 142.1mg; potassium 767.8mg; sodium 537.1mg; thiamin 0.4mg.

379. Seafood Stew

Total: 30 mins

Servings: 2

Ingredients

- 2 teaspoons extra-virgin olive oil
- 1 medium onion, chopped
- 1 clove garlic, minced

- ½ teaspoon dried thyme
- ½ teaspoon fennel seed
- ¼ teaspoon salt
- ¼ teaspoon freshly ground pepper
- Pinch of crumbled saffron threads
- 1 cup no-salt-added diced tomatoes, with juice
- ¼ cup vegetable broth
- 4 ounces green beans, cut into 1-inch pieces
- 4 ounces bay scallops, tough muscle removed
- 4 ounces small shrimp, (41-50 per pound), peeled and deveined

Instructions

- Heat oil in a large saucepan over medium heat. Add onion; cook, stirring constantly, for 3 minutes. Add garlic, thyme, fennel seed, salt, pepper, and saffron; cook for 20 seconds.
- Stir in tomatoes, broth, and green beans. Bring to a simmer. Cover, reduce heat, and simmer for 2 minutes.
- Increase heat to medium, stir in scallops, and cook, stirring occasionally, for 2 minutes. Add shrimp and cook, stirring occasionally, for 2 minutes more.

Nutrition

Serving Size: 1 3/4 Cups Per Serving: 213 calories; protein 19.7g; carbohydrates 19.7g; dietary fiber 4.4g; sugars 7.5g; fat 6g; saturated fat 1g; cholesterol 104.5mg; vitamin a iu 1283.1IU; vitamin c 31.1mg; folate 48.3mcg; calcium 114.4mg; iron 2mg; magnesium 46.8mg; potassium 370mg; sodium 1019.7mg; thiamin 0.1mg.

380. Easy Salmon Cakes

Total: 45 mins

Servings: 4

Ingredients

- 3 teaspoons extra-virgin olive oil, divided
- 1 small onion, finely chopped
- 1 stalk celery, finely diced
- 2 tablespoons chopped fresh parsley
- 15 ounces canned salmon, drained, or 1 1/2 cups cooked salmon
- 1 large egg, lightly beaten
- 1 ½ teaspoon Dijon mustard

- 1 3/4 cups fresh whole-wheat breadcrumbs, (see Tip)
- ½ teaspoon freshly ground pepper
- Creamy Dill Sauce, (recipe follows)
- 1 lemon, cut into wedges

Instructions

- Preheat oven to 450 degrees F. Coat a baking sheet with cooking spray.
- Heat 1 1/2 teaspoons oil in a large nonstick skillet over medium-high heat. Add onion and celery; cook, stirring, until softened, about 3 minutes. Stir in parsley; remove from the heat.
- Place salmon in a medium bowl. Flake apart with a fork; remove any bones and skin. Add egg and mustard; mix well. Add the onion mixture, breadcrumbs, and pepper; mix well. Shape the mixture into 8 patties, about 2 1/2 inches wide.
- Heat remaining 1 1/2 teaspoons oil in the pan over medium heat. Add 4 patties and cook until the undersides are golden, 2 to 3 minutes. Using a wide spatula, turn them over onto the prepared baking sheet. Repeat with the remaining patties.
- Bake the salmon cakes until golden on top and heat for 15 to 20 minutes. Meanwhile, prepare Creamy Dill Sauce. Serve salmon cakes with sauce and lemon wedges.

Nutrition

Per Serving: 350 calories; protein 34.4g; carbohydrates 25.8g; dietary fiber 5.7g; sugars 5.5g; fat 13.7g; saturated fat 1.4g; cholesterol 126.3mg; vitamin a iu 418.7IU; vitamin c 7.4mg; folate 26.4mcg; calcium 60.3mg; iron 2.2mg; magnesium 58.9mg; potassium 168.7mg; sodium 761.4mg; thiamin 0.2mg.

381. Easy Spicy Salmon Cakes

Active: 20 mins

Total: 20 mins

Servings: 4

Ingredients

- 1 1/2 cups flaked cooked salmon (see Associated Recipes)
- 2 eggs, lightly beaten
- ¼ cup finely chopped red onion

- ¼ cup chopped fresh cilantro
- 1 tablespoon chile-garlic sauce
- 1 tablespoon low-sodium soy sauce
- 1 teaspoon Chinese five-spice powder
- 1 cup panko breadcrumbs
- ¼ cup canola oil

Instructions

- Combine salmon, eggs, onion, cilantro, chile-garlic sauce, soy sauce, and five-spice powder in a large bowl. Fold in breadcrumbs. Form into four 3-inch-wide patties.
- Heat oil in a medium nonstick skillet over medium-high heat. Add the salmon cakes and cook, turning once, until browned on both sides, 4 to 6 minutes total.

Nutrition

Serving Size: 1 Cake Per Serving: 330 calories; protein 16.4g; carbohydrates 20.1g; dietary fiber 0.8g; sugars 3g; fat 19.8g; saturated fat 2.5g; cholesterol 118.1mg; vitamin a iu 358.3IU; vitamin c 3.4mg; folate 22.8mcg; calcium 46.8mg; iron 1.2mg; magnesium 22.9mg; potassium 276.2mg; sodium 412.4mg; thiamin 0.1mg; added sugar 1g.

382. Salmon-Stuffed Avocados

Active: 15 mins

Total: 15 mins

Servings: 4

Ingredients

- ½ cup nonfat plain Greek yogurt
- ½ cup diced celery
- 2 tablespoons chopped fresh parsley
- 1 tablespoon lime juice
- 2 teaspoons mayonnaise
- 1 teaspoon Dijon mustard
- ⅛ teaspoon salt
- ⅛ teaspoon ground pepper
- 2 (5 ounces) cans salmon, drained, flaked, skin and bones removed
- 2 avocados
- Chopped chives for garnish

Instructions

- Combine yogurt, celery, parsley, lime juice, mayonnaise, mustard, salt, and pepper in a medium bowl; mix well. Add salmon and mix well.
- Halve avocados lengthwise and remove pits. Scoop about 1 tablespoon flesh from each avocado half into a small bowl. Mash the scooped-out avocado flesh with a fork and stir into the salmon mixture.
- Fill each avocado half with about 1/4 cup of the salmon mixture, mounding it on top of the avocado halves. Garnish with chives, if desired.

Nutrition

Serving Size: 1/2 Avocado And 1/4 Cup Salmon Salad Per Serving: 293 calories; protein 22.5g; carbohydrates 10.5g; dietary fiber 7g; sugars 1.8g; fat 19.6g; saturated fat 3g; cholesterol 61.2mg; vitamin a iu 413IU; vitamin c 14.1mg; folate 94.1mcg; calcium 94.2mg; iron 1.1mg; magnesium 52mg; potassium 807.2mg; sodium 399.8mg.

383. Salmon Pita Sandwich

Total: 10 mins

Servings: 1

Ingredients

- 2 tablespoons plain nonfat yogurt
- 2 teaspoons chopped fresh dill
- 2 teaspoons lemon juice
- ½ teaspoon prepared horseradish
- 3 ounces flaked drained canned sockeye salmon
- ½ 6-inch whole-wheat pita bread
- ½ cup watercress

Instructions

Combine yogurt, dill, lemon juice, and horseradish in a small bowl; stir in salmon. Stuff the pita half with the salmon salad and watercress.

Nutrition

Serving Size: 1 Sandwich Per Serving: 239 calories; protein 24.8g; carbohydrates 19g; dietary fiber 2.3g; sugars 3g; fat 7.1g; saturated fat 1.4g; cholesterol 67.8mg; vitamin a iu 414.1IU; vitamin c 8.2mg; folate 21.6mcg; calcium 273.8mg; iron 1.5mg; magnesium

54.7mg; potassium 436.1mg; sodium 510.2mg; thiamin 0.2mg.

384. Salmon Tacos with Pineapple Salsa

Active: 20 mins

Total: 20 mins

Servings: 4

Ingredients

- 1 (1 pound) salmon fillet
- 1 teaspoon chili powder
- ¾ teaspoon salt, divided
- 1 tablespoon plus 1 teaspoon extra-virgin olive oil, divided
- 1 (9 ounces) package coleslaw mix (5 cups)
- ½ lime, juiced
- 8 (6 inches) corn tortillas, warmed (see Tip)
- ¾ cup purchased pineapple salsa (see Ingredient Note)
- Chopped fresh cilantro, for garnish
- Hot sauce for serving

Instructions

- Arrange oven rack in the upper third of oven so salmon will be 2 to 3 inches below heat source. Preheat broiler to high.
- Line a baking sheet with foil. Lay salmon on the foil, skin-side down. Broil, rotating the pan from front to back once, until the salmon is starting to brown, is opaque on the sides and the thinner parts of the fillet are sizzling, 5 to 8 minutes, depending on thickness.
- Sprinkle the salmon with chili powder and 1/4 teaspoon salt. Drizzle with 1 teaspoon oil and brush with a heatproof brush to moisten the spices. Return to the oven and continue broiling until the salmon just flakes and the spices are browned, 1 to 2 minutes more
- Meanwhile, toss coleslaw mix with lime juice, the remaining 1 tablespoon oil, and the remaining 1/2 teaspoon salt.
- Flake the salmon, discarding skin. Divide the salmon among tortillas and top with salsa. Serve with the coleslaw and garnish with cilantro and hot sauce, if desired.

Nutrition

Serving Size: 2 Tacos Per Serving: 320 calories; protein 25.5g; carbohydrates 29.5g; dietary fiber 3.8g; sugars 5.2g; fat 10.5g; saturated fat 1.7g; cholesterol 53mg; vitamin a iu 578.4IU; vitamin c 26.4mg; folate 40.7mcg; calcium 82.2mg; iron 3.5mg; magnesium 40.9mg; potassium 546.7mg; sodium 692.9mg; thiamin 0.1mg.

385. Dan Dan Noodles With Shrimp

Ingredients

- 12 ounces Chinese flat noodles
- 2 tablespoons sugar
- 2 tablespoons dark soy sauce
- 2 tablespoons reduced-sodium soy sauce
- 2 tablespoons Chinese sesame paste
- 2 tablespoons chile-garlic sauce
- 2 tablespoons low-sodium chicken broth
- 1 tablespoon cider vinegar
- 2 tablespoons Sichuan preserved vegetables or kimchi, rinsed and chopped
- 2 tablespoons peanut oil or canola oil
- 16 raw medium shrimp (10-12 ounces see Tips), peeled and deveined
- ¼ cup chopped unsalted roasted peanuts
- 3 scallions, finely chopped

Instructions

- Bring a large pot of water to a boil. Cook noodles according to package directions. Drain and rinse well. Transfer to a large shallow serving bowl.
- Meanwhile, combine sugar, dark soy sauce, reduced-sodium soy sauce, sesame paste (or tahini), chile-garlic sauce, broth, and vinegar in a small bowl. Place near the stove. Pat dry preserved vegetables (or kimchi) with a paper towel. Place near the stove.
- Heat a 14-inch flat-bottom carbon-steel wok or large cast-iron skillet over medium-high heat. Add peanut (or canola) oil and swirl to coat. When the first puff of smoke appears, add shrimp; cook, stirring until the shrimp just starts to turn pink, about 2 minutes. Stir in the vegetables (or kimchi), then add the sauce

mixture and cook, stirring, until the shrimp are just cooked through, 1 to 2 minutes.

- Pour the shrimp mixture over the noodles. Top with peanuts and scallions. Toss together at the table before serving.

Nutrition

Serving Size: About 1 1/3 Cups Per Serving: 387 calories; protein 19.9g; carbohydrates 51g; dietary fiber 3.6g; sugars 5.7g; fat 11.8g; saturated fat 1.9g; cholesterol 66.2mg; vitamin a iu 101IU; vitamin c 3.1mg; folate 181.9mcg; calcium 54.9mg; iron 2.7mg; magnesium 61.4mg; potassium 308.3mg; sodium 584.6mg; thiamin 0.5mg; added sugar 4g.

386. Walnut-Rosemary Crusted Salmon

Active: 10 mins

Total: 20 mins

Servings: 4

Ingredient

- 2 teaspoons Dijon mustard
- 1 clove garlic, minced
- ¼ teaspoon lemon zest
- 1 teaspoon lemon juice
- 1 teaspoon chopped fresh rosemary
- ½ teaspoon honey
- ½ teaspoon kosher salt
- ¼ teaspoon crushed red pepper
- 3 tablespoons panko breadcrumbs
- 3 tablespoons finely chopped walnuts
- 1 teaspoon extra-virgin olive oil
- 1 (1 pound) skinless salmon fillet, fresh or frozen
- Olive oil cooking spray
- Chopped fresh parsley and lemon wedges for garnish

Instructions

- Preheat oven to 425 degrees F. Line a large rimmed baking sheet with parchment paper.
- Combine mustard, garlic, lemon zest, lemon juice, rosemary, honey, salt, and crushed red pepper in a small bowl. Combine panko, walnuts, and oil in another small bowl.
- Place salmon on the prepared baking sheet. Spread the mustard mixture over the fish and

sprinkle with the panko mixture, pressing to adhere. Lightly coat with cooking spray.

- Bake until the fish flakes easily with a fork, about 8 to 12 minutes, depending on thickness.
- Sprinkle with parsley and serve with lemon wedges, if desired.

Nutrition

Serving Size: 3 Ounces Per Serving: 222 calories; protein 24g; carbohydrates 4g; sugars 1g; fat 12g; saturated fat 2g; cholesterol 62mg; sodium 256mg.

387. Salmon Pinwheels

Total: 30 mins

Servings: 4

Ingredients

- 1/2 cup coarse dry breadcrumbs, preferably whole-wheat (see Tip)
- 1 tablespoon extra-virgin olive oil
- 1 tablespoon whole-grain mustard
- 1 tablespoon chopped shallot
- 1 tablespoon lemon juice
- 1 teaspoon chopped rinsed capers
- 1 teaspoon chopped fresh thyme, or 1/2 teaspoon dried
- 1 ¼ pounds center-cut salmon fillet, skinned and cut lengthwise into 4 strips
- ❖ 4 teaspoons low-fat mayonnaise

Instructions

- Preheat oven to 400 degrees F. Coat a 9-by-13-inch baking dish with cooking spray.
- Mix breadcrumbs, oil, mustard, shallot, lemon juice, capers, and thyme in a small bowl until combined.
- Working with one at a time, spread each salmon strip with 1 teaspoon mayonnaise. Spread about 3 tablespoons of the breadcrumb mixture over the mayonnaise. Starting at one end, roll the salmon up tightly, tucking in any loose filling as you go. Insert a toothpick through the end to keep the pinwheel from unrolling. Place in the prepared dish. Repeat with the remaining salmon strips.

- Bake the pinwheels until just cooked through, 15 to 20 minutes. Remove the toothpicks before serving.

Nutrition

Serving Size: 1 Pinwheel Per Serving: 257 calories; protein 29.9g; carbohydrates 8.9g; dietary fiber 1.1g; sugars 0.6g; fat 10.3g; saturated fat 1.9g; cholesterol 67.5mg; vitamin a iu 254.7IU; vitamin c 3.7mg; folate 17.8mcg; calcium 57.2mg; iron 1.2mg; magnesium 41.2mg; potassium 537.8mg; sodium 204.6mg; thiamin 0.1mg.

388. Fish Amandine

Active: 15 mins

Total: 20 mins

Servings: 4

Ingredients

- 4 (4 ounces) fresh or frozen skinless tilapia, trout, or halibut fillets, 1/2- to 1-inch thick
- ¼ cup buttermilk
- ½ cup panko bread crumbs or fine dry bread crumbs
- 2 tablespoons chopped fresh parsley or 2 teaspoons dried parsley flakes
- ½ teaspoon dry mustard
- ¼ teaspoon salt
- ¼ cup sliced almonds, coarsely chopped
- 2 tablespoons grated Parmesan cheese
- 1 tablespoon butter, melted
- ❖ ⅛ teaspoon crushed red pepper

Instructions

- Thaw fish, if frozen. Preheat oven to 450 degrees F. Grease a shallow baking pan; set aside. Rinse fish; pat dry with paper towels. Measure the thickness of fish.
- Pour buttermilk into a shallow dish. In another shallow dish, combine bread crumbs, parsley, dry mustard, and salt. Dip fish into buttermilk, then into crumb mixture, turning to coat. Place coated fish in the prepared baking pan.
- Sprinkle fish with almonds and Parmesan cheese; drizzle with melted butter. Sprinkle with crushed red pepper. Bake 4 to 6 minutes per

1/2-inch thickness of fish or until fish flakes easily when tested with a fork.

Nutrition

Serving Size: 4 Ounces Per Serving: 209 calories; protein 26.2g; carbohydrates 6.7g; dietary fiber 0.9g; sugars 1g; fat 8.7g; saturated fat 3.2g; cholesterol 66.9mg; vitamin a iu 287.5IU; vitamin c 2.9mg; folate 34.2mcg; calcium 69.6mg; iron 1.1mg; magnesium 50mg; potassium 413.8mg; sodium 301.6mg.

389. Salmon Sushi Buddha Bowl

Active: 15 mins

Total: 15 mins

Servings: 1

Ingredients

- ½ teaspoon rice vinegar
- ½ teaspoon honey
- ½ cup cooked short-grain brown rice
- 3 ounces sliced smoked salmon
- ½ avocado, sliced
- ½ cup sliced cucumber
- 1 teaspoon reduced-sodium tamari or soy sauce (see Tip)
- 1 teaspoon toasted sesame oil
- 1/8-1/4 teaspoon wasabi paste
- 1 teaspoon sesame seeds for garnish

Instructions

Combine rice vinegar and honey in a small bowl. Stir in rice. Transfer the rice to a shallow serving bowl. Top with smoked salmon, avocado, and cucumber. Combine tamari (or soy sauce), sesame oil, and wasabi in a small bowl and drizzle over everything. Top with sesame seeds, if desired.

Nutrition

Serving Size: 1 Bowl Per Serving: 432 calories; protein 20.4g; carbohydrates 37g; dietary fiber 8.8g; sugars 4.4g; fat 23.8g; saturated fat 3.8g; cholesterol 19.6mg; vitamin a iu 275.3IU; vitamin c 11.5mg; folate 90.7mcg; calcium 40.6mg; iron 2.1mg; magnesium 96mg; potassium 801.1mg; sodium 771.6mg; thiamin 0.2mg; added sugar 3g.

390. Salmon & Avocado Poke Bowl

Active: 20 mins

Total: 20 mins

Servings: 4

Ingredients

- Poke
- 1 pound previously frozen wild salmon, skinned and cut into 3/4-inch cubes
- 1 medium ripe avocado, diced
- ½ cup thinly sliced yellow onion
- ½ cup thinly sliced scallion greens
- ½ cup chopped fresh cilantro
- ¼ cup tobiko (flying fish roe) or other caviar
- 3 tablespoons reduced-sodium tamari
- 2 teaspoons toasted (dark) sesame oil
- ½ teaspoon Sriracha
- Brown Rice Salad
- 2 cups cooked short-grain brown rice, warmed
- 2 cups packed spicy greens, such as arugula, watercress, or mizuna
- 2 tablespoons rice vinegar
- 2 tablespoons extra-virgin olive oil
- 1 tablespoon Chinese-style or Dijon mustard

Instructions

- Gently combine salmon, avocado, onion, scallion greens, cilantro, tobiko (or caviar), tamari, sesame oil, and Sriracha in a medium bowl.
- Combine rice and greens in a large bowl. Whisk vinegar, oil, and mustard in a small bowl. Add to the rice salad and mix well. Serve the poke on the rice salad.

Nutrition

Serving Size: About 1 3/4 Cups Each Per Serving: 442 calories; protein 29.5g; carbohydrates 34.3g; dietary fiber 7g; sugars 3.9g; fat 21.9g; saturated fat 3.4g; cholesterol 88mg; vitamin a iu 3496.1IU; niacin equivalents 17.1mg; vitamin b6 1.1mg; vitamin c 31.3mg; folate 65.2mcg; calcium 93.1mg; iron 2.7mg; magnesium 58.8mg; potassium 828mg; sodium 791.7mg; thiamin 0.6mg; added sugar 2g; calories from fat 197kcal.

391. Poached Salmon With Creamy Piccata Sauce

Total: 20 mins

Servings: 4

Ingredients

- 1 pound center-cut salmon fillet, skinned (see Tip) and cut into 4 portions
- 1 cup dry white wine, divided
- 2 teaspoons extra-virgin olive oil
- 1 large shallot, minced
- 2 tablespoons lemon juice
- 4 teaspoons capers, rinsed
- ¼ cup reduced-fat sour cream
- ¼ teaspoon salt
- 1 tablespoon chopped fresh dill

Instructions

- Place salmon in a large skillet. Add 1/2 cup wine and enough water to just cover the salmon. Bring to a boil over high heat. Reduce to a simmer, turn the salmon over, cover, and cook for 5 minutes. Remove from the heat.
- Meanwhile, heat oil in a medium skillet over medium-high heat. Add shallot and cook, stirring, until fragrant, about 30 seconds. Add the remaining 1/2 cup wine; boil until slightly reduced, about 1 minute. Stir in lemon juice and capers; cook 1 minute more. Remove from the heat; stir in sour cream and salt. To serve, top the salmon with the sauce and garnish with dill.

Nutrition

Serving Size: 3 Oz. Salmon & Scant 1/4 Cup Sauce Per Serving: 229 calories; protein 23.3g; carbohydrates 3.7g; dietary fiber 0.2g; sugars 0.9g; fat 8.3g; saturated fat 2.5g; cholesterol 58.9mg; vitamin a iu 293.3IU; vitamin c 5.1mg; folate 18.9mcg; calcium 68.1mg; iron 0.9mg; magnesium 41.7mg; potassium 506.2mg; sodium 285.6mg; thiamin 0.1mg.

392. Mustard-Crusted Salmon

Total: 20 mins

Servings: 4

Ingredients

- 1 ¼ pounds center-cut salmon fillets, cut into 4 portions
- ¼ teaspoon salt, or to taste

- ¼ cup reduced-fat sour cream
- 2 tablespoons stone-ground mustard
- 2 teaspoons lemon juice
- Freshly ground pepper, to taste
- Lemon wedges

Instructions

- Preheat broiler. Line a broiler pan or baking sheet with foil, then coat it with cooking spray.
- Place salmon pieces, skin-side down, on the prepared pan. Season with salt and pepper. Combine sour cream, mustard, and lemon juice in a small bowl. Spread evenly over the salmon.
- Broil the salmon 5 inches from the heat source until it is opaque in the center, 10 to 12 minutes. Serve with lemon wedges.

Nutrition

Per Serving: 198 calories; protein 29.2g; carbohydrates 2g; dietary fiber 0.3g; sugars 0.7g; fat 7.6g; saturated fat 2.4g; cholesterol 72.1mg; vitamin a iu 261.5IU; vitamin c 3.1mg; folate 17.8mcg; calcium 75.9mg; iron 0.9mg; magnesium 41.5mg; potassium 559.8mg; sodium 382.1mg; thiamin 0.1mg.

393. Seared Salmon With Green Peppercorn Sauce

Total: 15 mins

Servings: 4

Ingredients

- 1 1/4 pounds wild salmon fillet (see Tip), skinned and cut into 4 portions
- 1/4 teaspoon plus a pinch of salt, divided
- 2 teaspoons canola oil
- ¼ cup lemon juice
- 4 teaspoons unsalted butter, cut into small pieces
- 1 teaspoon green peppercorns in vinegar, rinsed and crushed

Instructions

Sprinkle salmon pieces with 1/4 teaspoon salt. Heat oil in a large nonstick skillet over medium-high heat. Add the salmon and cook until just opaque in the center, gently turning halfway, 4 to 7 minutes total. Divide among 4 plates. Remove the pan from the heat and immediately add lemon juice, butter, peppercorns, and the remaining pinch of salt; swirl the pan carefully to

incorporate the butter into the sauce. Top each portion of fish with sauce (about 2 teaspoons each).

Nutrition

Per Serving: 226 calories; protein 28.4g; carbohydrates 1.2g; dietary fiber 0.1g; sugars 0.4g; fat 11.4g; saturated fat 3.9g; cholesterol 76.4mg; vitamin a iu 327IU; vitamin c 7.6mg; folate 18.9mcg; calcium 57.8mg; iron 0.8mg; magnesium 40.8mg; potassium 543.1mg; sodium 269.3mg; thiamin 0.1mg.

394. Five-Spice Tilapia

Total: 15 mins

Servings: 4

Ingredients

- 1 pound tilapia fillets
- 1 teaspoon Chinese five-spice powder (see Tip)
- ¼ cup reduced-sodium soy sauce
- 3 tablespoons light brown sugar
- 1 tablespoon canola oil
- 3 scallions, thinly sliced

Instructions

- Sprinkle both sides of tilapia fillets with five-spice powder. Combine soy sauce and brown sugar in a small bowl.
- Heat oil in a large nonstick skillet over medium-high heat. Add the tilapia and cook until the outer edges are opaque about 2 minutes. Reduce heat to medium, turn the fish over, stir the soy mixture and pour into the pan. Bring the sauce to a boil and cook until the fish is cooked through and the sauce has thickened slightly, about 2 minutes more. Add scallions and remove them from the heat. Serve the fish drizzled with the pan sauce.

Nutrition

Per Serving: 180 calories; protein 23.9g; carbohydrates 9.4g; dietary fiber 0.4g; sugars 6.9g; fat 5.6g; saturated fat 0.9g; cholesterol 56.7mg; vitamin a iu 112.2IU; vitamin c 2.1mg; folate 34.5mcg; calcium 33.4mg; iron 1.5mg; magnesium 38.9mg; potassium 411.4mg; sodium 596mg; thiamin 0.1mg; added sugar 9g.

395. Dijon Salmon With Green Bean Pilaf

Total: 30 mins

Servings: 4

Ingredients

- 1 ¼ pound wild salmon, skinned and cut into 4 portions
- 3 tablespoons extra-virgin olive oil, divided
- 1 tablespoon minced garlic
- ¾ teaspoon salt
- 2 tablespoons mayonnaise
- 2 teaspoons whole-grain mustard
- ½ teaspoon ground pepper, divided
- 12 ounces pretrimmed haricots verts or thin green beans, cut into thirds
- 1 small lemon, zested and cut into 4 wedges
- 2 tablespoons pine nuts
- 1 8-ounce package precooked brown rice
- 2 tablespoons water
- Chopped fresh parsley for garnish

Instructions

- Preheat oven to 425 degrees F. Line a rimmed baking sheet with foil or parchment paper.
- Brush salmon with 1 tablespoon oil and place on the prepared baking sheet. Mash garlic and salt into a paste with the side of a chef's knife or a fork. Combine a scant 1 teaspoon of the garlic paste in a small bowl with mayonnaise, mustard, and 1/4 teaspoon pepper. Spread the mixture on top of the fish.
- Roast the salmon until it flakes easily with a fork in the thickest part, 6 to 8 minutes per inch of thickness.
- Meanwhile, heat the remaining 2 tablespoons of oil in a large skillet over medium-high heat. Add green beans, lemon zest, pine nuts, the remaining garlic paste, and 1/4 teaspoon pepper; cook, stirring, until the beans are just tender, 2 to 4 minutes. Reduce heat to medium. Add rice and water and cook, stirring, until hot, 2 to 3 minutes more.
- Sprinkle the salmon with parsley, if desired, and serve with the green bean pilaf and lemon wedges.

- All wild salmon--and now some farmed--is considered a sustainable choice. For farmed, ask for fish that's raised in the land- or tank-based systems. For more information about sustainable seafood, go to seafoodwatch.org.

Nutrition

Serving Size: 4 Oz. Fish & 1 Cup Pilaf Per Serving: 442 calories; protein 32.2g; carbohydrates 21.6g; dietary fiber 3.8g; sugars 1.7g; fat 24.8g; saturated fat 3.8g; cholesterol 69.2mg; vitamin a iu 795.2IU; vitamin c 13.4mg; folate 46.2mcg; calcium 99.3mg; iron 1.7mg; magnesium 67mg; potassium 705.9mg; sodium 605.2mg; thiamin 0.2mg.

396. Greek Roasted Fish With Vegetables

Active: 35 mins

Total: 55 mins

Servings: 4

Ingredients

- 1 pound fingerling potatoes, halved lengthwise
- 2 tablespoons olive oil
- 5 garlic cloves, coarsely chopped
- ½ teaspoon sea salt
- ½ teaspoon freshly ground black pepper
- 4 5 to 6-ounce fresh or frozen skinless salmon fillets
- 2 medium red, yellow, and/or orange sweet peppers, cut into rings
- 2 cups cherry tomatoes
- 1 ½ cups chopped fresh parsley (1 bunch)
- ¼ cup pitted kalamata olives, halved
- ¼ cup finely snipped fresh oregano or 1 Tbsp. dried oregano, crushed
- 1 lemon

Instructions

- Preheat oven to 425 degrees F. Place potatoes in a large bowl. Drizzle with 1 Tbsp. of the oil and sprinkle with garlic and 1/8 tsp. of the salt and black pepper; toss to coat. Transfer to a 15x10-inch baking pan; cover with foil. Roast 30 minutes.
- Meanwhile, thaw salmon, if frozen. Combine, in the same bowl, sweet peppers, tomatoes, parsley, olives, oregano, and 1/8 tsp. of the salt

and black pepper. Drizzle with remaining 1 Tbsp. oil; toss to coat.

- Rinse salmon; pat dry. Sprinkle with remaining 1/4 tsp. salt and black pepper. Spoon sweet pepper mixture over potatoes and top with salmon. Roast, uncovered, 10 minutes more or just until salmon flakes.
- Remove zest from the lemon. Squeeze juice from lemon over salmon and vegetables. Sprinkle with zest.

Nutrition

Serving Size: 4 Ounces Salmon And 1 1/2 Cups Vegetable Per Serving: 422 calories; protein 32.9g; carbohydrates 31.5g; dietary fiber 5.7g; sugars 6.6g; fat 18.6g; saturated fat 2.4g; cholesterol 78mg; vitamin a iu 2990IU; vitamin c 232.7mg; folate 130.8mcg; calcium 103.5mg; iron 4mg; magnesium 102.1mg; potassium 1740.6mg; sodium 593.1mg.

397. Moqueca (Seafood & Coconut Chowder)

Active: 30 mins

Total: 30 mins

Servings: 8

Ingredient

- 1 pound fresh crabmeat (preferably claw meat), cleaned and picked over
- 1 pound raw shrimp (16-20 per pound), peeled and deveined if desired
- ¼ cup lemon juice
- 1 ½ tablespoons dendê (red palm oil; see Tip) or canola oil
- 3 cups sliced red bell peppers
- 2 ½ cups sliced green bell peppers
- 2 ½ cups sliced red onions
- ½ cup minced fresh cilantro, plus more for garnish
- 4 large cloves garlic, minced
- ¼ cup tomato paste
- ¾ teaspoon salt
- ¾ teaspoon ground pepper
- 2 14-ounce cans of coconut milk
- 2 cups clam juice or fish stock
- 4 cups cooked brown rice

Instructions

- Combine crab, shrimp, and lemon juice in a medium bowl.
- Heat oil in a large pot over medium-high heat. Add red peppers, green peppers, and onions; cook, stirring occasionally, until beginning to soften, about 4 minutes. Add cilantro, garlic, tomato paste, salt, and pepper; cook, stirring, for 1 minute. Add coconut milk and clam juice (or fish stock) and bring to a simmer. Reduce heat to maintain a simmer, cover, and cook until the peppers are softened, 8 to 10 minutes.
- Add the crab and shrimp and return to a simmer over medium heat. Cover and cook until the shrimp is cooked through, 3 to 4 minutes more. Serve the chowder over rice. Garnish with cilantro, if desired.

Nutrition

Serving Size: 1 ⅓ Cups Chowder & ½ Cup Rice Per Serving: 485 calories; fat 26g; cholesterol 112mg; sodium 686mg; carbohydrates 39g; dietary fiber 5g; Protein 28g; sugars 5g; saturated fat 20g

398. Herby Mediterranean Fish With Wilted Greens & Mushrooms

Active: 25 mins

Total: 25 mins

Servings: 4

Ingredients

- 3 tablespoons olive oil, divided
- ½ large sweet onion, sliced
- 3 cups sliced cremini mushrooms
- 2 cloves garlic, sliced
- 4 cups chopped kale
- 1 medium tomato, diced
- 2 teaspoons Mediterranean Herb Mix (see Associated Recipes), divided
- 1 tablespoon lemon juice
- ½ teaspoon salt, divided
- ½ teaspoon ground pepper, divided
- 4 (4 ounces) cod, sole, or tilapia fillets
- Chopped fresh parsley, for garnish

Instructions

- Heat 1 Tbsp. oil in a large saucepan over medium heat. Add onion; cook, stirring occasionally, until translucent, 3 to 4 minutes. Add mushrooms and garlic; cook, stirring occasionally until the mushrooms release their liquid and begin to brown, 4 to 6 minutes. Add kale, tomato, and 1 tsp. herb mix. Cook, stirring occasionally until the kale is wilted and the mushrooms are tender 5 to 7 minutes. Stir in lemon juice and 1/4 tsp. each salt and pepper. Remove from heat, cover, and keep warm.
- Sprinkle fish with the remaining 1 tsp. herb mix and 1/4 tsp. each salt and pepper. Heat the remaining 2 Tbsp. oil in a large nonstick skillet over medium-high heat. Add the fish and cook until the flesh is opaque, 2 to 4 minutes per side, depending on thickness. Transfer the fish to 4 plates or a serving platter. Top and surround the fish with the vegetables; sprinkle with parsley, if desired.

Nutrition

Serving Size: 1 Piece Fish + 1/2 Cup Vegetables Per Serving: 214 calories; protein 18g; carbohydrates 11g; dietary fiber 3g; sugars 4g; fat 11g; saturated fat 2g; cholesterol 45mg; potassium 736mg; sodium 598mg.

399. Spicy Jerk Shrimp

Active: 5 mins

Total: 50 mins

Servings: 4

Ingredients

- 1 ½ pound fresh or frozen large shrimp in shells
- 4 (1/4 inch thick) slices peeled and cored fresh pineapple, halved
- 2 cups bite-size strips red sweet pepper
- 2 cups sliced red onions
- 1 fresh jalapeño chile pepper, halved lengthwise, seeded, and sliced (see Tip)
- 2 tablespoons olive oil
- 1 tablespoon Jamaican jerk seasoning
- ½ cup coarsely snipped fresh cilantro
- 1 ⅓ cups hot cooked brown rice
- Lime wedges

Instructions

- Thaw shrimp, if frozen. Preheat oven to 425 degrees F. Line two 15x10-inch baking pans with foil.
- Peel and devein shrimp, leaving tails intact if desired. Rinse shrimp; pat dry. In an extra-large bowl combine shrimp and the next six ingredients (through jerk seasoning); toss gently to coat. Divide mixture between the prepared pans. Roast 15 minutes or until shrimp are opaque.
- Sprinkle with cilantro and serve with brown rice and lime wedges.

Nutrition

Serving Size: 5 Ounces Shrimp And 1 Cup Pineapple Mixture Per Serving: 351 calories; protein 33.5g; carbohydrates 37.2g; dietary fiber 5.1g; sugars 12.1g; fat 8.5g; saturated fat 1.3g; cholesterol 238.3mg; vitamin a iu 2078.4IU; vitamin c 118.6mg; folate 62.2mcg; calcium 134mg; iron 1.9mg; magnesium 101.2mg; potassium 787mg; sodium 411.3mg.

400. New England Fried Shrimp

Total: 20 mins

Servings: 4

Ingredients

- 1 cup pale ale, or other light-colored beer
- 1 cup whole-wheat pastry flour, (see Ingredient Note) or all-purpose flour
- 1 teaspoon Dijon mustard
- ½ teaspoon salt, divided
- 2 tablespoons canola oil, divided
- 1 pound raw shrimp, (13-15 per pound; see Ingredient Note), peeled and deveined, tails left on
- Freshly ground pepper, to taste

Instructions

- Whisk beer, flour, mustard, and 1/4 teaspoon salt in a medium bowl until smooth.
- You'll need to cook the shrimp in two batches. Wait to batter the second batch until the first is cooked. For the first batch, heat 1 tablespoon oil in a large nonstick skillet over medium-high heat. Hold shrimp by the tail and dip in the

batter one at a time. Let any excess batter drip off, then add the shrimp to the hot oil, making sure they aren't touching. Cook, turning once and adjusting the heat as necessary to prevent burning, until golden brown on the outside and curled 3 to 4 minutes total. Transfer to a platter.

- Wipe out the pan. Add the remaining 1 tablespoon oil to the pan and heat over medium-high. Batter and fry the remaining shrimp. Season all the shrimp with the remaining 1/4 teaspoon salt and pepper and serve immediately.

Nutrition

Per Serving: 173 calories; protein 16.2g; carbohydrates 6.6g; dietary fiber 0.7g; fat 8.3g; saturated fat 0.8g; cholesterol 142.9mg; vitamin a iu 204.5IU; folate 21.6mcg; calcium 61.7mg; iron 0.3mg; magnesium 25.1mg; potassium 129.1mg; sodium 825mg.

401. Chef John's Salmon Cakes

Prep Time: 15 mins

Cook Time: 10 mins

Additional Time: 30 mins

Total Time: 55 mins

Servings: 4

Ingredient

- 1 (14.75 ounces) can red salmon, skin, and bone removed, drained, and flaked
- 2 eggs
- ½ lemon, juiced
- 1 tablespoon chopped capers
- ½ teaspoon salt
- ½ teaspoon ground black pepper
- ½ teaspoon cayenne pepper
- 12 saltine crackers
- 1 tablespoon bread crumbs, or as needed
- 1 tablespoon butter
- 1 tablespoon olive oil

Instructions

- Stir salmon, eggs, lemon juice, capers, salt, black pepper, and cayenne pepper together in a bowl until well-combined.
- Crush saltine crackers with your hands into the

salmon mixture and mix well. Wrap the bowl with plastic wrap and refrigerate, 30 minutes to overnight.

- Dust a plate with half the bread crumbs. Divide salmon mixture into 4 portions and shape into patties; place onto a prepared plate and sprinkle remaining bread crumbs atop the salmon patties.
- Melt butter and oil in a large skillet over medium heat. Cook patties in hot oil until cooked and heated through, about 5 minutes per side.

Nutrition Facts

- Calories: 305; Protein 30.9g; Carbohydrates 14.6g; Fat 14.6g; Cholesterol 174.2mg; Sodium 1019.9mg.

402. Garlicky Appetizer Shrimp Scampi

Prep Time: 15 mins

Cook Time: 6 mins

Total Time: 21 mins

Servings: 6

Ingredient

- 6 tablespoons unsalted butter, softened
- ¼ cup olive oil
- 1 tablespoon minced garlic
- 1 tablespoon minced shallots
- 2 tablespoons minced fresh chives
- Salt and freshly ground black pepper to taste
- ½ teaspoon paprika
- 2 pounds large shrimp - peeled and deveined

Instructions

- Preheat grill for high heat.
- In a large bowl, mix softened butter, olive oil, garlic, shallots, chives, salt, pepper, and paprika; add the shrimp, and toss to coat.
- Lightly oil grill grate. Cook the shrimp as close to the flame as possible for 2 to 3 minutes per side, or until opaque.

Nutrition Facts

- Calories: 303; Protein 25g; Carbohydrates 0.9g; Fat 21.8g; Cholesterol 261mg; Sodium 460.8mg.

403. Grilled Fish Steaks

Prep Time: 10 mins

Cook Time: 10 mins

Additional Time: 1 hr 10 mins

Total: 1 hr 30 mins

Servings: 2

Ingredient

- 1 clove garlic, minced
- 6 tablespoons olive oil
- 1 teaspoon dried basil
- 1 teaspoon salt
- 1 teaspoon ground black pepper
- 1 tablespoon fresh lemon juice
- 1 tablespoon chopped fresh parsley
- 2 (6 ounces) fillets of halibut

Instructions

- In a stainless steel or glass bowl, combine garlic, olive oil, basil, salt, pepper, lemon juice, and parsley.
- Place the halibut fillets in a shallow glass dish or a resealable plastic bag, and pour the marinade over the fish. Cover or seal and place in the refrigerator for 1 hour, turning occasionally.
- Preheat an outdoor grill for high heat and lightly oil grate. Set grate 4 inches from the heat.
- Remove halibut fillets from marinade and drain off the excess. Grill filets 5 minutes per side or until fish is done when easily flaked with a fork.

Nutrition Facts

- Calories: 554; Protein 36.3g; Carbohydrates 2.2g; Fat 43.7g; Cholesterol 62.5mg; Sodium 1259.3mg.

404. Mussels Mariniere

Prep Time: 35 mins

Cook Time: 15 mins

Total Time: 50 mins

Servings: 4

Ingredient

- 4 quarts mussels, cleaned and debearded
- 2 cloves garlic, minced
- 1 onion, chopped
- 6 tablespoons chopped fresh parsley
- 1 bay leaf
- ¼ teaspoon dried thyme
- 2 cups white wine
- 3 tablespoons butter, divided

Instructions

- Scrub mussels. Pull off beards, the tuft of fibers that attach each mussel to its shell, cutting them at the base with a paring knife. Discard those that do not close when you handle them and any with broken shells. Set aside.
- Combine onion, garlic, 4 tablespoons parsley, bay leaf, thyme, wine, and 2 tablespoons butter in a large pot. Bring to boil. Lower heat, and cook for 2 minutes. Add mussels, and cover. Cook just until shells open, 3 to 4 minutes. Do not overcook. Remove mussels from the sauce, and place in bowls.
- Strain liquid, and return to pot. Add remaining butter and parsley. Heat until butter melts. Pour over mussels.

Nutrition Facts

- Calories: 298; Protein 18.6g; Carbohydrates 10.3g; Fat 10.1g; Cholesterol 69.6mg; Sodium 329.6mg.

405. Chef John's Baked Lemon Pepper Salmon

Prep Time: 10 mins

Cook Time: 15 mins

Additional Time: 30 mins

Total Time: 55 mins

Servings: 2

Ingredient

- 2 tablespoons lemon juice
- 1 tablespoon ground black pepper
- 1 ½ tablespoons mayonnaise
- 1 tablespoon yellow miso paste
- 2 teaspoons dijon mustard
- 1 pinch cayenne pepper, or to taste
- 2 (8 ounces) center-cut salmon fillets, boned, skin on
- Sea salt to taste

Instructions

- Whisk together lemon juice and black pepper in a small bowl. Add mayonnaise, miso paste, Dijon mustard, and cayenne pepper to lemon-pepper mixture; whisk together.
- Spread the lemon-pepper mixture over salmon fillets. Reserve about a tablespoon for later use.
- Cover salmon with plastic wrap and refrigerate for 30 minutes.
- Preheat oven to 450 degrees F (230 degrees C). Line a baking sheet with parchment paper or a silicone baking mat.
- Place fillets on the prepared baking sheet. Spread the remaining lemon-pepper mixture on fillets without letting it pool around the base. Sprinkle with a pinch more black pepper and a generous amount of sea salt.
- Bake in the preheated oven until the fish flakes easily with a fork, 10 to 15 minutes.

Nutrition Facts

- Calories: 488; Protein 49.5g; Carbohydrates 7.1g; Fat 28.1g; Cholesterol 156.6mg; Sodium 784.3mg.

406. Rockin' Oysters Rockefeller

Prep Time: 30 mins

Cook Time: 30 mins

Total Time: 1 hr

Servings: 16

Ingredient

- 48 fresh, unopened oysters
- 1 ½ cups beer
- 2 cloves garlic
- seasoned salt to taste
- 7 black peppercorns
- ½ cup butter
- 1 onion, chopped
- 1 clove garlic, crushed
- 1 (10 ounces) package frozen chopped spinach, thawed and drained
- 8 ounces Monterey Jack cheese, shredded
- 8 ounces fontina cheese, shredded
- 8 ounces mozzarella cheese, shredded
- ½ cup milk

- 2 teaspoons salt, or to taste
- 1 teaspoon ground black pepper
- 2 tablespoons fine bread crumbs

Instructions

- Clean oysters, and place them in a large stockpot. Pour in beer and enough water to cover oysters; add 2 cloves garlic, seasoned salt, and peppercorns. Bring to a boil. Remove from heat, drain, and cool.
- Once oysters are cooled, break off and discard the top shell. Arrange the oysters on a baking sheet. Preheat oven to 425 degrees F (220 degrees C.)
- Melt butter in a saucepan over medium heat. Cook onion and garlic in butter until soft. Reduce heat to low, and stir in spinach, Monterey Jack, fontina, and mozzarella. Cook until cheese melts, stirring frequently. Stir in the milk, and season with salt and pepper. Spoon sauce over each oyster, just filling the shell. Sprinkle with bread crumbs.
- Bake until golden and bubbly, approximately 8 to 10 minutes.

Nutrition Facts

- Calories: 248; Protein 16.4g; Carbohydrates 5.3g; Fat 17.4g; Cholesterol 65.7mg; Sodium 652.2mg.

407. Sesame Seared Tuna

Prep Time: 10 mins

Cook Time: 10 mins

Total Time: 20 mins

Servings: 4

Ingredient

- ¼ Cup soy sauce
- 1 tablespoon mirin (japanese sweet wine)
- 1 tablespoon honey
- 2 tablespoons sesame oil
- 1 tablespoon rice wine vinegar
- 4 (6 ounces) tuna steaks
- ½ cup sesame seeds
- Wasabi paste
- 1 tablespoon olive oil

Instructions

- In a small bowl, stir together the soy sauce, mirin, honey, and sesame oil. Divide into two equal parts. Stir the rice vinegar into one part and set aside as a dipping sauce.
- Spread the sesame seeds out on a plate. Coat the tuna steaks with the remaining soy sauce mixture, then press into the sesame seeds to coat.
- Heat olive oil in a cast-iron skillet over high heat until very hot. Place steaks in the pan, and sear for about 30 seconds on each side. Serve with the dipping sauce and wasabi paste.

Nutrition Facts

Calories: 422; Protein 44.1g; Carbohydrates 13.2g; Fat 20.7g; Cholesterol 77.2mg; Sodium 1045.5mg.

408. Dinah's Baked Scallops

Prep Time: 20 mins

Cook Time: 15 mins

Total Time: 35 mins

Servings: 4

Ingredient

- 20 buttery round crackers, crushed
- black pepper to taste
- 1 teaspoon garlic powder
- 1 pound sea scallops, rinsed and drained
- ½ cup butter, melted
- ¼ cup dry white wine
- ½ lemon, juiced
- 1 tablespoon chopped fresh parsley, for garnish

Instructions

- Preheat oven to 350 degrees F (175 degrees C). Lightly grease an 8x8 inch baking dish.
- Combine crushed crackers, black pepper, and garlic powder in a small bowl. Press scallops into the mixture so that they are evenly coated, and place them in the greased baking dish.
- In a separate bowl, mix melted butter, wine, and lemon juice; drizzle mixture over scallops.
- Bake in the preheated oven until scallops are lightly browned, about 15 minutes. Garnish with chopped parsley.

Nutrition Facts

- Calories: 431; Protein 19.7g; Carbohydrates 15.3g; Fat 31.5g; Cholesterol 96.5mg; Sodium 530.1mg.

409. Easy-Bake Fish

Prep Time: 15 mins

Cook Time: 20 mins

Total Time: 35 mins

Servings: 4

Ingredient

- 3 tablespoons honey
- 3 tablespoons Dijon mustard
- 1 teaspoon lemon juice
- 4 (6 ounces) salmon steaks
- ½ teaspoon pepper

Instructions

- Preheat oven to 325 degrees F (165 degrees C).
- In a small bowl, mix honey, mustard, and lemon juice. Spread the mixture over the salmon steaks. Season with pepper. Arrange in a medium baking dish.
- Bake 20 minutes in the preheated oven, or until fish easily flakes with a fork.

Nutrition Facts

- Calories: 368; Protein 33.5g; Carbohydrates 15.6g; Fat 18.2g; Cholesterol 99.1mg; Sodium 381.1mg.

411. Seared Scallops With Jalapeno Vinaigrette

Prep Time: 5 mins

Cook Time: 10 mins

Total Time: 15 mins

Servings: 4

Ingredient

- 1 large jalapeno pepper, seeded and membranes removed
- ¼ cup rice vinegar
- ¼ cup olive oil
- ¼ teaspoon dijon mustard
- Salt and freshly ground black pepper to taste

- 1 tablespoon vegetable oil
- 12 large fresh sea scallops
- 1 pinch sea salt
- 1 pinch cayenne pepper
- 2 oranges, peeled and cut in between sections as segments

Instructions

- Place jalapeno, rice vinegar, olive oil, and Dijon mustard in a blender. Puree on high until mixture is completely liquefied, 1 to 2 minutes. Season with salt and black pepper to taste.
- Season scallops with sea salt and cayenne pepper. Heat vegetable oil in a skillet over high heat. Place scallops in skillet and cook until browned, 2 to 3 minutes per side. Transfer to a plate. Garnish scallops with orange segments and drizzle jalapeno vinaigrette over the top.

Nutrition Facts

- Calories: 307; Protein 30.1g; Carbohydrates 5.9g; Fat 18g; Cholesterol 72.4mg; Sodium 472mg.

412. Hudson's Baked Tilapia With Dill Sauce

Prep Time: 10 mins

Cook Time: 20 mins

Total Time: 30 mins

Servings: 4

Ingredient

- 4 (4 ounce) fillets tilapia
- Salt and pepper to taste
- 1 tablespoon cajun seasoning, or to taste
- 1 lemon, thinly sliced
- ¼ cup mayonnaise
- ½ cup sour cream
- ⅛ teaspoon garlic powder
- 1 teaspoon fresh lemon juice
- 2 tablespoons chopped fresh dill

Instructions

- Preheat the oven to 350 degrees F (175 degrees C). Lightly grease a 9x13 inch baking dish.
- Season the tilapia fillets with salt, pepper, and Cajun seasoning on both sides. Arrange the seasoned fillets in a single layer in the baking

dish. Place a layer of lemon slices over the fish fillets. I usually use about 2 slices on each piece so that it covers most of the surface of the fish.
- Bake uncovered for 15 to 20 minutes in the preheated oven, or until fish flakes easily with a fork.
- While the fish is baking, mix the mayonnaise, sour cream, garlic powder, lemon juice, and dill in a small bowl. Serve with tilapia.

Nutrition Facts

- Calories: 284; Protein 24.5g; Carbohydrates 5.7g; Fat 18.6g; Cholesterol 58.9mg; Sodium 500.5mg.

413. Angy Lemon-Garlic Shrimp

Prep Time: 10 mins

Cook Time: 10 mins

Total Time: 20 mins

Servings: 4

Ingredient

- 16 large shrimp - peeled, deveined, and tails on, or more to taste
- 3 large cloves garlic, smashed, or more to taste
- 1 teaspoon crushed red pepper, or to taste
- 2 teaspoons seafood seasoning (such as old bay®), or to taste
- Salt and ground black pepper to taste
- 2 tablespoons lemon juice
- 3 tablespoons chopped fresh parsley
- 3 teaspoons lemon zest

Instructions

- Heat a large skillet over medium-low heat until warm, about 3 minutes. Add shrimp, garlic, and crushed red pepper all at once and stir together. Add seafood seasoning, salt, and black pepper. Mix everything.
- Cook over medium heat until shrimp are fully cooked, 3 to 5 minutes. Pour lemon juice into skillet and stir again. Reduce heat to low; add parsley and lemon zest. Transfer only shrimp to a serving platter.

Nutrition Facts

- Calories: 76; Protein 14.2g; Carbohydrates 2.4g;

Fat 0.9g; Cholesterol 127.7mg; Sodium 460.3mg.

414. Parmesan-Crusted Shrimp Scampi With Pasta

Prep Time: 25 mins

Cook Time: 20 mins

Total Time: 45 mins

Servings: 6

Ingredient

- 2 cups angel hair pasta
- ½ cup butter, divided
- 4 cloves garlic, minced
- 1 pound uncooked medium shrimp, peeled and deveined
- ½ cup white cooking wine
- 1 lemon, juiced
- 1 teaspoon red pepper flakes
- ¾ cup seasoned bread crumbs
- ¾ cup freshly grated Parmesan cheese, divided
- 2 tablespoons finely chopped fresh parsley

Instructions

- Bring a large pot of lightly salted water to a boil. Cook angel hair pasta in the boiling water, stirring occasionally, until tender yet firm to the bite, 4 to 5 minutes. Drain and set aside.
- Set an oven rack about 6 inches from the heat source and preheat the oven's broiler.
- Heat 1/4 cup butter over medium heat in a large, deep skillet. Add garlic; cook and stir until fragrant. Add shrimp, white wine, and lemon juice; continue to cook and stir until shrimp is bright pink on the outside and the meat is opaque about 5 minutes. Stir in red pepper flakes until well combined. Remove from heat and set aside.
- Place remaining 1/4 cup butter, bread crumbs, 1/2 the Parmesan cheese, and parsley in a bowl. Stir until well combined. Set aside.
- Place cooked pasta into shrimp scampi mixture; toss until fully coated in sauce. Add remaining Parmesan cheese and toss well. Top with bread crumb mixture.
- Broil in the preheated oven until golden brown, 3 to 4 minutes. Serve immediately.

Nutrition Facts

- Calories: 419; Protein 22.6g; Carbohydrates 33.4g; Fat 20.8g; Cholesterol 164.7mg; Sodium 731.6mg.

415. Chef John's Fresh Salmon Cakes

Prep Time: 20 mins

Cook Time: 15 mins

Additional Time: 1 hr

Total Time: 1 hr 35 mins

Servings: 4

Ingredient

- 1 tablespoon extra-virgin olive oil
- ¼ cup minced onion
- 2 tablespoons minced red bell pepper
- 2 tablespoons minced celery
- Salt and pepper to taste
- 1 tablespoon capers
- 1 ¼ pound fresh wild salmon, coarsely chopped
- ¼ cup mayonnaise
- ¼ cup panko bread crumbs
- 2 cloves garlic, minced
- 1 teaspoon dijon mustard
- 1 pinch cayenne pepper
- 1 pinch seafood seasoning (such as old bay®)
- 1 tablespoon panko bread crumbs, or to taste
- 2 tablespoons olive oil, or as needed

Instructions

- Heat extra virgin olive oil in a skillet over medium heat. Cook and stir onion, red pepper, celery, and a pinch of salt in hot oil until onion is soft and translucent about 5 minutes. Add capers; cook and stir until fragrant, about 2 minutes. Remove from heat and cool to room temperature.
- Stir salmon, onion mixture, mayonnaise, 1/4 cup bread crumbs, garlic, mustard, cayenne, seafood seasoning, salt, and ground black pepper together in a bowl until well-mixed. Cover the bowl with plastic wrap and refrigerate until firmed and chilled, 1 to 2 hours.
- Form salmon mixture into four 1-inch thick patties; sprinkle remaining panko bread crumbs over each patty.

- Heat olive oil in a skillet over medium heat. Cook patties in hot oil until golden and cooked through, 3 to 4 minutes per side.

Nutrition Facts

- Calories: 460; Protein 31.6g; Carbohydrates 8.5g; Fat 33.5g; Cholesterol 101.6mg; Sodium 337.3mg.

416. Best Tuna Casserole

Prep Time: 15 mins

Cook Time: 20 mins

Total Time: 35 mins

Servings: 6

Ingredient

- 1 (12 ounces) package egg noodles
- ¼ cup chopped onion
- 2 cups shredded Cheddar cheese
- 1 cup frozen green peas
- 2 (5 ounce) cans tuna, drained
- 2 (10.75 ounces) cans condensed cream of mushroom soup
- ½ (4.5 ounces) can sliced mushrooms
- 1 cup crushed potato chips

Instructions

- Bring a large pot of lightly salted water to a boil. Cook pasta in boiling water for 8 to 10 minutes, or until al dente; drain.
- Preheat oven to 425 degrees F (220 degrees C).
- In a large bowl, thoroughly mix noodles, onion, 1 cup cheese, peas, tuna, soup, and mushrooms. Transfer to a 9x13 inch baking dish, and top with potato chip crumbs and remaining 1 cup cheese.
- Bake for 15 to 20 minutes in the preheated oven, or until cheese is bubbly.

Nutrition Facts

- Calories: 595; Protein 32.1g; Carbohydrates 58.1g; Fat 26.1g; Cholesterol 99.2mg; Sodium 1061.1mg

417. Good New Orleans Creole Gumbo

Prep Time: 1 hr

Cook Time: 2 hrs 40 mins

Total Time: 3 hrs 40 mins

Servings: 20

Ingredient

- 1 cup all-purpose flour
- ¾ cup bacon drippings
- 1 cup coarsely chopped celery
- 1 large onion, coarsely chopped
- 1 large green bell pepper, coarsely chopped
- 2 cloves garlic, minced
- 1 pound andouille sausage, sliced
- 3 quarts water
- 6 cubes beef bouillon
- 1 tablespoon white sugar
- Salt to taste
- 2 tablespoons hot pepper sauce (such as tabasco®), or to taste
- ½ teaspoon cajun seasoning blend (such as tony chachere's), or to taste
- 4 bay leaves
- ½ teaspoon dried thyme leaves
- 1 (14.5 ounces) can stewed tomatoes
- 1 (6 ounces) can tomato sauce
- 4 teaspoons file powder, divided
- 2 tablespoons bacon drippings
- 2 (10 ounces) packages frozen cut okra, thawed
- 2 tablespoons distilled white vinegar
- 1 pound lump crabmeat
- 3 pounds uncooked medium shrimp, peeled and deveined
- 2 tablespoons worcestershire sauce

Instructions

- Make a roux by whisking the flour and 3/4 cup bacon drippings together in a large, heavy saucepan over medium-low heat to form a smooth mixture. Cook the roux, whisking constantly until it turns a rich mahogany brown color. This can take 20 to 30 minutes; watch heat carefully and whisk constantly or roux will burn. Remove from heat; continue whisking until the mixture stops cooking.
- Place the celery, onion, green bell pepper, and

garlic into the work bowl of a food processor, and pulse until the vegetables are very finely chopped. Stir the vegetables into the roux, and mix in the sausage. Bring the mixture to a simmer over medium-low heat, and cook until vegetables are tender, 10 to 15 minutes. Remove from heat, and set aside.

- Bring the water and beef bouillon cubes to a boil in a large Dutch oven or soup pot. Stir until the bouillon cubes dissolve, and whisk the roux mixture into the boiling water. Reduce heat to a simmer, and mix in the sugar, salt, hot pepper sauce, Cajun seasoning, bay leaves, thyme, stewed tomatoes, and tomato sauce. Simmer the soup over low heat for 1 hour; mix in 2 teaspoons of file gumbo powder at the 45-minute mark.
- Meanwhile, melt 2 tablespoons of bacon drippings in a skillet, and cook the okra with vinegar over medium heat for 15 minutes; remove okra with a slotted spoon, and stir into the simmering gumbo. Mix in crabmeat, shrimp, and Worcestershire sauce, and simmer until flavors have blended, 45 more minutes. Just before serving, stir in 2 more teaspoons of file gumbo powder.

Nutrition Facts

- Calories: 283; Protein 20.9g; Carbohydrates 12.1g; Fat 16.6g; Cholesterol 142.6mg; Sodium 853.1mg.

418. Shrimp Scampi With Pasta

Prep Time: 20 mins

Cook Time: 20 mins

Total Time: 40 mins

Servings: 6

Ingredient

- 1 (16 ounces) package linguine pasta
- 2 tablespoons butter
- 2 tablespoons extra-virgin olive oil
- 2 shallots, finely diced
- 2 cloves garlic, minced
- 1 pinch red pepper flakes (optional)
- 1 pound shrimp, peeled and deveined
- 1 pinch kosher salt and freshly ground pepper

- ½ cup dry white wine
- 1 lemon, juiced
- 2 tablespoons butter
- 2 tablespoons extra-virgin olive oil
- ¼ cup finely chopped fresh parsley leaves
- 1 teaspoon extra-virgin olive oil, or to taste

Instruction

- Bring a large pot of salted water to a boil; cook linguine in boiling water until nearly tender, 6 to 8 minutes. Drain.
- Melt 2 tablespoons butter with 2 tablespoons olive oil in a large skillet over medium heat. Cook and stir shallots, garlic, and red pepper flakes in the hot butter and oil until shallots are translucent, 3 to 4 minutes. Season shrimp with kosher salt and black pepper; add to the skillet and cook until pink, stirring occasionally, 2 to 3 minutes. Remove shrimp from skillet and keep warm.
- Pour white wine and lemon juice into skillet and bring to a boil while scraping the browned bits of food off of the bottom of the skillet with a wooden spoon. Melt 2 tablespoons butter in a skillet, stir 2 tablespoons olive oil into butter mixture, and bring to a simmer. Toss linguine, shrimp, and parsley in the butter mixture until coated; season with salt and black pepper. Drizzle with 1 teaspoon olive oil to serve.

Nutrition Facts

- Calories: 511; Protein 21.9g; Carbohydrates 57.5g; Fat 19.4g; Cholesterol 135.4mg; Sodium 260mg.

421. Easy Garlic-Lemon Scallops

Prep Time: 10 mins

Cook Time: 10 mins

Total Time: 20 mins

Servings: 6

Ingredient

- ¾ cup butter
- 3 tablespoons minced garlic
- 2 pounds large sea scallops
- 1 teaspoon salt
- ⅛ teaspoon pepper

- 2 tablespoons fresh lemon juice

Instructions

- Melt butter in a large skillet over medium-high heat. Stir in garlic, and cook for a few seconds until fragrant. Add scallops, and cook for several minutes on one side, then turn over, and continue cooking until firm and opaque.
- Remove scallops to a platter, then whisk salt, pepper, and lemon juice into butter. Pour sauce over scallops to serve.

Nutrition Facts

- Calories: 408; Protein 38.5g; Carbohydrates 8.9g; Fat 24.4g; Cholesterol 152.4mg; Sodium 987.9mg.

420. Perfect Ten Baked Cod

Prep Time: 10 mins

Cook Time: 25 mins

Total Time: 35 mins

Servings: 4

Ingredient

- 2 tablespoons butter
- ½ sleeve buttery round crackers (such as Ritz®), crushed
- 2 tablespoons butter
- 1 pound thick-cut cod loin
- ½ lemon, juiced
- ¼ cup dry white wine
- 1 tablespoon chopped fresh parsley
- 1 tablespoon chopped green onion
- 1 lemon, cut into wedges

Instructions

- Preheat oven to 400 degrees F (200 degrees C).
- Place 2 tablespoons butter in a microwave-safe bowl; melt in the microwave on high, about 30 seconds. Stir buttery round crackers into melted butter.
- Place remaining 2 tablespoons butter in a 7x11-inch baking dish. Melt in the preheated oven, 1 to 3 minutes. Remove dish from oven.
- Coat both sides of cod in melted butter in the baking dish.
- Bake cod in the preheated oven for 10 minutes.

Remove from oven; top with lemon juice, wine, and cracker mixture. Place back in the oven and bake until fish is opaque and flakes easily with a fork, about 10 more minutes.
- Garnish baked cod with parsley and green onion. Serve with lemon wedges.

Nutrition Facts

- Calories: 280; Protein 20.9g; Carbohydrates 9.3g; Fat 16.1g; Cholesterol 71.5mg; Sodium 282.3mg.

421. Marinated Tuna Steak

Prep Time: 10 mins

Cook Time: 11 mins

Additional Time: 30 mins

Total Time: 51 mins

Servings: 4

Ingredient

- ¼ cup orange juice
- ¼ cup soy sauce
- 2 tablespoons olive oil
- 1 tablespoon lemon juice
- 2 tablespoons chopped fresh parsley
- 1 clove garlic, minced
- ½ teaspoon chopped fresh oregano
- ½ teaspoon ground black pepper
- 4 (4 ounces) tuna steaks

Instructions

- In a large non-reactive dish, mix the orange juice, soy sauce, olive oil, lemon juice, parsley, garlic, oregano, and pepper. Place the tuna steaks in the marinade and turn to coat. Cover, and refrigerate for at least 30 minutes.
- Preheat grill for high heat.
- Lightly oil grill grate. Cook the tuna steaks for 5 to 6 minutes, then turn and baste with the marinade. Cook for an additional 5 minutes, or to the desired doneness. Discard any remaining marinade.

Nutrition Facts

- Calories: 200; Protein 27.4g; Carbohydrates

3.7g; Fat 7.9g; Cholesterol 50.6mg; Sodium 944.6mg.

422. Seared Ahi Tuna Steaks

Prep Time: 5 mins

Cook Time: 12 mins

Total Time: 17 mins

Servings: 2

Ingredient

- 2 (5 ounces) ahi tuna steaks
- 1 teaspoon kosher salt
- ¼ teaspoon cayenne pepper
- ½ tablespoon butter
- 2 tablespoons olive oil
- 1 teaspoon whole peppercorns

Instructions

Season the tuna steaks with salt and cayenne pepper.

Melt the butter with the olive oil in a skillet over medium-high heat. Cook the peppercorns in the mixture until they soften and pop about 5 minutes. Gently place the seasoned tuna in the skillet and cook to desired doneness, 1 1/2 minutes per side for rare.

Nutrition Facts

- Calories: 301; protein 33.3g; carbohydrates 0.7g; fat 17.8g; cholesterol 71.4mg; sodium 1033.6mg.

423. Easy Paella

Prep Time: 30 mins

Cook Time: 30 mins

Total Time: 1 hr

Servings: 8

Ingredient

- 2 tablespoons olive oil
- 1 tablespoon paprika
- 2 teaspoons dried oregano
- Salt and black pepper to taste
- 2 pounds skinless, boneless chicken breasts, cut into 2-inch pieces
- 2 tablespoons olive oil, divided
- 3 cloves garlic, crushed
- 1 teaspoon crushed red pepper flakes

- 2 cups uncooked short-grain white rice
- 1 pinch saffron threads
- 1 bay leaf
- ½ bunch italian flat-leaf parsley, chopped
- 1-quart chicken stock
- 2 lemons, zested
- 2 tablespoons olive oil
- 1 spanish onion, chopped
- 1 red bell pepper, coarsely chopped
- 1 pound chorizo sausage, casings removed and crumbled
- 1 pound shrimp, peeled and deveined

Instructions

- In a medium bowl, mix 2 tablespoons of olive oil, paprika, oregano, and salt and pepper. Stir in chicken pieces to coat. Cover, and refrigerate.
- Heat 2 tablespoons olive oil in a large skillet or paella pan over medium heat. Stir in garlic, red pepper flakes, and rice. Cook, stirring, to coat the rice with oil, about 3 minutes. Stir in saffron threads, bay leaf, parsley, chicken stock, and lemon zest. Bring to a boil, cover, and reduce heat to medium-low. Simmer 20 minutes.
- Meanwhile, heat 2 tablespoons olive oil in a separate skillet over medium heat. Stir in marinated chicken and onion; cook 5 minutes. Stir in bell pepper and sausage; cook 5 minutes. Stir in shrimp; cook, turning the shrimp until both sides are pink.
- Spread rice mixture onto a serving tray. Top with meat and seafood mixture.

Nutrition Facts

- Calories: 736; Protein 55.7g; Carbohydrates 45.7g; Fat 35.1g; Cholesterol 202.5mg; Sodium 1204.2mg.

424. Simple Garlic Shrimp

Prep Time: 15 mins

Cook Time: 10 mins

Total Time: 25 mins

Servings: 4

Ingredient

- 1 ½ tablespoon olive oil
- 1 pound shrimp, peeled and deveined

- Salt to taste
- 6 cloves garlic, finely minced
- ¼ teaspoon red pepper flakes
- 3 tablespoons lemon juice
- 1 tablespoon caper brine
- 1 ½ teaspoon cold butter
- ⅓ cup chopped italian flat-leaf parsley, divided
- 1 ½ tablespoon cold butter
- Water, as needed

Instructions

- Heat olive oil in a heavy skillet over high heat until it just begins to smoke. Place shrimp in an even layer on the bottom of the pan and cook for 1 minute without stirring.
- Season shrimp with salt; cook and stir until shrimp begin to turn pink about 1 minute.
- Stir in garlic and red pepper flakes; cook and stir for 1 minute. Stir in lemon juice, caper brine, 1 1/2 teaspoon cold butter, and half the parsley.
- Cook until the butter has melted, about 1 minute, then turn heat to low and stir in 1 1/2 tablespoon cold butter. Cook and stir until all butter has melted to form a thick sauce and shrimp are pink and opaque about 2 to 3 minutes.
- Remove shrimp with a slotted spoon and transfer to a bowl; continue to cook butter sauce, adding water 1 teaspoon at a time if too thick, about 2 minutes. Season with salt to taste.
- Serve shrimp topped with the pan sauce. Garnish with remaining flat-leaf parsley.

Nutrition Facts

- Calories: 196; Protein 19.1g; Carbohydrates 2.9g; Fat 12g; Cholesterol 188.1mg; Sodium 243.7mg.

425. Baked Haddock

Prep Time: 10 mins

Cook Time: 15 mins

Total Time: 25 mins

Servings: 4

Ingredient

- ¾ cup milk
- 2 teaspoons salt

- ¾ cup bread crumbs
- ¼ cup grated Parmesan cheese
- ¼ teaspoon ground dried thyme
- 4 haddock fillets
- ¼ cup butter, melted

Instructions

- Preheat oven to 500 degrees F (260 degrees C).
- In a small bowl, combine the milk and salt. In a separate bowl, mix the bread crumbs, Parmesan cheese, and thyme. Dip the haddock fillets in the milk, then press into the crumb mixture to coat. Place haddock fillets in a glass baking dish, and drizzle with melted butter.
- Bake on the top rack of the preheated oven until the fish flakes easily, about 15 minutes.

Nutrition Facts

- Calories: 325; Protein 27.7g; Carbohydrates 17g; Fat 15.7g; Cholesterol 103.3mg; Sodium 1565.2mg.

426. Pan-Seared Tilapia

Prep Time: 10 mins

Cook Time: 8 mins

Total Time: 18 mins

Servings: 4

Ingredient

- 4 (4 ounce) fillets tilapia
- Salt and pepper to taste
- ½ cup all-purpose flour
- 1 tablespoon olive oil
- 2 tablespoons unsalted butter, melted

Instructions

- Rinse tilapia fillets in cold water and pat dry with paper towels. Season both sides of each fillet with salt and pepper. Place the flour in a shallow dish; gently press each fillet into the flour to coat and shake off the excess flour.
- Heat the olive oil in a skillet over medium-high heat; cook the tilapia in the hot oil until the fish flakes easily with a fork, about 4 minutes per side. Brush the melted butter onto the tilapia at the last minute before removing it from the skillet. Serve immediately.

Nutrition Facts

- Calories: 249; Protein 24.6g; Carbohydrates 11.9g; Fat 10.8g; Cholesterol 56.3mg; Sodium 50.9mg.

427. Classic Fish And Chips

Prep Time: 10 mins

Cook Time: 25 mins

Additional Time: 10 mins

Total Time: 45 mins

Servings: 4

Ingredient

- 4 large potatoes, peeled and cut into strips
- 1 cup all-purpose flour
- 1 teaspoon baking powder
- 1 teaspoon salt
- 1 teaspoon ground black pepper
- 1 cup milk
- 1 egg
- 1-quart vegetable oil for frying
- 1 ½ pounds cod fillets

Instructions

- Place potatoes in a medium-size bowl of cold water. In a separate medium-size mixing bowl, mix flour, baking powder, salt, and pepper. Stir in the milk and egg; stir until the mixture is smooth. Let mixture stand for 20 minutes.
- Preheat the oil in a large pot or electric skillet to 350 degrees F (175 degrees C).
- Fry the potatoes in the hot oil until they are tender. Drain them on paper towels.
- Dredge the fish in the batter, one piece at a time, and place them in the hot oil. Fry until the fish is golden brown. If necessary, increase the heat to maintain the 350 degrees F (175 degrees C) temperature. Drain well on paper towels.
- Fry the potatoes again for 1 to 2 minutes for added crispness.

Nutrition Facts

- 782 Calories: 787; Protein 44.6g; Carbohydrates 91.9g; Fat 26.2g; Cholesterol 124.6mg; Sodium 860.7mg.

428. Linguine With Clam Sauce

Prep Time: 20 mins

Cook Time: 12 mins

Total Time: 32 mins

Servings: 4

Ingredient

- 2 (6.5 ounces) cans minced clams, with juice
- ¼ cup butter
- ½ cup vegetable oil
- ½ teaspoon minced garlic
- 1 tablespoon dried parsley
- Ground black pepper to taste
- ¼ tablespoon dried basil
- 1 (16 ounces) package linguini pasta

Instructions

- Bring a large pot of salted water to boil. Cook pasta according to package directions.
- Combine clams with juice, butter, oil, minced garlic, parsley, basil, and pepper in a large saucepan. Place over medium heat until boiling. Serve warm over pasta.

Nutrition Facts

Calories: 88; Protein 37.2g; Carbohydrates 84.6g; Fat 42.7g; Cholesterol 92.3mg; Sodium 189.6mg.

429. Pan Seared Salmon I

Prep Time: 10 mins

Cook Time: 10 mins

Total Time: 20 mins

Servings: 4

Ingredient

- 4 (6 ounces) fillets of salmon
- 2 tablespoons olive oil
- 2 tablespoons capers
- ⅛ teaspoon salt
- ⅛ teaspoon ground black pepper
- 4 slices lemon

Instructions

- Preheat a large heavy skillet over medium heat

for 3 minutes.

- Coat salmon with olive oil. Place in skillet, and increase heat to high. Cook for 3 minutes. Sprinkle with capers, and salt and pepper. Turn salmon over, and cook for 5 minutes, or until browned. Salmon is done when it flakes easily with a fork.
- Transfer salmon to individual plates, and garnish with lemon slices.

Nutrition Facts

- Per Serving: 371 Calories; Protein 33.7g; Carbohydrates 1.7g; Fat 25.1g; Cholesterol 99.1mg; Sodium 299.8mg.

430. Easy Extremely Garlic Shrimp

Prep Time: 10 mins

Cook Time: 10 mins

Total Time: 20 mins

Servings: 4

Ingredient

- ⅓ cup butter
- 2 teaspoons minced garlic
- 1 pound large shrimp, peeled and deveined
- 3 tablespoons garlic salt, or to taste
- 3 tablespoons garlic powder, or to taste
- ½ lemon, juiced, or to taste

Instructions

- Melt butter in a large skillet over medium heat; cook and stir minced garlic until lightly browned. Add shrimp; season with garlic salt and garlic powder. Pour lemon juice over shrimp. Continue to cook and stir until shrimp are bright pink on the outside and the meat is no longer transparent in the center, 5 to 10 minutes.

Nutrition Facts

- Calories: 254; Protein 20.1g; Carbohydrates 6.9g; Fat 16.4g; Cholesterol 213.2mg; Sodium 4386.4mg.

431. Spicy Grilled Shrimp

Prep Time: 15 mins

Cook Time: 6 mins

Total Time: 21 mins

Servings: 6

Ingredient

- 1 large clove garlic
- 1 teaspoon coarse salt
- ½ teaspoon cayenne pepper
- 1 teaspoon paprika
- 2 tablespoons olive oil
- 2 teaspoons lemon juice
- 2 pounds large shrimp, peeled and deveined
- 8 wedges lemon, for garnish

Instructions

- Preheat grill for medium heat.
- In a small bowl, crush the garlic with the salt. Mix in cayenne pepper and paprika, and then stir in olive oil and lemon juice to form a paste. In a large bowl, toss shrimp with garlic paste until evenly coated.
- Lightly oil grill grate. Cook shrimp for 2 to 3 minutes per side, or until opaque. Transfer to a serving dish, garnish with lemon wedges and serve.

Nutrition Facts

- Calories: 164; Protein 25.1g; Carbohydrates 2.7g; Fat 5.9g; Cholesterol 230.4mg; Sodium 585.7mg.

432. Sheet Pan Salmon and Bell Pepper Dinner

Prep Time: 20 mins

Cook Time: 10 mins

Total Time: 30 mins

Servings: 4

Ingredient

- 2 tablespoons olive oil
- 4 (3 ounce) fillets salmon fillets
- 2 red bell peppers, chopped
- 1 yellow bell pepper, chopped
- 1 onion, sliced

Sauce:

- 6 tablespoons lemon juice
- 3 tablespoons olive oil
- 2 tablespoons water
- 1 tablespoon maple syrup
- 5 cloves garlic
- 1 ½ teaspoons salt
- 1 ½ teaspoon red pepper flakes
- 1 teaspoon ground cumin
- ½ bunch fresh parsley, chopped
- 1 lemon, sliced

Instructions

- Preheat oven to 400 degrees F (200 degrees C). Grease a sheet pan with 2 tablespoons olive oil.
- Place salmon fillets, red and yellow bell peppers, and onion on the prepared sheet pan.
- Combine lemon juice, 3 tablespoons olive oil, water, maple syrup, garlic, salt, red pepper flakes, cumin, and parsley in a small bowl. Drizzle 2/3 of the sauce over the ingredients on the sheet pan.
- Bake in the preheated oven until salmon is cooked through and flakes easily with a fork, 10 to 15 minutes.
- Serve with lemon slices and remaining sauce.

Nutrition Facts

- Calories: 337; Protein 18.8g; Carbohydrates 16.9g; Fat 22.9g; Cholesterol 47mg; Sodium 920.7mg.

433. Maple Sriracha Salmon

Prep Time: 30 Min

Cook Time: 15 Min

Total Time: 45 Min

Servings: 15

Ingredients

- 1 Tbsp. brown sugar
- 2 green onions, thinly sliced
- 2 Tbsp. lime juice
- 1 tsp. finely grated lime zest
- 1 Tbsp. maple syrup
- 3 lb. salmon fillet
- ½ tsp. salt
- 2 Tbsp. sriracha sauce

Directions

- Preheat your grill on setting #4. Whisk together sriracha, lime juice, maple syrup, brown sugar, lime zest, and salt. Brush over top of salmon and let stand for 20 minutes.
- Grill, covered and without turning, for 15 to 18 minutes or until grill-marked and fish flakes easily when tested with a fork. Sprinkle with green onions before serving.

Nutrition Facts

- Calories: 327; Protein 33.7g; Carbohydrates 4g; Fat 18.5g; Cholesterol 99.1mg; Sodium 810.8mg.

33. Lemon Garlic Tilapia

Prep Time: 10 mins

Cook Time: 30 mins

Total Time: 40 mins

Servings: 4

Ingredient

- 4 each tilapia fillets
- 3 tablespoons fresh lemon juice
- 1 tablespoon butter, melted
- 1 clove garlic, finely chopped
- 1 teaspoon dried parsley flakes
- 1 dash pepper to taste

Instructions

- Preheat oven to 375 degrees F (190 degrees C). Spray a baking dish with non-stick cooking spray.
- Rinse tilapia fillets under cool water, and pat dry with paper towels.
- Place fillets in baking dish. Pour lemon juice over fillets, then drizzle butter on top. Sprinkle with garlic, parsley, and pepper.
- Bake in the preheated oven until the fish is white and flakes when pulled apart with a fork, about 30 minutes.

Nutrition Facts

- calories: 142; protein 23.1g; carbohydrates 1.4g; fat 4.4g; cholesterol 49.1mg; sodium 93mg.

434. Szechwan Shrimp

Prep Time: 10 mins

Cook Time: 10 mins

Total Time: 20 mins

Servings: 4

Ingredient

- 4 tablespoons water
- 2 tablespoons ketchup
- 1 tablespoon soy sauce
- 2 teaspoons cornstarch
- 1 teaspoon honey
- ½ teaspoon crushed red pepper
- ¼ teaspoon ground ginger
- 1 tablespoon vegetable oil
- ¼ cup sliced green onions
- 4 cloves garlic, minced
- 12 ounces cooked shrimp, tails removed

Instructions

- In a bowl, stir together water, ketchup, soy sauce, cornstarch, honey, crushed red pepper, and ground ginger. Set aside.
- Heat oil in a large skillet over medium-high heat. Stir in green onions and garlic; cook for 30 seconds. Stir in shrimp, and toss to coat with oil. Stir in sauce. Cook and stir until sauce are bubbly and thickened.

Nutrition Facts

- Calories: 142; Protein 18.3g; Carbohydrates 6.7g; Fat 4.4g; Cholesterol 163.8mg; Sodium 499.5mg.

435. Lemony Steamed Fish

Prep Time: 15 mins

Cook Time: 30 mins

Total Time: 45 mins

Servings: 6

Ingredient

- 6 (6 ounces) halibut fillets
- 1 tablespoon dried dill weed
- 1 tablespoon onion powder
- 2 teaspoons dried parsley
- ¼ teaspoon paprika
- 1 pinch seasoned salt, or more to taste
- 1 pinch lemon pepper
- 1 pinch garlic powder
- 2 tablespoons lemon juice

Instructions

- Preheat oven to 375 degrees F (190 degrees C).
- Cut 6 foil squares large enough for each fillet.
- Center fillets on the foil squares and sprinkle each with dill weed, onion powder, parsley, paprika, seasoned salt, lemon pepper, and garlic powder. Sprinkle lemon juice over each fillet. Fold foil over fillets to make a pocket and fold the edges to seal. Place sealed packets on a baking sheet.
- Bake in the preheated oven until fish flakes easily with a fork, about 30 minutes.

Nutrition Facts

- Calories: 142; protein 29.7g; carbohydrates 1.9g; fat 1.1g; cholesterol 60.7mg; sodium 183.9mg.

436. Salmon With Fruit Salsa

Prep Time: 15 mins

Cook Time: 40 mins

Total Time: 55 mins

Servings: 4

Ingredient

- 1 pound salmon steaks
- 1 lemon, juiced
- 1 tablespoon chopped fresh rosemary
- Salt and pepper to taste
- 1 lemon, sliced
- ⅓ cup water
- ¼ cup diced fresh pineapple
- ¼ cup minced onion
- 3 cloves garlic, minced
- 2 fresh jalapeno peppers, diced
- 1 tomato, diced

- ½ cup pineapple juice
- ¼ cup diced red bell pepper
- ¼ cup diced yellow bell pepper

Instructions

- Preheat oven to 350 degrees F (175 degrees C).
- Arrange salmon steaks in a shallow baking dish, and coat with lemon juice. Season with rosemary, salt, and pepper. Top with lemon slices. Pour water into the dish.
- Bake for 30 to 40 minutes in the preheated oven, or until easily flaked with a fork.
- In a medium bowl, mix pineapple, onion, garlic, jalapeno, tomato, pineapple juice, red bell pepper, and yellow bell pepper. Cover, and refrigerate while fish is baking. Top fish with salsa to serve.

Nutritional Value

- Calories: 217; Protein 25.9g; Carbohydrates 15.7g; Fat 7g; Cholesterol 50.4mg; Sodium 198.3mg.

437. Mainely Fish

Prep Time: 30 mins

Cook Time: 20 mins

Total Time: 50 mins

Servings: 6

Ingredient

- 6 (3 ounce) fillets haddock
- salt and pepper to taste
- 4 Roma (plum) tomatoes, thinly sliced
- 1 red bell pepper, thinly sliced
- 1 yellow bell pepper, thinly sliced
- 1 small onion, thinly sliced
- 5 tablespoons capers
- 8 tablespoons chopped fresh parsley
- 6 tablespoons fresh lemon juice
- 6 tablespoons extra virgin olive oil

Instructions

- Preheat oven to 400 degrees F (200 degrees C).
- Center each piece of fish on an individual piece of aluminum foil (large enough to enclose the fish when folded). Sprinkle each piece of fish with salt and pepper. Divide the sliced

tomatoes, onion, and red and yellow peppers between the 6 pieces of fish, and place them on top of the fillets. Sprinkle evenly with the capers and parsley. Drizzle each fillet with 1 tablespoon of olive oil and 1 tablespoon of lemon juice.
- Fold and seal the foil into a packet and place on a baking sheet. Leave 2 inches between each packet for even cooking.
- Bake in preheated oven for 20 minutes.
- Let rest for 5 minutes and unwrap. One packet per person.

Nutrition Facts

- Calories;: 226 Protein 17.3g; Carbohydrates 7.1g; Fat 14.4g; Cholesterol 48.4mg;

438. Grilled Tuna Teriyaki

Prep Time: 15 mins

Cook Time: 10 mins

Additional Time: 30 mins

Total Time: 55 mins

Servings: 4

Ingredient

- 2 tablespoons light soy sauce
- 1 tablespoon Chinese rice wine
- 1 tablespoon minced fresh ginger root
- 1 large clove garlic, minced
- 4 (6 ounces) tuna steaks (about 3/4 inch thick)
- 1 tablespoon vegetable oil

Instructions

- Stir soy sauce, rice wine, ginger, and garlic together in a shallow dish. Place tuna in the marinade, and turn to coat. Cover the dish and refrigerate for at least 30 minutes.
- Preheat grill for medium-high heat.
- Remove tuna from marinade and discard remaining liquid. Brush both sides of steaks with oil.
- Cook tuna on the preheated grill until cooked through, 3 to 6 minutes per side.

Nutrition Facts

- Calories: 227; Protein 40.4g; Carbohydrates 1.5g; Fat 5.1g; Cholesterol 77.1mg; Sodium

328.6mg.

439. Anaheim Fish Tacos

Prep Time: 15 mins

Cook Time: 30 mins

Total Time: 45 mins

Servings: 6

Ingredient

- 1 teaspoon vegetable oil
- 1 anaheim chile pepper, chopped
- 1 leek, chopped
- 2 cloves garlic, crushed
- Salt and pepper to taste
- 1 cup chicken broth
- 2 large tomatoes, diced
- ½ teaspoon ground cumin
- 1 ½ pound halibut fillets
- 1 lime
- 12 corn tortillas

Instructions

- Heat the oil in a large skillet over medium heat, and saute the chile, leek, and garlic until tender and lightly browned. Season with salt and pepper.
- Mix the chicken broth and tomatoes into the skillet, and season with cumin. Bring to a boil. Reduce heat to low. Place the halibut into the mixture. Sprinkle with lime juice. Cook 15 to 20 minutes until the halibut is easily flaked with a fork. Wrap in warmed corn tortillas to serve.

Nutrition Facts

- Calories: 273; Protein 27.7g; Carbohydrates 29.9g; Fat 5.1g; Cholesterol 36.3mg; Sodium 285.8mg.

440. Batter Fried Basa Fish

Prep Time: 15 mins

Cook Time: 20 mins

Total Time: 35 mins

Ingredients

- Boneless Basa fillet – 2
- All-purpose flour (Maida) – 1 cup
- Egg – 2
- Milk – 1 cup
- Salt to taste
- Vegetable oil – 1 tsp + more for shallow frying
- Freshly crushed black pepper – ½ tsp or more as per taste

Instructions

- Wash the fish fillet well. I used frozen fillets, so I had to thaw them completely before starting. Season the fillet with a pinch of salt on both sides.
- In a big bowl, combine the flour, eggs, milk, salt [approximately a little less than ½ teaspoon will do], and 1 teaspoon of oil.
- Whisk them well to make a thick and smooth batter. The batter must be very smooth without any lumps. Consistency should be such that it should adhere to the fish fillet covering all sides and does not drip off completely. [See notes below for more details.]
- Heat oil in a non-stick frying pan. I didn't deep fry my fish; I did shallow frying which worked quite well.
- Dip a fillet into the batter. Take it out, let the excess batter drip off and when the oil is quite hot, tip in the batter-coated fish on the pan. If you find that the batter is flowing out of the fillet, take a little amount of batter from the bowl using a spoon and smear it on the top of the fillet. Do not move the fish for 2 minutes and let it cook on medium-low flame.
- When the bottom side of the fillet turns golden brown after about 5 minutes on medium flame, carefully flip the fillet and fry the other side till it turns golden brown. It will take around 5 to 6 minutes on each side but it also depends on the thickness of the fillets you are using. Mine took about 6 minutes on each side. To check the doneness, take a toothpick and prick the fish in the middle. If it goes in very easily without any resistance, your fish is done. Else give it two more minutes.
- Once done, take out the batter-fried basa fillets on a plate lined with an absorbent kitchen towel to soak the excess oil.
- Serve the batter-fried basa warm with tartar sauce on the side. Enjoy!

Nutrition Facts

- Calories: 142; Protein 18.3g; Carbohydrates 6.7g; Fat 4.4g; Cholesterol 163.8mg; Sodium 499.5mg.

441. Lemon-Garlic Marinated Shrimp

Total Time: 10 mins

Servings: 12

Ingredient

- 3 tablespoons minced garlic
- 2 tablespoons extra-virgin olive oil
- ¼ cup lemon juice
- ¼ cup minced fresh parsley
- ½ teaspoon kosher salt
- ½ teaspoon pepper
- 1 ¼ pounds cooked shrimp

Instructions

Place garlic and oil in a small skillet and cook over medium heat until fragrant, about 1 minute. Add lemon juice, parsley, salt, and pepper. Toss with shrimp in a large bowl. Chill until ready to serve.

Nutrition Facts

- Calories: 82; Protein 11g; Carbohydrates 1.9g; Dietary Fiber 0.1g; Sugars 0.2g; Fat 3.2g;; Calcium 49.3mg; Iron 0.3mg; Magnesium 19.1mg; Potassium 102.3mg; Sodium 495.3mg.

442. Shrimp Poke

Active Time: 30 mins

Total Time: 30 mins

Servings: 4

Ingredient

- ¾ cup thinly sliced scallion greens
- ¼ cup reduced-sodium tamari
- 1 ½ tablespoons mirin
- 1 ½ tablespoon toasted (dark) sesame oil
- 1 tablespoon white sesame seeds
- 2 teaspoons grated fresh ginger
- ½ teaspoon crushed red pepper (Optional)
- 12 ounces cooked shrimp, cut into 1/2-inch pieces

- 2 cups cooked brown rice
- 2 tablespoons rice vinegar
- 2 cups sliced cherry tomatoes
- 2 cups diced avocado
- ¼ cup chopped cilantro
- ¼ cup toasted black sesame seeds

Instructions

- Whisk scallion greens, tamari, mirin, oil, white sesame seeds, ginger, and crushed red pepper, if using, in a medium bowl. Set aside 2 tablespoons of the sauce in a small bowl. Add shrimp to the sauce in the medium bowl and gently toss to coat.
- Combine rice and vinegar in a large bowl. Divide among 4 bowls and top each with 3/4 cup shrimp, 1/2 cup each tomato and avocado, and 1 tablespoon each cilantro and black sesame seeds. Drizzle with the reserved sauce and serve.

Nutrition Facts

- Calories: 460; Protein 28.9g; Carbohydrates 40.2g; Dietary Fiber 9.9g; Sugars 4.5g; Fat 22.1g; Saturated Fat 3.2g;; Calcium 113.2mg; Iron 3.2mg; Magnesium 145.1mg; Potassium 939.3mg; Sodium 860.6mg.

443. Creamy Lemon Pasta With Shrimp

Active Time: 20 mins

Total Time: 20 mins

Servings: 4

Ingredients

- 8 ounces whole-wheat fettuccine
- 1 tablespoon extra-virgin olive oil
- 12 ounces sustainably sourced peeled and deveined raw shrimp (26-30 per pound)
- 2 tablespoons unsalted butter
- 1 tablespoon finely chopped garlic
- ¼ teaspoon crushed red pepper
- 4 cups loosely packed arugula
- ¼ cup whole-milk plain yogurt
- 1 teaspoon lemon zest
- 2 tablespoons lemon juice
- ¼ teaspoon salt
- ⅓ cup grated Parmesan cheese, plus more for

garnish
- ¼ cup thinly sliced fresh basil

Instructions

- Bring 7 cups of water to a boil. Add fettuccine, stirring to separate the noodles. Cook until just tender, 7 to 9 minutes. Reserve 1/2 cup of the cooking water and drain.
- Meanwhile, heat oil in a large nonstick skillet over medium-high heat. Add shrimp and cook, stirring occasionally, until pink and curled, 2 to 3 minutes. Transfer the shrimp to a bowl.
- Add butter to the pan and reduce heat to medium. Add garlic and crushed red pepper; cook, stirring often, until the garlic is fragrant, about 1 minute. Add arugula and cook, stirring, until wilted, about 1 minute. Reduce heat to low. Add the fettuccine, yogurt, lemon zest, and the reserved cooking water, 1/4 cup at a time, tossing well, until the fettuccine is fully coated and creamy. Add the shrimp, lemon juice, and salt, tossing to coat the fettuccine. Remove from the heat and toss with Parmesan.
- Serve the fettuccine topped with basil and more Parmesan, if desired.

Nutrition Facts

- Calories: 403; Protein 28.3g; Carbohydrates 45.5g; Dietary Fiber 5.8g; Sugars 3g; Fat 13.9g;; Calcium 207.5mg; Iron 3mg; Magnesium 124.7mg; Potassium 626.4mg; Sodium 396.3mg.

444. Grilled Blackened Shrimp Tacos

Active Time: 20 mins

Total Time: 20 mins

Servings: 4

Ingredient

- 1 ripe avocado
- 1 tablespoon lime juice
- 1 small clove garlic, grated
- ¼ teaspoon salt
- 1 pound large raw shrimp (16-20 count), peeled and deveined
- 2 tablespoons salt-free Cajun spice blend
- 8 corn tortillas, warmed
- 2 cups iceberg lettuce, chopped

- ½ cup fresh cilantro leaves
- ½ cup prepared pico de gallo

Instructions

- Preheat grill to medium-high.
- Mash avocado with a fork in a small bowl. Add lime juice, garlic, and salt and stir to combine.
- Pat shrimp dry. Toss the shrimp with Cajun seasoning in a medium bowl. Thread onto four 10- to 12-inch metal skewers. Grill, turning once until the shrimp are just cooked through, about 4 minutes total.
- Serve the shrimp in tortillas, topped with guacamole, lettuce, cilantro, and pico de gallo.

Nutrition Facts

- Calories: 286; Protein 24g; Carbohydrates 30.4g; Dietary Fiber 6.0g; Sugars 3.5g; Fat 9.3g; Calcium 117.8mg; Iron 1.6mg; Magnesium 87.2mg; Potassium 662.1mg; Sodium 442.7mg;

445. Moqueca (Seafood & Coconut Chowder)

Active Time: 30 mins

Total Time: 30 mins

Servings: 8

Ingredient

- 1 pound fresh crabmeat (preferably claw meat), cleaned and picked over
- 1 pound raw shrimp (16-20 per pound), peeled and deveined if desired
- ¼ cup lemon juice
- 1 ½ tablespoons dendê (red palm oil; see Tip) or canola oil
- 3 cups sliced red bell peppers
- 2 ½ cups sliced green bell peppers
- 2 ½ cups sliced red onions
- ½ cup minced fresh cilantro, plus more for garnish
- 4 large cloves garlic, minced
- ¼ cup tomato paste
- ¾ teaspoon salt
- ¾ teaspoon ground pepper
- 2 14-ounce cans of coconut milk
- 2 cups clam juice or fish stock
- 4 cups cooked brown rice

Instructions

- Combine crab, shrimp, and lemon juice in a medium bowl.
- Heat oil in a large pot over medium-high heat. Add red peppers, green peppers, and onions; cook, stirring occasionally, until beginning to soften, about 4 minutes. Add cilantro, garlic, tomato paste, salt, and pepper; cook, stirring, for 1 minute. Add coconut milk and clam juice (or fish stock) and bring to a simmer. Reduce heat to maintain a simmer, cover, and cook until the peppers are softened, 8 to 10 minutes.
- Add the crab and shrimp and return to a simmer over medium heat. Cover and cook until the shrimp is cooked through, 3 to 4 minutes more. Serve the chowder over rice. Garnish with cilantro, if desired.

Nutrition Facts

- Calories: 485 Fat 26g; Cholesterol 112mg; Sodium 686mg; Carbohydrates 39g; Dietary Fiber 5g; Protein 28g; Sugars 5g; Saturated Fat 20g.

446. Brodetto Di Pesce (Adriatic-Style Seafood Stew)

Active Time: 45 mins

Total Time: 1 hr 15 mins

Servings: 8

Ingredient

- ¼ Cup extra-virgin olive oil, plus more for serving
- 1 medium yellow or red onion, finely diced
- ⅓ cup finely diced celery
- ⅓ cup finely chopped flat-leaf parsley, plus more for serving
- 4 cloves garlic, lightly crushed, divided
- ½ teaspoon crushed red pepper
- ¾ cup dry white wine
- 3 sprigs of fresh oregano
- 3 fresh bay leaves
- 2 1/2 cups clam juice or seafood stock, divided
- 2 cups petite diced or crushed canned tomatoes
- 2 pounds littleneck clams, scrubbed
- 1 pound mussels, scrubbed
- 1 pound cleaned squid tubes or tentacles, tubes cut into rings
- 1 pound meaty white fish, such as cod, monkfish, rockfish, snapper, or a combination, cut into 2-inch pieces
- 2 tablespoons lemon juice
- 8 diagonal slices whole-grain baguette (1/2 inch thick), plus more for serving

Instructions

- Cook oil, onion, celery, parsley, 3 cloves garlic, and crushed red pepper in a large pot over medium-low heat, stirring occasionally, until the vegetables are very tender, about 15 minutes.
- Increase heat to medium-high and add wine; cook for 1 minute. Add oregano and bay leaves; cook for 30 seconds. Add 2 cups clam juice (or stock) and tomatoes and bring to a boil over high heat. Reduce heat to a simmer and cook until slightly thickened, 20 to 25 minutes.
- Add clams and mussels; cover and cook for 5 minutes. Add squid, fish, and the remaining 1/2 cup clam juice (or stock). Cover and cook until the fish is just cooked through, 8 to 12 minutes. Remove from heat and gently stir in lemon juice.
- Meanwhile, preheat the broiler to high.
- Place bread on a rimmed baking sheet and broil until lightly browned for 1 to 2 minutes. Immediately rub with the remaining garlic clove.
- Place one slice of bread in each of 8 shallow bowls and top with the stew. Serve with more oil, parsley, and bread, if desired.

Nutrition Facts

- Calories: 334; Protein 31g; Carbohydrates 25.7g; Dietary Fiber 2.1g; Sugars 4.2g; Fat 10.2g; Saturated Fat 1.5g; Calcium 97.2mg; Iron 5.3mg; Magnesium 77.1mg; Potassium 902.6mg; Sodium 770.3mg.

447. Seafood Linguine

Total Time: 35 mins

Servings: 4

Ingredient

- 8 ounces whole-wheat linguine, or spaghetti
- 2 tablespoons extra-virgin olive oil
- 4 cloves garlic, chopped
- 1 tablespoon chopped shallot
- 1 28-ounce can diced tomatoes, drained
- ½ cup white wine

- ½ teaspoon salt
- ¼ teaspoon freshly ground pepper
- 12 littleneck or small cherrystone clams, (about 1 pound), scrubbed
- 8 ounces dry sea scallops
- 8 ounces tilapia, or other flaky white fish, cut into 1-inch strips
- 1 tablespoon chopped fresh marjoram or 1 teaspoon dried, plus more for garnish
- 1/4 cup grated Parmesan cheese, (optional)

Instructions

- Bring a large pot of water to a boil. Add pasta and cook until just tender, 8 to 10 minutes, or according to package directions. Drain and rinse.
- Meanwhile, heat oil in a large skillet over medium heat. Add garlic and shallot and cook, stirring, until beginning to soften, about 1 minute.
- Increase the heat to medium-high. Add tomatoes, wine, salt, and pepper. Bring to a simmer and cook for 1 minute. Add clams, cover, and cook for 2 minutes. Stir in scallops, fish, and marjoram. Cover and cook until the scallops and fish are cooked through and the clams have opened, 3 to 5 minutes more. (Discard any clams that don't open.)
- Spoon the sauce and clams over the pasta and sprinkle with additional marjoram and Parmesan (if using).

Nutrition Facts

- Calories: 460; Protein 34.5g; Carbohydrates 55.8g; Dietary Fiber 8.2g; Sugars 7.5g; Fat 9.5g; Saturated Fat 1.6g; Calcium 86.5mg; Iron 4.5mg; Magnesium 122.1mg; Potassium 474.9mg; Sodium 1173.3mg.

---

448. Seafood Paella With Spring Vegetables

Active Time: 1 hr 15 mins

Total Time: 1 hr 35 mins

Servings: 6

Ingredient

- 6 tablespoons extra-virgin olive oil, divided
- 2 cups diced onion
- 1 cup diced fennel

- 3 medium tomatoes, grated on the large holes of a box grater (skins discarded)
- 4 cloves garlic, thinly sliced
- 2 tablespoons white-wine vinegar
- 1 teaspoon sea salt, divided
- ½ teaspoon ground pepper
- ½ teaspoon crushed red pepper
- Pinch of saffron
- 1 large fresh artichoke
- 1 cup Calasparra rice or other paella rice
- 2 cups seafood stock
- 1 cup green beans, trimmed and cut into 2-inch pieces
- 4 ounces squid bodies, sliced into rings
- 6-12 clams and/or mussels, scrubbed
- 8 ounces skinned monkfish or cod, cut into 1-inch-thick pieces

Instructions

- Heat 3 tablespoons oil in a 13- to 14-inch paella pan over medium-high heat. Add onion and fennel; cook, stirring often, until the onion is translucent, about 5 minutes. Add tomatoes, garlic, vinegar, 1/2 teaspoon salt, pepper, crushed red pepper, and saffron. Reduce heat to maintain a simmer and cook, stirring occasionally, until the tomato liquid has evaporated, 20 to 25 minutes.
- Meanwhile, clean artichoke. Cut lengthwise into 6 wedges. Heat 2 tablespoons oil in a large skillet over medium heat until very hot but not smoking. Add the artichoke wedges; sprinkle with 1/8 teaspoon salt and cook until browned, about 2 minutes per side. Transfer to a plate.
- Preheat oven to 375 degrees F.
- When the tomato liquid has evaporated, add rice to the paella pan, increase heat to medium, and cook, stirring, for 2 minutes. Add stock. Turn on a second burner so both the front and rear burner on one side of the stove are on; bring to a boil over high heat.
- Spread the rice evenly in the pan and nestle the artichokes and beans into it. Reduce heat to maintain a low simmer and cook for 10 minutes, rotating and shifting the pan around the burners periodically to help the rice cook evenly. Season squid with 1/8 teaspoon salt and place on the rice. Cook, without stirring but continuing to

rotate the pan, for 5 minutes more.

- Nestle clams and/or mussels into the rice with the open edges facing up. Season fish with the remaining 1/4 teaspoon salt and place on top of the rice. Remove the paella from the heat and very carefully cover the pan with foil.
- Transfer the pan to the oven and bake for 10 minutes. Let stand, covered, for 10 minutes before serving.

To Prep A Fresh Artichoke:

1. Trim 1/2 to 1 inch from the stem end. Peel the stem with a vegetable peeler.

2. Trim 1/2 inch off the top.

3. Remove the small, tough outer leaves from the stem end and snip all spiky tips from the remaining outer leaves using kitchen shears.

4. Cut in half lengthwise and scoop out the fuzzy choke with a melon baller or grapefruit spoon.

Keep artichokes from browning by rubbing the cut edges with a lemon half or putting them in a large bowl of ice water with lemon juice.

Nutrition Facts

354 calories; protein 16.1g; carbohydrates 38.2g; dietary fiber 4.7g; sugars 5.2g; fat 15.3g; saturated fat 2.3g; calcium 65.6mg; iron 1.7mg; magnesium 51.4mg; potassium 695.1mg; sodium 695.3mg;

449. Spaghetti With Garlic & Clam Sauce

Total Time: 45 mins

Servings: 8

Ingredient

- 2 heads garlic
- 28 fresh littleneck clams, scrubbed and rinsed well
- ¾ cup cold water
- 5 tablespoons extra-virgin olive oil, divided
- 2 tablespoons all-purpose flour
- 1 cup dry white wine, such as Pinot Grigio
- 1 cup chopped fresh parsley plus 2 tablespoons, divided
- 1 tablespoon chopped fresh tarragon
- ¾ teaspoon freshly ground pepper, divided
- 1/8 teaspoon crushed red pepper (optional)
- 1 pound whole-wheat spaghetti or linguine

Instructions

- Put a large pot of water on to boil.
- Peel 1 head of garlic, separate cloves, and halve any large ones. Peel the second head and chop all the cloves.
- Place clams in a Dutch oven or large saucepan with cold water. Cover and cook over high heat, stirring frequently, until the shells just open, 6 to 10 minutes. Transfer to a bowl as they open, making sure to keep all the juice in the pan. Discard any unopened clams. Reserve 16 whole clams in their shells. Then, working over the pot so you don't lose any of the juice, remove the meat from the remaining clams. Coarsely chop the meat; set aside separately from the whole clams. Pour the clam juice from the pan into a medium bowl, being careful not to include any of the sediment. Rinse and dry the pan.
- Heat 4 tablespoons of oil in the pan over medium heat. Add all the garlic and cook, stirring, for 1 minute. Stir in the chopped clams and cook for 15 seconds. Add flour and cook, stirring, for 15 seconds. Increase heat to high, stir in wine and the reserved clam juice. Bring the sauce to a simmer, stirring constantly to prevent the flour from clumping. Once it's simmering, reduce the heat to medium and stir in 1 cup parsley, tarragon, and 1/2 teaspoon pepper. Cook, stirring often, until slightly thickened, 6 to 8 minutes. Add crushed red pepper, if using. Add the reserved clams in shells and stir to coat with the sauce.
- Meanwhile, cook pasta in boiling water until al dente, 10 to 13 minutes, or according to package directions. Stir 2 tablespoons of the pasta-cooking water into the clam sauce, then drain the pasta and transfer to a large serving dish. Stir the remaining 1 tablespoon oil and 1/4 teaspoon pepper into the pasta. Spoon the clams and sauce over the pasta. Sprinkle with the remaining 2 tablespoons parsley.

Nutrition Facts

Calories: 371; Protein 17.8g; Carbohydrates 49.6g; Dietary Fiber 7.3g; Sugars 2.5g; Fat 10.3g; Saturated Fat 1.5g;; Calcium 83mg; Iron 3.8mg; Magnesium 97mg; Potassium 431.8mg;

Prep Time: 30 mins

Cook Time: 15 mins

Total Time: 45 mins

Ingredient

- ½ cup all-purpose flour
- 1 ½ teaspoon ground black pepper
- 2 large eggs
- ⅔ cup unsweetened flaked coconut
- ⅓ cup panko bread crumbs
- 12 ounces uncooked medium shrimp, peeled and deveined
- cooking spray
- ½ teaspoon kosher salt, divided
- ¼ cup honey
- ¼ cup lime juice
- 1 serrano chile, thinly sliced
- 2 teaspoons chopped fresh cilantro

Instructions

- Stir together flour and pepper in a shallow dish. Lightly beat eggs in a second shallow dish. Stir together coconut and panko in a third shallow dish. Hold each shrimp by the tail, dredge in flour mixture, and shake off excess. Then dip floured shrimp in egg, and allow any excess to drip off. Finally, dredge in coconut mixture, pressing to adhere. Place on a plate. Coat shrimp well with cooking spray.
- Preheat air fryer to 400 degrees F (200 degrees C). Place 1/2 the shrimp in the air fryer and cook for about 3 minutes. Turn shrimp over and continue cooking until golden, about 3 minutes more. Season with 1/4 teaspoon salt. Repeat with remaining shrimp.
- Meanwhile, whisk together honey, lime juice, and serrano chile in a small bowl for the dip.
- Sprinkle fried shrimp with cilantro and serve with dip.

Nutrition Facts

- Calories: 236; Protein 13.8g; Carbohydrates 27.6g; Fat 9.1g; Cholesterol 147.1mg; Sodium 316.4mg.

Made in the USA
Columbia, SC
04 March 2021